TRANSLATING INVESTMENTS

TRANSLATING INVESTMENTS

Metaphor and the Dynamic of Cultural Change
in Tudor-Stuart England

Judith H. Anderson

Fordham University Press
New York 2005

Library of Congress Cataloging-in-Publication Data

Anderson, Judith H.
    Translating investments : metaphor and the dynamic of cultural change in Tudor-Stuart England / Judith H. Anderson.— 1st ed.
        p.   cm.
    Includes bibliographical references and index.
    ISBN 0-8232-2421-X
    1. English literature—Early modern, 1500–1700—History and criticism.
2. Translating and interpreting—England—History—16th century.
3. Translating and interpreting—England—History—17th century.
4. English language—Early modern, 1500–1700—Rhetoric.
5. England—Civilization—16th century.   6. England—Civilization—17th century.   7. Renaissance—England.   8. Metaphor.   I. Title.
PR428.T7A53   2005
808′.042′094209031—dc22   2005001889

Printed in the United States of America
08 07 06 05   5 4 3 2 1
First edition

For Nancy Cridland and Harry Berger, Jr.

Contents

Acknowledgments

This project began in 1995–1996 at the National Humanities Center, where I was appointed the National Endowment for the Humanities Fellow. I subsequently spent two months on a grant from the Huntington Library for additional work on its third chapter. Essentially, I finished the book, working especially on the rhetorical tradition, John Foxe, and Gerrard de Malynes, as the National Endowment for the Humanities-Newberry Library Fellow. Indiana University provided supplemental support in the form of a Research-Leave Grant and two Summer Faculty Fellowships. I am grateful to each of these institutions and particularly thank the National Endowment for the Humanities, without whose support I would be writing this page ten years from now, if at all.

My book engages the interests of a considerable number of disciplines: for this reason, helpful conversations, queries to colleagues in other fields, and experimental previews figure strongly in its background. At one stage or another, many chapters had readings by friends and colleagues in various settings: the second chapter by Leah Marcus and Mary Thomas Crane and, at the National Humanities Center, by Denis Donoghue and Paul Hunter; the third by Michael Allen and Tamara Goeglein, who read the sixth as well; the second, third, and fifth by Debora Shuger; the fifth also by Susan Felch and Carole Levin; the sixth by John Watkins and Anne Lake Prescott; the seventh by John Watkins and Eleanor Winsor Leach, the latter my colleague in Classics; and the eighth by Richard John, an economic historian whose fellowship at the Newberry Library coincided with my own. Lowell Gallagher read and commented on the whole manuscript, as did my colleague in Religious Studies, Constance Furey. Harry Berger, Jr., read early chapters when they were published, middle chapters as they were written, and then commented extensively on the two final chapters and introduction. Others, colleagues at Indiana University, offered expert information and leads when consulted: Paul Spade in Medieval Philosophy; Alvin Rosenfeld, Herbert Marks, Alfred David, and William Hansen in various Classical languages;

Nicholas Williams and Patricia Ingham in their special areas of literary theory, respectively, Marxism and psychoanalysis; and above all, often, and extensively, Nancy Cridland, librarian, in history. I wish to thank all who offered their help, but of course without implying their responsibility for any of my final views. I am additionally grateful to Jessica Sisk, who helped me verify the accuracy of notes and compiled the bibliography. One other colleague I also wish to mention: the late Albert Wertheim, my friend since graduate school. Al's quite unexpected critique of my last application for research support led to its considerable improvement and ultimate success. In a sense, he belongs in the first paragraph of these acknowledgments.

In whole or, more often in earlier part, nearly all the chapters that follow were tested in various forums: two seminars of the Shakespeare Association, two Donne Society talks, two talks for the International Spenser Society, followed by another in Kalamazoo; talks on Foxe at Ohio State and the Sixteenth-Century Studies Conference; a talk about the copula and the Eucharist at a meeting of the Renaissance Studies Association, and a talk on Malynes at the Renaissance Prose Conference. Particularly helpful and enjoyable was the opportunity to present my work on metaphor and metonymy and subsequently on vestments and Foxe to a colloquium and a seminar at the Newberry Library during my fellowship there. None of these presentations went without at least minor revision, and some led to considerably more.

In an earlier form and a significantly different context, several of my chapters have also seen publication and have benefited from the resulting feedback: chapter 2, "Translating Investments: The Metaphoricity of Language, *Hamlet* and *2 Henry IV*" in *Texas Studies in Literature and Language*, 40 (1998), 231–67; chapter 3 as "Language and History in the Reformation: Translating Matter to Metaphor," in *Renaissance Quarterly*, 54 (2001), 20–51; chapter 4 as "Donne's Tropic Awareness and *Devotions upon Emergent Occasions*," in the *John Donne Journal*, 21 (2002), 11–34; chapter 6 as "Busirane's Place: The House of Rhetoric," in *Spenser Studies*, 17 (2003), 133–50. I thank the University of Texas Press, the Renaissance Society of America, the *John Donne Journal*, and AMS Press, respectively the holders of copyright, for permission to incorporate these materials here. A small portion of chapter 5 was published as "Metaphors, Metonyms, Vestments, and Foxe," in *Reformation*, 8 (2003), 63–77; and bits of chapter 8 as "Mixed Metaphor and the Cultural Watershed of Gerrard de Malynes," in *Prose Studies*, 25 (2002), 27–37. I thank Ashgate Publishing Ltd. and the Taylor and Francis Group, respectively, holders of copyright, for permission to incorporate these materials as well. The cover design is taken from *Consuetudo, vel Lex Mercatoria, or The Ancient Law-Merchant*, by Gerrard de Malynes, and printed by permission of the Folger Shakespeare Library.

In closing, I want to return to the important role played in the life of this book by two special friends of longstanding, Harry Berger and Nancy Cridland. Harry first suggested to me in the early 1990s that I write a book on metaphor, and over the years since then we have shared our different but related work on this subject. Nancy, who is also my neighbor, has read and responded to my manuscript at every stage. That I singled out these two generous friends for particular acknowledgment of a heartfelt debt at the end of my last book is not meant to go unnoticed. Here I do so again with a continuing but even deeper sense of affection and gratitude.

J.H.A.

Bloomington, 2004

1. Renaissance Metaphor and the Dynamic of Cultural Change: An Introductory Road Map

This book studies the functioning of metaphor in Tudor and early Stuart culture. Accordingly, its chapters treat a range of disciplines, including language, religion, rhetoric, politics, literature, and economics. Also and inevitably, it touches the present, raising questions about the position of language and rhetoric within post-structuralism and neo-cognitivism and doing so in a way that highlights the connection between intellectual problems active in our own culture and those manifested in the sixteenth- and seventeenth-century texts, controversies, and crises that I discuss. *Translating Investments* is thus conceived as simultaneously a critical and a historical study.

In it, I am recurrently concerned with the issues of conceptualization, abstraction, and transcendence that can be encapsulated in the Hegelian concept of sublation—*Aufhebung*, or, "raising," as both Jacques Derrida and Paul Ricoeur have understood this concept. More expansively, sublation can be rendered as "translation to a higher level incident on partial cancellation of the physical" and thus at once a plus or surplus beyond it, a partial continuity with it, and a partial loss of it.[1] The problem of sublation traditionally has occurred in relation to the physical roots of philosophical abstractions, such as *Idea* (from Greek *eido*, "to see") or *concept* itself (from Latin *com* + *capio*, "to seize together"). These roots threaten the transcendence of thought built on abstractions derived from them. By extension, the problem of sublation informs broader issues of symbolism and conception, for example, those surrounding the Eucharist in the sixteenth century, those realized in poetic vision, or even those evident in attitudes to currency exchange under the early Stuarts.

As I have indicated, sublation, as raising, involves translation, or a transfer from one dimension (one place) to another. Fundamentally tropic and more specifically metaphoric, the process of translation itself, whether from lower to higher or otherwise, is known in traditional rhetoric by the Latin term *translatio*, literally a "carrying across," and this traditional term is also a synonym for the arch-trope metaphor. In sum, the raising that is sublation is fundamentally implicated in the problematic of metaphor: its structure, workings, and effects in theory and cultural history. More specifically, sublation is inseparable from the viability of metaphor, its productive life as distinct from its death in code or cliché, and from the related linguistic issues of diachrony and synchrony and in particular of etymology and polysemy. Underlying, generating, shaping such issues and relationships, metaphorical language will emerge in my argument as a constructive force in the historical development of cultural meaning.

When transferred to the more humanistic forms of cognitive science, to which I refer in this study as neo-cognitivism, sublation reappears as surplus, continuity, and loss in such a concept as Andy Clark's "scaffolding." Clark conceives "language and culture" as advanced forms of "external scaffolding 'designed' to squeeze maximum coherence and utility" from otherwise limited, embodied, physical "minds."[2] Scaffolding is the means by which physical "minds," or more precisely, brains, go higher. Neo-cognitivism posits that thought is "materially possible," but without a metaphorical concept like scaffolding, its impulse is insistently downward and backward to a physical or purely material base; that is, its impulse is to level cultural development and flatten cultural nuance.[3] When the neo-cognitivists George Lakoff and Mark Johnson, for example, assert that even an amoeba "categorizes" by distinguishing food from non-food and cite this "fact" as evidence that abstract concepts are primarily "body-based" and therefore metaphorical, one might question, partly in jest, whether the amoeba also "classifies" according to a conceptual scheme, makes a predication, or speaks in the assembly (Greek *katagoreuein*), all more complex meanings that attach over time to the human concept *categorization*.[4] With such historical development and nuance, the question of "raising" (*Aufhebung*) returns and brings with it the problematic of metaphor. Even cursorily examined, the metaphor of scaffolding, or laddering, itself also has obvious physical, conceptual, and explanatory limits. In this respect, it resembles the Tower of Babel, whose material limits vie with its height and with the purely human aspiration (sinful to traditional religion) that it embodies.

Problems like these play in and out of discussion in the chapters that follow. My intention is to *explore* the relation of these problems to the cultural texts in which they inhere and thus both to ground abstractive issues and to render textual ones more significant. The ensuing conversation between them is meant to be mutual rather than merely one-sided: history and text have as much to tell theory as the reverse. I also intend to be suggestive rather than definitive and hope to be provocative rather than prescriptive or dogmatic. Each chapter has a thetic issue and an unfolding thesis, however, and their outcome shows metaphor, as constructive exchange, to be essentially and powerfully creative, a source of code-breaking conceptual power. This is not to overlook what metaphor conceals, loses, and costs, but to acknowledge and emphasize what it enables.

In the penultimate sentence of the preceding paragraph, I initially wrote "upshot," rather than "outcome," but I replaced the more distinctly metaphorical term that first came to mind, since it was not clearly apt for the context: a very minor example of metaphorical grounding and contextualized abstraction, perhaps. Historically, the term "upshot" derives from archery and refers to the last shot in a contest; in the twenty-first century, it appears to be a partially sublated term, clearly metaphorical but for a reason no longer clearly apparent. Thinking of it, I was remembering an image that occurs in the seventh chapter of this book when the Renaissance rhetorician John Hoskins conceives the creativity of metaphor as an archer's taking aim "on this side or beyond his mark" because he knows his bow will overcast or carry short of the target. "Upshot" is what I really mean to say.

While each of the seven chapters to follow treats a different site of metaphorical activity, language and rhetoric, religion, and economics are conspicuous and recurrent connections among them. "Translating Investments," the punningly entitled second chapter, initially examines the basic conditions of linguistic meaning in the Tudor and early Stuart periods; then it assesses the crucial debate between Ricoeur and Derrida concerning sublation and dead metaphor, relating these issues to neo-cognitivism; and finally it explores their enactment in Shakespeare's deployment of the word *invest/ment*. Etymologically based on clothing, *investment* historically comes to signify trading, finance, and more broadly, a psychological stake or interest. The Ricoeur-Derrida debate is essentially whether the meaning of a metaphorical word is tied to the implications of its material origin or whether, within a conceptual, syntactic, or temporal structure, it can exceed or truly differ from them. This chapter, like the Ricoeur-Derrida debate itself, is fundamental to my exploration of cultural metaphor.

"Language and History in the Reformation: Translating Matter to Metaphor in the Sacrament," the third chapter, begins with the pre- and recorded history of the copula *is*, which is a story of changing and controverted significations, as well as of substantive and figurative ones. It proceeds to the role of the copula in Reformation argument and specifically in the reform of the English church under Archbishop Thomas Cranmer. This role centers in the words of institution, particularly, "This is my body," and more exactly in the word *is*. Language and rhetoric were at the heart of Cranmer's basic challenge, which was effectively to convey a metaphorical conception of presence. Positions taken by Cranmer, his supporters, and his opponents, especially the conservative Bishop Stephen Gardiner, variously parallel modern ones concerning the meaning and nature of metaphor, as again evident, for example, in the writings of Derrida and Ricoeur. Since Ricoeur's theory of metaphor involves a "quasi-bodily externalization" and "a figurability . . . [that] make[s] discourse appear," it also has an obvious relation to the view that human cognition is fundamentally and definitively embodied, and thus to neo-cognitivism.[5] Derrida's theory does as well, since he would tie concepts firmly to their material bases, yet with this difference: for Derrida, these bases are already—indeed always already—within language.

Whereas my second and third chapters, both basic to this study as a whole, deal with broad linguistic histories and contexts, the next two focus on more immediate and local contexts, namely, John Donne's *Devotions upon Emergent Occasions* in chapter 4, and in chapter 5, the vestiarian controversy over the use of traditional ecclesiastical vestments that erupted in the reign of Edward VI and continued well into the next century. Chapter 4, which culminates with Donne, begins with a reconsideration of the relation and distinction between metonymy and metaphor, the one referential, substitutive, coded, ideological; the other deviant, constructive, creative–code-breaking. It then analyzes the play of these figures in theological controversy among three landmark figures of the Reformation, namely, Luther, Zwingli, and Calvin, and finally it examines the enactment of a metaphorical view, which is also from an ideological perspective metonymic, at the crucial center of Donne's *Devotions*. In history and within belief, the distinction between metaphor and metonymy, two nodes of theoretical controversy in the later twentieth century, simply vanishes. Donne's sublating tropology, which arises from the physical world but also takes flight from it, also focuses a challenge to neo-cognitivism of Lakoff and Johnson's totalizing kind. It does so less by its transcendence (although it aspires to this) than by the conscious agency of its transactions and by its implicit inclusion of loss.

Both Donne and the (in)vestments of chapter 2 make a reappearance in the fifth chapter, "Vesting Significance and Authority." This chapter tracks the tropic paradigms of metaphor and metonymy in the vestiarian controversy that show the fluid play of dominant and emergent political and reli-

gious perceptions. At its most fundamental level, the vestiarian controversy
is concerned not simply with cloth but, like controversies about the Eucharist, with the perception of symbolism and the control of meaning. In *Actes
and Monuments*, John Foxe's treatment of the principal actors in the origin
of this controversy in the Edwardine church—namely, Bishops John
Hooper and Nicholas Ridley, plus Cranmer himself—affords a case in point.
Foxe's metaphorizing appropriates, personalizes, and re-translates the public
symbol of vestments to an essentially moral end. In contrast, for Hooper,
Ridley, and Cranmer, all three of them Marian martyrs, the original vestiarian contest had essentially been between lawful authority and individual
conscience, and the question had finally come down to the right publicly to
interpret, and thus to represent, God's word, including its symbolic forms.
Ironically, Foxe, whose account of the controversy deliberately minimizes
or else mistakes these essential issues, in the end controls the final vestiary
"statements" of its major players: he uses his expressive and historical authority not just passively to recount what is seen but metaphorically, and
thus creatively and politically, to reinterpret it.

Like the first two couplings of chapters, the sixth and seventh chapters
are closely related. Both concern metaphor and catachresis, the latter a radical form of metaphor: the sixth chapter does so within an erotic context,
and the seventh more explicitly within the Roman tradition of rhetoric.
Focusing on the culminating cantos of Spenser's 1590 *Faerie Queene*, chapter
6, "Busirane's *Place*: The House of Abusive Rhetoric," recognizes the Enchanter Busirane's erotic creation as a "house" in the rhetorical sense—a
rhetorical place or topos—and Busirane himself, as *abusio* ("abuse"), a common name for the extreme form of figural translation known also as catachresis. In Busirane's House, *abusio* reigns, or "ranes," supreme. Busirane
abuses figuration outrageously, fantasizing that metaphor is the same as reality, feigning and faining rape. Within the conflicting interpretations his
House sponsors, the debate about dead metaphor and sublation that has engaged Ricoeur and Derrida dramatically resurfaces. Relevantly, Britomart
cannot destroy Busirane without killing what Amoret is, the cultural object
par excellence, and for this reason, it is not surprising that the poem has
trouble with the figure of Amoret thereafter or that, while Busirane's art
works may vanish, he must survive, even if bound by the very chain—a
traditional symbol of rhetoric—that he has abused. Cultural vacuums require forms to fill them.

The seventh chapter, "Catachresis and Metaphor," continues my concern with the relation of these tropes in the House of Busirane (and earlier

in chapter 4), extending it backwards in time to the Roman rhetorics, particularly to those of Cicero and Quintilian, and then following it forward
virtually to the end of the Elizabethan period when the rhetoric of John
Hoskins was written. Within deconstructive theory, the relation of metaphor and catachresis in these foundational Roman rhetorics has been taken
to evidence a rift at the heart of signification, but examination of the rhetorics themselves and of the influential, misleading translations of them that
underlie this assertion leads to adjustment and correction of it. These coin-
cide with recognition both of the potentially positive contribution of neo-
cognitivism to a theory of signification and of the linguistic and rhetorical
challenges that neo-cognitivism needs more fully to address. The mottoes
(or cumulative motto) Spenser's Britomart reads over the doors in Busirane's House, "Be bold, be bold, be not too bold," weaves in and out of this
chapter in connection with the recurring Latin word *audacia*, "boldness,"
in traditional discussions of tropology. Derived from rhetorical tradition, an
association of boldness with catachrestic metaphor wryly informs what Britomart sees.

In chapters 6 and 7, rhetoric clearly emerges as a form *and* a force shaping
human experience, and it continues to do so in the eighth and final chapter,
but now in the sphere of economics. In the Roman rhetorics, the concept
of exchange plays a significant role in defining the working of metaphor,
and when this concept is transferred to the title of chapter 8, "Exchanging
Values," it refers primarily to the foreign currency exchanges. To the merchant and assay master, Gerrard de Malynes, whose life spans the Elizabethan and Jacobean periods, these exchanges lay at the heart of the economic
woes of England in the early 1620s. My interest in Malynes focuses on the
pervasive metaphoricity of his capacious world view, particularly in *Lex
Mercatoria, or The Antient Law-Merchant*, his *opus*, and less surprisingly, in *St.
George for England*, his quaint chivalric allegory about socio-economic problems. Malynes' view is in every way mixed. He straddles two worlds, one
passing and one emerging, and they are rhetorical as well as social, religious,
political, and economic. His attitude to and analysis of the economy of his
day intersect with his problems with metaphor. This intersection is not passively reduplicative, uni-directional, or, strictly speaking, homologous; it is
instead *transactive*—in sum, itself a vital exchange.[6] Although even contemporaries of Malynes remark his conspicuous use of similitudes, however, he
actually distrusts creative exchange or what I would call real metaphor. Issues that occur in earlier chapters resonate throughout his writing: among
them, abuse, imagination, substance, denomination, control, usurpation, in-

vestment, and, as already noted, exchange. In the eyes of a modern reader, his depiction of the world he sees occupies a position in the end like that anciently ascribed to metaphor by Cicero: this position is *locus alienus*, a strange or foreign place, one not "natural" to the world as *we* have come to understand it.

What emerges at the end of this book is a heightened, analytical sense of the dynamic of metaphor in cultural history. This dynamic operates not only within history itself but also within our reading of it. In both, it is, or at least it can be, powerfully and validly constructive. Whether it is validly so in our reading depends a good deal on the recursive self-consciousness of our construction, on its doubling back to observe and enunciate its own operation, the fact of its constructedness. Ricoeur's discussion of metaphor makes much of an expression he finds in the preambles of Majorcan storytellers: "*Aixo era y no era* (it was and it was not)." This expression captures the "split reference" characteristic of metaphor—a kind of bi-focality that doubles and productively disrupts, rather than merely canceling, the world as we know it.[7] I would not only recognize the necessity of this bifocality in the function of the interpreter of cultural history; I would also insist on the necessity of its recognition.

2. Translating Investments: The Metaphoricity of Language, Hamlet, and 2 Henry IV

In this chapter, my argument, which is historical in orientation, suggests a way of conceiving language that informs the metaphoricity of Renaissance writings and bears on our reading of them. In doing so, it also addresses contemporary debates about the metaphoricity of language and their application to the early modern period. Ultimately it treats Shakespeare's use of the word *investment* in *2 Henry IV* and *Hamlet* as telling instances of the linguistic character of early modern metaphor, whose conditions of meaning differ in significant ways from our own. What follows in this chapter is an effort to make history, theory, and textual practice converse and mutually inform one another. Its purpose is also to identify historical and theoretical contexts that explain and validate the existence of analyzable spaces between the vexed poles of fixed meaning and total unfixity in the Renaissance. Margreta de Grazia's *Shakespeare Verbatim* provides a historical backdrop for this effort: de Grazia traces the fixing of Shakespearean meaning to the search for historical certainty that motivated Edmond Malone, the eighteenth-century Shakespearean who instituted a methodology of editing still influential today.[1] Insofar as my argument would free Renaissance meaning from narrow, anachronistic lexicalization, it supports and extends de Grazia's, yet it would also balance this freedom with a responsiveness to systemic and local contexts, even in the extreme but significant instances in which these are overruled. Thus my point is not to jettison historical context but to contribute to its definition in a way that renders it pertinent to the claims of modern theory, as well as the more commonly assumed reverse. My story of the past is not Malone's, but it *is* grounded in the historical conditions of Renaissance meaning.

In the early modern period, metaphor was also called *translatio*, or "translation," a term with a broad range of meanings that exceed synonymy yet resist designation as unmotivated polysemy. These meanings exemplify the figurality and cultural embeddedness of language. *Translation* refers to the carrying of something (anything) from one place to another; as the trope *translatio* it indicates a transfer of words and a likely transformation of meaning. Despite attention to the concepts *translatio studii* and *translatio imperii*—diachronic translations of cultural wisdom and power—and attention to the ideology of translation from one language to another, the parameters within which early modern metaphor, or *translatio* as trope, is usually discussed have excluded other meanings of the term, which are rich and varied.[2] In English, they include the transfer of an official from one ecclesiastical jurisdiction to another, the transmigration of a soul to heaven, the transformation or refashioning of apparel, the transfer (or alienation) of money or property from one person to another, and the movement of a tradesman from one company to another (e.g., baker to draper). Any expression of one thing in terms of another, whether relatively neutral explication or more intrusive interpretation, might also be termed "translation."[3] What is constant in all these significations is some degree of modification or change. Historically, linguistic and tropic translations are—to borrow a term from George Lakoff—"radial" instances of such changes, that is, motivated and conceptual, rather than haphazard, and potentially metaphorical in extension.[4] This constant, change, suggests more than the mere substitution of meaning that so knowledgeable and influential a theorist as Paul Ricoeur has found characteristic of rhetorical definitions of metaphor such as those of the early modern period.[5]

The force of the term *translation* is inseparable from the variously lived contexts to which its historical meanings testify. These provide a living resonance for the trope, a kind of associative or paradigmatic nuancing that the meanings of *translation* or *metaphor* would not now suggest to speakers of English: in the early modern period *translation* is an implicitly metaphorical, multivocal pun just waiting to happen. Whether then or now, moreover, the very word *translation*—the phonically close English translation of a phonically less obvious Latin translation of Greek *metaphora*—is not merely a linguistic "carry-over" but also a spatial metaphor to begin with, one of movement and, more exactly, of dis*place*ment, since it derives from *trans* and *fero (latum)*, "across," "beyond," and "carry," "bear."[6] Indeed, in our own time, it is pleasant to suppose that I. A. Richards' seminal analysis of metaphor into tenor and vehicle was inspired by the automotive "transporters" of things—trucks labeled *metaphorai*—that wheel daily through the streets of modern Greece. Herein, a relevant modern instance of the intersection of linguistic figurality and cultural embedding—yet presumably one that would be a purely vernacular, synchronic coincidence for a modern speaker of Greek.[7]

As already noted, however, the conditions of meaning in which the trope *translation* is discussed and practiced in early modern English differ considerably from our own, and for more than one reason. Of these, the most obvious relates to the prominent role of Latin in such areas as Renaissance schooling, scholarship, and diplomacy.[8] Yet the prominence of Latin is coupled with the enhancement of the status and use of the vernacular in such other areas as poetry and drama, religion, and commerce. In this linguistic climate the use of Latin necessarily becomes more visible and deliberate— less simply "natural"—and at least in religion and pedagogy, noticeably controversial as well.[9]

Culturally, the period is both more in touch with the Latin origins and etymological or "literal" (*litteralis*, "of letters," or component parts) meanings of English words than is our own and likely for other cultural reasons to have had a heightened awareness of them. Especially in the absence of monolingual vernacular dictionaries, even a degree of awareness that is virtually simultaneous and reflexive in the presence of neology and wordplay would be plausible among those with a grammar school education, which was basically concerned with Latin.[10] Indeed, the common practice of double translation in Renaissance grammar schools—Latin to English to Latin— would further have encouraged bilingual habits of mind. The same point holds for the pedagogical emphasis on morphology in these schools—for example, the compounding of words such as prepositions and verbs and the derivation of cognate terms—both as a mnemonic device and as an indication of linguistic rationality or "cause." If Latin, the language of grammar, is conceived as rational, it would only be reasonable to conceive of English in a related way, especially if countless words in English flaunted their kinship with Latin words, as they do for anyone with even a smattering of Latin and a dim awareness of relationship.

While this may not be the place to enter the fray about Renaissance literacy, in connection with that of a potential theater audience I would note the social breadth of the audience at which John Rider aims in advertising the contents of *Bibliotheca Scholastica*, his mainly English-Latin dictionary, and specifically the information it contains about Latin grammar, such as the cases governed by certain verbs. Among the readers he solicits are "Courtiers, Lawiers, Apprentices of London, Travailers [travelers, workers], and al Discontinuers, whoe haue lost the vse of their Grammar rules by discontinuance."[11] If "discontinuance" witnesses the increasing cultural status and use of English, the need or desire for the reminders of Latin meanings and usage that Rider's enterprise assumes also witnesses the persistent usefulness of Latin.

If nearer the cultural surface, however, literal meanings of words generally turn out to be closer to metaphor, as we have seen in the case of the word *translation* itself. The extent to which a reciprocal relation exists between literal meaning and metaphor in the period can be clarified and extended by recourse to Robert Estienne's *Thesaurus linguae Latinae,* an important Latin dictionary used for reference in England throughout the Tudor and Stuart periods.[12] If readers recognizing the kinship between the English word *vestment* and Latin *vestis,* "garment," for example, consulted Estienne's dictionary, they would have read that *vestis* derives from the verb *velo,* "cover, veil" or else from *vellus,* the "fleece of a sheep."[13] Or, making the obvious connection between English *monument* and Latin *monumentum,* they would have found that both were based on *moneo,* because monuments "remind or admonish." To help in understanding what is "legal," they might have turned to Estienne's entry on *lex/legis,* "law," and there have found that the origin of the word *legal* is actually *lego,* primarily in the sense "chosen, elected" yet chosen in accordance with Nature and thus also carrying something of the sense "gather, collect" and of a rule established by the prudent choices of many.[14]

If puzzled by Thomas Nashe's idiosyncratic use of *locupleatly* in English, they might have thought of Latin *locuples/-pletis,* "rich, abounding," but originally "rich in property," for *locuples,* according to Estienne, "comes from extended earth [*a lata humo*], which means *locorum plenus,* 'richly provided with grounds or estates.'"[15] In the same entry they would also have encountered a methodological justification of Estienne's procedure cited from Quintilian: "we may define a word either by its content [i.e., *lata humo*] . . . or by its etymology, for example, deriving . . . *locuples* from *copia locorum* [many places] or *pecuniosum* [wealthy] from *copia pecorum* [many cattle]." To these random examples of an underlying principle of *translatio* in language, readers could also add the very format of Estienne's dictionary, which advertises metaphoric cognation: the Latin nouns *usus,* "use" and *usura,* "interest, usury," for instance, are both subordinated etymologically beneath a primary entry for the verb *utor,* "use," rather than given separate entries as they normally would be in a modern dictionary. Estienne's format thus correlates with the morphological principles of early modern pedagogy.[16]

A final example from Estienne's *Thesaurus* illustrates the proximity of literal meaning to metaphor with unusual clarity. If we trace the English substantive *gravity* to its adjectival antecedent *grave* and thence to its Latin origin, we find the following entry under Latin *gravis/-e*, "heavy" or "weighty":

> In its own nature [*suapte natura*] . . . [*gravis*] signifies heavy: as a heavy stone, a heavy bundle, weighty arms, a weighty shield, clearly because it burdens us [*grauat nos*] in bearing it and because it is carried with difficulty and vexation [*cum molestia*]. Thence we transfer it through catachresis [*per abusionem transfferimus*] to age, illness, labor, grief: because these who feel the vexation of age, illness, and other things are oppressed, as it were, by an intolerable burden, which, even as a heavy weight, they ardently wish to put from them. And this transference [*translatio*] is applied not only to bodily vexations but also to those of the mind, . . . which oppress the spirit with a certain kind of weight. . . . And for the same reason *molestia*, "vexation," has been named from *moles*, that is, from a huge mass, heavy in weight. Another sense is that just as heavy rocks and huge tree trunks are not easily moved from a place but stand fixed in all changing times: so constant persons endowed with wisdom are justly and figuratively called grave [*graues*], because neither by entreaties, nor bribes, nor vainglory, nor promises are they budged from fairness and justice—as are these whom we call light [*leues*], who in likeness of dust and straws are stirred by every breeze.

As this entry indicates, lexical meaning in Estienne's *Thesaurus* is simultaneously rooted in objective phenomena and fundamentally tropic: a reproach is heavy because it is like a stone; judgments have weight because they are fixed and constant like rocks or tree trunks. Language is thus translational and transformative; its constant is change.[17]

The extent to which recourse to literal or etymological signification contributes to meaning in the early modern period would be difficult to exaggerate. In addition to the conspicuous appearance of etymology in Latin and bilingual lexicons employing Latin, other basic cultural texts, such as logics, dialectics, and rhetorics, call for its use to define terminology. Etymological definition and argument are as likely to be haggled about among debaters in the learned Thomas Wilson's *Discourse Uppon Usurye* as to be featured as grounding evidence in Sidney's courtly *Defence of Poesy*, and as likely to provide food for thought in a sermon by Andrewes or Donne as to prove a bone of contention between two merchants: for example, Gerrard de Malynes in his ambitious *Consuetudo, vel Lex Mercatoria* and Edward Misselden in *The Circle of Commerce*, his often sarcastic riposte.[18]

Wherever etymological definition occurs, and that seems to be every-where, it testifies to tropic displacement. Not coincidentally, I suspect, it frequently plays a salient role in narrative argument, as is evident even in Estienne's lexical explanation of *lex, locuples,* and *gravis.* One might choose to maintain, with Saussure, that etymological origins do not function as de-terminants of meaning in a synchronic system, yet choose also to maintain, with Derek Attridge, that in fact they do contribute to current meaning if we think they do and speak or write accordingly.[19]

Not surprisingly, the treatment of metaphor in early modern rhetorics acknowledges, if somewhat reluctantly at times, the translational character of language—its fundamental metaphoricity. In fact, it is the linguistic aspect of metaphor that most occupies early modern rhetoricians and, incidentally, casts light on Ricoeur's implicitly negative attitude toward them, a subject to which I'll return. Typically, Henry Peacham's *Garden of Eloquence* follows Cicero in basing the origin and rationale of tropes on a lack—a want of "words to expresse the nature and propertie of diuerse things"—and on the consequent borrowing of "the name of one thing, to signifie another" that resembles it in some way. Peacham explains that language-users, seeing mat-ters well expressed by this means, began to refuse "such words as were proper" and to substitute their own inventions for the nature of things. Em-bellishment now exceeds need, but where we might expect next to learn more about human obstinacy, Peacham adds that "proper" words either "had litle sweetnesse, or could not declare the nature of the thing so well." His conclusion reinforces the superiority of artfully "translated speech," ob-serving that men borrowed words "from like things, both for the grace sake of the similitude, and also *for the cause of perspicuitie of the thing* [subject matter or existent thing] *expressed."* Metaphorical art, at once more pleasing and more accurate, now compensates for the shortcomings of natural language.[20]

Significantly, Peacham notes the shortcomings of language and specifi-cally the lack of proper words, as do other rhetoricians, and it is precisely on the metaphorical word, which now represents the punningly lacking proper-ty, rather than on the dynamics of the sentence that they focus. Angel Day's *English Secretary* offers an example of the bearing of this focus on a "substitution theory" of metaphor from the practical context of use.[21] While Day does his best to see metaphor as the largely ornamental substitu-tion of one word for another, his statements and examples are not wholly consistent: "Betweene a Trope and a Scheme the difference is, that the Trope changeth the signification, as in these wordes *Generation of Vipers,* meaning thereby *homicides* of their own issue or antecessors, as the *Viper* devoureth her owne broode.''²² A "generation of vipers" does indeed change the signification, involving a natural world beneath the human one in a kind of self-slaughter. Like Day's, any Renaissance treatment of metaphor that attempts to describe the reason or cause of translation seems ultimately to express what Derrida has called the logic of the supplement: in this case, an ornament that in fact effects change.²³ Culturally, there is a considerable awareness of the basic metaphoricity of language in early modern England and, on balance, an ambivalent attitude toward it, whether it is conceived as filling a lack, as enhancing an argument, or as effecting a change in meaning.

Besides this basic linguistic metaphoricity, the emphasis on individual words and phrases, as distinct from sentences, also bears importantly on conditions of meaning in the early modern period, serving further to heighten the characteristics, etymological and otherwise, of the tropic word. Early modern grammar and education, which center on Latin, are word-based; whatever bilingual habits of mind they fostered would have been word-based as well.²⁴ Renaissance rhetorics, which do treat English directly, deal with figures of thought and speech and therefore prioritize word and figure, rather than sentence.²⁵ While I think we have not taken enough account of the profound implications of the prioritizing of words at these basic levels, I would emphasize that prioritizing certainly should not imply an ignorance of sentential structure or of context: Renaissance speakers and writers obviously had some sense of a formal sentence and of its larger contexts, and this awareness, as well as a specifically verbal awareness, played a significant role in theological dispute. My point, however, is that linguistic attention and interest were likely to focus on the rhetorical status of an utterance or on its component parts. Rather than being merely subordinate, these parts had claims of their own beyond those we would normally grant them.²⁶ For our century, in contrast, the sentence, not the word or idea, "serve[s] as the interface between the knowing subject and what is known."²⁷ As J. L. Austin has flatly declared in a paper much-cited, "the phrase 'the meaning of a word' is . . . dangerous nonsense"; "what alone has meaning is a *sentence*."²⁸ If not counter-intuitive (and I'm not persuaded it isn't), Austin's declaration is both challenged by history and questioned by popular usage.

On this note, I would turn for further clarification to contemporary readings of the metaphoricity of language, in which the sentence has most often dominated. These readings and the early modern emphases on the tropic

word that challenge them have considerable implications for the understanding and editing of early modern texts and notably of Shakespearean
texts, in which the metaphoricity of language is more frequently and complexly heightened than in most others, despite—or could it have been because of—their relatively popular form. The central debate can be instanced
in the arguments of Jacques Derrida and Paul Ricoeur concerning "dead
metaphor," a term that I would broaden (as they do) to mean metaphor
bearing the etymological trace of an archaic signature.

Since my purpose is to highlight the function of this specifically etymological trace, which figures centrally in the Ricoeur-Derrida disagreement,
two passages of emphatic summation occurring well into Derrida's "White
Mythology" are crucial. Arguing in the first that Aristotle's definitions of
metaphor employ metaphorical concepts—for example, *metaphora* and
epiphora, each "a transfer in space"; *eidos*, "a visible figure, an outline and
a form"; *genos*, "a line of consanguinity, the stock of a birth, an origin, a
family"—and that these definitions are thereby informed and circumscribed
by what they would define, Derrida continues,

> One sees everything that these tropes maintain and sediment in the tangle of
> their roots. But our task is not to trace back the function of a concept along
> a line to the etymology of a word. Indeed it was to avoid this etymologism
> that we concerned ourselves with the inner, systematic, and synchronic artic-
> ulation of Aristotelian concepts. Nonetheless, none of these has a conven-
> tional and arbitrary "x" as a name, so that the historical or genealogical (not
> to say etymological) link which ties the concept signified to its signifier (to
> language) is not a contingent link which can be set aside [54–55][29]

Concerned with the systematic, synchronic functioning—with the logic
(Greek *logos*, Latin *ratio*)—of the concepts within Aristotle's argument, Derrida is not simply pursuing the etymological origins of words. He observes
a problem in this argument, for example, in the fact that metaphor can be
involved in defining what a thing truly is, and therefore that it is involved
in what is "proper," although perhaps not "essential," to the thing (48, 50);
it might be said, again punningly, to define a proper-ty. Coincidentally but
pertinently, his observation illuminates and glosses the ambivalent rational-
izations of tropic invention by Renaissance rhetoricians (e.g., Peacham, as
cited earlier). It also parallels suggestive arguments in the reformed and
notably metaphorical theologies of the Eucharist to be scrutinized in my
two following chapters.

What I would especially stress in the Derridean passage quoted, however, is its final sentence, beginning, "Nonetheless, none of these [concepts] has a conventional and arbitrary 'x' as a name." In this sentence it turns out that etymology itself operates as the parenthetically present-but-rationally-absent trace of the diachronic "link which ties the concept . . . to its signifier." Presumably Derrida's examination of the true character of Aristotelian argument has exposed the history and genealogy of its concepts in a larger sense, but everywhere the initial clue, part of the intermediate evidence, and the summary shorthand for the examination has been etymological. The salience of the trace is linguistic.

The second passage from "White Mythology" is an even more painstaking balance between asserting and rejecting the significance of what I have termed "the etymological trace." The passage is lengthy, but its many qualifiers—adverbial, adversative, and adjectival—deserve quotation in full:

> In drawing attention . . . to the history of the signifier *idea* [from Greek *eido*, "to see"], we do not mean to give etymology an importance which it has already been denied. We recognize the specific function of a term within its own [synchronic] system, but we must not suppose the signifier to be perfectly conventional [neutral, synchronically isolated, without diachronic motivation]. No doubt, Hegel's Idea is not Plato's; no doubt the effects of the system in which these notions exist are irreducible, and must be understood accordingly. But the word *Idea* is not an arbitrary "x," and it has a traditional burden which continues Plato's system into Hegel's, and must also be investigated as such, through a stratified reading: neither pure etymology or origin, nor homogeneous continuum, nor the absolute synchronism or simple interiority of a system to itself [56–57].

Derrida's is always a thought in process, and between the preceding passage cited and this one there is a slight but significant movement. The latter half of this passage, as of the last, is again what interests me, beginning with the repeated assertion that the particular word (or name) is not arbitrary or neutral and that it has a systemic meaning, relying, however, on Derrida's own analysis of that meaning, which has itself been informed, if not circumscribed, by etymology. Perhaps recognizing this contingency, in the same passage Derrida writes, instead of "neither etymology," "neither *pure* etymology," a phrase I take to mean "neither etymology without 'inner, systematic, and synchronic' validation"—"ni étymologie ni origine pures."[30] Etymology, rather than being itself the origin or cause, is thus again a vestigial mark, a mere trace, of these. Derrida's hedged denial only of "*absolute*

synchronism [*synchronisme absolu*]" to any system likewise balances and qualifies the diachronic claims that he has once more made so cautiously; he
thus grants rights to synchronism, as well as to the diachronic trace, although
the extent to which he can honor all these rights and the balance he can
maintain between them are at best problematical.

Before turning to Ricoeur, whose response justifies Derrida's caution, I
should note that Derrida extends his arguments regarding the metaphorical
genesis of Platonic and Aristotelian concepts to the Saussurian distinction (if
that is the proper word for the nominal or culturally conceptual difference
between the recto and the verso of a single page) between the acoustic
image and the concept in the sign, and thence to any distinction between
word and meaning—that is, between the physically sensible and the figurative sense (27–28). In other words, the ramifications of his arguments are
not limited to metaphysics or more generally to philosophy, their immediate
concerns, but extend to everything that language touches.

Lucid and direct where Derrida is elusive and poetic, Ricoeur's *Rule of
Metaphor*—more pointedly, *La métaphore vive* or "living metaphor" in Ricoeur's original title—ignores Derrida's qualifiers and goes right to what he
sees as the center of controversy: etymology.[31] Ricoeur rejects Derrida's exposure of a material supplement in Aristotelian concepts that can be traced
in their systemic and linguistic past, and, against it, he defends the Hegelian
"raising" of conceptual meaning or *Aufhebung,* "sublation," translation to a
higher level incident on partial cancellation. In Ricoeur's (mis)interpreta-
tion, Derrida ignores the "innovation of meaning" in Hegel's *Aufhebung,*
which Derrida actually understands as an economic "surplus"—hence a
plus—that masks its (material) source.[32] Instead, Ricoeur argues, Derrida
"sees *only* the wearing away of metaphor and a drift towards idealization
resulting from the dissimulation of this metaphorical origin," a dissimulation
attested by the etymological trace (286: my emphasis).[33] Ricoeur holds conversely—and here really is the point in dispute—that this "origin" has become a dead issue, canceled by usage: "dead metaphors are no longer
metaphors, but instead are associated with literal meaning, extending its
polysemy" (290). They have become merely synchronic—in actuality,
traceless.

For Ricoeur, the death of metaphors is marked by lexicalization: thus "it
is only by knowing the etymology of the word that we can reconstruct the
Latin *testa* ('little pot') in the French *tête* [head]. . . . In current usage the
metaphor has been lexicalized to such an extent that it has become the
proper word; . . . the expression now brings its lexicalized value into dis-

course, with neither deviation nor reduction of deviation" (290). The literal sense is the current, usual, lexical one; in this sense, not in an originary sense, it is the proper meaning (290–91). Moreover, "the reanimation of a dead metaphor," is a "positive operation" of de-lexicalization: thus it is contextual and predicative, and it "amounts to a new production of metaphor and, therefore, of metaphorical meaning" (*Rule*, 291; *Vive*, 370: "sens métaphorique").

In the course of this polemic, Ricoeur appears at one point to glance as much at conceptions of metaphor resembling those of the early modern period as at his immediate opponent Derrida. "The effectiveness of dead metaphor can be inflated," he suggests, "only in semiotic [i.e., merely word-centered] conceptions that impose the primacy of denomination, and hence of substitution of meaning" to explain metaphor (290; cf. 4, 44–47, 69). His suggestion returns us to the conditions of meaning in the early modern period with which we began. These conditions present an apparent difficulty for Ricoeur's tension theory of metaphor, which depends on the primacy of the sentence: basic grammatical education in England was word-based and its rhetoric subsentential. While Ricoeur endeavors not only to include a semiotic emphasis on the word in his theory but actually to locate metaphor in the tension between word and sentence, naming and predication, verbal focus and sentential frame, his polemic against Derrida indicates that inclusion remains at best problematic and likely subsumptive of the word.[34]

The very meaning of lexicalization in the early modern period presents another problem for Ricoeur's metaphorics. What would Ricoeur make of Robert Estienne's highly tropic, etymologized lexicalization of *gravis*, for instance? What would he use as a lexical measure of English in the absence of a comprehensive lexicon representing the word-stock of the language? Although the Renaissance witnesses the compilation of numerous bilingual dictionaries and these take a quantum leap toward "lexicality," they do not overnight create the monolingual mindset in the vernacular that Saussurean linguistics requires and the other conditions and criteria of standard usage that Ricoeur envisions. Language is nothing in the early modern period if not in a ferment: "an analysis of 40 pages of the *Shorter Oxford Dictionary*," for example, shows "that of every 100 [English] words in use in 1600, 39 were introduced between 1500 and 1600."[35] It has been claimed that Shakespeare alone introduced 1700 Latinate neologisms, including compounds, of which two-thirds now survive.[36] Perhaps Ricoeur's definition of the literal sense as the "current, 'usual'" one affords the alternative to an exclusively lexical definition, but it does not indicate where and how currency and use will be adjudicated in the absence of "proper" monolingual vernacular lexicons. Various forms of linguistic canonization in the early modern period, such as Ciceronianism, education, the pronouncements of grammarians (interpreters), and the practice of lexicographers might have ensured considerable regularization for Latin, a "dead" or "immortal" language, but the determination of acceptable English usage was hardly general, stable, or effective to the same extent. And even with Latin or Greek, stability of signification was notably qualified by theological debate and sectarian translation of the Bible, not to mention such a display of the evolving tropicality of language as Robert Estienne's definition of Latin *gravis* (heavy).

Lexicons, too, are only part of the historical and cultural problem. If it is "only by knowing the etymology" of French *tête* that we would see Latin *testa* behind it, we would see it more readily in the old and early modern French form *teste* or if training had made it second nature for us to think in terms of translations from the one language to the other, and we would be especially prone to do so if the meaning or use of a word were unusual. The popularity and authority of etymological compendia such as those by Varro, Isidore of Seville, and, in the first decades of the seventeenth century, John Minsheu, would further have sanctioned this habit. Popular beliefs about the origin and power of language could also have played a part: Adamicism, for some a religiously sanctioned belief in the iconic language of our Edenic ancestors; Cratylism, its more secular Platonic form; and various forms of mysticism and magic.

Studying the metaphoricity of language from the aspect of the analogous meanings of words, J. F. Ross observes in passing that "the real interest in . . . diachronic manifestations of analogy" is how they reveal the "expressive capacity of natural language." This is an obvious way, he notes, in which natural languages, especially living ones, differ from artificial languages; it is "the most evident strength through which natural languages expand to incorporate new ideas and by which . . . language performs some of our thinking for us" (17, 51). Although Ross, like Ricoeur, is committed to the synchronous control of meaning, his awareness of "expressive capacity" in these statements suggests an opening for history, both in the study of language itself and of its changing historical sites. As Ross reminds us in another connection, "capacity is prior to function" or, for that matter, to use (12).

The capacity, or expressive potential, of language provides a resistant context for the alternative to an etymological trace that Ricoeur's argument offers: "dead metaphors are no longer metaphors, but instead are associated [*s'adjoignent*] with literal [stable, non-figurative] meaning, extending its polysemy" (*Rule*, 290; *Vive*, 368). In this alternative, polysemy emerges both as the gravesite of metaphor and seemingly also as its metempsychosic form. Despite the care Ricoeur has earlier taken to define "polysemy" as a "heterogeneity [that] does not destroy the identity of the word," his claim about the relation of dead metaphor to it asks for additional clarification. Let me venture a modest paraphrase of his alternative: "Dead metaphors are stabilized as lexical meanings, which are just further instances of a usage that increases the word's synchronic multivalence without destroying its recognizability."[37] I hope that helps, but it sounds a bit tautological to me and thus provokes freer translation: "Dead metaphors are to be taken at the face value set by the *Thesaurus linguae Anglicanae*—the lexical Treasury of English. The debts and loans that once underlay them have been canceled by usage, worn out of mind—unless, in Derridean wordplay on derivatives of Latin *usus*, 'use,' they have been canceled in kind by a usurious surplus. Reentering the exchange, they may fluctuate freely in synchronic financial markets" (i.e., a resurrected dead metaphor is a new metaphor).

To translate Ricoeur's statement into Derrida's terms serves two ends.[38] The first is again to highlight the sticking point between their theories, the means and effects of cancellation and in it the highly contingent factor of historical time: my extended financial metaphor (indeed, my allegory) collapses into literal translation when it tries to account for the cancellation of debts by usage and then by mnemonic wear and tear—hardly the way debts get canceled in a real world—unless, that is, we have recourse, as I did, to the etymological pun on "usury" (from Latin *usus*, "use") that at least proves systemic to the rest of the Derridean story. The second is simply to show the extent to which radical metaphorical translation conveys the problem but fails to resolve whether or in what sense it is really there. Translation only returns us to the metaphoricity of language and to a story constructed about it.[39]

As such translation might have suggested, my purpose has not been to endorse one side of the Ricoeur-Derrida dispute regarding etymology at the expense of the other, particularly since I presently find Ricoeur's theory of metaphor, which does not necessarily require the uncompromised sublation, or "raising," that he seeks to recover for metaphysics, among the more powerfully suggestive ones available. Nonetheless, I think that to overlook the relevance of Derrida's emphasis on the etymological trace (*not* to be confused with mere etymologism) to meaning and especially to the metaphoricity of language in the early modern period is a denial of what history indicates. Before proceeding to a Renaissance test case, however, I want to extend this dispute about dead metaphor to the more recent neo-cognitivism of Lakoff and Johnson, not only because of the currency of this theory but also because of its importance. By comparison, Lakoff and Johnson's theory further clarifies the issues of language, history, and the agential control of meaning at stake in Derrida's and Ricoeur's.

Lakoff and Johnson's theory shares some ground with Derrida's, since it suppresses the notion of dead metaphor, and otherwise it contrasts with Ricoeur's in focus and dynamic complexity. Whereas Ricoeur's theory of metaphor focuses on the structure and dynamics of language and rhetoric, Lakoff and Johnson attend almost exclusively to its conceptual function. They argue for the metaphorical "mapping of a subject domain onto a target one (e.g., war onto conversation) that is one-directional and therefore opposed to Ricoeur's bi-directional tension between word and sentence, or, to anticipate a later stage of my discussion, even to his eventual subsumption of word by synchronic context. In contrast to Ricoeur's painstaking linguistic and structural analyses of metaphorical creativity, they distinguish loosely between codified and innovative metaphor on the grounds of cognitive novelty: their codified metaphor often looks like metonymy, or code. Their conception of language is so indiscriminately "metaphorical" that such a word as *obviously* participates in what they identify as the "argument is war" metaphor (e.g., Obviously this is an extreme view: see *Metaphors,* 64). They argue that most "conventional" (their word) or codified metaphors (e.g., "at a cross roads") are systemic and therefore living. Faintly echoing Ricoeur's argument that a reawakened metaphor is a brand new one, they explain the life of conventional metaphors by noting our ability to extend them or to generate additional ("new" but still systemic) metaphors from them (54–55). Contrastingly, in my view, extension and generation are active and productive, not merely neutral, processes: try playing with or on a "dead" metaphor (even the expression *dead metaphor* itself), and it wakes up, often comically; try using a dead metaphor (as is) in a poem and it either snores or else sounds ironic: witness e. e. cumming's poem "next to of course god america," for a strong example. Such reawakening is likely to exploit, not to deny, the metaphor's past.

At first glance, Lakoff and Johnson thus appear to share with Derrida the sense that systemic metaphor is *ipso facto* alive and perhaps to share an indiscriminate metaphoricity with him, as well. What strikes me in Derrida's "White Mythology," however, is precisely his use of Plato's philosophy as his prime example. That is, I am struck by the contextualization of Derrida's argument, whether *de facto* or deliberate. Plato's philosophical system, as

Derrida and most others perceive it, is idealistic; virtually by definition, it sublates. However misguided (or not) it might be, it is dynamic; it builds, scaffolds, and in short, it is constructive. In other words, Derrida implicitly attributes creativity to Plato's systemic metaphors. The same might be said of Aristotle, by modern standards just another, if variant, idealist, since he believed that our abstract conceptions of nature actually exist in things outside the mind (*universalia in rebus*); like Plato's concepts, in this view Aristotle's are systemically metaphoric and creative. On the contrary, systemic metaphors, as Lakoff and Johnson construe them, are essentially passive. They proliferate in a denial of truly creative metaphor, reproducing mirrors of themselves, altered expressions with just the same meaning. Again, as Lakoff and Johnson describe these "metaphors," they are "conventional," to which I would again add, with a glance forward, coded and metonymic.[40]

Implicitly, Lakoff and Johnson also share with Ricoeur a concept of sublation that suppresses anything but elevation. Paradoxically, this oversimplification both denies the uncompromising reality of the physical and the actual significance of "raising." Where Ricoeur, against Derrida, refuses the continuity of the sublated term with its past, Lakoff and Johnson refuse the reality of loss in its partial cancellation of the physical, and thus the work of abstraction. In time, the following section of my discussion will further engage Ricoeur's refusal, and chapter 4, that of Lakoff and Johnson.

In distinguishing Lakoff and Johnson's position on dead metaphor from Derrida's, I have invoked Platonic and Aristotelian contexts, and more specifically systems, in a resistance to unlimited semiosis that perhaps only seems non-Derridean. Context, like system, necessarily injects an element of rationality, order, judgment—*logos*—no matter how eventual or tenuous this element might be. In textual practice, the extent to and way(s) in which a sentential or larger context can co-exist and, indeed, co-operate with radical metaphoricity remain in question. With this in mind, I now turn from a lengthy preamble to a tale about Shakespearean metaphor, looking first at the history of the word *invest* and its cognate forms and then at their working in several passages of Shakespeare's plays. My tale is meant to be a test case for the Ricoeur-Derrida dispute about dead metaphor and for its implications in understanding the historical action of language in texts.

Invest, deriving from Italian and Latin *investire* and thence from Latin *in* and *vestis*, "in clothes," has a specific, fairly narrow meaning in the Middle Ages. It occurs in the nominal form *investiture* and indicates the conferring

of an office or a benefice on a churchman. The cognate noun *vestment,* signifying the garment of a king, official, priest, or ecclesiastic, is also found in
the Middle Ages. Another cognate, the verb *vest,* likewise derived from *vestis,* signifies still more generally the bestowal of estates, rights, titles, and the
like on a person or else a person's being established in legal possession of
these; it makes its appearance in the fifteenth century.[41] During the sixteenth
and early seventeenth centuries, various forms of the word *invest* occur with
notably greater frequency and with a broader range of meanings than before: for example, "to clothe . . . envelop," or "surround"; "to clothe or
endue with attributes, qualities, or a character"; "to clothe *with* or *in* the
insignia of an office" and hence "*with* the dignity itself"; "to endow *with*
the dignity itself"; "to endow or furnish with power"; "To settle, secure,
or vest (a right or power)"; "to enclose or hem in . . . to lay siege to"; "to
occupy or engage"; and "to laie out or emploie ones money vpon anie bargaine for aduantage."[42]

This last meaning, found in Italian as early as the fourteenth century, is
cited here from John Florio's Italian-English dictionary of 1598.[43] It evidently expresses the idea that invested capital is given another cover or
form—clothed otherwise, as it were, or vested elsewhere—and it appears to
have "passed from the Levant or Turkey Company to the East India Company," in whose transactions the *OED* first records its English use in 1613.[44]
Although this meaning in English probably originated in Italian methods of
bookkeeping, the idea of a capital investment (or reinvestment) in cloth and
wool would have been easy to adopt in England insofar as these were the
country's major exports.[45] Interestingly in this regard, two other English
verbs besides *invest,* namely *wear* ("don clothing," "wear out") and archaic
ware ("spend, lay out" money or goods), together combine significations of
clothing and money and also share orthographic forms, common ancestors,
and multi-lingual relatives in the early modern period. Among the relatives
of *wear* is *vestis,* the etymological parent of *invest/ment*[46] Small world, it
would seem, culturally and lexically speaking.

To consider a historical analysis of the origin and various meanings of
invest/ment is not only to realize that they all derive from the idea of clothing
(or enclosing) but also to see metaphorical associations both within the cultural lexicon and between it and the larger culture. The idea of investment
as the bestowal, possession, or acquisition of rights and powers, for example,
slides readily into the idea of investment as dressing for advantage and
thence into that of financial investment. Dress as symbolic capital similarly
invites a connection with the increased interest in sumptuary laws under the

Tudors.[47] The association of clothing with rights and powers, with defining a space or enclosure, and specifically with financial transactions appears to have afforded a fundamental metaphorical code that affected still other applications—the comparison of rhetoric to clothing, for instance.

While the Renaissance image of rhetorical clothing has commonly been taken to indicate the view that language is merely an external adornment and not constitutive of meaning, the realization that clothing itself is materially defining in such broad and basic ways transforms—indeed translates—the force of the image.[48] Consider, for example, Edmund Spenser's *View* that "theare is not a litle in the garment to the fashioninge of the minde and Condicions": clothing shapes, in-forms, mental and social status rather than merely reflecting it.[49] Historically language and clothing have proved peculiarily symptomatic when representation is in flux, whether in the later sixteenth century or in the last decade of our own.[50] The renewed interest in the legislation of dress under Henry VIII and even more under Elizabeth, the conspicuously symbolic sartorial politician of the portraits (and the 2,000 dresses), merely highlights a fundamental category of social perception that is metaphorical (and in time metonymic) to its verbal core.[51]

Generally in Shakespeare, forms of the word *investment* refer basically to clothing, even when their primary meaning might sensibly be glossed otherwise by editors—for instance, as the bestowal of power.[52] Moreover, they do so in a way that is not appropriately described as dead or dormant or conversely as reawakened or resurrected.[53] "Invest me in my motley," a familiar line spoken by Jaques in *As You Like It*, perhaps affords the easiest interesting example.[54] Taken at face value, the line means "clothe me in the insignia of my office, the motley of a fool." The word *motley*, a metonymic sign of folly, co-operates with the translative, basically metaphoric sense of *invest* in which a literal act of clothing becomes a bestowal of office. But given Jaques' character and the "expressive capacity" of the verb *invest*, the potential for meaning it offers, his line suggests additional translative nuances, his own cathected investment in the fool's role and the privileged status he gains by it. These nuances reside in the constructive capacity of the word within its historical context and not in what Ricoeur calls its "vagueness," a negative value that, with almost unavoidably gendered suggestions, endures meaning rather than contributing positively to it.[55] This constructive capacity, which is also translative or metaphorical, is grounded in *clothing* and becomes relevant contextually, with *context* understood not simply as syntax, or form, but also as history, or matter. In this sense it does not exist until realized, but once realized it is seen to have existed already.

As any writer knows who has replaced a perfectly appropriate word with one radically more resonant, perhaps even with a pun, the word makes sense where it is not simply because it is in a sentence; rather it is there because it makes sense that it should be there (as is the case with the word "radically" in this sentence). The difference in emphasis may be slight and intuitive, but it is also significant. The modern practice of deliberate writing—the complexity of crafted use as well as of lexical usage—is likely closer to the model of speaking as well as of writing that Renaissance rhetorics assume, quite in contrast to the assumptions of most modern theories of metaphor.

What I want to call a surplus of nuance is more clearly evident in a line from *Othello* that remains puzzling without a translative metaphor of clothing; it comes just before the Moor's seizure in the fourth Act: "Nature would not *invest* herself in such shadowing passion without some instruction. It is not words that shakes me thus. Pish! Noses, ears, and lips" (IV.i.39–42: my emphasis). Nature invests or clothes herself in but in doing so also commits herself to, or stakes herself on, Othello's darkly prophetic passion. Again the clothing metaphor, actively invoked, passes into financial, rhetorical, and psychological senses, not the least of which involves the confusion of a supportive Nature with the conception of a subversive Desdemona: it is a personified, feminine Nature's investment in passion that instructs him to kill his wife. In so passing, the clothing metaphor literally and regeneratively re-verberates.[56]

In the first scene of *King Lear*, a similar movement is still more obvious. Having disowned Cordelia, Lear addresses Cornwall and Albany: "I do invest you jointly with my power, / Pre-eminence, and all the large effects / That troop with majesty" (I.i.130–32). Lear not only invests his sons-in-law with rights and powers but also invests in them, seeking to clothe his majesty in another form, at once to relinquish and to extend it. If it were really true that the financial or advantageous meaning of *investment* only enters English usage in 1613, in a very real sense this meaning is already there. The language of the play chronicles and reflects a deeply ingrained structural parallel in the culture between an investment, this time in dignity—human "worth"—and economics. Since the idea of "worth"—tantamount to desert, value, property, excellence—also carries legal and theological as well as political weight in the period, historically the parallel is a troubled and unstable one: exactly the sort of systemic parallel to attract an enterprising playwright, who can make it evident and, in effect, bring it to realized life.

In readings of Shakespeare to this point, I have tried to keep the lines that are cited as isolated as a meaning responsible to each play would allow, but these readings have obviously been informed by sentential and larger contexts, whether specifically textual or cultural in other ways. Yet the expressive capacity of the word has played at least an equal role—in any case not a subsumptive one. Keeping Estienne's highly metaphorical definition of *gravis* in mind and the fact that *invest* in the sense "clothe capital in another form," or, "invest for advantage," is novel in the English Renaissance, I find it hard to see the realization of this capacity as simply an expression of polysemy. What would be the difference between the metaphorical extension of this word's etymological core and polysemy? Ricoeur argues that the "identity" or synonymy of the word—for Estienne its etymological core—persists despite a heterogeneity of meaning. Fair enough, but does it not do so through a *translation*—whether a comparison, a catachrestic leap, an imaginative association, or, to use Puttenham's term, even a kind of inversion (e.g., *invest* as "besiege")?[57] In the instances we have examined, this translation has had an identifiable basis, given its past—a past still audible, still visible, still present in the early modern period. This basis has enabled an extension of verbal senses and nuances that occurs over time—not only within the temporal context of Shakespeare's syntagm(s), plot(s), and literary corpus, but also within the larger context of his culture and its relation to the linguistic past, whether as his contemporaries conceived this relation or as we do. Its diachronic occurrence, moreover, is not simply abstract as in the listings of the *OED* but real and significant within the historical context of early modern meaning. Polysemy, in contrast, is merely a description of a synchronic phenomenon and not an explanation of a translation that is culturally diachronic and that Renaissance rhetoricians and lexicographers, who were aware in their practices of its diachrony, considered fundamentally metaphoric.[58] Quite in contrast to Shakespearean drama, in fact, it engages neither the history nor the story of language.

Considering the status of etymology after Saussure, Attridge observes that "Synchrony is an impossible fiction, not [only] because language is always changing . . . but [also] because even as a methodological hypostatisation it's not consistent with itself," as Saussure's inconsistent statements and practices regarding it amply demonstrate.[59] Attridge also asserts that "the only way in which history [and specifically linguistic history] *can* [and *does*] intervene in the present . . . [is] as a theory or story of the past" (198). Truly "the present is always inhabited and modified by theories (or stories) of the past, *popular and scholarly*," and, I would add, the fundamental conditions of linguistic meaning in the early modern period—pedagogical, grammatical, rhetorical, logical, and lexical—are everywhere rife with them.[60]

Before turning to *2 Henry IV* and *Hamlet*, I want briefly to look at two occurrences of *invest* in *Macbeth* that offer a degree of negative control and contrast for the others discussed. Both instances are one dimensional in meaning, neither in context inviting significant translation, except perhaps in non-specific relation to the clothing imagery that informs the whole play. This exception aside, both lack the complexity of multiple registers or of etymological re-verberation. In the one, Macduff informs Rosse that Macbeth has been named king and has "gone to Scone / To be invested" (II.iv.31–32). In the other, Duncan tells Macbeth that Malcolm has become Prince of Cumberland, "which honor must / Not unaccompanied invest him only" (I.iv.39–40). Since honor does not normally clothe anyone with the insignia of office or dignity, the latter citation involves explicit metaphor, unless we prefer to specify it further as personification, the translating of an abstraction into a person. But even this citation, like the preceding one, asks for a merely conventional response to the metaphorical identification of office or dignity with a garment that has been embedded in the word *(in)vest/ment* since medieval times. Instead of describing this identification in metaphors of death or dormancy, however, I am inclined to regard it as implicit and available but inconsequential except in the large symbolic patterns of the play already noted (e.g., nature/civilization or truth/illusion). Like the preceding example, this is one of the flat, convenient, and, indeed, metonymic sort too often favored over more complex ones in philosophic and linguistic approaches to the metaphoricity of language: perhaps the hard truth is that the variousness of language tends to resist the finalizing form toward which theory yearns.

In *2 Henry IV,* as in the instances cited earlier from *As You Like It, Othello,* and *Lear,* awareness of the history—indeed the story—of the word *invest* facilitates meaning more distinctly and even contributes directly to it, enlarging and reshaping its nuances. At the same time, an awareness of the word is embedded more resonantly in its immediate context. *Invest* occurs four times in this play, all in the fourth Act. The first is at Gaultree Forest when Westmerland questions the Archbishop of York,

> Whose white *investments figure* innocence,
> The dove, and very blessed spirit of peace,
> Wherefore do you so ill *translate* yourself
> Out of the speech of peace that bears such grace,
> Into the harsh and boist'rous tongue of war?
> Turning your books to graves, your ink to blood,

Your pens to lances, and your tongue divine
To a loud trumpet and a point of war?

(IV.1.45–52: my emphasis)

Distinguished by a flourish of metaphors more appropriate to a rhetorical textbook than to imminent battle, Westmerland's question focuses on representation and explicitly addresses the Archbishop's figuration or "translation" of his office. The Archbishop's "investments" are his symbolic garments, their whiteness associated with innocence, yet the context also implies the corruption of their meaning to advantage: clothing or appearance—investments—for another purpose. The Renaissance debate about ecclesiastical vestments, which was very much alive in Shakespeare's lifetime, adds a sharper edge to Westmerland's challenge, and the very conspicuousness of the rhetorician's craft in the passage enforces the suggestion of deceptive manipulation, even while leaving open the deceiver's identity (speaker or addressee).

The word "investments" does not actually cause the rest of this remarkably metaphorical passage but figures crucially in it; even this word's position in the sequence suggests that it motivates what follows. Coincidentally, the *OED* cites this instance of *investment* as its earliest figurative use; the second being *Hamlet*, I.iii.128 (discussed below); for whatever reason, the figurative capacity of the word appears to have been becoming Shakespearean. With this figurative usage, the "plot" of the speech thickens—a claim that reflects the popular saying and the perception it embeds that much of what happens in language is a story. Here it is part of another story, in the first instance called *2 Henry IV*, in the second, called Shakespeare's, and in yet a third, the one we call our own.

Like all the other reverberant occurrences of *invest* in the play, the next after that of the royal emissary Westmerland belongs to King Henry himself. It too conveys the suggestion of deception, even as the context in which it occurs glances at the subject of metaphor. In words that recall the opening of *I Henry IV*, Henry announces his ever already deferred intention to lead a holy crusade, were it not for home-grown rebellion:

Now, lords, if God doth give successful end
To this debate that bleedeth at our doors,
We will our youth lead on to higher fields,
And draw no swords but what are sanctified.
Our navy is address'd, our power collected,
Our *substitutes in absence well invested,*

And every thing lies level to our wish.
Only, we want a little personal strength;
And pause us till these rebels, now afoot,
Come underneath the yoke of government.

(IV.iv.1–10: my emphasis)

Here "invested" means "furnished or vested with powers" or "clothed in the insignia and power of office," as Angelo will be in *Measure for Measure.* But it also means "clothed in another form or guise" and may even refer to "power laid out for advantage." Taken whole, the line in which "invested" occurs means that the king has taken care to be well represented—well invested—in his planned absence. If "invested" implies advantage, however, and the line is read with a pause after "substitutes," it isn't clear who will gain most from investment in Henry's absence, Henry himself or his ambitious substitutes, enough of an ambiguity to make any politic king think twice before departing the realm. (Notably, Henry is not careless enough to authorize a single substitute.)

The phrase "substitutes in absence" can also be read as a single unit without the pause after "substitutes"; on first sight this is actually the easier reading. It accentuates the fact that Henry's representatives—his substitutes in absence—are stand-ins, figures or figureheads for him, with a recollection for us of his counterfeits in the battle of Shrewsbury at the end of *1 Henry IV.*[61] In the cultural context of Tudor England, "substitutes in absence" for this king figure the possibility of his essential insubstantiality, his being merely an image of a king, a mocking fiction, an empty metaphor, and not the real thing: *mere* investment. As we have seen, for Renaissance rhetoricians a metaphor can be considered a replacement, sometimes a violent catachrestic one, for a lack; or as Calvin put a similar perception, "*humanly* devised symbols . . . [are] images of things absent rather than marks of things present."[62] Thus a metaphor or even a word is, from this perspective, an image of what is missing. Both are vestments, and in them perception itself is invested.

Invest occurs twice more in Act IV of this *Henry* play within little more than a dozen lines, first when the dying King discovers that his son has taken the crown from his bedside and reflects with poignant, self-pitying bitterness on filial ingratitude and greed:

See, sons, what things you are!

How quickly nature falls into revolt
When gold becomes her object!

For this the foolish over-careful fathers
Have broke their sleep with thoughts, their brains with care,
Their bones with industry;
For this they have engrossed and pil'd up
The cank'red heaps of strange-achieved gold;
For this they have been thoughtful to *invest*
Their sons with arts and martial exercises;
When like the bee tolling from every flower
[The virtuous sweets],
Our [thighs] pack'd with wax, our mouths with honey,
We bring it to the hive, and like the bees,
Are murd'red for our pains. The bitter taste
Yields his engrossments to the ending father.

                              (IV.v.64–79: my emphasis)

The underlying pun on crown, the symbol of kingship, and crown, a gold coin, operates throughout the passage. Accompanying words like "gold," "industry," "tolling," "engrossed," and "engrossments" and the memorable image of apian husbandry, all of which suggest the strongly economic nuancing of these lines, the word *invest*, meaning only "endow," "equip," or even "educate" would sit somewhat oddly. But this context again cooperates with a more self-interested potential already resident in the word than Henry openly intends, namely, "invest in" and implies the father's projection and substitution in the son.

When, sixteen lines later, *invest* occurs again, Henry accuses the Prince of stealing the crown in words that reinforce these earlier resonances. Recalling the bees' "mouths [filled] with honey" that they bring to the hive, he demands of the Prince: "Dost thou so hunger . . . That thou wilt needs invest thee with my honours" (IV.v.94–95)? Clothed or invested by himself in the dignity of the father, the son's power becomes wholly his own. As earlier Hal replaced Hotspur in the battle of Shrewsbury, investing himself with the "budding honours" cropped from Percy's head and thereby refiguring himself, in Henry's fear he now becomes not merely the substitute invested in the approaching absence that will be Henry's death but also the present reality of investment and the translation of power: that is, investment despite the absence or present non-fulfillment of death.[63] The fundamentally metaphorical, translative operation of *investment*, earlier hinted, comes fearfully to light, as does the ironic reality of substitution.

The word *invest/ment* also occurs twice in the third scene of the initial Act of *Hamlet*, the farewell between Laertes and Ophelia, joined less than midway by Polonius and thereafter dominated by him. Although its occurrence belongs to a lower key than that in *2 Henry IV,* it further clarifies the translative capacity of the metaphoric word and its etymological trace. In the first occurrence, in which Polonius tells Laertes, "The time invests you; go, your servants tend," *invest* is often glossed "besieges," since Polonius has earlier told Laertes that the wind is right for sailing, and he is "stay'd for" (56–57, 83).[64] This gloss is possible, but "invest" properly understood as "besieges" in the sense of hemming in or inclosing (inclothing?) does not seem as desirable a reading as "endows you with power," "clothes you with opportunity, advantage," a meaning that also suits better both the immediate sequel to Polonius' worldly precepts—"the apparel oft proclaims the man"—and the final words he speaks to his son (72). Attention to the underlying metaphor of clothing, which neither the framing sentential structure and predication nor the larger context requires, again proves useful both immediately and in non-specific relation to the imagery of clothing blatant elsewhere in the play. Although thoroughly conventional, however, the clothing-metaphor is here neither dead nor in a context novel enough to reanimate it had it been so.

A more complex linguistic context in which the word *investment* occurs comes shortly after in the same scene, when Polonius warns Ophelia about Hamlet's intentions. Once more, as before in Henry's words to Hal, the context is laced with financial diction: "Be something scanter of your maiden presence, / Set your entreatments at a higher rate . . . In few, Ophelia,"

> Do not believe his vows, for they are brokers
> Not of that dye which their investments show,
> But mere [implorators] of unholy suits,
> Breathing like sanctified and pious bonds,
> The better to [beguile].
>
> (I.iii.121–31)[65]

This passage, in which sex, religion, and commerce intertwine, has been much discussed, and many editors have emended their copytext's financial "bonds" to Theobald's sexual "bawds." I will not rehearse the arguments for either reading here, except to note that either yields an acceptable sense. I would register my own vote for "bonds," however, both on the editorial principle of *durior lectio* and on the basis of Thomas Clayton's capaciously persuasive analysis.[66] "Vows" in the passage are pledges, whether of lovers (secular or religious) or borrowers, and "brokers" are reputedly dishonest middlemen or mediators, with "broke," the past tense of *break*, providing a reinforcing homonymic echo—broken vows. "Dye," a hue or shade, suggests also the stamp for a coin, and "investments" are either garments or commercial transactions, the whole line suggesting related controversies about clerical morality, the coinage, the cloth trade, and financial exchange that are endemic in the period. Just conceivably, if distractingly, "investments" could also glance at the meaning "sieges," this time in the proper translative sense of "hemming in" for which the clothing metaphor calls.[67] "Unholy suits" are duplicitous pleas or else misleading clothes, hence deceptive appearances; "breathing" could modify "vows," "brokers," or even "suits," the first and last of these semi-personified; and "bonds" (or bands) are conceivably clerical bands (collars) or marriage banns / bands / bonds but are more clearly financial commitments or legal agreements, again semi-personified like so much in the passage—unless, of course, we decide to emend them to "bawds," or brokers of passion.[68] Throughout the passage, words themselves—the clothes or "vestments" of thought, as they are so commonly regarded by Renaissance writers—are irreducibly duplicitous. As elsewhere in the play, they clothe and hide, express and obscure whatever "passes show" or claims to (I.ii.85).

In a passage as densely, inextricably, and coherently full of wordplay as this one, even irrational puns that cannot sustain syntactical scrutiny may be audible (or visible), inescapable, and relevant; that is, they may be at once systemic *and* creative. Syntax is a rational ordering of language that a word-centered grammar and figure-centered rhetoric may reinforce, supplement, or fully subvert. This is not to say that we are misguided in pursuing the syntactical sense of such passages but that we are misled in suggesting that it alone is there or always dominant. In the overdetermined punning of this passage, sentential and predicative meaning is nearly overwhelmed by connections and tensions among senses of the words themselves. The words are, as it were, "lifted" into another realm of possibility, a simultaneity of meanings that allows comprehension even while exceeding and frustrating it.[69] Metaphor that is both systemic and in context creative operates here as an instrument of textual sublation.

Although directly invoking neither side of the Ricoeur–Derrida dispute about Hegel's sublation (*Aufhebung*), Pierre Bourdieu's interpretation of Heidegger's sublation of words bears at once on this dispute and on the related metaphoricity of words in the same *Hamlet* passage. Bourdieu's theory of language accommodates both sides of the dispute, effectually accepting Ricoeur's uncompromising assertion of generic and systemic constraints on meaning and Derrida's equally strong sense of the word's past or multiple registers. For Bourdieu, as for Ricoeur, "the incorporation [l'insertion] of a word into the system of philosophical language . . . brings about the *negation* of its primary meaning," but Bourdieu also adds, inclining now toward Derrida, that the meaning "the tabooed word assumes with reference to the system of ordinary language . . . continues to lead a clandestine existence [*une existence souterraine:* 'underground']." Synthesizing the two emphases, he continues, "the imposition of form makes it both justified and unjustified to reduce *negation* to what it negates. . . . Because of the fact that this 'lifting [*Aufhebung*] of repression' . . . simultaneously denies and maintains both the repression and the repressed, it allows for a doubling of profits [*cumuler tous les profits*]: the profit of saying and the profit of denying what is said by the way of saying it."[70] Like my prior description of the connections and tensions among the senses of words in the *Hamlet* passage, Bourdieu's understanding of Heidegger's linguistic practice might be described as a *full* extension to the word, including the etymologized word, of Ricoeur's tension between word and sentence.[71] If for Heidegger, having meaning both ways pays off in the philosophical market of Weimar Germany, for Shakespeare, the Renaissance stage, a more popular site and a market differently constituted, is equally receptive to linguistic duplicity.[72]

But Bourdieu apparently underestimates the popularity of verbal play and other phenomena like folk etymology and does not extend tension within the word to ordinary language.[73] Too restrictively even for a modern context, he regards "the ability to grasp simultaneously the different senses of one word . . . and, *a fortiori*, the ability to manipulate them practically (for example, by recovering the original [or etymological] sense of ordinary words, as philosophers like to do)" as typifying the "scholarly ability to remove oneself from a situation and to disrupt the practical relation which links a word to practical context, restricting the word to one of its senses."[74] The word "practical" is now curiously limited by him, if not to a subsistence market, to one that is material in too reduced a sense. Whereas Bourdieu is led by his conception of the marketability of linguistic competence narrowly to limit punning and a practical etymological awareness to scholars and lexicographers (whose readers surely expand the market), my argument has been that many of the basic conditions of early modern linguistics such as grammar and rhetoric would have encouraged these same characteristics to a remarkable degree.[75] With a familiar, ordinary early modern word like *investment,* whose etymological trace and metaphoric force are everywhere available and often active—in these senses alive rather than dead—and whose meaning is as much in process as the social and economic phenomena it reflects, the implication of metaphor in verbal punning re-verberates potently. It is with the occurrence of this word that the three major foci of meaning in the *Hamlet* passage, namely clothing, commerce, and religion, converge axially.

Although from a modern point of view, Renaissance theories of metaphor might have been sententially weak, the rhetoricians who expressed them knew something else in their heightened awareness of the metaphoricity of words. Such awareness suggests that Ricoeur's masterful theory might not have the balance between words and sentences quite right. Perhaps more exactly, when Ricoeur faces the radical implications of Derridean wordplay for philosophy, he does not maintain the balanced tension he envisions ideally. After all, he does grant the word a degree of "semantic autonomy," finds "potential for meaning" in its "semantic kernel," and sees it as the focus of "the dynamism" of the framing sentence (*Rule*, 128, 130, 132). Conditionally, he even acknowledges in polysemy a more or less "diachronistic character" that is "difficult to contain within the limits of synchronistic description" (122–23). And does he not conclude that "[metaphor's] place in language is *between* words and sentences"?[76] Yet every one of these affirmations or admissions is so quickly and heavily qualified by the reassertion of sentential control as to become doubtful in meaning. "Semantic autonomy" in actuality turns into immediate "contextual values"; the kernel or potency of the word becomes in a single sentence "nothing real or actual [*rien de réel ni d'actuel*]"; and if the focus of sentential dynamism is the word, "the reverse is no less true" and, in fact, because actually prior, is truer (128–30, 132). The diachronic character of polysemy excludes its "sources" (e.g., historical and etymological) and is not manifest anyway unless realized in the synchronic "domain," where it becomes a "variety of polysemy" subject to the sentence (122–23). Even Ricoeur's final statement situating metaphor between words and sentences is attached by a semicolon to another sentence, which asserts "that metaphor is the outcome of a debate between *predication* and *naming*"; the crux—in fact the focal word—of this metaphor of debate is "outcome," one in which the name or word is never to dominate nor really to come in an honest draw (133).

The point is not to urge instead an unlimited semiosis, which would be meaningless, or to embrace wordplay without contextual awareness and a resulting degree of constraint. But it is to recognize the variable character of terms like "contextual awareness" and "degree of constraint" and the historical and cultural values informing them. More specifically, at least in the early modern period, it is to argue the possibility of a salience in the metaphoric word, a persistence of its etymological trace, and, in short, a constructive capacity in the word that can markedly defer or exceed subsumption by the sentence: witness *investment* in the Shakespearean lines examined. Perhaps the word, more generally understood in this way, could also realize the truly radical tension toward which Ricoeur's theorizing of metaphor gestures boldly but on which it seems to renege in practice and life.

3. Language and History in the Reformation: Translating Matter to Metaphor in the Sacrament

What follows further concerns two interlocking interests: the involvement of language in history, history in language, and herein the particular role of language, especially figurative language, in the early reforms of the established church in Tudor England. Still more specifically, my concerns in this chapter will focus on explanations of eucharistic belief during the archbishopric of Thomas Cranmer. As Diarmaid MacCulloch, Cranmer's recent biographer, has observed, Cranmer's basic problem "was how best to convey a metaphorical notion of presence."[1] Language and rhetoric, the language art, were at the heart of this problem.

Linguistic history is the larger backdrop against which the theological Reformation of the sixteenth century acquires a meaning that appears at moments prophetic. From a modern perspective, Reformation debates about tropology that center on the sacrament, the defining issue of the Reformation itself, at once mask and express the older linguistic displacements that underwrite their inevitability. These displacements—actually, translations—involve the verb *is* in the words of institution, "This is my body," and they are basically metaphoric. They transfer meaning from one language to another and from one mode of conception to another. Instead of being transparent or truly equivalent, they involve shifting registers of meaning.

As controversialists on both sides of the Reformation note, the argument for real presence rests essentially with the verb *is*, traditionally known as the substantive verb and taken to indicate a real and present existence. Understandably, the Swiss reformer Huldrych Zwingli therefore bases his seminal denial of real presence on a tropic understanding of the verb "is," taking it to mean "represents" or "figures."[2] Zwingli's associate Johannes Oecolampadius, responding to linguistic argument and historical precedent, merely transfers Zwingli's tropic initiative to the predicate nominative, "my body." He translates it as "a representation—or figure—of my body."[3] In either of these cases, real presence is displaced in and by "a certaine maner of [figurative] spech," a phrase I borrow from Cranmer and his antagonist Stephen Gardiner about three decades later.[4] This manner, or mode, inheres not simply in Zwingli's trope, but also in a second concept of being inherent in the verb *to be* itself, one that is rather "fictive" (from *fingere*: "to form, make; to conceive, imagine") than substantive.

Not long before the clashes of Zwingli with Martin Luther in the 1520s over the meaning of the words of institution, Erasmus' annotations of the New Testament provoked controversy about these words, specifically calling attention to variants of them in the Greek codices. On the traditional Latin rendering of 1 Corinthians 11:24, *Hoc est corpus meum*, Erasmus remarks that the substantive verb is absent in the Greek, although, he notes circumspectly, "I find it added (*additum*) in certain [manuscripts]."[5] His Greek sources read, "*τουτό μου σῶμα*," or, in his Latin rendering, "hoc meum corpus." Citing Erasmus, Luther, although a proponent of bodily presence and willing enough to invoke the authority of the substantive verb to support it, offers in his *Confession concerning Christ's Supper* a verbatim translation of the statement of institution without the substantive verb, namely, " 'Take, eat this my body which is broken for you' " (331–32). Luther considers this version theologically acceptable.

The linguistic issue Erasmus and Luther directly or obliquely address is what linguists know as the nominal sentence. This is defined by Emile Benveniste as "a predicate nominative, without a verb or copula," which is "the normal expression . . . where a possible verbal form would have been the third person of the present indicative of 'to be.' "[6] Examples are *Omnis homo mortalis*, "Every man mortal," or *Verbum satis sapienti*, "A word enough for a wise man," or, indeed, *Hoc meum corpus*: "This my body," rather than "This is my body." The nominal sentence is found in ancient Semitic (including Aramaic), which actually lacks a copulative form of the verb *to be*, and in Greek and Latin, where it co-exists with alternative verbal expressions employing *esti* and *est*, respectively, both forms equivalent to English *is*.[7] Zwingli, acknowledging that "There is no word for 'is' and 'are' " in Hebrew, explains that this is "simply because the Hebrew language is not the same as the German." Instead, he adds, there are other "expressions [in Hebrew] which have the same sense as in German."[8] In other words, while the statement of institution is a nominal assertion, for Zwingli its appropriate translation in a western European language lacking the nominal sentence employs the verb *to be*. Significantly, it does so despite the fact that the absence of this verb in the text could have been used to support his denial of substantive presence, had he not embraced the particular convention of translation at issue. The absence of the verb, of course, is the reason that Oecolampadius transfers the trope from the verb to the predicate nominative, "my body."

According to Benveniste, the nominal sentence, which necessarily lacks such verbal modalities as time and person, is inherently "beyond all temporal or modal localization and beyond the subjectivity of the speaker," and it is therefore improper to translate this expression of "semantic content alone" into the third person present of the verb *to be* (137–38).[9] Establishing a total or partial "equivalence . . . between two nominal elements," the nominal sentence differs in nature, and not simply in degree, from an utterance employing this verb (137, 144). Benveniste further suggests that, besides having the syntactic function and morphological marks of a verb, *to be* originally had a definite lexical meaning, approximating "to exist, to have real substance," before it fell—"at the end of a long historical development—to the rank of copula" (138). While Benveniste grants that it is impossible to attain the earlier meaning of *es (Indo-European prototype of *be*) directly, he observes that "*bhu 'to put forth, to grow,' furnished part of the forms of *es [and therefore] gives an inkling of it" (138). In other words, *to be* is fundamentally a verb and historically one with substantive meaning, a description to which the nominal sentence does not answer. Indeed, from a rhetorical perspective, the *total or partial equivalence between the two nominal elements* of the nominal sentence has, as its very description suggests, a structural predisposition to metaphor.

In contrast to Benveniste's argument, although with some resemblance to Zwingli's, Charles Kahn's study of the Greek verb *to be*, which is based on transformational grammar, recognizes the nominal sentence "as a phenomenon of surface structure only."[10] The essential principle of Kahn's theory is "that all syntactical operations or transformations be defined as relations between sentence forms," which necessarily include a verb (193). But as Kahn acknowledges, "reinterpretation of the nominal sentence as a phenomenon of zeroing or deletion of the copula follows almost inevitably from the very nature of the transformational enterprise" (436). System thus overrides difference, whether real or merely apparent, in what would itself appear to be a metaphorical transaction—the translation of nominal to verbal sentence structure. The difference between Benveniste's and Kahn's views of the linguistically nominal sentence approximate those between philosophic nominalism and realism: the apparent phenomenon is significant for Benveniste, only the underlying reality (or grammatical fiction?) for Kahn.

Kahn, a Classicist taking the Homeric system of uses of *be* for his primitive datum, also rejects any diachronic arguments about the development of this verb. All its forms are synchronic ab ovo in his view.[11] He is intent on the ideally triadic structure of the Greek verb *be*, which combines the copula, the veridical meaning, and the existential meaning—or predication, truth, and existence—and thereby avoids the "tyrannical influence of [post-Cartesian] epistemology," with its vexing questions about how we know and how we can be certain and, indeed, with its characteristically early-modern entanglement in seeming (400, 404). In the Greek system he describes, "problems of reality or existence were . . . inseparable from problems of truth and . . . predication." In fact, it is "Precisely because εἰμί was basically understood as copula, but also functioned like our verb *exist*, [that] the major Greek philosophers were never seriously tempted to conceive existence as a predicate" (403–04). Kahn's target, it should be noted, is the *priority* of the existential to the copulative meaning, not the difference between them, which he never doubts.

Other statements Kahn and Benveniste make regarding the nominal sentence prove further relevant to Reformation debate about the words of institution. Benveniste distinguishes between the communication of a fact by the verb *to be* and the assertion of a general truth by the nominal sentence: in Homer, Pindar, Hesiod, or Herodotus, for example, "The nominal sentence and the sentence with ἐστί ['is'] do not make assertions in the same way and do not belong on the same plane. The first is from discourse, the second, from narration. The one establishes an absolute; the other describes a situation" (142). In a modern language like Spanish, which has supplemented the nominal by the verbal sentence, Benveniste also notes a differentiation within the verb *to be* that corresponds to an earlier one between the nominal and verbal sentence: that Spanish *ser* means "to be essentially," and Spanish *estar* "to be existentially or circumstantially," he believes, "is doubtless not by chance" (144). A parallel development occurs in late Latin, where "*esse* assumes the role of the copula while the notion of existence passes to *existere, extare*" (167).

Kahn's Homeric evidence suggests to him that Benveniste's argument about the uses of *be* is too sweeping here. Kahn finds that as a "general rule . . . the verb [*be*] may be omitted [in Homer] wherever it is uninformative" and that it is often omitted for metrical reasons, which, I might add, are a very considerable complication in poetry for either side of the argument

(441, 449). He also indicates that omission correlates "with at least two distinct stylistic tendencies [in Greek], the high style of tragedy and solemn orations and the more relaxed usage of conversation, whereas ἐστί is more often expressed in the formally correct prose of courtroom speeches and historical narrative" (444). This distinction looks very much like Benveniste's more extremely stated one between absolute and situational and between aphoristic and narrative uses. Yet Benveniste is clearly more inclined to see content in the nominal structure than is Kahn, who sees it in the verb, and interpretative biases that historically have proved recurrent are again evident in their differences regarding the structures of predication and being.

Notwithstanding them, Zwingli's observation about the translation of Hebrew, or indeed, of Greek, holds true, however: in western European countries, whose modern languages generally lack the nominal sentence—acknowledged even by Kahn as an *apparent* phenomenon—its translation customarily will, and arguably must, employ the verbal form *is* and will thereby open the words of institution to the ambiguity inherent in the history of this verb, not only in its original relation to the nominal sentence but also in its subsequent relation to itself—to the two concepts of being, essential and existential, nominal and truly verbal, copulative and substantive, within it. Insofar as the word *translation*—Latin *translatio*, literally "a carrying over or across"—is an early modern word for the arch-trope metaphor, a translation from Hebrew or Greek is potentially a tropic transfer of meaning, and in the biblical translations of western Europe, this metaphorical potential similarly exists within the verb of being itself.

Discussing this same bifunctionality of the verb *to be* from a modern philosophical perspective, Ernst Cassirer, like Benveniste, responds to the significance of the nominal sentence for meaning. He employs the opposed terms "predicative" and "existential" or "relational" and "absolute" or even "formal" and "sensuous" in his characterization of it, associating the latter term in each pair—existential, absolute, sensuous—with the languages of early and "primitive" peoples who employ the nominal sentence, "lacking . . . a copula in our logical-grammatical sense" and perceptually having "no need of one."[12] Intent on the Kantian rationality of the copula, he agrees with Benveniste that the apparent copula of the nominal sentence is only apparent but disagrees with the linguist's sense of the formal (grammatical) timelessness, impersonality, and essentiality of such sentences. To the contrary, the missing copula in the nominal sentence "is not a universal term, serving to express relation *as such*, but . . . designates existence in this or that place, a being-here or being-there, or else an existence in this or that

moment. . . . Formal 'being' and the formal meaning of relation are replaced
. . . [in the nominal sentence] by more or less materially conceived terms
which still bear the coloration of a particular sensuously given reality" (314–
15). Cassirer cites examples of nominal assertion such as "The city big" or
"I man," rather than the more aphoristic examples that Benveniste favors,
albeit not exclusively.[13]

Even in languages with a sharply developed sense of "the logical singularity of the copula," Cassirer continues, the underlying sensuous signification
of the verb *to be* itself—namely, "to exist," "to occur in reality"—persists.
But he also finds that this underlying meaning "comes ultimately to be so
permeated with the relational" one that it emerges as "the sensuous vehicle
of a purely ideal signification" (318). In this way, the material and formal,
the existential and essential, and the sensuous and "the spiritual" (ideal) become reciprocally determined, and "language shows itself to be *at once* a
sensuous and an intellectual form of expression" (318–19). The philosopher's observations are not historically precise, but by "ultimately" he
hardly intends a period prior to the Enlightenment. In Reformation terms,
however, the reciprocal determination he describes might be approximated
to, or recognized as a translation of, something between the substantive verb
of real presence and the figurative verb of absence, and thus between the
extremes of Luther and Zwingli. This is the middle ground eventually oc-
cupied by Calvin, whose preeminence in England is a somewhat later story
than the one that will centrally concern me in this chapter, namely, the con-
flicted ground that Cranmer and several of the figures associated with him
inhabited.

Benveniste and Cassirer, the linguist and the philosopher, approach the
content of the nominal sentence-form from different perspectives and with
different criteria of assessment, and, as we have seen, they differ regarding its
nature: timeless, impersonal, and essential, on the one hand, and temporal,
concrete and specific, on the other. They agree, however, on the fact of its
historical relevance to the verb *to be*, into which historically it is folded, and
they align it with one or the other concept of being this verb expresses,
Benveniste with the essential and copulative, Cassirer with the sensuous and
existential. Their differences bear a curious resemblance to that between *langue* and *parole*, language as system and as actual speech, and they exemplify
the charged debate for which the verb of being has proved a lightning rod
over the centuries. Whatever the validity of these particular differences,
which must also be weighed against Kahn's view that the nominal sentence
is insignificant, they, too, parallel the linguistic history of eucharistic debate

that the Renaissance inherits and Reformation debate regarding the Eucharist itself. Roughly speaking, Cassirer's view of the nominal sentence has affinities with the older, Catholic position; Benveniste's with the new, reformed one. Their differing views also have farther-reaching alignments with the realisms and materialisms that interpenetrate late medieval and early modern culture, but here I again anticipate a stage of my story that will build on mid-century English debates about the Eucharist.

Observing the history of eucharistic theology from the early Fathers to Thomas More, Brian F. Byron has noted a shift involving the verb *to be* "from expressions of identity (or essence) to those of presence," which is also a shift from the copulative to the substantive mode of *is*.[14] As Byron explains the difference,

> "Essence" is from the Latin *esse*, the copulative "to be." This copulative *esse* is to be distinguished from the substantive *esse* meaning "to exist." "Presence" is from *praeesse*, "to be before," in which *esse* has the substantive meaning. (430)

Byron maintains that in the New Testament (language unspecified) the verb "to be" referring to the Eucharist "is always the copula," as it is in the writings of the Fathers (430). But where the Fathers affirm "*what the eucharist is*," or "This IS my body," the Scholastics translate the copulative *is* to the substantive one: "This my body IS." They "assert . . . that the Body of Christ is *present* or is 'contained' in the Eucharist," and their assertions reappear in the eucharistic arguments of early modern controversialists, such as Thomas More and Stephen Gardiner.[15] The particular realism of presence or presence within, is further heightened, he also suggests, by a concomitant "shift from the Semitic concept of 'flesh'" (e.g., flesh of my flesh, flesh and bone, flesh and blood) to the less elemental and more "holistic term 'body'" (434, 436). In general terms, the shifts Byron characterizes illustrate the transfer within culture of linguistic to doctrinal history, and in more specific ones, they reverberate within the Reformation debates about the words of institution. Crucially, the translation from copulative to substantive *is* that he identifies reveals a historical instance in which the metaphoric potential within the verb *to be* is realized, and language becomes history.

As argument about the sacrament proceeded at mid-century in Reformation England, there was general agreement, according to Cranmer, the reform-minded Archbishop of Canterbury, that "the very pith of the matter, and the chief point whereupon the whole controversy hangeth, [is] whether in these words, 'This is my body,' Christ called bread his body." Cranmer noticeably shifts the issue from being to calling, from object to language, truth to interpretation. Elsewhere he complains that his conservative opponents "still repeat and beat upon [the same words, 'This is my body']. . . . And this saying they make their sheet-anchor."[16] Although the term "saying" could apply to any utterance, it more familiarly refers to an adage, a proverb, a motto, or an axiom, the very sense that Cranmer's "sheet-anchor" assumes; the Archbishop insinuates the issue of being into a figure known to rhetoric as paroemia, literally translated, a "byword" or "proverb."[17]

Peter Martyr, a Continental expatriate who lived in England, experienced Cranmer's hospitality, and influenced his thinking, makes the related point that "oure aduersaries as we dooe holde that . . . [Christ's eucharistic saying] is a true proposicion or sentence. And all oure contencion and striefe is onelye aboute the sense or meanynge of it." This sense concerns "howe and in what mannier it is his bodye."[18] Of course the larger issue here is how words mean. Since in Martyr's reading the manner of Christ's saying is figurative and the meaning is spiritual, truth and figuration come enticingly—perhaps also deceptively—close in it. Just how they are related remains central throughout the Reformation debate about meaning.

Again and again, the reformers confront the conservative insistence that "all these aduerbes, really, substancially with the rest [e.g., 'vnfaynedly'], be conteyned in the one worde (is) spoken out of his mouthe" (*Explication*, sig. D4r). This literalist claim by Stephen Gardiner, Bishop of Winchester, complements his earlier denial that *est* in the same instance signifies "a resemblaunce, (& not the beynge, as the verbe substantiue properly doth signifie)."[19] For him, the bread and wine are "not bare tokens" both because Christ is "spiritually present in them" and because his presence is necessarily "real and substanciall" (*Explication*, sigs. B1r–v, B5v). Emphatically, he *is* there physically, and he is *in* the elements. The word also has a real relation to the material thing, not just a figurative relation, and not just to a spiritual thing.

Linguistic literalism—what both sides considered the "plaine . . . signification of the wordes"—aligns with objective, physical reality, and tropology with the subject and spirit (Martyr, fol. 44r). Either side recognizes the other dimension of meaning, but secondarily and less crucially. While the English reformers assert the figurative character of Christ's whole statement regarding the bread, they put less emphasis on any single part of it. Their focus has become rather rhetorical and contextual than grammatical and logical, and this shift has made a very real difference. With it, the underlying linguistic issue within the verb of being is avoided, as in Cranmer's shift of focus from being to naming, or calling, and to figuration, or else its focus is broadened to the sentence and beyond. At the same time, this linguistic issue is diachronically present in the reformers' reliance on the writings of the early Fathers, not to say on the Bible itself. A fundamental diachrony, while not unique to Reformation Christianity, is a heightened characteristic of it, the linguistic dimensions of which await further exploration. Scholastic argument, in which the assertions of Peter Lombard, Augustine, Bonaventure, Albertus Magnus, and a few others regularly provide points of departure and reference, is nonetheless marked by a degree of presentism—in part the result of methodological abstraction—that is missing from the arguments of more historically oriented theologians like Cranmer.

Cranmer and those minded like him, however, also read Patristic writings in ways inconceivable without the Luther-Zwingli debates about real presence and particularly without Zwingli's seminal insight into the metaphoricity inherent in the verb of being. Although taking a variety of forms, the reformed understanding of the words of institution as "tropical, figurative, analogical, allegorical" is derived from Zwingli's earlier linguistic claim, as Oecolampadius' version of it prototypically instances.[20] The linguistic diachrony implicit in such reformed claims does not always or necessarily result in the right reading of a Patristic text, but it finds sustenance in texts that often exhibit a different use and signal a divergent understanding of the verb *to be* from that of the Scholastics.

A significant defense against the conservative assertion of substantiation by the verb comes in the reformers' countercharge that the verb of being in the old religion is actually the vehicle of change or transubstantiation: the Catholics "dooe muche abuse the latine verbe substantif, *Est*, and muche contrarie to the propre significacion that [*est*]" should have caused it "to signifie *transubstanciatur*[,] is chaunged in substaunce, or to stand for *conuertitur* . . . or for *transmutatur*. . . . [If] thei should take *est*, in his true and propre significacioun: they should speake that thyng, whiche is false and not true" (Martyr, fol. 15r). Thus it is the conservatives' *est* that is fundamentally metaphorical, a *translatio* or carrying of one thing across to another, and in this case a substantial translation, to boot. Perhaps the crucial difference is that for the conservatives, the translation is objective and real, whereas for the reformers, transubstantiation occurs merely in language. Their charge is the obverse of Gardiner's charge that the allegories of the reformers will subvert truth, "and all our religion [will be] reduced to significations," to mere language.[21] While both sides assert spiritual presence, the conservatives crucially in the elements of bread and wine, the reformers definitively in the believer, what finally and most fundamentally separates them is the spiritual status of the material realm, and what joins them is a fear of mere language—language unmoored to a material or spiritual reality outside it—which is precisely and ironically the linguistic condition their arguments and counter-arguments work to expose. This irony may have more to do with the subtleties about being and figuration in Renaissance literature that continue to fascinate us than we have recognized.

The fear of language is manifest in the very intensity of the reformers' scorn for the metaphoricity of transubstantiation and in their anxious effort to distinguish their own figuration from that of the poets and playwrights. For example, John Hooper, a prelate-martyr whose fiery fate was a prelude to Cranmer's, compares the conservative interpretation of the words of institution to a Canterbury Tale or an Ovidian metamorphosis. The words "*Hoc est corpus meum,*" he declares, "make no more for the transubstantiation of the bread . . . than *In nova fert animus mutatas dicere formas corpora* [the beginning of Ovid's *Metamorphoses*], proveth *Verbum caro factum est, et habitavit in nobis* [the beginning of the gospel of St. John]." Eager to disqualify appeals to the troublesome *est*, Hooper, a relatively radical voice among the reforming English prelates, insists that this verb proves nothing, unless the bread is really and substantially the body of Christ to begin with.[22] He rejects a role for language even correlative with, let alone causal of, real change. While the verb of being is his immediate, primary concern, the realism of conservative analogy, another mode of metaphor, is a secondary one. More than once we have seen the two related.

Reform-minded writers like Peter Martyr and Nicholas Ridley, a prelate close to Cranmer who shortly preceded him to the stake, are at pains to distinguish their own interpretation of a sacrament, or figure, from a merely fictive one, or, in Ridley's words, "a bare sign, or a figure, to represent Christ, none otherwise than the ivy-bush doth represent the wine in a tavern; or as a vile person gorgeously apparelled may represent a king or a prince in a play" (*Declaration*, 10). Martyr similarly distances the sacramental figuration he embraces from dramatic fiction as he seeks to rationalize why some of the Patristic writers spoke of the sacrament in an "vnpossible" or realistic way. He suggests three reasons: they sought merely to echo Scripture, not to explain it; they were attempting to move the people more powerfully; and they wished to show "this signification was not like to thynges signifyed in a comedie or tragedie. For in such enterludes, any of the players beyng disguised in his players apparell maye represente the person of Hector or Priamus, . . . but whan he hathe placed [*sic:* played] his parte he is the same man that he was before": indeed, to borrow a question from Hamlet's response to the players, "What's Hecuba to him, or he to Hecuba [then]?" In contrast, the worthy actor in a sacramental rite is more, if not wholly other, than before, because he is "made one thing with Christ" (fol. 61v). The difference lies in the intensifying, transmuting effect of the sacrament rather than in its fictive or physical nature. This effect is psychological but also spiritual; it is assured—warranted by divinity and not simply imagined. But it is hardly a wonder that fiction per se could seem so threatening, lacking, as it did, a warrant of truth in either the material world or that of the spirit, but otherwise one with the sacrament.

The perceived, though threatening, proximity of truth to fiction and psychology to spirit (threats that linger in more than one quarter today) produced debate that shows considerable sensitivity to language. In an exchange with the conservative Richard Smith, who has argued that if Christ merely called bread his body, then bread was "given to death for you," Cranmer mocks a literalism baffled by metalepsis and metonymy; at the same time, his examples attest to the figurality even of ordinary language: And so "a man may not take a loaf in his hand made of wheat that came out of Dantzic, and say this is wheat that grew in Dantzic, but it must follow, that the loaf grew in Dantzic. And if the wife shall say, this is butter of my own cow, Smith shall prove by this speech that her maid milked butter" (*Answer*, 33). Cranmer's wit seems merely commonsensical, until we recall that it occurs in a treatise in which the correspondence of words to things is becoming less clear and in a context in which blatantly realistic language—the language of Catholicism—occurs with nothing but a figurative referent unless its psychic effect is confirmed by the spirit: thus, Cranmer writes, "we receive the body of Christ with our mouths, see him with our eyes, feel him with our hands, break him and tear him with our teeth, eat him and digest him (which speech I have also used in my catechism;) but yet these speeches must be understood figuratively" (*Answer*, 55–56). The eating is "as it were," "as though," or "as if," and in a word, it is metaphoric.[23] Cranmer exaggerates its realism both to convey the actuality of spiritual hunger and to make literal interpretation unreasonable, indeed, horrific.[24] Yet the danger of inconsistency or deception, of mere subjectivity and solipsism, is also apparent in his use of such language, and ironically in a religion that has given new primacy to the plain word, this danger suggests its unreliability. Later in the same century, Edmund Spenser's *Faerie Queene* will aptly describe the cave of Error, a monster that vomits volumes of religious writing, as a place "Where plaine none might her see, nor she see any plaine": exactly what "plaine" *is* and what *is* "plain" are everywhere the issues underlying, and sometimes undermining, the linguistic surface (I.i.16).

The conservative Gardiner displays a sophistication about language every bit as developed as that of Cranmer and his associates, but he marshalls it in the interest of containment. For example, he readily makes the seemingly modern admission that "There is no speache so plaine and simple, but it hath somne peice of a figuratiue speache," but then he adds, "the common vse of the figure causeth it to be taken as a common propre speache" (*Explication*, sig. G6v). His explanation can be paralleled in standard rhetorics of the Renaissance, whether under "trope," "metaphor," or "catechresis," where it is often accompanied by an apology for the shortcomings of "natural," as distinct from figurative, language. While Cranmer appeals to usage as evidence of figuration, however, Gardiner cancels his own recognition of its extent by invoking usage and thereby dead metaphor or cliché. For a modern reader, their arguments have a faintly familiar ring, recalling the highly charged debate between Paul Ricoeur and Jacques Derrida over dead metaphors and living ones, canceled debts as opposed to synchronic ones.[25]

Gardiner also calls on figure to evidence its self-cancellation: since Christ "was the body of al the shadowes & figures of the law . . . We must vnderstand his wordes in the institucion of his sacraments without figure in the substaunce of the celestial thyng of them" (*Explication*, sig. D3v). His statement is ambiguous in a striking way: in it, the word "substaunce" refers equally well to the substance (subject matter) of the words or of the sacraments (material reality), and in this way it mirrors the real relation he sees between them. Here, neither word nor correspondent thing turns out to be substantially figurative. Analogy, which the reformers saw as rhetoric, has also a real, causal relation to a present effect in Gardiner's statement: since Christ was the body implicit in the shadows, we *must* see the substance at once in his words and the thing.

The reformers are the ones who open a (pre)Cartesian chasm between the mind's figures and a world that is materially real. Oddly, for Gardiner they do so because they are materialists. For him, their understanding is "carnall" since it answers to the testimony of their senses regarding the bread. To Gardiner's adversaries, of course, his literal understanding of *est* is carnal because it requires material presence to be real and is therefore impervious to the truth of the spirit. The issues, indeed the categories, here are at once confused and important. The eucharistic debates of the earlier half (roughly) of the sixteenth century constitute an epistemological watershed between the earlier age and the one to come. Alone, they hardly cause this overdetermined cultural crisis, but even aside from their contribution to its content, they critically organize and crucially express it.[26]

Consider the subject of matter itself, for instance. Gardiner complains that Cranmer "hath diffamed as it were the termes carnally, and corporally, as termes of grossenes, to whom he vsed alwaies to put as an aduersatiue, the term spiritually, as thoughe carnally, and spiritually might not agre in one" (*Explication*, sig. G8r). This idea, that matter, here the redeemed flesh, and spirit are complementary and that both obtain for salvation, is at least in theory the dominant late medieval position. It relates to belief in a visible church and thence to a theory of the Papacy. In reference to modern scholarship, it includes Caroline Bynum's radical revaluing of the flesh in medieval devotional beliefs and practices. But the visible church was also materially restrictive and corruptible, whether in historical or geographical terms, and Bynum's view grants no rights to the "real" body—the material body as *we* know it—which is to be suppressed, abused, or actively tortured in order to attain political and spiritual ends. The medieval notion of matter, physical and specifically fleshly as it can be in practice, is still conceived *sub spiritu*. Although a material body can contribute to spiritual honor and resist lesser societal codes through privation and abuse, its behavior is nonetheless authorized by, and bound to, the spirit. It inevitably resists within the same dominant societal field in which it is expressed. This is a field in which matter can be transvalued, and its intractability to the mind greatly lessened.[27]

At least in Reformation England, the materiality of the substance a conservative like Gardiner defends also turns out to be qualified, and heavily so. Engaging Cranmer's question as to why we might not believe our senses with respect to the substance of the bread, as well as to the accidents or appearance, Gardiner offers as his answer a witty, imagined encounter between a scholar and a "rude[, 'sensuall'] man," the latter an obvious stand-in for the learned Archbishop. This "rude" (that is, ignorant) man asks the scholar to show him the difference among the substances of bread, cheese, and ale, and the scholar first explains the fundamentals, namely, that "the substance is the inwarde nature, wherin those that be accidentes do naturally staye, the quantite immediatly, and the rest by meane of quantite." Impatiently, the rude man demands, "Callest thowe not this substance, this goode rownde thicke piece [of bread] that I handle?" He hears the reply that substance, properly understood, is neither seen nor felt by itself, "yet by reason,

[is] comprehended truely to be in that we fele & see" and "in comen speach
. . . is vsed to signifie that is seen or felt, & so ye may say ye see the substance
or feale the substance of bread, & yet ye [do] . . . in deade[28] see but the
colour, and by it the largenesse, and feale the heate, or coldenes, moysture,
or drynes, weight, or lightnes, hardenes, or softnes, thicknes, and thynnes."
Implicitly glossing the meaning of the substantive verb, Gardiner then ad-
vises, "If ye will learne what substance is ye must leue your outwarde
sences & considre in your vnderstandyng howe in euery thynge that is, there
is a staye [support or base], whiche we call a substance, beyng the principall
parte of euery thyng, whiche fayling we saye that speciall thyng not to be."
To be or not to be, after all, is still the question, yet "The rude man I thinke
would herat say, here is sophistrie in deade, for here is substance & no substance, matter of bread & no bread, apparance of bread & no bread, called
bread and no bread, this is to playe iugling where it happeneth."[29]

Cranmer's version of this same "sophistrie" concerning the transubstan-
tiated bread affords the model for what Gardiner parodies: "there remaineth
whiteness, but nothing is white: there remaineth colours, but nothing is col-
oured therewith: there remaineth roundness, but nothing is round: and
there is . . . breaking, without any thing broken; division without anything
divided: and so other qualitites and quantities, without anything to receive
them" (*Answer*, 45). Cranmer's objection operates within Gardiner's terms,
insisting only that accidents must inhere in their proper substance and not
questioning the basic division of objects into substance and accident. But
the Archbishop goes further when he exclaims, "take away the accidents,
and I pray you what difference is between the bodily substance of the sun
and the moon, of a man and a beast, of fish and flesh, between the body of
one beast and another, one herb and another, one tree and another, between
a man and a woman? yea, . . . between any one corporal thing and another?" (*Answer*, 260). Even if in theory not essential to a thing, the accidents in this view are nonetheless proper to its identity and necessary to its
definition. To recall an earlier discussion, we might employ an Aristotelian
paradox or, for that matter, a Derridean pun and term them essential
proper–ties.[30] The vexed question of Cranmer's nominalism aside, fictive
theory yields in his argument to the evident facts of material reality.[31]

The roots of the dispute between Cranmer and Gardiner reflect confla-
tions of essence and substance in the philosophic tradition. Essence (from
esse, "to be") is the identity of a thing—what it is—and this is defined by
Aristotle as its form, which is necessary and unchanging, as distinct from
matter. In Aristotle substance can mean the concrete individual thing but

primarily means the genus and species, and, for further complication, essences also occur secondarily as substances. The fact that Aristotle's account of substance is "obscure and probably inconsistent" illuminates the later history of these categories. For example, Augustine attributes the same meaning to the terms *essence* and *substance*, and Boethius translates the one as the other. Aquinas regards a substance as an existent essence, or in terms of physical bodies, as a form that has received matter. Literally, *substance* (from Latin *substo*) means "standing under," hence support or base (material, with reference to animal existence) for the accidents that inhere in it.[32] It is only within this confused philosophic tradition that Gardiner's distinction between "the accidentes of bread[, which] maye be called the matter of breade," and "the materiall breade"—the thing itself for him—makes sense. Cranmer's claim (as reported by Gardiner) that "to saye the materiall breade and the matter of breade" is "all one" again shows that he participates in the same tradition, if only to deny it in the name of physical reality (*Explication*, sig. P3r). It is as if Cranmer knew (though I'm not claiming he did) that Greek *ousia*, "essence" or "substance," also occurs in the philosophic tradition as a synonym for Greek *physis*, "stuff of which things are made," or as we might say, "physical nature."[33] Common sense (literal usage) or some shade of nominalism could have suggested the same conclusion to him.

If the status of the material realm, theoretical and physical, fictive and real, is one focus of debate, that of the spiritual realm is another. This focus, too, involves debate about fiction and specifically about tropes. More than once, as we've seen, Gardiner objects that even as Cranmer has sundered the carnal from the spiritual, he has equated the terms "figurative" and "spiritual." In interpreting a passage from Chrysostom, for example, Cranmer allegedly "vseth a sleight to ioyn figuratiuely to spiritually, *as though they were always all one, whiche is not so*" (*Explication*, sig. G1r: my emphasis). Gardiner also catches Cranmer rendering Augustine's description of the sacrament as Christ's body "(secundum quendam modum) after a certaine maner" as "after a certaine maner of spech" and thus translating what Gardiner interprets as a real change to a merely figurative and linguistic one—precisely the characteristic shift I have earlier remarked in Cranmer's writing (*Explication*, sig. G4r).

Had Gardiner been able to make his charges stick, then he would indeed have convicted his opponent of reducing spiritual truths to significations. His reading of Cranmer is obviously biased, however. Although there are places in Cranmer's writings where he appears to equate the terms *figuratively* and *spiritually* through a kind of shorthand, there are more telling ones in which he insists that "figuratively . . . [Christ] is in the bread and wine, and spiritually he is in them that worthily eat and drink the bread and wine" (*Answer*, 139). Here, the real analogy is not between word and matter, but between linguistic figure and internal affect. The change is *psychic* (from Greek *psyche*), a word I invoke for its poise between the meanings "mind" and "soul." Here, too, the crucial argument between Cranmer and Gardiner also reverts to the status of the object: in Cranmer's words, "Christ is not there [in or under the bread], neither corporally, nor spiritually," whereas, in Gardiner's, he is "there really & substancially," by which he intends corporally, "but in a spirituall maner" (*Answer*, 54; *Explication*, sig. F3r). Thus we are back to the meaning of Christ's assertion "This is my body."

If Gardiner's corporeality is to be understood in a spiritual manner, the firmness of Cranmer's distinction between outward symbol and inward effect is elsewhere qualified as well. In Cranmer's fateful disputation on the sacrament at Oxford in 1554, where he is obliged significantly to engage with logical terms and structures, his statements about figuration suggest that the reformed object is touched, at least conditionally, by the spiritual effect. This is the other side of the debate, one no longer between the conservative juncture of matter and spirit and the reformed separation of them, but now between magical object and naked sign, or bare token—Lear's "thing itself," in an analogous manner of speaking. On this side of the debate, because the political tide has turned with the death of Edward VI and the accession of Queen Mary, the reformers are on the defensive.

According to John Foxe's account of the Oxford disputation, Cranmer declares at one point to Owen Ogelthorpe, a conservative, "You know not what tropes are" (1433). Ogelthorpe, an arbiter of the disputation, has objected, "*qualis est corpus? qualis est predicatio* [what is the body? what is the predication]?" to Cranmer's answer that Christ, as Ogelthorpe puts it, "gaue his body in bread." First correcting Ogelthorpe's Latin to "*Quale corpus*," Cranmer affirms, "It is the same body which was borne of the virgin, was crucified, ascended: but tropically, & by a figure. And so I say, *Panis est corpus* [bread is the body: the predication at issue], is a figuratiue speache, speaking sacramentally, for it is a sacrament of his body" (1432). Reserving the condition "speaking sacramentally" (i.e., *sub specie fidei*), I would pursue what Cranmer intends by a trope or figure, which sequent exchanges clarify.[34]

Ogelthorpe next rebuts Cranmer in a syllogism: the word "body," being predicated, signifies substance; but "substance" is not predicated denominatively; therefore, "it is an essential predication, and so it is his true body, and not the figure of his body." To this, Cranmer counters, "*Substantia* [substance] may be predicated denominatiuely in an allegory, or in a metaphore, or in a figuratiue locution." It is to Ogelthorpe's then objecting that Christ would not use tropes in his last testament because they merely obfuscate and lie that Cranmer retorts, "Yes, he may vse them well enough. You know not what tropes are" (1432–33).

What Cranmer means by a denominative predication in an allegory, metaphor, or (other) figurative speech—metonymy, for a relevant example—is of greater interest than Ogelthorpe's familiar assumption that figurative language is deceptive. Glossing *denominative* contextually as "non-essential, insubstantial, or figurative" is useful but also redundant, since it repeats the text instead of explaining it. The logical usage "derivative" or "in a derivative sense" may offer a more enlightening alternative. In Aristotle, something can be denominated black that is not wholly so if it has enough black to justify the term; in such a case it can also be said to be black derivatively, insofar as the appropriateness of using the term black is *derived* from how much blackness there is in the thing.[35]

In a related example at the beginning of Aristotle's *Categories*, some things are said to be "paronymous," which has been translated *denominativa* [denominative] in the Latin tradition and becomes a theory of connotation in such nominalists as William of Ockham and Jean Buridan. The term "denominative" applies when a noun or adjective makes a kind of oblique reference to something else: for example, the words "just" and "justice" are derived one from the other (opinions differ on which from which), and there is some kind of systematic connection between what is called "justice" (the actual virtue itself) and what can be called "just" (just people, just governments). Here the appropriateness of calling something "just" is *derived* from the justice it has in it or exhibits. Put otherwise, something is called "just" denominatively.[36] In both examples—black and just(ice)—the propriety of the term derives from a thing's having a substantial amount or expressing a significant degree of the attribute in question.

In the eucharistic allegory, metaphor, or (other) figurative locution to which Cranmer attributes substance denominatively, or in a derivative sense, he affirms that the body is not essentially, and therefore not "really," a substance. At the same time, however, he affirms something more regarding its substantiality than if he had flatly asserted that the sacrament is merely bread. In logical terms, the connection between a figurative body and a real one is, if derived, systematic and appropriate; in this limited sense, it is proper, as his responses to Ogelthorpe imply. The figurative body has or expresses something derived from the real one that is substantial, though also equivocal, in the instance in question.

Metonymy is the figure invoked by reformers of different stripes and with different intentions perhaps more often than any other to explain the words of institution, and at times in the disputation at Oxford, as elsewhere, Cranmer appears to invoke it: Christ "calleth the sacraments by the names of the things: for he vseth the signes for the things signified: and therefore the bread is not called bread, but his body, for the excellencie and dignitie of the thyng signified by it" (1439). The usual emphasis on calling is here, along with association, but arguably little more. Here, it would seem, is neither identity nor predication—neither the absolute stability of Benveniste's nominal sentence nor even the predication necessary to Ricoeur's conception of metaphor—and thus denomination only in the simplest, least technical sense of verbal substitution or mere metonymic "naming."

Metonymy can be understood otherwise, however, as it variously had been by Scholastic theologians. In Thomas Aquinas, for example, extension, which is metonymic, is "an analogical mean between the extremes of . . . univocal and equivocal meaning." Such an extensive or metonymical relationship corresponds in Thomas' view "to something in the reality outside the mind."[37] The meaning or mode of signifying of the extended term—its "*denominating* form"—corresponds to this reality.[38] Metonymy, as explained here, participates in Thomas' realism and contrasts with equivocation and metaphor. In the view of Duns Scotus, for a different example, *denomination*, another metonymic conception, relevantly occurs in discussion of the *communicatio idiomatum* or exchange of the names "Word" and "man" in reference to Jesus. According to Scotus, "god" can be designated man denominatively—by *denominatio*, in rhetoric defined as "the substitution of the name of an object for that of another to which it has some relation, as the name of the cause for that of the effect, [or] of the property for that of the substance, [as in] . . . a metonymy."[39] Scotus argues that the Word, which subsists in Jesus' human nature as its supposit (from *supponere*, "to place under"), is formally man and that both the names "god" and "man," being common to several persons, are "ordered denominatively [*ordinatur denominative*]" in any one of them.[40] Scotus' theological position is unexceptional: Jesus' humanity and divinity and the distinction, crucial to salvation, between them are real. What is notable, however, is his use of *denominative* to characterize a statement that is correct given a certain qualifying under-standing, in this case of defining form. Within the later context of nominal-ist thought, the question its language focuses is whether what Scotus regards as the denominative order (an order of naming *properly*) is also an order of *being* that corresponds to something in a reality outside the mind or whether it belongs essentially to the mind, to an order of logic, rhetoric, and faith.[41] On the face of it, this question again gets us closer to Cranmer's careful, constrained, and somewhat equivocal responses in Oxford.

Through comparison, related statements by Cranmer and his associates, such as Nicholas Ridley, John Hooper, and Peter Martyr, can further clarify his argument in the disputation, albeit not without suggesting some variance in their views or at least in their expression of them. These views had, after all, changed in the course of their adult lives and, specifically in Cranmer's, from a Catholic to a Lutheran position and then to one sufficiently Zwin-glian for him to have stated near the end of his *Defence*, "we make no sacri-fice of him [Christ], but *only* a commemoration and remembrance of that sacrifice."[42] Yet if Cranmer's assertion to Ogelthorpe regarding the denomi-native predication of substance were to be read in connection with state-ments by Ridley, the friend and personal chaplain Cranmer credited with having led him to his final reformed belief, it would lend a positive quality to his responses that is reminiscent of metonymic extension and of the logi-cal derivation I've described, and then some.[43]

In Foxe's rendering of the disputation on transubstantiation licensed for Cambridge in 1549, during the heyday of reform under Edward VI, Ridley asserts that Christ's "body is there onely in a signe *vertually*, by grace, in the exhibition of it in spirite, effect, and fayth, to the worthy receiuer of it." Presuming the qualifications "by grace . . . in spirite, effect, and fayth," he later acknowledges not Christ's "reall substance to be there, but the proper-tie of hys substance," as would be the case in a metonymy. He then adds as a relevant condition that "the proprietie of essence in the deitie is the very essence, and what soeuer is in God, is God."[44] Since "vertually" (from Latin *virtus*) means "by virtue or power of [grace, in this instance]," Ridley argues that in divinity "property" or "propriety," part of what is proper to a sub-stance or being (Latin *proprietas*), amounts to much the same thing as that in which it inheres: what is effected by grace is so by a property of God's es-sence, which is in God, or as Ridley puts it, Christ's real substance is not there but the property of his substance is. Moreover, this property is present "onely in a signe vertually, by grace," and "in the exhibition of it in spirite, effect, and fayth" and to a "worthy receiuer."[45] Yet, with all these qualifications, there is a systematic, proper connection between the virtual, figurative eucharistic substance and divinity.[46] The body is, in a sign and by grace and in spirit, effect, and faith, virtually and derivatively present.

For a modern reader, the concept of virtual reality is an inescapable analogue to Ridley's argument, but this concept falls short of the realization (in both inner and outer senses) that is attributed to faith. Ridley's extreme virtualism stops short of Calvin's mature thought in lodging the communication of Christ's power in spirit and faith with merely derivative attention to the object, yet the difference between them is finally slight—more a matter of reference and emphasis, focus and rhetoric, and certainly not of substantial or bodily presence on Calvin's part.[47] Far from being a trivial or merely external matter, however, rhetoric, including Ridley's careful, multiple qualifications, proves surprisingly—I would say, incredibly—essential both to reformed belief in general and to its many subtle variations. As Heiko Obermann demonstrated long since, Reformation thinking is to a significant extent the offspring of late medieval nominalism, and the very age that derived the slur "dunce" from the name of Duns Scotus, *doctor subtilis* ("the subtle doctor"), is very much his descendant.[48] Another, it would seem, is the Derridean critique of Aristotle's concepts and specifically of the presence of metaphor in defining what a thing truly is, and therefore in what is "proper," although perhaps not "essential," to the thing—namely and punningly, a proper-ty ("Mythology," 48, 50).

Although the prelate Hooper, a more radical ecclesiastical reformer than Ridley, thinks of sacraments as "nothing else but a [Zwinglian] badge and open sign of God's favour," his explanation to Gardiner of how the sacrament is "not a bare sign and token of his [Christ's] death only" helps by comparison with Ridley's virtualism to define further what Cranmer's denomination (derivation) means.[49] Hooper distinguishes between all the sacraments of Christ and other signs as he does "between the seal of a prince, that is annexed unto the writing or charter that containeth all the prince's right and title . . . unto his realm, and the king's arms painted in a glass window." The matter of the seal is simply wax and the land is not "corporally nor really contained in the writing, nor annexed to the writing." Yet the seal on a charter, though lacking power in itself, "confirms" the king's title, whereas the arms in the window are merely a representation (*Answer*, 190–91). In a transferred or derivative sense, the seal could be considered efficacious, although the word seems almost to lose its charge in this context. Any other man's seal would similarly afford confirmation of his property, if not of a kingdom.

Examining Zwinglian metaphors for the Eucharist, Peter Martyr complains that they are "to[o] cold," and his complaint highlights a difference between his own views and the Zwinglians' to which I'll apply the ambiguous term "substantial" (fol. 105r). His complaint applies equally well to the metaphor of the seal as Hooper develops it, which strikes me rather as declarative and indicative than properly instrumental. Hooper's metaphor fails to appeal to divine right or regal power as such and thus to convey a sense of the special force invested in the sign. Right after unambiguously rejecting the possibility of Christ's body being "naturally, corporally, & really conteyned in the . . . breade," Peter Martyr also objects that the Zwinglians "seldome make mencion of the sacramental mutation of the breade & the wyne, which yet is no small matter," and his objection approaches Cranmer's position in Oxford when Cranmer holds, "'Panis est corpus' is a figurative speech, speaking sacramentally"—a figure, indeed, but given certain conditions, one that truly effects a change (fols. 106r–07r).

Predictably, this same, elusively poised affirmation of substantial significance and effect characterizes Cranmer's position in his Oxford disputation regarding the issue underlying figuration—the status and function of the words, as such, of institution. Conservative disputants argue that if these words are figurative, they have no efficacy; the speech they constitute "worketh nothing"; in contrast, "the [eucharistic] speach of Christ is a working thing" and therefore it cannot be figurative. In rebuttal, Cranmer replies, "I sayd not, that the words of Christ do worke, but Christ himselfe: and he worketh by a figuratiue speache." Rephrasing slightly, he stresses, "the speach doth not worke, but Christ, by the speache, doth worke the sacrament" (Foxe, 1438). This is clearly the charged "instrumentalism" identified by B.A. Gerrish with Calvin and by Diarmaid MacCulloch, citing Gerrish, with Cranmer.[50]

Notably, however, there are almost no references to Cranmer's familiarity with Calvin's writings in MacCulloch's capacious and enlightening biography, which abounds with references to relevant divines, and Basil Hall notes that Cranmer "never mentions Calvin in his published writings on the eucharist" (254).[51] Although Gerrish's work is immensely helpful in evaluating Cranmer's position, his command of Calvin's many revisions, including Calvin's most mature view in the final edition of the *Institutes* in 1559, three years after Cranmer's death, invites caution. As Archbishop from 1533–56, Cranmer was often embroiled in controversy and political maneuvering, and however genuine his scholarly credentials and theological achievements, he cannot have had unlimited time for them. Certainly he employed ghostwriters and relied on intermediaries like Martin Bucer and Peter Martyr to keep abreast of Continental developments (MacCulloch, 488). Compared to Calvin's theological position, Cranmer's appears more in process, more variable, and at times more elusive. In my reading, the status of the object is more focal for Calvin and its mystical nature considerably more pronounced.[52] In the relatively controlled confines of Geneva, he could perhaps afford to have it so.

In another exchange at Oxford about the "vertue of Gods word" in the sacrament, Cranmer affirms, "with the [Catholic] Church, that the bodye of Christ is in the sacrament effectually" (Foxe, 1430). When a conservative disputant challenges that the words " 'This is my body' " refer to the substance and not to the effect, Cranmer grants, as Ridley will, that "he spake of the substaunce, and not of the effect after a sorte [derivatively and figuratively, I assume]," and he again asserts that Christ's body is in the sacrament most effectually, albeit not in or under the bread, to which he refuses to confine the meaning of *sacrament* (1431). This looks again like presence of some sort, but definitely not a material presence. Perhaps Cranmer's clearest answer regarding the words of institution comes in the last revised response he made to Gardiner from prison: here, in a memorable phrase, he describes "Christ's words in the supper" as having "effectual signification." But the reason he gives unambiguously indicates what he means: "For he is effectually present . . . *in* the godly receivers" of the bread and wine (*Answer*, 34–35: my emphasis).[53] A page later, he adds, "to the godly eater," the words of the supper "be effectuous and operatory," and "so to the wicked eater, the effect is damnation and everlasting woe" (*Answer*, 36). The object is subject to the condition of its recipient. Christ is not absent but "present in his sacraments, as . . . in his word, when he worketh mightily by the same in the hearts of the hearers" (*Answer*, 11). This looks more like a dynamic presence than even an instrumental one, and it is radically interiorized.

Substance was a code word in eucharistic debate, as has been evident, and analogies between the sun, its sunbeams, and Christ's substantial presence are recurrent in it as well. In 1539, Calvin added to the images of the chain and the channel the rays radiating from the sun to convey the idea of a power that comes from Christ in the sacraments: thus in *Institutes* 4.17.8, the sun " 'casts its substance' " on the earth by shining its rays. Our union with Christ through faith is "substantial" and a "*substantialis vigor*" flows from him as head to us as members.[54] Gardiner is attracted to the use of the solar analogy by Bucer, another expatriate reformer influential in England and specifically on Cranmer, since it also makes the point that the sun is "substantially present" on earth by means of its sunbeams.[55] Of course "substantially" means "really" or "bodily" to Gardiner. What Cranmer repeatedly stresses, however, is that "as the sun corporally is ever in heaven, and no where else, and yet *by his operation and virtue* . . . is here in earth, . . . so likewise our Saviour" (*Answer*, 89: my emphasis).[56]

It would not be hard to imagine the puzzled frustration of Gardiner's uneducated layman—his "rude man"—if faced with the subtleties of denomination, derivation, virtuality, and propriety or with nuanced distinctions among various conceptions of substance and essence; nor to imagine this layman's yearning instead for a "goode rownde thicke piece" of bread and for the familiarity and reassurance of the visible, tangible sacred object.[57] But there is another side to the reformers' efforts to express their metaphorical notion of presence that brings the abstraction of their conceptual thought down to earth. This side is affective, and it is especially invested in language and rhetoric, indeed in a way that resonates suggestively with the great literature of the early modern period. Or perhaps it is more accurate to describe the two sides merely as different aspects of a single conception, insofar as the efforts of reformers such as Cranmer, Ridley, and Martyr to explain the cognitive aspect of their metaphorical presentism not only always includes, but also requires, and even depends on the affective, psychological one.

Attention to psychology is inevitable in a theology of the sacrament that crucially locates its effect within the recipient. Both the psychological effect of the sacrament and the words conveying it are inseparable from the "efficacye which is due vnto" (i.e., results from) the "sacramental mutation of the breade & the wyne," for, as Martyr explains, "these thynges are not made vulgare or comon signes, but suche signes as maye myghtily & strongly stiere vp the mynde."[58] Memorably glossing Theophylactus, Cranmer makes this mutation explicitly a change "into the virtue" of Christ's being for the faithful recipient: "as hot and burning iron is iron still, and yet hath the force of fire; and as the flesh of Christ, still remaining flesh, giveth life, as the flesh of him that is God; so the sacramental bread and wine remain still in their proper kinds; and yet to them[59] that worthily eat and drink them, they be turned not into the corporal presence, but into the virtue of Christ's flesh and blood" (*Defence*, 187). Martyr's sense that the similitudes favored by Zwinglians are too cold to "weorke any alteracion or chaunge . . . in the thynker" or to feed and nourish "hys mynde" illuminates Cranmer's attention to affect: his adaptation—apparently with Luther's help—of Theophylactus' vivid image of hot iron; his use, cited earlier, of realistic, "Catholic" language to dramatize the truth of the sacrament; or more generally, his justly admired liturgical compositions.[60] Among these, Cranmer's "most enduring monument" remains the *Book of Common Prayer,* a widely disseminated book whose language had an enormous influence on the development of English both in this period and beyond it.[61]

Ricoeur's theory of metaphorical imagination and feeling bears suggestively on Cranmer's and Ridley's scholastic language of efficacy, illuminating what they seek to convey. Ricoeur conceives of the psychlogical features of metaphor—images and feelings—as having a semantic or meaningful function that complements that of its cognitive features. Good metaphors do not simply convey content, they enable "its mental actualization"; they " 'set before the eyes' the sense they display." If Ricoeur's description of metaphor were not already suggestive enough in relation to the function the reformers assigned to the metaphoric elements of bread and wine, it becomes even more so: "it is as though the tropes gave to discourse a quasi-bodily externalization," one that is there and not there. "By providing a kind of figurability to the message, the tropes [*figures,* after all, of speech] make discourse appear."[62] The Reformation commonplace that the sacraments are "words visible," "speakyng signes" that give visible form to God's words, resonates in the background of Ricoeur's explanation, along with derivation and virtual presence.[63] It is as if the reformers' conception had taken this explanation one step further, conceiving of figuration in dramatic terms as an actual performance of metaphor, in this case at a table or altar.

Seeing Cranmer's communion rite as sacred drama, Julia Houston has noted its iconic aspect, and Ricoeur, after Charles Sanders Pierce and Paul Henle, has argued for an iconic aspect of metaphor, of which virtually visible words are an expression.[64] But as Ricoeur asserts—and as Houston also grants with respect to Cranmer's rite—the verbal element, particularly the words of predication, must control the iconic if the latter is to be meaningful or to belong in a semantic theory.[65] Ricoeur, now following Marcus Hester, refers in this connection to " 'bound' images, that is, concrete representations aroused by the verbal element and controlled by it" (148–49). This is a point about which the reformers were similarly adamant, insisting that exhibition of the sacramental signs be accompanied by the explication and preaching of God's word. Like Ricoeur's theory, their theology of efficacy is finally poised between a semantics of metaphor and a psychology of imagination.

Ricoeur also distinguishes between emotions and what he calls "genuine feelings." The latter, which he also terms "poetic," in fact "imply a kind of *epoché* [suspension] of our bodily emotions"; for example, "When we read, we do not literally feel fear or anger," and Aristotelian catharsis entails "both the denial and the transfiguration of the literal feelings of fear and compassion" (155–56). Feelings are "not merely inner states but interiorized thoughts." Far from being opposed to thought, feeling "is thought made ours." It involves a "felt participation" that is part of the meaning of metaphor or of metaphoric structure (154). As Martyr put it, the sacraments, metaphorical to their core, are "such signes as maye myghtily & strongly stiere vp the mynde," and as Cranmer protests, Christ is not absent but "present in his sacraments, as . . . in his word, when he worketh mightily by the same in the hearts of the hearers" (*Answer*, 11).

The most perceptive ideas about metaphor, as about close reading in the Renaissance, are often to be extracted from the writings of the theologians, rather than from those of the rhetoricians (if the distinction is tenable). These are the ideas that resonate most strongly with the practice of the great poets and playwrights of the period. Metaphor is finally the conception and inseparably the form upon which a historical reformation of human perception and belief is founded and which remains very much with us in contemporary epistemological argument. The relevance of its early modern background is clearly evident in the Ricoeur-Derrida dispute about metaphorical meaning, for one telling example related to the founding assumptions of either's epistemology. Knowing more of this background is instructive and exhilarating in a peculiarly academic way, and yet the implication of language in history and history in language is, in the main, deeply sobering, a witness to a kind of inevitability in even brilliantly rational arguments that gestures toward larger structures. Having looked at these in the last two chapters, I want to turn to the possibilities of their local and immediate manipulation through metaphor in the two that follow.

4. *Donne's Tropic Awareness: Metaphor, Metonymy, and* Devotions upon Emergent Occasions

To ask in what ways and to what extent John Donne might have been aware of the dazzling tropes he used would seem a question whose answer is self-evident. Historically, however, this is a real question, and one bearing on faith and ideology. To take an obvious instance, the correspondences invoked so often in Donne's writing are to us metaphoric fiction, but as extensions of a single, celestial power, hence valid and real parallels, they presumably meant more for Donne and his immediate audience, even in their more skeptical moments. They assume the familiar centered universe organized hierarchically from low to high and dense to rare: what exists on one level really corresponds to what exists on another. Through the culturally sedimented extensions of meaning available in word play—puns, metonymic substitutions, and the like—perception can move vertically or horizontally among recognized correspondences with the assurance of meaningful relationship or, at the very least, of a meaningful denial of relationship insofar as this belongs to the same field or paradigm.

But no trope is so innocent of complicating consequences. All involve some degree of translation, *translatio*, the name normally, but perhaps also misleadingly, reserved for the arch-trope metaphor in traditional rhetorical classification. If names have real and not simply conventional references, tropology, including even metonymic extension and other forms of word-play, disturbs this relationship; a trope, after all, is literally a "turn" away from the true, original, or "natural" referent. For the purpose of illustration, take an obvious metonymy from the presumably less centered modern universe, such as the lunch counter waitress' calling to another server, "The ham sandwich wants a cup of coffee."[1] As the Renaissance rhetorician George Puttenham remarked, such a metonymic "misname[ing]" carries "an alteration of sence," by which he intends only a shift into tropic register, but an alteration, a swerving, it nonetheless remains (191). For someone who is outside the lunch counter code, the substitution of "ham sandwich" for the customer is comic on the face of it: if the ham sandwich wants a cup of coffee, well, why not give it one? Outside the lunch counter code, either we literalize the ham sandwich in blank puzzlement or else we personify it, converting it to metaphor and cartoon. Here, metonymy, as Umberto Eco has argued, is essentially the language of codes and, in a broader sense, of ideology, and metaphor becomes our rational appropriation of whatever is alien and other.[2] With all the analytical and theoretical ink spilled in the past two centuries over metaphor and metonymy as master tropes and over the paradigmatic differences between them—Friedrich Nietzsche, Roman Jakobson, and Paul de Man come conspicuously to mind—this common conversion of the one to the other has too often been unremarked, as has its relation to shifts in ideological audience and historical context and thus to coding and decoding.[3]

Metaphor, of course, is a great deal else besides rational appropriation, including the ability to alter and create new codes and thus to use the traditional resources of language in a way that exceeds them. This, to my mind, is characteristically what Donne does. But as a way of thinking about the nature of his awareness of contemporary codes as at least potentially distinct from that I bring to his text as a modern reader and more crucially about the relation of metaphor and metonymy—as creative fiction and referential coding—I would look at some landmarks, not to say mountains, on the tropological landscape of the Renaissance period. These are theological landmarks that Donne knew personally or at least knew about, namely Luther, Zwingli, and Calvin. These theologians engage tropology as substance or content and not merely as form, and their assertions and affirmations inform the culture in which Donne thinks and writes.

The seemingly arcane subject of the *communicatio idiomatum*, the communication of divine and human properties in the God-man, which Luther's influence virtually bonded to consideration of the Eucharist, affords a rich and pertinent example of tropological context. Departing from the traditionally firm distinction between the human and divine natures of Christ, Luther insists that the glorified body of Christ shared modes of presence *proper* to his divine nature, specifically omnipresence. Luther presumably did so because his conception of the Eucharist required that this body be present along with the bread. His understanding of Christ's unity and ministry also led him, in another break with the dominant earlier tradition, to argue that the whole person of Christ, "who is God, suffer[ed]," although, he conceded, in his humanity.[4] Engaged with Zwingli in a series of arguments regarding these views, he expended his wrath on Zwingli's copious rhetorical concepts, singling out for particular scorn the figure "alleosis." Zwingli had found this trope in Plutarch and defined it as "that leap or transition or . . . interchange, by which, when speaking of one of Christ's natures, we use the terms that apply to the other."[5] As a leap, transition, or interchange, alleosis is not only tropic but clearly also translative and therefore, as Luther intuits, ominously metaphoric and fictive. In Luther's colorful writing, alleosis takes on a notably gendered life of its own, becoming a virtual character for a parodic allegory. For example, Luther dismisses "the old witch, Lady Reason, alloeosis' grandmother," for suggesting "that the Deity surely cannot suffer and die," or he invokes "Lady Alleosis" to "stand godmother" for an interpretation of scripture that he thinks wrongheaded (210, 235). He asks why, if Zwingli "is so fond of tropes, . . . isn't he satisfied with the old trope which Scripture and all teachers up to now have used," namely synecdoche, and he offers as an example to buttress his own view " 'Christ died according to his humanity,'" a synecdoche in which "humanity" stands for the composite whole, the indivisible God-man of Luther's conception (211).[6] Notably, Luther's trope, understood within the context of his thinking, is self-canceling—contained, inconsequential, strictly nominal. Luther later charges Zwingli with dividing the person of Christ, with the result that a mere man—indeed a mere body—died for us without accomplishing redemption, and then he continues, "we recognize here no alleosis, no heterosis [Zwingli's synonym for alleosis], no ethopoeia [a related Zwinglian variant], nor any other trick that Zwingli produces out of his magician's kit" (231). The magician's rhetorical art is illusory, merely fictive; it lacks a referent that is true or real.

Against Zwingli's objection to "identical predication" or the simultaneous presence of two substances in one, in this instance the presence of both bread and body in the Lutheran celebration of the Eucharist, Luther responds by citing relevant instances of personal, natural, and effectual union, respectively the hypostatic union in Christ—two natures in one person— "the union of natures" in the triune Godhead, and an angel in a flame. The last of these examples, which is based on Psalm 104—"He makes his angels winds and his ministers flames of fire"—Luther discusses at some length: "Here also there are two kinds of being, angels . . . and flames of fire, just as in the sacrament[,] bread and body. Yet here Scripture makes a single being out of the two, . . . so that one must say of these . . . flames, 'This is an angel.' . . . Now no one can see an angel in his intrinsic nature but only in his form of flame or brightness; moreover, this form of brightness does not have to vanish if one points to it and says, 'This is an angel,' as the sophists insist that the bread in the sacrament is annihilated; rather, it must remain" (298).

No Donnean could read Luther's exposition of an angel in a flame without remembering the beginning of "Aire and Angels":

> Twice or thrice had I loved thee,
> Before I knew thy face or name;
> So in a voice, so in a shapelesse flame,
> *Angells* affect us oft, and worship'd bee.[7]

While Donne didn't need Luther to conceive of angels as flames—the key reference, after all, comes in a Psalm[8]—the rest of Donne's poem suggests the extent to which it is informed by the theological issues of his time and especially by those that bear on Christology, on the Eucharist, and more generally on religious representation and its effectual working:

> But since, my soule, whose child love is,
> Takes limmes of flesh, and else could nothing doe,
> More subtile then the parent is,
> Love must not be, but take a body too.

Donne's speaker concludes that love can "inhere" (that is, dwell, with a pun on the earthly "here" and now) "nor in nothing, nor in things / Extreme, and scattring bright" and thus neither in no thing nor merely in things. Arguably, a word I use deliberately with this much-argued poem, the speaker ends with a compromise in which his love assumes angelic purity, while its earthly expression, like wind, flame, or the containing love of a woman, becomes relatively more material.[9] When the love poem is viewed as *simultaneously a participant* in the theological issues of its time, however, the speaker's assertion of male and spiritual ascendancy has also the unexpected consequence of gendering the human subject himself feminine in relation to deity's ministering spirits. But isn't this consequence always potentially available to such hierarchized religious thought, ironically as yet another coded or metonymic expression of the very correspondences that subordinated women? To ask what activates it within a particular piece of writing is to question the awareness evinced there. In "Aire and Angels" the answer, necessarily interpretative, derives from the speaker's tone, which is witty, even teasing, while seriously speculative: *serio ludere*. The translation—the metaphorizing—of the terms of theological dispute to the affairs of human lovers here ensures a vision that is stereoscopic. The fabric of this poem displays a sophisticated awareness of issues, terms, and codes. Their use in its context quite literally and creatively puts them in play.[10]

But just when I've signaled a focus on Donne and a turn to his *Devotions*, my eventual goal, I need to return once more to the tropological matrix and specifically to the ongoing Luther-Zwingli debate: again, my larger concern is to take some measure of the tropological landscape, first looking at Zwingli and then at Calvin. In my reading, Zwingli is among the more rhetorically learned, indeed more linguistically sophisticated, of the key Reformation theologians, and from this perspective it is not so surprising that his is also one of the least realist explanations of the controverted issues of them all. As we know, Zwingli's view of the Eucharist was also the least mystical or even sacramental. He saw it as a memorial celebration, although his view developed deeper and more fertile, ecclesiological nuances over time.[11]

Leaving aside Zwingli's argument with Luther about Christ's nature, which my earlier discussion has indicated, I want to look at his use of rhetoric in discussing the Eucharist or Supper. He believes that the words of institution in the Supper, "This is my body," mean "This represents my body." But here I would turn directly to the terms of his argument:

> How almost all kinds of figures are formed all through the Hebrew writers, I have often told elsewhere, and since it is only metonymy and catachresis that we have need of for the present purpose, I will speak here of these only. Metonymy, according to the various significations of the preposition *meta*, which sometimes means "after," or "with" or "across," can sometimes be called "denomination," or the substituting of one name for another, as when we put on an invention or an institution the name of its originator. . . . Thus we call wine, Bacchus; wheat, Ceres; the supper or symbol of commemoration, the body of Christ. . . . Sometimes it can be called "cognomination" or the applying of the name of a person (or thing) to something that represents the same, as when we call a statue Cocles or Cloelia, because the statue represents one or the other. . . . Sometimes it can be called "transnomination," or the exchanging of the names of things; when opposites are given the names of each other, as when law is put for the sin which is committed against the law. (355–56)

Zwingli goes on to explain that the trope catachresis—a radical form of metaphor, such as Hamlet's "I will speak daggers to her"—must be considered further,[12] because if anyone chooses to interpret the word "is" as "signifies," we can call in that variety of figure and quote passages from Scripture in which it is used in this way. Catachresis is a figure by which the literal and natural signification of anything is applied to a thing to which the literal signification does not belong. I will not speak here of the battle I fought with Billicanus as to whether substantive verbs admit tropes or not, for language existed before the name "trope" was invented. This word "is," then, is transferred from its natural signification to one not literally belonging to it, when I point to a statue of Caesar and say, "This is Caesar." (356)

Then Zwingli considers Luther's charge that the interpretations of the words of institution by the radical reformers are at odds with one another, thus discrediting them. Zwingli's reply has a remarkable degree of sophisticated skepticism about the very terms of argument. After indicating his immediate influences, contemporaries such as Hoen of Holland, John Rhodius, and George Saganus, and noting his own reading of Fabius, Cicero, and Plutarch, he explains that the "simple explanation which anyone could understand pleased me: 'This bread signifies my body which is given for you.' For everybody does not know what a trope is. I saw, also, that by whatever kind of trope we explain the words, the point is simply this, that the force of the word 'is' undergoes modification and has the value, 'is a signification or representation of'" (357). He goes on to say that he followed the simplest path and therefore "explained the thing as an example of catachresis" (357). But Zwingli adds that his associate Oecolampadius, following Tertullian, instead took the words to signify "This is the figure of my body," understanding the word "figure" to mean image and thus "representation, or reflection of something that has sometime really been" (357).

Zwingli concludes that Tertullian and Oecolampadius must have taken the words of institution "as a metonymy, of the variety cognomination, by which that is called the body which is an image or representation of the body, or a means of recalling it to remembrance." But he notes that Luther and others have tried to exploit this seeming disagreement, since "Oecolampadius says this is metaphor, while I say it is metonymy" (357). The cultural code itself, at least as it pertains to the finer distinctions of rhetoric, seems to be coming apart here, but Zwingli takes it in stride with what I'll call *rhetorical relativism*. He observes that any expression "may be explained by different kinds of figures, and these may also be considered from different points of view. Hence even among the rhetoricians, we very often find the same form of expression elucidated by different tropes" (357). After extensive discussion of his own and Oecolampadius' equally reasonable points of view, he asks, "what difference . . . is there in the essentials of the opinion," if he calls the tropic expression catachresis or, from another point of view, metonymy and Oecolampadius calls it from still others metonymy or metaphor (357–58)? "Why [should] we . . . impute a quarrel to people, that, while espousing one and the same opinion, . . . explain words by tropes with different names," all of which "are consistent with the apostolic writings and with the analogy of faith, indeed, . . . [they] look to the one and only union and harmony of Christ's body" (358). Zwingli appears to have grasped the essential of translation at the heart of all rhetorical tropes. Little wonder that the unconvinced Luther mocked the radical reformers' understanding of the words of institution, "*Hoc est corpus meum,*" with the declaration "*Hoc est tropus meus*" (259). In the spirit of Luther's mock and Zwingli's insight, I would translate "*tropus meus*" as "my metaphor"—as *translatio*, the tropic denominator common to them all.

Although neither the first nor the only theologian to argue that the words of institution are tropic, Zwingli is the figurehead and the lightning rod in this period for the tropic view. His interest in the fundamentals of signification and his awareness of the relative value of all rhetorical distinctions suggest a suppleness of intellect at some distance from Luther's more rigid and more scholastic insistence on absolute, a priori truths. To this extent, perhaps, Luther still looks back and Zwingli forward. The latter's discussions of meaning, in which metonymy, the conservative figure that underlies coding, and metaphor, the creative violator of codes, are themselves interchangeable, equally suggest either the enlarged awareness or, perhaps, the seemingly tolerant insensitivity of an age in transition, poised between old beliefs and new ones.

Calvin's awareness in this particular resembles Zwingli's. Invoking the Schoolmen for support, Calvin affirms an essentially traditional understanding of the *communicatio idiomatum* and rejects Luther's assertion that "wherever Christ's divinity is, there also is his flesh, which cannot be separated from it." In Calvin's view, this is to remove "the distinction between the natures" and so to urge "the unity of the person" as to make "man out of God and God out of man."[13] Quite unlike the Schoolmen, however, Calvin endorses a figurative interpretation of the words of institution. Although admitting that by these words, "the name of the thing was given to the symbol" and also recognizing the appropriateness of the resulting analogy, he declines to explain it as allegory or parable—both forms of extended metaphor, hence fiction—"lest someone accuse" him of "seeking a place to hide and of digressing from the present issue"; this issue is presumably the reference, or truth, of the words themselves, and for us it recalls by contrast Cranmer's equivocal invocation of allegory in his fatal disputation at Oxford.[14] Interestingly, Calvin's explanation does not suggest that he thinks such metaphorical explanations unsuitable but only that they might be misunderstood by hostile readers. His choice of one rhetorical figure over another therefore looks more tactful and strategic than substantive.

In fact, as Calvin's explanation proceeds, the metaphor he has put out the one door, he readmits at the other. He asserts that the statement "This is my body" is "a metonymy, a figure of speech commonly used in Scripture," and explains that "you could not otherwise understand such expressions as 'circumcision is a covenant'" or "'the lamb is the passover'" or "'the rock from which water flowed in the desert . . . was Christ,' unless you were to take them as spoken with meanings transferred."[15] *Transferred* is as much as to say translated, since this word, like the word *translatio*, metaphor itself, derives from the Latin verb *transfero/translatus*. In fact, Calvin's Latin reads, *nisi translatitie dictum*, "unless spoken tropically," and indeed, "metaphorically." Calvin's wish that his adversaries would stop heaping "unsavory witticisms" (*insulsas facetias*) on the beliefs he represents and stop calling such believers "tropists" (*tropistas*) may be justified on the first count, wit, but tenuously so on the second, tropistry.[16] Metonymy is itself a trope, and when pressed, as I have earlier suggested, it will likely reveal the archtrope metaphor at its base, as it does here.

Calvin has more to say about overlapping and interchangeable figures of speech and the kind of awareness they enable. His explanation of what he calls a metonymic transfer, or translation, of meaning continues, clearly displaying an active, transformative role, therefore properly speaking a metaphorical role, rather than one that is merely nominal and inert: by the metonymy in the words of institution,

> Not only is the name transferred [*transfertur*] from something higher to something lower, but, on the other hand, the name of the visible sign is also given to the thing signified . . . For though the symbol differs in essence from the thing signified (in that the latter is spiritual and heavenly, while the former is physical and visible), still, because it not only symbolizes the thing that it has been consecrated to represent as a bare and empty token, but also truly exhibits it, why may its name not rightly belong to the thing [*in ipsum iure*]?[17]

To ask rhetorically why the physical name might not rightly belong to the spiritual thing is in this period to indicate that the transfer of names should not be considered equivocal. Yet to transfer meaning from higher or spiritual to lower or physical, or the reverse, is "truly" also a change, and if not, in Calvin's terminology, an essential change, then essentially an equivocation, a doubling, a swerving, a leap in signification: "For . . . the symbol differs in essence [substance?] from the thing signified."[18] Calvin goes on to explain more specifically that physical things might borrow the names of those higher "things of which they always bear a definite and not misleading signification," by which he can only mean a figurative signification, indeed a tropic and more specifically metaphoric one. Here his hedged, slightly negative wording, in the original Latin, "certam minimeque fallacem significationem"—more literally, "a certain and minimally fallacious signification"—suggests his Augustinian distrust of the materiality of language and specifically of tropes, even while it makes evident his acute awareness of, and dependence on, them. Of course Calvin adds, even before the sentence is finished, that such symbols also have "the reality joined with them": "adiunctam habent secum veritatem."[19] In this thoroughly equivocal and thoroughly metaphysical addition, he simply asserts the necessarily irrational sine qua non of faith. Calvin's awareness of language is here neither mystified nor mystifying as Richard Waswo has urged; rather, his awareness of the necessity of faith involves a leap of a different order and into another register.[20]

But even Calvin's final wording in the passage from which I have been quoting makes his recognition of a trope evident. So great, therefore, is their similarity and closeness that transition from one to the other is easy: "Tanta est similitudo et vicinitas alterius ad alterum, ut proclivis ultro citroque sit deductio."[21] Here Calvin's learned translator suggestively renders "ultro citroque . . . deductio" as "transition," a word, which, like "transfer" and "translate," signals a tropic exchange. More literally, however, *deductio* indicates a conducting, a leading, perhaps a traffic, up and down, "ultro citroque," between heavenly and earthly realities. Of course, *deductio*, meaning "deduction," is also a word associated with logic, but instead of a logical conclusion, it suggests in this context a movement of the psyche as both mind and soul and thus a trafficking that is essentially perceptual—insightful and intuitive. Here, the very presence of such a rational word actually highlights its distance from syllogistic usage. The phrase "[of the] one to the other" (*alterius ad alterum*) in the same sentence likewise testifies to two distinct realms of meaning, one higher and one lower, whose relation *openly* requires an irrational and personal shift into another register. This openness is also awareness, and it underlies the central Reformation tenet that only faith justifies. It is similarly evident and helpfully illustrated in the leap between an earthly and an enlightened grasp of enigmatic symbols experienced in the white space between two stanzas by Spenser's Redcrosse Knight on the Mount of Contemplation in *The Faerie Queene*.[22]

Two points are important for my purposes. The first is Calvin's rhetorical relativism, his merging of fine rhetorical distinctions in a common, translative denominator. The second is his awareness that the movement from higher to lower or lower to higher term is essentially, materially rhetoric's, if finally and spiritually faith's. Where in Luther there is a middle term—a presence "real" or physical as well as spiritual and symbolic—in Calvin there is a trope, an exchange or transfer, indeed a sleight of name, and with it there is an assertion of faith. These are the defining alternatives neither of the Middle Ages nor of the Lutheran version.

Furnished with this awareness, I would turn to the centerpiece of Donne's twenty-three *Devotions*, namely, Station XII: "They apply Pidgeons, to draw the vapors from the Head": "Spirante Columba, Supposita pedibus, Revocantur ad ima vapores."[23] Most clearly for me, this station marks a shift in register—a realization or breakthrough—and the reason may partly be that I find its movements strange and exotic, with the danger that I will find creative metaphor—the magician's fictive art—where a Renaissance reader would find an assertion of code.[24] Notably, however, only on the further side of this station come those passages so openly describing a metaphor-making God: for immediately relevant examples, "when one Man dies, one *Chapter* is not *torne* out of the *booke*, but *translated* into a better *language*; and every *Chapter* must be so *translated*; *God* emploies severall *translators*; . . . [but His] hand is in every *translation*"; and perhaps the best known of these, "thou art a *figurative*, a *metaphoricall God* too; A *God* in whose words there is such a height of *figures*, such *voyages*, such *peregrinations* to fetch remote and precious *metaphors*, such *extensions*, such *spreadings*, such *Curtaines of Allegories*, such *third Heavens of Hyperboles*, . . . as all *prophane Authors* seeme of the seed of the *Serpent*, that *creepes*; thou art the *dove*, that flies" (XVII, 86; XIX, 99). Metaphor underwrites all the figures Donne names, including extensions and spreadings, or metonymies, in the hands of the divine creator—"the *dove*, that flies" and Donne's model in Station XII.

In this Station, Donne's mind plays over the medically diagnosed vapors and the curative *columba* ("dove") named in its heading, variously considering them as physical things, ideas, words, figures, and spiritual things. The Station moves from a meditation grounded in the physical and the political, to an expostulation in which he transacts a movement up and down—"ultro citroque"—in Calvin's phrasing, and finally to faith in prayer. In the presence of faith, necessarily understood as an ideology, the distinction between metaphor and metonymy effectually disappears, thereby, as in Zwingli and Calvin, challenging theories that assume its necessity. Noticeably in the first stage of Station XII, Donne's meditation, the cure specifically named is a very material "pigeon,"or, in what I'm tempted to term Anthony Raspa's fowl gloss, "pigeon poultice." Such a poultice is made by halving a live pigeon or pigeons and applying the bleeding halves to the fevered patient's feet. Presumably these halves, while still warm and wet, are quite dead when applied, yet Donne's Latin heading, perhaps proleptically, describes the pigeon as "spirante" or "breathing," and thus with a participial form of the same Latin verb (*spiro*) that underlies the words *spirit* and *spiritual*.[25] But my speculation flies ahead of the bleeding pigeon conspicuously named as such only in the twelfth meditation, the first stage, and there appropriate to what might be described as a horizontal focus—one earthly and physical.

Meditation XII opens with a series of metonymic analogies at once feverish in their quickness, bizarre in their extension, and reasonable in their constant, the destructive power of small things over large ones: "What will not kill a man, if a *vapor* will? how great an *Elephant*, how small a *Mouse* destroyes? to dye by a *bullet* is the *Souldier's dayly bread*; but few men dye by *haile-shot*: A man is more worth, then to bee sold for *single money*; a *life* to be valued above a *trifle*" (62). The next sentence, despite its subordinated, faith-based demurrer, accuses God's agent Nature of unkindness, a murderous denial of herself:

> If this [vapor] were a violent shaking of the Ayre by *Thunder*, or by *Canon*, in that case the *Ayre* is condensed above the thicknesse of *water*, of water baked into *Ice*, almost *petrified*, almost made stone, and no wonder that that kills; but that that which is but a *vapor*, and a *vapor* not forced, but breathed, should kill, that our *Nourse* should overlay us, and *Ayre*, that nourishes us, should destroy us, but that it is a *halfe Atheisme* to murmure against *Nature*, who is *Gods immediate Commissioner*, who would not think himselfe miserable to bee put into the hands of *Nature*, who does not only set him up for a *marke* for others to shoote at, but delights her selfe to blow him up like a *glasse*, till shee see him breake, even with her owne breath? (62)

Donne's question is followed by another series of negative analogies, suggesting what we are not—a volcano, a mine-shaft, a calumny. These are increasingly metaphoric, issuing in the devastated realization that we are all these things as the source of our mortal, or deadly and (un)natural, vapors.

Whereas his initial analogies—mouse, bullet, and single money—give substance to a vapor, now he concludes that if he "were asked again, what is a *vapour*, I could not tell, it is so insensible a thing; so neere *nothing* is that that reduces us to *nothing*" (63). As if to escape this cul-de-sac of mortal nothingness, Donne suggests that we "extend this *vapour*, rarifie it," from "our *Naturall bodies*, to any *Politike body*" and thus that we extend our meditation on physical vapors to the pestilent rumors and libels that afflict the state. The metonymic refinement of body to body politic, of private to communal entity, could hardly assert a more traditional or more Donnean correspondence, although Donne's particular application of it here to vapors, rumors, and libels seems an original twist.[26]

Donne next expands his anatomical figure into a little allegory, making the heart of the body politic the king, the brain his council, and "the whole *Magistracie*" his "*Sinewes*," or nerves, and he concludes with the observation that "sometimes *vertue*, and alwaies *power*, be a good *Pigeon* to draw this *vapor* from the *Head*, and from doing any deadly harme there"(64). Formerly the heart, now the head is king as Donne shifts from the moral primacy of the one to the physiological primacy of the other at the end of his meditation.[27] The odd phrasing that gives superiority to "*power*" over "*vertue*," the latter a subtler efficacy that is at least punningly moral, would appear to enforce the emphasis on the physical evident in the identification of the *columba*, not as a dove, but as a common pigeon. At the same time, however, the extended anatomical analogy has held us for roughly the last third of the meditation—in notable contrast to the immediately preceding third—in a figurative medium between two dimensions of meaning, one physical and one political. While physically grounded, we have not, in fact, remained wholly on the ground. We have been in a metaphorical medium. In this way, the final movement of the meditation prepares for Expostulation XII, the second stage of the Station.

This stage continues to focus on vapor but casts it at once in a more religious light and treats it less as natural, physical, or political phenomenon than as an enigmatic symbol, or in Donne's own word as a "hieroglyph," linking the physical and spiritual realms, as well as image and word.[28] Yet emphasis now, as compared to the preceding stage, is also distinctively more verbal, indeed stereovocal, and in a manner typical of Donne, *vapor*, as symbolic verbal sign, effects a dynamic exchange, a traffic, between heaven and earth. After an urgent invocation of God, Expostulation XII begins with the answer to the apostle James's question "*what is your life*," namely, that "*It is even a vapor, that appeareth for a little time, & then vanisheth away*" (64). In this answer, Donne discovers a definition of death as well and thus in *vapor* an "indifferent . . . thing, . . . the *Hierogliphique*" of divine blessings and judgments. Moving through scriptural passages via a *catena*, or verbal chain, of beneficent vapors, he considers the vapor in Genesis that rose from the earth to water the ground, the sacrificial vapors in Leviticus that rose to God in a cloud of incense, and "*the vapor of the power of God*," identified in Wisdom with the Son. Playing further on the meaning of *vapor* as "breath," he then asks God how something "perfumed . . . with thine own breath, . . . in thine own *word*," should receive "an ill, and infectious sense" (65). His question leads to his recognition that sin is also a vapor or blinding smoke fittingly punished with the vapors of sickness and there follows a parallel chain of noxious vapors in scripture: for example, the "*breathing vapors*" of beasts, "*pillars of smoke*," translated to "*vapors* of smoke" in Acts; the terrible "*smoke*" that "*went out . . . at his Nostrils*," the "*smoke*" from "*the bottomlesse pit*" that will rise to darken the sun and breed locusts with the power of scorpions.

Seeking a relief from such vapors, Donne envisions an exchange between heaven and earth similar to that in the "Hymne to God my God," in which the way down and the way up are one: "ultro citroque" in Calvin's phrasing. When the angels fell, he observes, God created earth, "assuming" and "drawing" us heavenward, and when we fell, He "assum[ed: (from Latin *assumo*, 'take up, adopt')] . . . us another way, by descending down to assume our nature" in the Son. "So that though our last act be an ascending to glory, (we shall ascend to the place of *Angels*) yet our first act is to goe the way of thy *Sonn, descending*, and the way of thy blessed *spirit* too, who *descended in the Dove*" (65). In this context the descent of the Son to human nature activates the favored Donnean pun on "sun" and further enforces the seeming logic of an essentially rhetorical relationship between heaven and earth. Shades of Ramus here, perhaps, but of Calvin, too. Conceptually, and not merely in form, the perception that down is up is metaphorical and, more precisely, both catachrestic and naturally, physically counter-intuitive.[29] The conceit—oxymoric, too—effects an *exchange of value*. In it, to recall Calvin's words, "transition from one to the other is easy" or, more accurately, it is *made*, crafted metaphorically to be, surprisingly so. What Calvin asserts, Donne enacts in rhetorical experience.

Now Donne returns to his immediate physical plight, thankful that God has "afford[ed] us this remedy in *Nature*, by this application of a *Dove*, to our lower parts, to make these *vapors* in our *bodies*, to descend, and to make that a *type* to us, that by the visitation of thy *Spirit*, the *vapors* of sin shall descend, & we tread them under our feet" (65–66). The dove, no longer mere pigeon but now a natural vehicle of divine intervention, has become the fulcrum of the salvific descent that raises. More simply, its presence *translates*, or metaphorizes, God's power.

Donne continues from our treading on the vapors of sin to end his expostulation: "At the baptisme of thy *Son*, the *Dove* descended, & at the exalting of thine *Apostles* to preach, the same spirit descended. Let us draw down the *vapors* of our own *pride*, our own *wits*, our own *wils*, our own *inventions*, to the *simplicitie* of thy *Sacraments*, & the obedience of thy word, and these *Doves*, thus applied, shall make us live" (66). At the end of the Expostulation, Donne thus explicitly takes leave of his own art, his wit and invention, his own highly creative imagination, to rest in a renewed appreciation of God's art, God's writing in and with both natural objects and historical events. Donne's naming human pride, along with wit and invention, as baggage to be left behind in turning to the simplicity and simple affirmation of God's sacraments renders his awareness of his own tropological making in the Expostulation explicit.

The final stage of Station XII, Prayer, focuses no longer on vapors but instead on the dove. Indeed, vapors, disobedient vapors, appear only once, to be trampled. This stage begins in humility, a prayer that God might prosper both a bodily remedy and a spiritual one. Quickly, Donne then encapsulates the significance of the typological dove, at once "naturally proper to conduce medicinally to our *bodily health*," and through the Law "a *sacrifice for sinne*," and "through the *Gospel* . . . [with] thy spirit in it, a witnes of thy *sonnes baptisme*," and he asks that the qualities of the dove be imprinted—written—in his own soul (66). He prays that in this way "all vapours of all disobedience to thee, being subdued under my feete [i.e., in the dove], I may in the power, and triumphe of thy *sonne*, treade victoriously upon my *grave*, and trample upon the *Lyon* and *Dragon*, that lye under it, to devoure me" (66). This is the point where, in my reading, Donne might be said to take flight, but very much on the wings of scripture: "Thou O *Lord*, by the *Prophet* callest the *Dove*, the *Dove of the Valleys*, but promisest that *the Dove of the Valleyes shall bee upon the Mountaine*: As thou hast layed mee low, in this *Valley* of sickenesse, so low, as that I am made fit for that question, asked in the field of bones, *Sonne of Man, can these bones live*, so, in thy good time, carry me up to these *Mountaynes*, of which, even in this *Valley*, thou affordest mee a prospect, the Mountain where thou dwellest, the holy Hill" (66–67). This passage, while a scriptural pastiche, truly translates meaning into another language. Understood in the context of Station XII, it expresses the transition from literal to spiritual called faith. Whether it should also be called metonymic, the language of codes, which it surely is, or metaphoric, the language of creative perception, which in the total context of Station XII it surely is as well, I'm not sure: the difference between them has vanished.

But of two things I am sure: the first is that if we read only Donne's Prayer, the impact of his translations is quite lost: his tropes build on the previous stages. The second is that Donne commits the final stage to a spiritual meaning only nominally literal: the last passage cited, in which the "*Dove of the Valleys*" is raised to the mountain, continues, describing further the holy hill of God's dwelling "unto which none can ascend but *hee that hath cleane hands*, which none can have, but by that one and that strong way, of making them cleane, in the blood of thy Sonne *Christ Jesus*" (67). This ending indicates blood guilt and the redeeming blood of redemption and also seals the passage totally and simultaneously into metaphor and faith.[30] Now the transition from physical object to spiritual meaning is not so easy, except in faith, since the terms no longer pretend to a paradoxical and rhetorical logic that is rational at its base but instead to a more symbolic one. Abruptly, the dove has been raised to as purely symbolic a register as that to which a creature can attain: here, as the humble *columba* sacrificed for a curative poultice, in a conspicuously metaphysical leap that is also metaphorical and metonymic, it is understood as a figure of Christ. Within the figural terms of Station XII, perhaps this is no more scandalous than a piece of bread's being so.[31] Yet, for me, what still remains the most fascinating, though not finally the most moving, stage of this Station is the second, since this is where Donne openly *transacts* the shift into another register and thereby initiates the sublation so fundamental to the reformers' understanding, and indeed to their performing, of the sacraments and specifically of Communion, as I have argued in the preceding chapter.

I have been trying to locate a historical sensibility, one available to but also different from our own. It is at once strongly rhetorical and sophisticated in its awareness of rhetorical translation. Yet this is also a religious sensibility, quite distant from the dominant medieval one, that is willing to see rhetoric as a vehicle or instrument of truth. This sensibility shares ground at once with Calvin's tropic assertion of faith and also with Sir Philip Sidney's relatively more modern endorsement of fiction—"poesy" in his idiom—which includes Plato's dialogues. But the real difference between Donne's age and our own seems to me to come with his Prayer, which truly effects the flight of the Dove on the translated wings of faith. Here, that final affirmation of faith is fully realized. Here, too, in the presence of faith and therefore of historical and ideological context, a sharp distinction between metaphor and metonymy no longer signifies. This necessity is itself exposed as ideological, too, and therefore at least potentially as a forced choice between linguistic coding and linguistic creativity. Pushed to an extreme, as it has been in the past several decades, this is a choice between a master trope of conceptual passivity and one of conceptual power.

Before leaving Donne's *Devotion*, I would like to see its ending in another light, one that relates this ending more specifically to my continuing concern with the Ricoeur-Derrida dispute about dead metaphor and the relevance to it of neo-cognitivism. Earlier, following Derrida and Ricoeur, I identified the crucial concept of sublation with the Hegelian "raising" of conceptual meaning and then defined it as translation to a higher level incident on partial cancellation. It is thus at once positive, neutral, and negative; gain, preservation, and loss; surplus, continuity, and lack. It is also a further way to understand the raising of Donne's pigeon, the "Dove of the Valleys," to the mountain. When the significance of the physical bird extends upward to the Godhead, the physical life of the bird is obviously lost, and the bird translated to another, higher dimension of significance: here creative metaphor becomes *the agent of sublation*. Within faith, continuity is maintained, however, and in a further, specifically Christian development of translative signification, even the resurrection of physical life for humanity (if not for the bird) is intimated. From this perspective, the reformers were right: by faith alone, however.

But Donne's amazing metaphorical transactions also have meaning within the material confines of contemporary neo-cognitivism. A theory of embodied cognition that is radical and totalizing, such as Lakoff and Johnson's, for example, bases human categorization and conceptualization primarily but not exclusively on physical experience. Categorization and conceptualization, so construed, raise and continue, although apparently without loss or cancellation, or at least without confronting it. Lakoff and Johnson finally aim at a basic empathy of the human with the rest of the natural world—in their words, an "ecological spirituality."[32] Within this ecology, such a sacrifice as that of Donne's bird, whether to seventeenth-century sympathetic medicine or to Hegel's sublation, would prove a basic and familiar problem. This problem is even evident in the concern of Jeremy Taylor, roughly Donne's contemporary, about using halved pigeons to cure fever. Taylor observes the prohibition of such cruelty to beasts in the Old Testament, although he excuses it in the name of "necessity" and the higher order of "charity to men" (IX, 357). In contrast, either Lakoff and Johnson don't deal with arguably necessary rarefication or unavoidable loss or else they simply don't get off the physical or literal ground.

Partly through focus and balance, the self-styled "ecumenicism" of the neo-cognitivist Andy Clark rings truer to Donne's tropology. Although Clark embraces explanations of "mind" that are material, if not simply phys- ical, he also acknowledges that "Minds may be essentially embodied and embedded and *still* depend crucially on brains which compute and repre- sent," and he finds "cases involving reasoning about the distant, the nonex- istent, or the highly abstract" the "most compelling" with regard to "the representational approach" (143, 175). As indicated earlier, Clark also con- ceives metaphorically of what he terms "scaffolding," strategies that involve "the use of some type of external structure . . . to mold and orchestrate behavior." He singles out "language," as well as culture more generally, as "advanced species of external scaffolding."[33] His concept of "scaffolding" is itself a metaphor that uplifts or raises and continues, but as I have earlier suggested, it also has material limits (like the Tower of Babel) and therefore aligns provocatively with sublation. When Clark speaks of scaffolding as also molding and orchestrating, however, he has shifted into mixed metaphor, which, read sympathetically, indicates not only a mind in constructive proc- ess but additionally suggests his awareness of the artistry of metaphor and indeed—insofar as his mixed metaphor invokes sculpture and orchestral performance—specifically his awareness of its creativity, as well.

By any measure, Donne's vision, arising from the physical world but also taking flight from it, remains humanly compelling. Perhaps its power can be reduced to a physical process, but if it can, the reduction is very real. Ladders that start in "the foul rag-and-bone shop of the heart" are still worth the climbing, whether metaphorized by the poet Yeats or the scaf- folding philosopher Clark. The perspective from the top, if only a possibility ever translative, carries a powerful psychic charge, indeed an uplift, that is beyond the ordinary. Like the quasi-visualization of metaphor that is there and not there, this perspective, as Ricoeur characterizes it, is at once imag- ined and felt, and thus at once in mind and in body. Similarly, the "masterful [and thoroughly metaphorical] images" that "*Grew in pure mind*," to which Yeats refers in the same poem, *also* rise in the poem from below.[34]

5. *Vesting Significance and Authority: The Vestiarian Controversy under Cranmer and Its Treatment by Foxe*

That a particular outfit or a more general style of clothing should make a "statement" is a familiar enough idea in the twenty-first century. It assumes that clothing, like language, participates in a system of signs, and that plain clothing, such as chinos or blue jeans, can be every bit as much a statement as can a dark suit, a pink dress, or a tuxedo. But when we take clothing to be making a "statement," rhetorically we are using a metaphor, or possibly a metonymy, or both. Only figuratively does clothing speak and whether it speaks metonymically or metaphorically depends on whether its statement is—or more accurately, is perceived to be—a metonymic expression of a societal norm or a deliberate metaphorical deviation from it, and thus on whether it is perceived to answer to a conservative language of codes or to a marked difference from them.

Distinguishing between metaphor and metonymy helps to track and to explain the process of historical development, even while history further clarifies the potential for dynamic relationship between these two tropic paradigms. Their relationship is particularly sensitive to the fluid play of dominant and emergent perceptions and, when these are sufficiently distinct, to ideologies. As the Renaissance historiographer Sir Francis Bacon realized both in theory and practice, symbols, like battles, have histories. Symbolic language informs and shapes, rather than simply expresses, history as event and as account and does so in ways that can resist and alter totalizing abstractions, whether these pertain to history or to literary theory.[1] Accordingly, my interest in this chapter lies less in drawing fine distinctions between metaphor and metonymy than in the *lived* play of these figures in historical experience.

When we see clothing as a statement, we are likely also assuming the societal function of role-playing or possibly of deliberate role-playing, even masking, which within some contexts is recreation or constructive play and within others is simply hypocrisy—the last a word from Latin *hypocrisis*, "imitation, mimicry," and thus historically connected with the theater:

compare Greek *hypocrites*, "actor." If the societal function of clothing is controverted, what Gramsci termed "the language question," as invoked in my second chapter, figuratively urges its presence as well, which "in one mode or another . . . signifies that a series of other [ideological] problems are beginning to impose themselves" (Steinberg, 206). Gramsci's "language question" comes in one mode or another, which might be understood as one representational mode or another, such as clothing or language per se, and not simply in one or another mode still more materially productive. A system of signs, metaphor and metonymy, role-playing, masking, and hypocrisy—the last three common accusations in Reformation polemics—would be hard to beat as modes and points of reference for the vestiarian controversy over the use of traditional ecclesiastical vestments during the Tudor-Stuart period.

As M. M. Knappen observed in a "magisterial" study of puritanism some sixty years ago, the vestiarian controversy was "more than a . . . quibble about a piece of cloth."[2] John Udall (1560?-92), writing, or at least published, in the early 1590s, would pointedly have agreed that the heart of "the controuersie is not about goates wooll (as the Prouerbe saith) neither light & trifling matters . . . but about no lesse matter then this, whether Iesus Christ shall be King or no."[3] This controversy first became urgent in England in 1550, when the Zwinglian reformer John Hooper openly resisted the wearing of traditional ecclesiastical vestments for his consecration as bishop, and it actively persisted through most of Elizabeth's reign, to reemerge, together with larger issues, under the Stuarts.[4] In the broadest sense, the relation of a Protestant church to its Roman Catholic precursor was figuratively (and visually) at issue in Hooper's resistance and with it the priesthood of every believer, to which an anointed and hierarchical priesthood distinguished by power and symbolic dress is clearly inimical and an egalitarian ministry (Latin *minister*, "servant") in common dress is congenial. Even more exactly, however, interpretation of the eucharistic celebration as the renewal of Christ's sacrifice and thus a propitiatory offering for the quick and the dead, as opposed to its interpretation in Archbishop Thomas Cranmer's words, as "only a commemoration and remembrance of that sacrifice," had over centuries been woven into the history and symbolism of the traditional vestments (*Defence*, 227). Although interpretation of the vestments is a traceable evolution and accretion through constructive metaphor, these metaphors had long been absorbed into a normative code in the Roman Church—in fact, so normative that some of them had become part of the initiatory rite for the priesthood. The significance of the vestments had become fixed, recognizable, even separable from the wearer—metonymic. The vestments were instinct with a dignity of their own, as happens to an extent with the metonymic value of any uniform, military or judicial, for example, but happens more radically with the elaborations of cultic dress.[5] Thus perceived, their metonymic life, although initially derived from metaphor, came with the metaphor's death. Their value was coded and fixed, more referential than imaginative, more metonymic than metaphoric.

Reformers like Hooper sought to reinterpret the vestiary metonym, seeing it as a symbol of the Old Law, of corruption, and above all as fiction. In effect, they thus reinterpreted it as merely disguised metaphor and therefore as the mask or pageant of hypocrisy.[6] They not only sought to expose but simultaneously to reclothe the metonym in copious, abusive metaphor of their own making—for example, in "feathers," the colors of a "[mag]-pie," "Aaronical" habits, "shewes, and trifles," "menstrous cloathe[s]," the costumes of "stage-players and fools," and the "livery of Antichrist"—and more generally to characterize the cultic vestments as "popish pageauntes" or as barbaric "monuments of superstition."[7] Ultimately, they sought to create a new metonym, to recode the vestments in a lasting way. At its most fundamental level, the dispute about vestments, like that about the Eucharist itself, concerned not cloth but the perception of symbolism and the control of meaning.[8]

Traditional Christian *vestments*, a term designating both distinctive liturgical and non-liturgical ecclesiastical garments, originated in the civilian dress reserved for persons of status and rank in the late Roman Empire, rather than in the vesture of the Jewish priesthood, as often supposed.[9] But Christian interpreters as early as the fourth to sixth centuries drew connections between the presumed symbolism of Jewish priestly vesture and the vestments and practices of Christianity: for example, one Chrysostom (likely not the saint) explained that the Jewish high priest wore a tiara on his head to show he is "made head of all," but his head was also covered in order that he "may learn that he too hath a Head (in heaven). For this cause in the [Christian] church also, in the ordaining of priests, the gospel of Christ is laid upon their heads, that he who is ordained may learn that he then receiveth the true tiara of the Gospel; and may learn this also, that though he be head of all, yet doth he act in subjection to God's laws."[10] In another example, St. Jerome explains the alb or long, white, linen sacerdotal tunic worn by all clergy until the eleventh century and thereafter by principal clergy with reference to Leviticus, where God commands Moses to wash Aaron and his sons. He compares this act of purification to baptism, and he continues, "It is by God's commandments that we are to be washed clean, and when, being made ready for the garment of Christ, we shall have laid aside our garments made of skins, then shall we be clad in the linen robe [or alb] which hath in it nothing which is of death, but is wholly bright and pure" (Marriott, 21). As Christa Mayer-Thurman notes, flax, "from which linen is made[,] is the only one of the four natural fibres which was a direct product of the ground and . . . not the product of an animal" that "savour[s] of mortality and corruption."[11]

From the point of view of the English Reformation, the widespread influence of such early analogies between ancient Jewish practices and Christian ones bears on Reformation charges that the traditional liturgical vestments of the Roman Catholic Church were Aaronic vestiges of the Old Law. Oddly, both support for these charges and refutation of them could be found in the late medieval Sarum rite for consecrating a bishop. This rite explicitly invokes the example of Aaron's vesture and pointedly internalizes its significance:

> God who holding private familiar converse with thy servant Moses hast also decreed, among the other patterns of heavenly worship [*coelestis documenta culturae*], concerning the disposition of priestly vesture; and didst command that Aaron thy chosen should wear a mystical robe [*mystico amictu vestiri*] during the sacred rites, so that the posterity to come might have an understanding of the meaning of the patterns [*de exemplis*: "models"] of . . . [*priorum*: "former times"], lest the knowledge of thy teaching be lost in any age; and as the very outward sign of these symbols [*significationum species*: "the seeing of signs"] obtained reverence among thy former folk, also among us there might be a knowledge of them more certain than types and shadows [*aenigmata figurarum*: "enigmatic forms, allegories"]. For the adornment of our mind [*habitus nostrae mentis ornatus est*: "the habit—dress but also inner disposition—of our mind"] is as the vesture of that earlier priesthood; and the dignity of robes no longer commends to us . . . pontifical glory [*pontificalem gloriam*: "the glory of a high priest"], but rather the splendour of spirits, since even those . . . things, which then pleased fleshly vision, [*carnalibus blandiebantur obtutibus*] depended rather on these truths [*ea potius . . . poscebant*: "needed, asked urgently for"] which in them were to be understood.[12]

The Sarum rite is representative of English practices and indeed of those in Western Christendom on the eve of the Reformation. It is the precursor from which even the first of Archbishop Thomas Cranmer's Ordinals sharply diverges but which the more radical Hooper (not irrelevantly a monk in his younger years) found still offensively present therein.[13] Given the distinction made between the carnal vision of an earlier time and the inner understanding of Christianity in the passage just cited, one can equally well imagine either Hooper's view of the sacerdotal vestments as merely a superstitious adherence to Aaronic practices or the more conservative argument that vestments are both sanctioned by precedent and understood spiritually.

The ambiguous potential evident especially in the word *instructum* in the next passage in the Sarum rite only increases the opportunity for a conflict of interpretations: in it, the celebrant beseeches God "that whatsoever it was that those veils signified in radiance of gold, in sparkling of jewels, in variety of diverse workmanship, this may show forth in the conversation and deeds of these men. Complete the fullness of thy mystery in thy . . . [*sacerdote*: "priest"], and equipped [*instructum*: "provided, prepared, instructed"] with all the adornments of glory, hallow . . . [him] with the dew of heavenly unction" (Porter, 21; Maskell: II, 276). Inner and outer perspectives oscillate unstably in the passage, depending on how we see them: now simultaneous, now alternating, now sequential—now metaphorical and contingent and now metonymic and coded, to boot. They align both with the traditional belief that the character of the priesthood is indelible and conversely with the tendency historically evident to identify it with the external trappings of priesthood that are conferred in ordination and removed in degradation.

According to historians of liturgy, the distinction of vestments from lay attire developed gradually between about the fourth and ninth centuries as vestments became more traditional and relatively unchanging relative to lay garb and as particular ones were more specifically prescribed and reserved exclusively for liturgical use, worn over non-liturgical clothing, and marked with a special blessing.[14] Symbolism was attached to the vestments as early as the fourth century, but its heyday came between the ninth and thirteenth centuries, appearing from the twelfth century on in missals, sacramentaries (office-books with the rites and prayers for sacraments), and pontificals (office-books for episcopal rites and ceremonies). As might be expected, symbolic interpretations became increasingly rich and various, and only toward the end of the Middle Ages did greater agreement arise between the "symbolism of the liturgists and what might be called the official symbolism" of church prayers (Braun [symbolism]). The two major kinds of symbolism that developed were moral and Christological, the one focusing on the virtues of the wearer and the other on his role as a representative of Christ. Of these, moral symbolism appears to have had the greater and more enduring effect, as evidenced in the alb, the chasuble, and the surplice, three vestments I select as examples for more detailed discussion, because the alb plays a significant role in Cranmer's first revision of the Ordinal and in Hooper's resistance to it; because the chasuble is the garment particularly associated with the Roman Catholic Eucharist and compromised, then rejected, in Cranmer's Prayer Books of 1549 and 1552; and because the surplice, alone retained for Communion in the Prayer Book of 1552, became the symbolic cause célèbre of the purifying Reformers in Elizabethan England.[15] Awareness of the background of the traditional vestments contributes to a historical understanding of, and indeed, a feeling for, the intense engagement of the issues represented in the vestiarian controversy and its aftermath in the reigns that followed.

Between roughly the sixth and thirteenth centuries, the alb, whose formal bestowal appears to be among relatively later additions to ordination rites in England, is variously interpreted on the basis of its whiteness, material, style, length, and closeness to the body as a layer of clothing. For example, Isidore of Seville, the sixth- to seventh-century writer whose work was widely known in the Renaissance, explains, in a reminiscence of Jerome, that deacons assist at the altar in white garments ("albis") in order "that a heavenly life may be theirs, and that bright and pure, and without stain, they may approach unto the holy offerings, being clean in body and in chasteness undefiled." About two centuries later, Rabanus Maurus associates the linen and close fitting cut of the alb ("strictam lineam") especially with continence and chastity and thence with the spiritually meritorious work of faith. Interpreting Ezekiel in the ninth century, Amalarius Metensis cites Jerome approvingly to the effect that priests may not wear the polluted garments ("pollutis vestibus") of daily life in God's inner sanctum ("sancta sanctorum") but should be clad in a special linen tunic when they know the secrets and mysteries of God, for these mysteries, Jerome adds, "are not to be shown to the vulgar, nor proffered to the people, who are neither sanctified nor prepared for the sanctity of God." Surely the sentiment that Amalarius here endorses would have confirmed the worst of puritan fears regarding the threat of sacerdotal vestments to the priesthood of every believer. Almost comically, however, Amalarius hastens from Jerome to reassure his clerical audience that we understand the letter according to the spirit and therefore that if they should use a woolen vestment "secundum spiritum" (according to the spirit) that their practice is not a whit opposed to truth ("non abhorret a vero").[16] Wintry drafts and uncertain supplies doubtless argued against rigid prescription until a relatively later period. Before the thirteenth century, tradition largely set the norms for vestments; only after that did these norms begin "to be written into church law" (Kavanagh, 13).

By the thirteenth century, elaborations of the significance of the vestments had increased, and the need of legislation was likely becoming both more evident and more feasible. In the eleventh to twelfth centuries, one Alcuin (not the familiar British Alcuin of three centuries earlier) sees in the alb perseverance in good action ("actione") which he describes as the end or goal ("finis") of the body—a description implying more worldly engagement than does Rabanus' emphasis on the spirit. Yet in the same period, Honorius Augustodunensis, more like the earlier Rabanus, still finds in the alb's white linen only the holiness of chastity.[17] More imaginatively, the thirteenth-century Bishop Gulielmus Durandus elaborates the spiritual significance of seven articles of episcopal wear in an allegory whose material vehicle consists of armor: thus the alb, like a cuirass, envelops the entire body ("pro lorica totum corpus cooperit"), and the chasuble, or cloak, covers it as might a shield ("clypeo").[18]

To jump to the sixteenth century, Erasmus' character Folly, observing a discrepancy between the practices of popes, cardinals, and bishops and the symbolism of their vestments, affords a handy summation of other kinds of symbolism, even as she begins with an apparent memory of Isidore's etymological gloss on the alb. She asks facetiously what would happen if any of these prelates "were to reflect on the meaning of his linen vestment, snow-white in color to indicate a pure and spotless life, or of his two-horned mitre, both peaks held together by a single knot, signifying perfect knowledge of both Old and New Testaments; of his hands, protected by gloves, symbolic of purity, untainted by any contact with human affairs, for administering the sacrament; of his crozier, a reminder of his watchful care of the flock entrusted to his keeping, or the cross carried before him as a symbol of his victory over all human passions?"[19] Even while invoking and honoring a long tradition of symbolism, Folly's ironic question clearly indicates a major reason why the purifying Reformers charged the vestment-clad priesthood with corruption, hypocrisy, and empty pageantry. The question asked Shakespeare's Archbishop of York, "Whose white *investments figure* innocence, / The dove, and very blessed spirit of peace," in *2 Henry IV* comes again to mind: "Wherefore do you so ill *translate* yourself / Out of the speech of peace that bears such grace / Into the harsh and boist'rous tongue of war?" (IV.1.45–49: my emphasis). The Archbishop's translation is not only a physical movement onto the battlefield but also a metaphorical refiguration of the metonymic meaning still visible in the vestments that the Archbishop wears, or at least should wear.

Relatively more agreement seems to exist among medieval interpreters regarding the symbolic significance of the chasuble and linen surplice, insofar as the latter's significance can be distinguished from that of the alb: the surplice is a wide-sleeved, ample version of the alb, originally of ankle-length but progressively shortened. Most interpreters, such as Rabanus, Alcuin, Hugh of Saint Victor, and Pope Innocent III, take the chasuble to signify charity, very likely because of the encompassing style of this garment, which, in Hugh's eyes, makes it the perfection of the priestly ensemble and the signifier of the greatest of all the virtues, according to the Bible.[20] The same signification is given the chasuble in the Sarum ordination rite, where, immediately after putting it over the shoulders of the candidate for ordination to the priesthood, the bishop tells him, "Accipe vestem sacerdotalem, per quam caritas intelligitur: potens est enim Deus augere tibi caritatem, et opus perfectum [Receive the sacerdotal vestment, by which charity is understood; for God is powerful to increase charity in you, and perfect work]."[21] As earlier noted, the chasuble is the priestly vestment par excellence that came to be associated distinctively with the sacrificial Mass and, in a medieval addition, to be bestowed on the priest at his ordination (Echlin, 10). Although the connection or lack of connection between the historical development of liturgical dress and that of eucharistic doctrine has proved controversial, the two were clearly coincident between the ninth and thirteenth centuries, a fact that in retrospect likewise appears suggestively relevant to the vestiarian controversy in the sixteenth.[22] Cloth is implicated, but again, much more than cloth is centrally and fundamentally at issue.

Although the shape of the third vestment to be examined, the surplice, dates from at least the sixth century, the name "surplice" derives from the use of this garment in northern countries in the twelfth century, where it was worn over fur-lined cassocks: *superpelliceum*, its Latin name, signifies "over pelts, over fur." From the twelfth century on, "the surplice became the distinctive dress of the lower clergy and was worn by priests outside the mass" (Cope, 377–78). Thus the surplice was not associated specifically with the sacrifice of the Mass, and this fact is also of considerable importance to the controversy regarding the continued use of this vestment in England in the sixteenth century. Although "popish" to puritans, the surplice could be considered doctrinally neutral in the eyes of episcopacy.

Commentary on the surplice by the memorably imaginative Bishop Durandus will serve to indicate the range of moral and mystical significance that could be attached to it, as well as the exfoliation of meanings evident by the thirteenth century. Durandus explains that the surplice, on the basis of its whiteness, first designates the cleanness or purity of chastity and adds that the works of those ordained or ministering should be frank and decent. He bases his second signification on the name *superpelliceum*, which "figures mortification of the flesh," insofar as the surplice used to be worn "above the fur tunics made from the pelts of dead animals [super tunicas pellicias de pellibus mortuorum animalium factas]," which in turn represented Adam's having been clothed in skins after he sinned. The third signification is innocence: "therefore," Durandus adds, "often it is put on before [ante] all other sacred vestments." The great size or breadth ("latitudinem") of the surplice accounts for its fourth signification, charity, and its form in the shape ("modum") of a cross figures the passion of Christ. Finally, Durandus remarks the related facts that baptized infants are wrapped in linen, that Moses was so wrapped, and that Aaron and his sons wore linen vestments when they ministered in the sanctuary.[23] With these remarks, the association of the significance of the surplice with that of the alb is complete and, viewed this way, potentially a motivation of puritan objections.

Cranmer's directions regarding the use of vestments in the Prayer Book of 1549, the Ordinal of 1550, and the Prayer Book of 1552, with which the newly revised Ordinal was now bound, depend on his basic (re)conceptions of doctrine and reflect his desire to control the words, actions, and visual symbols that express it.[24] When Cranmer offers an explanation at the end of the 1549 Prayer Book as to why some liturgical ceremonies and practices, such as liturgical vesting, have been "abolished and some retayned," his reasons emphasize neither their inherent sanctity nor that of the priesthood, but the need to maintain "decent ordre" and "quyete dyscyplyne" and lawful calling and "autoriz[ation]," although they also include "edificacion" and "reuerence unto" the practices maintained "for theyr antyquitye."[25] Recalling at once the Pauline epistles and the language of the official Tudor homilies, Cranmer urges that "all thynges bee done emong you . . . in a semely and due ordre" (*PB*, 286). At least officially, the primary metonymic value of vestments is now to be order and authority. Cranmer seeks to capture the traditional vestiary metonym and to *translate* it to his own meaning. Translating, he is in fact metaphorizing it and thereby hoping in time to change the code. In the short term, under Edward, he succeeds; under Mary he loses; but under Elizabeth and the early Stuarts, he wins, although post-humously.

In a series of questions put to bishops and divines in 1540, Cranmer's own answers indicate that he thought ordination equivalent to appointment to civil office, for "'In the New Testament he that is appointed to be a bishop or priest, needeth no consecration by the Scripture, for election and appointing thereto is sufficient.'" In 1547, however, Cranmer appears to endorse the more traditional view that the "imposition of handes, and gyv-ynge of the Holy Ghost" by those already ordained constitute "the conse-cration, ordres and unction of the apostles, whereby they, at the begynnynge, made byshopes and pryestes."[26] In an effort to reconcile the evident discrepancy between Cranmer's two views, Paul Bradshaw suggests that Cranmer's statement in 1540 identifies the "consecration" he rejected with Catholic anointing and other such practices that will be omitted in Cranmer's Ordinals, and he thus maintains that Cranmer's view in 1547 is not a contradiction (15). In my reading, Bradshaw's suggestion is addition-ally supported by Cranmer's phrasing in 1547, where transmission of the grace of the Holy Ghost through hands and words is itself at once "conse-cration, ordres, and unction." His interpretation appears to be premised on the instrumentalism, or perhaps the dynamic presence, examined in my third chapter. Yet it also seems possible in view of Cranmer's high opinion of the civil power and his instrumental view of the communion bread that the Archbishop believed a particular form of Orders no more necessary for any value inhering in it than simply because "wythoute some Ceremonies it is not possible to kepe anye ordre or quyete dyscyplyne in the churche" (*PB*, 287). Cranmer is often found in a politic version of the *via media*, not to say on the ambiguous fence.

The directions or "ordres" for Communion and the ordaining of clergy in Cranmer's Edwardine Prayer Books and Ordinals bear significantly on changes in the role of vestments between the late Middle Ages and the Tudor state church. By the time these Books and Ordinals were published, Cranmer no longer believed in the Mass as a sacrifice or offering and there-fore a meritorious work, a belief that is fundamentally opposed to the basic Reformation tenet of justification by faith. In a rubric introducing the order for Communion, his first Edwardine Prayer Book directs that the "Priest . . . appoincted for that ministracion," namely, Communion, should wear only "a white Albe plain, with a vestement [chasuble, stole, and maniple] or Cope" (*PB*, 212).[27] Significantly, although the chasuble, "the distinctive mark of the sacrificing priest," remains an option, a cope having general ceremonial uses (e.g., for processions), but not specifically eucharistic ones, is equally so (*PB*, Porter, x). Assisting priests and deacons are also to wear plain albs, but with tunicles (over-tunics). A separate rubric immediately following Cranmer's apology for ceremonies directs that a bishop celebrating Communion in a church or executing any other public "minystracyon" should wear, "besyde his rochette [variant form of the alb with full sleeves gathered at the wrist], a Surples or albe, and a cope or vestment" and should also bear his pastoral staff or else have it borne by his chaplain (*PB*, 288).

In marked contrast, the second Edwardine Prayer Book directs that "the minister at the tyme of the Communion and all other tymes in his ministracion, shall use neither albe, vestment, nor cope: but being archbishop or bishop, he shall have and wear a rochet; and being a preest or deacon, he shall have and wear a surplice onely" (*PB*, 347). Both rochet and surplice lack traditional symbolism that is specifically eucharistic. In this revision, the rubric for priestly Communion wear is put at the outset of the initial section on prayer rather than with the order for the Sacrament itself and is therefore as undistinctive in placing as in content; it, too, implies that Communion is no more an event than prayer, quite in contrast to the centrality of the eucharistic celebration in Catholicism. To take one crucial example of the change in the wording that this change in vestments accompanies, compare the priest's description of the bread that he distributes to communicants in 1549 with that in 1552: "The body of our Lorde Jesus Christe whiche was geuen for thee, preserue thy bodye and soule unto euerlasting lyfe" in 1549, and in 1552, "Take and eate this, in remembraunce that Christ dyed for thee, and feede on him in thy hearte by faythe, with thankesgeuing" (*PB*, 225, 389). Stephen Gardiner, Cranmer's conservative episcopal nemesis, found it possible to read a fairly orthodox Catholic meaning in the ambiguous words of 1549 and vexed his Archbishop by saying so.[28] But in 1552, any likelihood of such an understanding has vanished. For good measure, of course, in 1552 a table replaces the altar and the notorious "black rubric" appears, explaining that although communicants kneel, their doing so does not signify "any adoracion . . . eyther unto the Sacramentall bread or wyne there bodily receyued, or unto anye reall and essencial presence there beeyng of Christ's naturall fleshe and bloude" (*PB*, 393).

Cranmer's two Ordinals witness even more dramatically a movement away from the past and particularly from the notion of sacrifice, which permeates earlier rites of ordination. In comparison to Cranmer's, the Sarum rites are elaborately symbolic. For example, they feature comparisons between priests and the sons of Aaron, who are dedicated to offer sacrifices

("ad hostias salutares"); the unction of the priestly initiate's hands, symbolizing the power to consecrate; the imposition of a stole and chasuble, suggesting on the one hand the yoke and the dignity of office, and on the other,
charity and sacrificial power; and the *porrectio instrumentorum*, or presentation
to the initiate of a paten with wafers and a chalice with wine, the very instruments and indeed the means of sacrificial renewal.[29] With this presentation, or more literally this extending (*porrigere*: to extend), of the
instruments, the presiding bishop tells the new priest, "Receive the power
to offer sacrifice to God and to celebrate the Mass on behalf of the living as
of the dead (Accipe potestatem offerre sacrificium Deo, missamque cele-
brare tam pro vivis quam pro defunctis)" (Maskell, II, 226). Here are instruments, but in marked contrast to the Calvinist instrumentalism discussed in
my third chapter, the sacrificial power they represent is primarily embodied
in the celebrant, who receives it from the bishop.

Edward Echlin summarizes concisely the significance of Cranmer's omis-
sions from the Sarum rite in 1550: "no references to the altar, no analogies
with the sons of Aaron, no comparison of priests to levites, no unction or
references to the priest's hands, no tradition of stole and chasuble" (98). Although Cranmer retains the *porrectio instrumentorum*—a medieval accretion—he radically alters its form and meaning, which a number of
contemporary clergymen thought essential to the Sarum rite of ordination.[30]
In Cranmer's rite, the bishop presents the priest with "the Bible in the one
hande, and the Chalice or cuppe with the breade, in the other," saying,
"Take thou aucthoritie to preache the word of god, and to minister the holy
Sacramentes in thys congregacion, where thou shalt be so appointed" (*PB*,
312). Gone is the propitiatory, sacrificial offering, and in addition, blood is
now balanced by book and sacrament by sermon. Power and cultus have
shifted subtly in the wording to authority and appointment, as well. Especially notable in these shifts is the psychological understanding and the politic awareness with which Cranmer handles charged symbols. He retains
their traditional form but alters their content and thereby challenges the idea
that the content of a form is fixed. His politic moves are impressive and
instructive.

In 1552, Cranmer's Ordinal goes much farther. Whereas in the 1550 Ordinal those to be ordained deacon or priest wear a plain alb, and archbishops,
bishops, and bishops to be consecrated wear a surplice and cope, in 1552 the
mention of vestments is simply absent. Vestments have become invisible but
decidedly not inaudible as a statement, variously metaphorical or metonymic and thus dependent on what we think we hear in the sound of this

silence. Missing as well is the medieval form of the *porrectio instrumentorum*, the cup and bread now replaced by the presentation of a Bible alone, accompanied by the same words used in 1550. Three names are inseparable from these changes—Cranmer's, of course, as that of the primary authority behind them; Cranmer's friend and chaplain Nicholas Ridley's, as that of a key episcopal player in the relevant doctrinal and procedural changes of the period—one of the Archbishop's "company of learned men"; and above all, John Hooper's, as that of the candidate for episcopal consecration who objected vigorously and stubbornly to the Ordinal of 1550, losing the battle, but by 1552 apparently winning the war, at least for a brief time.[31] Insofar as the interwoven stories of these three prelates bear on the vestiarian controversy and culminate with their final appearances in John Foxe's Martyrology, they will occupy my attention in the remainder of this chapter.

Hooper, an exile in Zurich during the waning years of Henry VIII's reign, returned to England in 1549, the year Cranmer's first Edwardine Prayer Book was published. Having quickly established a reputation as a preacher and divine, early in 1550 he was ordered by Cranmer to preach before the King.[32] In a series of Lenten sermons on the prophet Jonah, he edified the Court by reflecting on various failings in the English church, conspicuous among them "the use of such vestments or apparel, as obscure the ministry of Christ's church, and representeth the form and fashion of the Aaronical ministry of the old law, abrogated and ended in Christ."[33] Obscuring a true ministry for him, vestments signal the distinctive status of a cultic priesthood. Elsewhere in the sermons, Hooper somewhat facetiously takes broader aim at Cranmer's Ordinal of 1550:

> I happened to see of late a certain book for the making of deacons, priests, and bishops, wherein is required an oath by saints; whereat I did not a little wonder. And how it is suffered, or who is the author of that book, I well know not. I am led to think it to be the fault of the corrector in the printing, for two causes: one is, because in the oath for the bishop is no mention made of any saints; the other cause is, that in the same book the minister must confess, at the receiving of his vocation, that the book of God, the holy scripture, to be perfect and sufficient for the salvation of man. Yet do I much marvel that in the same book it is appointed, that he that will be admitted to the ministry of God's word or his sacraments, must come in white vestments; which seemeth to repugn plainly with the former doctrine, that confessed

the only word of God to be sufficient. And sure I am, they have not in the word of God, that thus a minister should be apparelled, nor yet in the primitive and best church. It is rather the habit and vesture of Aaron and the gentiles, than of the ministers of Christ. Further, where, and of whom, and when have they learned, that he that is called to the ministry of God's word, should hold the bread and chalice in one hand and the book in the other hand? Why do they not as well give him in his hand the fount and the water? for the one is a sacrament as well as the other. If the fount be too great, take him a basin with water, or such like vessel [*An Oversight*, 478–79]

At the end of this passage, Hooper sees the primacy of communion over baptism as a vestige of the centrality of sacrifice to the priesthood. Earlier in it, vestments again figure as Aaronic or even pagan inheritances unauthorized by the New Testament, and at its outset, Hooper criticizes the oath of the King's supremacy in the 1550 Ordinal, which concludes, "so help me God, all Saints and the holy Evangelist."[34] Throughout, he transgresses the Act of Uniformity of 1549, which forbade speaking against the Prayer Book, as well as refusing to abide by it.

Hooper was next offered a bishopric despite his temerity (or for it, since he found an admirer in young Edward VI), but he refused to accept it, since he would not take the oath or wear the vestments required of a bishop for Communion by the 1549 Prayer Book and by the 1550 Ordinal for episcopal consecration. Arguing his view before the King's Council, Hooper was excused from taking the objectionable form of the oath or wearing "Aaronic" vestments, although both he and his episcopal opponents were required to acknowledge the vestments to be matters of indifference—*adiaphora* or non-essentials—in religion. But Cranmer, still declining to consecrate Hooper, then passed responsibility for doing so to Ridley, who, instead of complying, persuaded the Council that since everyone concerned had agreed vestments to be a matter of indifference, it was proper for the Crown to order their use, as had already been done in the Prayer Book and Ordinal. The issue vestments represented—Ridley, like Cranmer, would like to have thought "metonymized"—was now one of authority and governance, as distinct from Aaronic vestiges and the scruples of the individual conscience, and the Council agreed with Ridley. Cranmer's apology for ceremonies in the 1549 Prayer Book had already afforded a prescient commentary on the issue disputed and its outcome: "the willful and contemptuous transgression, and breakyng of a common ordre, and disciplyne, is no small offence before God"; moreover, "The appoyntemente of the whiche ordre pertayneth not to pryuate menne: Therefore no manne ought to take in hande nor presume to appoynte or alter any publyke or common ordre in Christes Churche, excepte he be lawfully called and autorized thereunto" (*PB*, 286).

Although six months had now elapsed since Hooper had been offered the bishopric, instead of capitulating, he wrote to the Council to explain his reasons for refusing. Ridley then replied in writing as well, and in my reading of their two responses, he managed to convict Hooper of inconsistency and unreasonableness. Hooper's primary premise is that anything employed in the church should be the express word of God or else should be wholly indifferent, that is, not profitable if used and not harmful if not used ("nihil prosit . . . praetermissa nihil obsit").[35] Thus *adiaphora* (indifferent things) do no good and their omission does no harm—seemingly an oddly restrictive, largely negative definition of this important Reformation concept. "Priuata" (individuating, distinctive) and "peculiaria" (peculiar, extraordinary, singular) vestments, Hooper continues, are neither commanded by God nor indifferent. He goes on to argue that even *adiaphora* should have their origin and foundation in the word of God and that their use or lack of use should depend on the individual conscience: thus, individuating and singular ("priuata et peculiaria") vestments, by which he describes the *traditional* metonym, the vestments of a privileged priesthood, are opposed to a like conscience, individual and singular and freely metaphorizing the traditional vestments and their defenders on the basis of God's word.

In a more apparent contradiction of his earlier definition of things indifferent, Hooper next asserts that *adiaphora* should have an open and manifest utility and should edify rather than harm.[36] As things indifferent, they also ought not to be introduced by means of deception and guile ("fraude ac dolo") or imposed by an impetuous tyranny ("violenta quadam Tyrannide"!) that restricts the liberty of a Christian and violates the freedom of the church (197). Such imposition compromises their very status as things indifferent, he argues. He concludes the body of this forceful and at times rashly phrased argument by suggesting that the civil authority should not concern itself with this matter, warning the magistrates against the bishops who sanction vestments, challenging his opponents to find a scriptural basis for their position, and promising to maintain his own view to the death.

Clearly not one to mince words, Hooper laces his closing comments with scorn. He notes the "vestium pompa in Ecclesia" (the pomposity of vesture, the parade of garments), which Ridley's indignant reply notably renders as "masking," and he refers to the bishops' blind and superstitious church

("Vestram superstitiosam et caecam Ecclesiam").[37] He implies that the opposing bishops are at once enemies ("Inimicos") and children of this world ("filios huius saeculi") who merely dream ("somniant") they are conserving decorum and order and providing edification. Appending supplemental commentary on vestments, Hooper repeatedly denounces their use as the misguided antiquations of Aaronic and papist rites and contrasts them with Christ's nakedness on the cross ("Notes," 198–99).

To read Hooper's letter in Latin is both to grasp something of the force of his conviction and better to understand the harsh, exasperated tone of Bishop Ridley's reply (ironically and symbolically in plain English instead of prelatical Latin) and why Ridley, who actually had a history of tolerating or even committing infractions of church rule in the interest of further reform, should have resisted so firmly the position of Hooper and the desire of the King and the Council for resolution.[38] For Ridley—aside from an obvious clash between two stubborn personalities—the issue appears to have involved the extremity and the openness of Hooper's defiance of lawful authority, which, Ridley goes so far as to intimate, savors of Anabaptism, the panic button of the Tudor period. With Hooper intended, Ridley darkly suggests that the schismatics "in our days" to be feared are

> the Anabaptists, who, considering neither the diversity of times concerning the external ecclesiastical polity, nor the true liberty of the Christian religion in extern rites and ceremonies, in matters neither commanded nor forbidden in God's law, nor the power of magistrates in the Christian congregation concerning the same, have boldly enterprised to stir up many heinous errors; as to make that necessary, and of necessity unto salvation, which though the apostles did it, yet they thought it to be left free to be done or not done, as the Holy Ghost should teach Christ's congregation . . . or to forbid and to make that sin which God never forbade, wickedly thus bringing in bondage the Christian liberty, and ungodly adding unto God's word ["Reply," 382].

Whereas the requirements and restrictions Ridley describes distort God's word, he stresses that "wholesome ordinances" regarding "things [deemed] indifferent by lawful authority"—by Church, King, Council, and Parliament—namely, vestments, do not ("Reply," 382). The confrontation, then, is not just between lawful authority and individual conscience; it is also about publicly interpreting—representing—God's word, including its symbolic forms. Even at this early date, the underlying issue is conformity.

Lawful authority, as distinct from and even opposed to individual conscience, is nonetheless the keynote of Ridley's reply, as when, for example, he answers Hooper's claim "that the thing indifferent is to be left free to use it or not use it, . . . [according] unto the conscience of the user." He agrees that this is true if no command or order pertains to indifferent things but adds, "in public ordinance it is not lawful, except in a lawful urgent cause, or in a case of necessity, to break the same; for then thou showest thyself a disordered person, disobedient, . . . [a] contemner of lawful authority, and a wounder of thy weak brother his conscience" ("Reply," 377). In a subsequent passage, he asserts even more strongly, "to teach that Christian liberty is free to use and not use, even as every man list, ordinances well made by lawful authority, is a seditious doctrine and liable to confound a good order" ("Reply," 378).

Hooper certainly was no Anabaptist, and his regard for lawful authority was great enough to lead him actively to support Mary Tudor's claim to the throne three years later, yet in the issue of conscience versus established authority that is revealed within the ample folds of the vestiarian controversy, a pressure that will build during the second half of the century and explode in the next is already apparent.[39] In the course of its emergence, the vested value of the vestiary metonym will finally shift from a dominantly cultic to a dominantly political meaning. In this shift, the vestments become a cultural plaything: their value, increasingly relativized, is also emptied out as it is subjected to the crosswinds of rival interpretations. As earlier remarked, symbols, like battles, have histories. Consider even the cross—the cross! the crucial symbol—emblazoning the armor of Spenser's Red Cross Knight at the outset of *The Faerie Queene*: when in only the second canto of Book I the villainous Archimago, masking in the armor of the Red Cross Knight, passes for him with the narrator's ironical assent, any attentive reader feels the ambiguating, relativizing, ironizing pertinence of the contests about signification in the preceding decades.[40]

Ridley, nearing the end of his reply to Hooper, declares it "a slanderous lie" to suggest that Cranmer and "the company of learned men with him that appointed the apparel judged the same to be a thing of necessity [to faith and doctrine], and not a thing indifferent, to be done for order's sake, without any opinion of necessity, or of superstition in the same" (389–90).[41] Ridley then makes a curious offer, which clearly indicates that for him the vestments are merely a figure for the real issue of lawful authority and the right to determine indifferent things: "Let him [Hooper] revoke his errors, and agree and subscribe to the doctrine, and not to condemn that for sin, that God never forbade, ungodly adding unto God's word, and I shall not, for any necessity that I put in these vestments, let [omit, delay] to lay my hands upon him and to admit him bishop, although he come as he useth to ride in a merchant's cloak, having the king's dispensation for the act, and my lord archbishop's commission orderly to do the thing" (390). "For any necessity that I put in these vestments" is surely ambiguous, suggesting both "Despite any necessity" and thereby implying a measure of commitment to them, or the more colloquially idiomatic "For all I care about them" and thereby implying virtually no commitment to them at all. In the context of a careful letter meant to sway the Council, the former seems the likelier, the latter simply peevish. Once again, as happened with the subtleties of Ridley's eucharistic virtualism, discussed in my third chapter, the complexity of his position is tinged with equivocation. But by either reading of Ridley's offer, if Hooper were only to grant the principle, he would be allowed to play his part. The legitimacy of authority and particularly of the authority to interpret reestablished, his scruples regarding vestments might charitably pass as a permissible idiosyncracy instead of a symbolic precedent with far-reaching implications.

Not surprisingly, Hooper did not accept Ridley's offer. Instead, he appealed for the support of Johannes à Lasco (Jan Laski), Martin Bucer, and Peter Martyr, three influential expatriates from the Continent resident in England and, particularly in the instances of the last two, familiar with Cranmer. The Archbishop himself consulted Bucer, whose draft rite had had a major influence on Cranmer's Ordinal. With à Lasco the odd man out, Martyr and Bucer advised Hooper to yield. Bucer wrote that he would prefer to see vestments abolished, since they are a source of superstitious belief, but that he does not "believe . . . there is anything about them which in itself is wicked"; moreover, he thinks that unless and until the people are properly taught, "the use and removal of vestments will do equal damage."[42] Eventually, Bullinger, Hooper's influential mentor, wrote to him and to the King, and even Calvin appears to have weighed in, telling Hooper that "his opposition to vestments was not worth it" (Hunt, 129–37, here 136). Striking in all these conciliatory responses is the tendency to neutralize and literalize the vestments and thus to reduce their significance as a charged, disputed cultural symbol—to turn them into mere cloth and thus to escape the issues Hooper and Ridley saw in them.

Hooper's obduracy led eventually to house arrest, which in spirit, if not in fact, he promptly violated by publishing *A godly Confession and protestacion of the christian faith*.[43] In it, he endorses the principle *sola scriptura* to a provocative extreme, holding that "the church is bound to no sort of people, or any ordinary succession of bishops, cardinals, or such like, but unto the only word of God." So much for the hands with which Ridley would symbolically pass on the succession in consecrating him. Hooper further holds that no such ecclesiastics should be "believed but when they speak the word of God" (90). Glancing at Ridley's reliance on lawful, and finally on civil, authority and Cranmer's politic commitment to gradual change, he regrets with all his "heart to see the church of Christ degenerated into a civil policy," and with seeming inconsistency, he states his view that the people "owe their duty and obedience to God, to their king and magistrates, unto their neighbours, and unto themselves" (90–91). Ministers of the church are conspicuously absent from this statement, as is an answer to the exasperated questions in Ridley's earlier reply, which have been triggered by Hooper's reiteration of the inflammatory word *tyrannis* (tyranny): "I pray you, who hath appointed now and instituted our vestments in the church of England; and who hath established them? Hath not the archbishop and his company of learned men thereunto appointed by the king his highness and his majesty's council appointed them? Hath not the king his majesty and the whole parliament established them?" ("Reply," 387). *Sola scriptura* and lawful authority clash conspicuously here, and all (barely) under the aegis of the variously metonymic and metaphorical vestments, their variousness dependent on the disputants' points of view.

Hooper soon found himself in prison, where he recanted sufficiently to win release. His consecration as bishop—in surplice and cope—quickly followed, but he was excused from the further wearing of ecclesiastical vestments except " 'when he preached before the King, or in his Cathedral, or in any publick place.' "[44] Notably, no issue is made specifically about his subsequent garb for Communion, once again underlining the extent to which for church authorities the controversy concerned lawful power, not vestments per se. For Hooper, as we have repeatedly seen, it concerned *both* Aaronic papal vestiges and the rights of private conscience.

John Foxe recounts the next time on record when the new Bishop Hooper played the public role now his: "appoynted to preach before the king, as a new player in a strange apparel, he commeth forth on the stage. His upper garment was a long scarlet Chymere [outer, sleeveless robe of silk] downe to the foote, and under that a white linnen Rochet that couered all his shoulders. Vpon his head he had a Geometrical, that is, a four squared cap, albeit that his head was round." Had the term "Roundhead," apparently a coinage of the English Civil War, been current when Foxe wrote, he would be found here in an unFoxian moment of gratuitous levity. Instead, implying the unnatural pretension of the squared cap, he invites our sympathy, continuing, "What cause of shame the straungenes hereof was that day to that good preacher, euery man may easily iudge." The rash and head-strong Hooper becomes a Foxian figure of patient, private suffering for the "publike profite of the Church." Referring obliquely to Hooper's opponents, most notably Ridley, Foxe then exclaims, "And I would to God in lyke maner, they which tooke vpon them the other part of that tragedy, had yelded their priuate cause whatsoeuer it was, to the publike concord and edifieng of the Church: for no man in all the Citie was one haire the better for that hote contention" over vestments (1504). What is striking is the distance between Foxe's attitude and Ridley's or Hooper's. Between Protestants, the pacific Foxe would have the vestments mere cloth, and the whole dispute a private matter of predilections and personalities. Here the vestments, as objects, are again subject to a variant reading.

Because Foxe's attitude to the vestments controversy bears on his accounts of the degradations of Hooper, Ridley, and Cranmer from priestly office and symbolic dress, to which I'll next turn, his view of the eruption of this controversy over Hooper's scruples is worth further pause. Removed by time and place from the actual degradations, Foxe's narrative provides a different perspective on the relation of these three prelates to vestments, which for all its bias conveys an affecting awareness of human engagement and a sense of the power of metaphor to transform the perception of official symbols and ritual acts. Vestments are a focal point in Foxe's development of a sartorial motif in the falls of these prelates. Each prelate finally becomes what Sir Philip Sidney describes as "a speaking picture"—the "fusion of moral abstraction . . . with [an] actual character," and thus a lived metaphor.[45] In this way Foxe arrests and through metaphor redirects the increasingly volatile vestiary symbol to an essentially moral and personal end.

More than once in *Actes and Monuments* Foxe deliberately minimizes or else fails to grasp the significance of the vestiarian controversy to the principals, or indeed, to the principles, involved:

> But I cannot tell what sinister & vnlucky contention concerning the ordering and consecration of Bishops, and of their apparell, with suche other like trifles, began to disturbe the good & lucky beginning of this godly byshop [Hooper, appointed but unconsecrated]. For notwithstanding that godly reformation of religion then begon in the church of England, besides other ceremonies more ambitious than profitable or tending to edification, they

vsed to weare suche garmentes and apparrell as the popish Bishops were
wont to doe: first a Chymere, & vnder that a white Rochet: then a Mathematicall cap with iiij angles, deuiding the whole world into foure partes.
These trifles tending more to superstition then otherwyse, as he could neuer
abide, so in no wise could he be perswaded to weare them [1504].

Notably, the ecclesiastical garments Foxe specifies do not include those in
the Ordinal over which battle was joined, the surplice and cope. His phrase
"vsed to weare" is notable as well, and its antiquating force at odds with the
continuing friction over vestments under Elizabeth, with eruptions around
1566 (Parker's "Advertisements") and 1584 (Whitgift's "Subscription").[46] In
this latter period, just after the 1583 edition of *Actes and Monuments*, Foxe's
"letter of some five thousand words" to Whitgift regarding clerical subscription, a letter described by Patrick Collinson as "betraying hardly an
ounce of sympathy for . . . [the puritan dissidents] he called 'thoughtless
youths' and 'restless innovators,'" likewise contrasts with his dismissive dis-
tancing in the passage cited.[47]

Most generally notable of all in the passage is Foxe's (re)interpreting presence, which initially represents itself through an assertion of ignorance
("But I cannot tell"), a kind of negation that fails to mask his outright disap-
proval of contention over such "trifles" as vestments. Like Bucer, Martyr,
Bullinger, and Calvin, he would again neutralize the vestments, preferring
to overlook the more fundamental investments in them. Given Foxe's access to registers and informants and the relative recency of a fairly public
controversy, it seems reasonable to suppose that he could have discovered
more about the controversy had the incident interested him for a purpose
beyond representing Hooper in a favorable, long-suffering light and trivial-
izing the charged issues the vestments represented.[48] In the passage at hand,
he clearly considers the controversy merely a distraction from the true business of Reformation. When, under Queen Mary, vestments reappear as part
of a variant script, however, the shift in Foxe's tone and angle of representation is again notable, if hardly surprising. The Marian vestments once more
have a highly charged value *in themselves*, a value Hooper had sensed even
while acknowledging their indifferent status but Ridley had denied to them
in their earlier debate. Now, at once registering and shaping response, they
are again a Catholic metonym for the Christ-like power to offer sacrifice,
and they bid fair to become a competing Protestant metonym for Antichrist.

When the former monk Hooper is haled before the Marian commission
that is to examine him and thus to prepare for his degradation, the commis-

sioners are interested first in his commitment to his own marriage and second in his belief about the Eucharist. These become the sufficient grounds for depriving him of his bishopric, and when subsequent interviews fail to persuade him to accept papal authority and doctrine, the Bishop of London delivers in Latin the sentence of excommunication and degradation from the priesthood. Foxe reports the sentence in full but does not translate it, although on the same folio page he renders from Latin an affecting letter of reconciliation from Ridley to Hooper. Foxe's omission is in itself symbolic. For simple readers or semi-literate viewers of his book in their parish churches, the Latin in such a context would in itself have conveyed the mystification and alienation of a "foreign" religion. Where the Latin is also set in a different font, these effects are strengthened.[49] Following this Latin document, Foxe reports the "forme and maner" of Hooper's degradation, repeating this phrase no less than three times in four sentences (1508). Since medieval discussions of the rite of ordination, which degradation reverses, characteristically employ the terms "matter" and "form" (essential action and verbal formula) to describe what constitutes the rite, the tautology of Foxe's repeated doublet conveys to the knowing the suggestion of empty formality.[50] Foxe also omits any reference to the accompanying verbal formula from the acts of degradation he reports, which consequently have as much likeness to charade as to ritual.

Foxe lingers, if only briefly, over Hooper's degradation, as he customarily does in other occurrences of the same "trifles" in his Martyrology, where one or two instances of the "forme and maner" might have been enough for summary reference thereafter. The formulaic, if not fixated, strangeness of the whole repetitious procedure, as Foxe repeatedly represents it, is fascinating, however briefly.[51] Perhaps its being so reflects not simply the magical strangeness of the rite but also the danger of imitative form or textual contamination by what is depicted.[52] Foxe's account of Hooper's degradation is relatively short in comparison to his accounts of Ridley's and Cranmer's, and it refers at once to Hooper and to a second priest who is being degraded at the same time. First the Bishop of London

> put vpon [each of them] . . . all the vestures and ornaments belonging to a Priest, with all other things to the same order appertainyng, as though (beyng reuested) they should solemnly execute in their office. Thus they beyng apparelled and inuested, the Bishop beginneth to plucke of, first the vttermost vesture, and so by degree and order, comming downe to the lowest vesture, . . . and so, beyng stript and deposed, he depriued them of all order,

benefite, and priuiledge belonging to the Clergy: and consequently, that beyng done, pronounced, decreed, and declared the sayd parties so disgraded, to be geuen personally to the secular power [1508].[53]

Despite Hooper's earlier participation in the vestiarian controversy and in marked contrast to Foxe's treatment of the degradations of Ridley and Cranmer, this account indicates nothing of Hooper's response to degradation—to the imposition of vestments on him only to remove them again—a nonsensical act except in a ritual context in which the vestments participate in the vested power. It is as if Hooper simply had done with these vanities of cloth, and this might be exactly Foxe's point: the formality of Hooper's degradation contrasts markedly with passages that precede and follow it, which involve an account of Hooper's exemplary conduct as bishop, practical arrangements for the execution of his sentence, human interaction, and emotional response—Hooper's rejoicing at the news that he is to be burned in his own diocese of Gloucester, Kingston's tearful farewell, the visits of the faithful blind boy and the wicked papist to Hooper. In the context Foxe provides, the act of vesting and devesting, empowering and disempowering, symbolic making and unmaking, is made to witness its own emptiness.

Stripped and virtually naked at the end, resembling the Christ whose near nudity Hooper invoked in his letter to the Council about vestments, Hooper is again on a stage that is not of his own making: fastened to the stake, "he looked vpon the people, of whom he might be wel sene (for he was both tal, and stoode also on an high stoole) and behelde rounde about him" (fol.1510). Tortured for three-quarters of an hour by the fire, "as a Lambe, paciently he aboade the extremitie therof, neither mouing forwardes, backwards, or to any side: but, hauing his nether partes burned, and his bowels fallen out, he died as quietly as a childe in his bedde" (1511). At the end, Foxe represents Hooper as an unbearably human emblem of patience, a resounding rebuke to any trivial concern with vestments.

Ridley's execution follows Hooper's in the same year and makes the patterns of Foxe's narrative that are relevant to the controversial vestments more distinct. Ridley's examination before the commissioners, which provides the immediate context for his degradation, is coupled with that of one-time bishop Hugh Latimer, the two interlacing with one another and reinforcing the overall tonal effect. The highlight of Ridley's examination, as Foxe narrates it, involves his four-squared clerical cap. At first, Ridley stands "bare headed, humblye expecting the cause of that hys appearaunce" before the commission, but as soon as he hears "the Cardinall named, and the Popes holines," he puts on his cap (1757). John White, Bishop of Lincoln and an examiner, challenges Ridley to doff his cap at mention of Cardinal Pole, the Pope's representative in England:

> M. Ridley, although neyther I, neyther my Lordes here, in respecte of our owne persones doe looke for cappe or knee, yet because we beare & represent, such persones as we doe, that is my Lorde Cardinalles grace, Legate a latere to the popes holinesse, as well in that he is of a noble parentage, and therewith mayster Ridley mooued hys cappe with lowly obeysaunce,[54] descendyng from the regall bloud, as in that he is a man worthy to be reuerenced with all humility, for hys great knowledge and learning, noble vertues, and godly lyfe, and especially in that he is here in Englande deputye to the popes holynesse, it should haue beccommed you at his name, to haue discouered your head [1757].

Bishop White then tells Ridley that he must either "discover"(irresistibly, a pun) his head at the naming of cardinal and pope or have it uncovered for him. To this alternative, Ridley offers an elaborate response that mirrors White's admonition closely enough to verge on parody. The exaggerated formality of Ridley's manner requires substantial quotation:

> As touching that you sayd (my Lord [Bishop]) that you of your owne persones desire no cappe nor knee, but only require the same, in consideration that you represent the Cardinalles graces persone, I doe you to wit, and therevpon make my protestation, that I did put on my cappe at the naming of the Cardinalles grace, neither for anye contumacye that I beare towardes your own persones, neither for any derogation of honour towarde the Lorde Cardinalless grace. For I know him to be a man worthy of all humilitie, reuerence, and honour, in that he came of the most regall bloud, & in that he is a man endued wyth manifolde graces of learning and vertue, and as touching these vertues and poynts, I, with all humility (therewith he put of his cap, and bowed his knee) and obeysance that I may, will reuerence, and honour his grace: but, in that he is Legate to the Byshop of Rome (and therewith put on his cap) whose usurped supremacy, and abused authoritie, I utterly refuse and renounce, I may in no wise geue any obeysaunce, or honour vnto him [1757].

Having admonished Ridley thrice to no avail, White has a beadle remove Ridley's cap. These players know exactly what game they are playing here, and it is on this note of rehearsal that the examination proper begins. It focuses on Ridley's understanding of the Eucharist, and whenever Ridley strays from the examiner's script, as he is bound by his beliefs to do, he is interrupted.

Ridley having been dismissed until the following morning, the commissioners summon Latimer into their presence. In one of Foxe's more celebrated descriptions, Latimer's apparel and accoutrements certainly make an arresting statement about age, poverty, and a change in fortune: "Master Latimer bowed his knee downe to the ground, holdyng his Hat in his hand, hauing a kerchefe on his hed, and vpon it a night cap or two, and a great cap (such as Townes men vse, with two broad flaps to butten vnder the chin), wearyng an olde thred bare Bristowe fryse gown gyrded to his body with a peny leather gyrdell, at the which hanged by a long string of leather his Testament, and his spectacles without case, depending about his necke vpon his brest" (1762). Although at description's end, Latimer may resemble a holy old hermit, the proliferation of his head coverings—particularly the "night cap or two"—suggests more than protection against the cold. For Latimer, a master of "anecdotes, jibes, digression, and simple vituperation," mockery is not out of the question.[55]

Though coming hat in hand, at least one hat in hand, and with knee bowing, Latimer is not a docile prisoner: his first words reprove the commissioners for having left him, an old man, so long in the cold while they examined Ridley, and they evoke an apology from the Bishop of Lincoln, their spokesman. Although Latimer is cautioned against "rayling or tauntes" before he ever says anything substantive (the examiners evidently know their man), he soon turns the tables on one of them, more than once evoking laughter from the audience with his wit, and causing the examiner in question to defend himself (1762–63). At the end of the examination, Latimer again spoils the script by requesting immediate sentencing rather than waiting for a reappearance the next day. He thereby implies that the result of the proceeding has been predetermined and that its justice is a sham.

Ridley and Latimer are further examined the following day with little change: Ridley's examination begins with another hat episode in virtually identical language, and Latimer's with another complaint requiring and receiving apology. Foxe then recounts Ridley's degradation, whose lack of dignity befits yet exceeds that in the passages looked at so far. Affording ironic reflection on Ridley's role in the controversy with Hooper, vestments play a conspicuous part in this scene, as Foxe's predilection for poetic justice, an intimation of divine order, hovers not quite offstage. James Brooks (or Brookes), Bishop of Gloucester, is the official degrader, accompanied by numerous others. Having made a final, fruitless offer of the Queen's mercy to Ridley if he recants, Brooks reminds him of the inevitable burning to follow his degradation from the priesthood. Foxe's narrative now switches to a passage of unmediated dialogue, which begins this way:

> *Ridley*—Do with me as it shall please God to suffer you, I am well content
> to abide the same with all my heart.
> *Brooks*—Put of your cap, M. Ridley, and put vppon you this surples.
> *Ridley*—Not I, truly.
> *Brooks*—But you must.
> *Ridley*—I wyll not.
> *Brooks*—You must: therefore make no more a do, but put this surples vpon
> you [1764].

The impasse continues, until, in Foxe's words, "they put vppon the sayde Doctor Ridley the surples, with all the trinkettes appertaynyng to the Masse." As they vest Ridley, he "vehemently inuey[s] . . . against the Ro- mysh Bishyp, and all that foolysh apparell, callyng hym Antichrist, and the apparell foolysh and abominable, yea, to fond for a vice in a play" (1767). The value of the vestments now having shifted, poor Ridley sounds for all the world like Hooper *redivivus*. That symbolic value is relative is becoming ever more painfully clear. Equally evident is the political analogue to the rhetorical relativism of Zwingli's arguments in my previous chapter.

The threat of gagging leads Ridley to contain, though not wholly to cease, his remarks, but when they reach the point where he is to hold the chalice and wafer-bread, he declares, "They shal not come in my handes; for, if they do, they shall fall to the ground for all me." An attendant is then "appoynted to hold them in his hand [whether his own or Ridley's is unclear]," while Bishop Brooks reads "a certaine thyng in Latine, touching the degradation of spirituall persones, accordyng to the Popes law." Then "they put a booke [the gospel] in hys hand, and withall red (as is before sayd) a certayne thing in Latin, the effect therof was: We do take from you the office of preachyng the Gospel, etc. At which wordes D. Ridley gaue a great sigh, lookyng vp towards heauen, saying: O Lorde God, forgeue them this their wickednes" (1768). Foxe's ignorance of what book is put into Ridley's hand and what is said in Latin at every stage is unconvincing. This information was available to one with access to bishops and universities, and, indeed, to one with access to a copy of "the popes booke, called Pon- tificale," as Foxe indicates he is in his account of Cranmer's degradation in his "first booke of Monuments."[56] Here, however, such particularity would interfere with the focus on hocus pocus and ruin the farce.

Foxe returns his attention to the vestments and continues, "as they put vppon hym the Masse geare, so they began with the vppermost garment in taking it away agayne, reading a thyng in Latine, accordyng to the order contayned in the sayd booke of the Popes law."[57] When nothing but a surplice remains, "as they were readyng and takyng it away," Ridley exclaims in frustration, " 'Lord God, what power be you of, that you can take from a man that which he neuer had: I was neuer singer in all my lyfe.' " In a final blundering touch, the Bishop's "uncreating word" has apparently removed from Ridley a minor clerical order never conferred on him.[58] Foxe's inclusion of this unglossed exclamation again indicates his considerable knowledge of the Roman rites. Hard on it, his summation of the whole procedure affords a final palette of rhetorical colors: "So when all this their abhominable and ridiculous degradation was ended very solemnely, D. Ridley sayde vnto D. Brookes, haue you done?"—a quiet but deflating question (1768). First in Foxe's summation comes outright condemnation, then in its wake, heavy irony ("solemnely"), and finally Ridley's dramatic understatement.

Going to the stake in Oxford, Ridley and Latimer, the academic theologian and the popular preacher, are still paired and still visually contrasting statements. Latimer comes in his "poore Bristow freeze frocke all worne, with hys buttened cap, and a kerchiefe on his hed," a costume fitting his persona as son of a yeoman, preacher of "The Sermon on the Plough," popularizer of the Reformation, and simple proponent of active virtue, as against theological abstraction. Ridley comes for all the world in the public dress of a divine: "M. Ridley had a faire blacke gowne furred, and faced with foins [sables], such as he was woont to weare beyng Bish. and a tippet [long black scarf] of veluet furred likewyse about his necke, a veluet night cap vpon his hed, & a corner cappe vpon the same, goyng in a paire of slippers to the stake, & going betweene the Maior and an Alderman" (1769). To my reading, Ridley's garb firmly declares once again that to him distinctive dress is appropriate to lawful order and discipline. But this is not Foxe's reading, for he juxtaposes the lines just cited immediately with the description of Latimer in his "freeze frocke" and does not indicate that Latimer is accompanied by anyone, such as officers or friars, as would likely have been the case. Instead, Latimer's image alone comes into focus. Given Foxe's earlier impatience with distinctive ecclesiastical dress, Latimer follows after Ridley like a rebuke of such worldly vanities as cloth.[59] And it is Latimer, Foxe tells us, who stirs men's hearts to pity both of them, beholding in Ridley "the honour they sometyme had," and in Latimer "the calamitie whereunto they were fallen": these emblematic images "Before" and "After" are fitting mementos in the *de casibus* tradition (1769).[60] "Mere cloth" turns up in Foxe with moral and metaphorical value, after all.

Although Ridley had the spotlight during the first dramatic eruption of the vestiarian controversy, Diarmaid MacCulloch indicates that Cranmer and Ridley worked closely together to oppose Hooper. Like that of the other two principals, Cranmer's final engagement with distinctive clerical dress predictably draws Foxe's attention when Cranmer appears in his narrative to answer the commission appointed to examine him on charges that he has violated his oath of celibacy by marriage, held and disseminated heresies regarding the Eucharist, and fomented England's schism with Rome. Appearing before the commission, Cranmer wears "a faire blacke gowne, with his hoode on both shoulders, suche as Doctors of diuinity in the Vniuersity vse to weare," since he has been deprived of a prelate's vestments (1872). Much as did Ridley, he takes off his cap and bows to representatives of the King and Queen, but he puts it on again to face Bishop Brooks, who represents papal jurisdiction, and thereby offends Brooks officially. Foxe is interested enough in this sort of vestiary gesture to add pages later, after a series of exchanges between Brooks and this time, significantly, the two commissioners representing royal authority on the one side, and on the other, Cranmer, "All this while his cappe was on his head" (1875). In retrospect, Foxe's sensitivity even to this quiet gesture by Cranmer makes his lack of appreciation of the issues represented in the earlier controversy over vestments the more notable by contrast. Foxe's interest lies rather in the immediate, individualizing gesture than in the impersonal continuity of tradition, in the signification of drama, not ritual.

The examination of Cranmer in *Actes and Monuments* generally has a less rehearsed quality than that of Ridley, despite the prepared orations that occur in Cranmer's. Perhaps this is an inevitable result of its length and complexity, but Cranmer's having a relatively greater opportunity to respond and his taking advantage of it fairly economically and effectively contribute to this impression. There is no denying Cranmer's ecclesiastical status in the eyes of Rome, as there was the episcopal status of Hooper and Ridley, both of whose consecrations as bishop postdated the schism. Cranmer must therefore be dealt with more carefully. A precedent for degrading and burning the ecclesiastical primate of all England was not easy to come by. This was to be a judicial murder, not an illegal, royal attack on another Becket.

Accordingly, the second commission appointed to deal with Cranmer, headed by Thomas Thirlby, Bishop of Ely, and Bishop Bonner, comes with an order from the Pope for proceeding with deprivation, degradation, and excommunication of him, since Cranmer's archbishopric had originally derived its authority from Rome.[61] The bishops, having read their commission, proceed with the degradation: "first," Foxe tells us, they "clothed and disguised him: putting on hym a surplis, and then an Aulbe: after that the vestiment of a Subdeacon, and euery other furniture, as a Priest ready to Masse." Cranmer seems at first to respond to these vestments with surprise, "What . . . I thinke I shall say Masse," although his response looks more ironic after we learn that the vestments are made of canvas and clouts (rags) and are thus *merely* a costume—for Catholic viewers a realization of Cranmer's hypocrisy and for Protestant readers an expression of the empty pageantry of the Mass. The degraders continue, investing Cranmer "in all manner of Robes of a Bishop and Archbishop, as he is at his installing, sauing that as euery thing then is most riche and costly, so euerye thing in this was of Canvas and olde cloutes, with a Miter and a Pall of the same sute downe [done] vppon hym in mockery, and then the crosier staffe was put in hys hand. This done after the Popes pontificall *forme and maner*," Foxe adds scornfully (1881–82: my emphasis). For an instant, the mocking of Cranmer with a staff brings to mind that of Christ with a reed or mock scepter.[62] More quietly than Ridley and with more help from Foxe, Cranmer interferes again with the ceremony, for at this point Bonner tries to make a living exemplum of the hapless Archbishop ("'Thys is the man . . . This is the man . . . This is the man,'"), but he is first interrupted by Cranmer regarding a matter of fact, and then convicted of interminable and dishonest "Rhetoricall repetition" by Foxe (1882). Given Cranmer's mock staff, the emphatic repetitions "This is the man" in Foxe's rendering may also recall Pontius Pilate's phrase *Ecce homo* and the variants *Ecce eum, Ecce rex vester* rung on it during the examination and exhibition of Jesus (John 19.4–5, 14: "Behold the man," "Behold him," "Behold your king").[63]

After the exchange between Bonner and Cranmer, Foxe reports how the bishops "began then to *bustle* toward his disgrading, and first to take from him hys Crosiar Staff out of his hands, which he held fast and refused to deliuer, & withall, imitiating the example of Martin Luther, pulled an Appeal oute of his left sleeue vnder the wrest, which hee there and then deliuered vnto them, saying: I appeale to the next general Councel: and herein I haue comprehended my cause and forme of it, whych I desire may be admitted" (1882: my emphasis). Foxe then prints a copy of the appeal. That he should have done so, I applaud. That he intrudes the content of this document into the scene he purports to represent historically, I notice. Once again, whether rightly or wrongly, this *narrative* is far from just history.

Following further byplay, the degradation proceeds, with Foxe omitting in 1583 an account of "the perfect forme wherof, withal the rites & ceremonies therto appertaining," and thereby enforcing the parodic effect of what was supposed by the persecuting side to be a solemn ritual. Rather then include this extensive ritual as it was ordered and actually performed, Foxe simply (and not very helpfully) refers readers to his "first booke of Monuments . . . pag. 1493," where they have been "described at full" (1883).[64] Omission of the ritual may contribute to narrative coherence, but it also enables the narrator Foxe to bring the absent rites and ceremonies to a different, less dignified life: "Heere then to be short, when they came to take of hys Pall (which is a solemne vesture of an Archb.) then sayde he: Which of you hathe a Pall, to take off my Pall; whych imported as much as they being his inferiors, coulde not disgrade him.[65] Whereunto one of them said, in that they were but Bishops, they were his inferiors, and not competent iudges: but being the popes Delegates, they might take his Pall [the symbol of his office given him by the pope, albeit via Henry VIII—a vital difference for Cranmer], & so they did: and so proceeding tooke euery thing in order from him, as it was put on." They next have Cranmer's hair clipped to eliminate his tonsure symbolically, and they scrape his fingers—roughly, on Bonner's part—where he had once been anointed: "Whiles they were thus doing, All this (quoth the archbishop) needed not: I had my selfe done wyth this geare long ago" (1883).[66] Here *geare* could be taken either narrowly as a reference to cutting and scraping or more broadly as a reference to the entire ceremony of devestment and degrading. The word has a relevant range of meaning from "apparel, attire, dress, vestments" (*OED* example cited from another passage in Foxe); to "apparatus," including tools; or even to "toys." This is Cranmer's final statement on the accoutrements of ritual, however, and it confirms that for him, as for Ridley, they had long since become at most metonyms of lawful authority and no longer of a mystical priesthood.

The finale of "this pageant of degradation," as Foxe describes it, is the stripping of Cranmer even "out of his gown into his iacket," then replacing it with a poor yeoman-beadle's gown, along with a townsman's cap. It is at this point that Bonner tells Cranmer, "Nowe are you no Lord any more," and thus reasserts the power of symbolic clothing to make the man and, it would seem here, the priest, bishop, and archbishop (1883). When, not long after, Cranmer goes to the stake, he is another "speaking picture" in the *de casibus* tradition, in this fate, too, joining Ridley. The doomed Cranmer, Foxe tells us, now wears "a bare and ragged gowne" and an "olde square cappe," visually admonishing "men not onely of his owne calamitie, but also of theyr state and fortune" (1885). Thus clothed, at the end he has become Foxe's living metaphorical exemplum, of which his vesture is the substance, and like Ridley and Hooper, his associates in the vestiarian controversy, he is a Foxian rebuke to any dignity that is of this world, especially to one of mere cloth.

During the Tudor period the symbolic value of vestments focuses, blurs, shifts, and refocuses—mystical priesthood, lawful authority, Antichrist, worldly vanity, at once an alternation and a succession of metonym, transforming metaphors, competing metonyms, more metaphors, with an incremental, centrifugal weakening of symbolic force. Toward the end of this period, the poet John Donne metaphorically embodies religion in a female form that comments on the vestiary experience spanning the previous half century. He imagines one Mirreus, who seeks this elusive female at Rome "because hee doth know / That shee was there a thousand yeares agoe, / He loves her ragges so." The name Mirreus signals a merely superficial engagement with externals, variously suggesting incense, from "myrrh"; or else "mirror" and thus ironically the glass *through which* (in both senses) we should see darkly; or else the potentially superstitious act of gazing wide-eyed—Old French *mirer*, "to look at," derived in turn from Latin *mirari*, "to wonder at," both verbs being also roots of the noun *mirror* itself. He also imagines one Crants, whose North European name is harsh and crabbed in cadence, who loves instead

> her onely, who'at Geneva'is call'd
> Religion, plaine, simple, sullen, yong,
> Contemptuous, yet unhansome. As among
> Lecherous humors, there is one that judges
> No wenches wholesome, but course country drudges.[67]

This Lady Holy-Church-come-lately is in various states of overdress or undress, "richly painted" in Rome or "rob'd and tore" in Protestant countries, but she is nonetheless still depicted in terms of her outward appearance and accoutrements and easily recognized by them. She has visual authority, or its lack.

In the controversy over vestments is also the historical and political basis—the motivation and the root—of Donne's pronounced, abiding interest in the word and concept of *investment* (Latin *investire*, "to clothe, vest"). This interest extends to his coining the term *super-invest*, first for use in the *Devotions* and then with almost incredible complexity two years later, extends to its elaboration, together with the words *invest* and *devest*, in the culmination of his Second Prebend Sermon.[68] In this sermon, super-investment is spiritual and involves the putting on of heavenly glory, which is nonetheless still significantly conceived as a garment. In another, somewhat earlier sermon, Donne also describes "a double *Induere*, a twofold clothing;" since "we may *Induere*, 1. *Vestem*, put on a garment; 2. *Personam*, put on a person. We may put on Christ so, as we shall be *his*, and we may put him on so, as we shall be *He*" (V, 158). It is as if Donne had been reading St. Jerome or the Sarum ordination rite, in both of which vesting occurs inside and outside at once. Of course he has also been reading Luther and Calvin, who, while echoing St. Paul, use clothing as a more exclusively interiorized metaphor to describe our having been covered in the righteousness of Christ.[69] Donne distinguishes between putting on Christ as his servant— wearing his livery, as it were—and putting him on as our very being, yet he retains *both* senses.

More startling as a commentary on what might be called the continuing past of the vestiary symbol is George Herbert's poem "Aaron," which was published posthumously in *The Temple* in 1633, the year of William Laud's translation to Archbishop of Canterbury. This poem, too, seems almost to circle back to early commentaries on vestments like those of Chrysostom and St. Jerome, who saw in the alb both a memory of Aaron and the garment of Christ's redemption. But the fact that there is neither alb nor any other cloth garment in Herbert's poem is a very significant difference between it and these early commentaries. The garment Herbert's "Aaron" wears is wholly metaphorical:

> Holinesse on the head,
>   Light and perfections on the breast,
> Harmonious bells below, raising the dead
>   To leade them unto life and rest:
>   Thus are true Aarons drest.
>
>   Profaneness in my head,
>   Defects and darknesse in my breast,
> A noise of passions ringing me for dead

Unto a place where is no rest:
  Poore priest thus am I drest.

  Onely another head
I have, another heart and breast,
Another musick, making live not dead,
  Without whom I could have no rest:
    In him I am well drest.

  Christ is my onely head,
  My alone onely heart and breast,
My onely musick, striking me ev'n dead;
  That to the old man I may rest,
    And be in him new drest.

  So holy in my head,
Perfect and light in my deare breast,
My doctrine tun'd by Christ, (who is not dead,
  But lives in me while I do rest)
    Come people; Aaron's drest.[70]

While allusively evoking an "Aaronic" model, the poem actually offers only its inner realization. Like Herbert's *Temple*, his true church, the Christ-like power of the priesthood is found within. In Herbert's interiorizing Aaron is back, but without his distinguishing vestments of cloth.

Whether viewed retrospectively against the Tudor church or prospectively against the Laudian one, Herbert's "Aaron" is at once an idealized, symbolic expression and obliquely a political one. Unlike Hooper and Foxe, however, Herbert is not rejecting meanings woven into the warp and woof of the cloth or replacing the cloth with nakedness; instead, he is seizing such meanings and *translating* them radically inward. Such inwardness comes with a cost, however. His recovery of Aaron, for all its final intimation of a public ministry, is also a narrowing and personalizing of the power of the vestiary symbol, which no longer has even a separably or externally actualized form. Its power and authority are radically interiorized, much like the Eucharist's.[71] The inwardness is a gain and a sublation that intensifies significance, but the loss that accompanies it is, in both material and conceptual senses, substantial.

As the vestiarian controversy indicates, metaphor and metonymy, the latter as the encoded offshoot of metaphor, are fundamentally conceptual, rather than merely ornamental or descriptive, and therefore, to my mind, they are both in some sense always linguistic. Language is required even for categorization within a human culture and is certainly essential to the more advanced forms of abstraction from the singular, immediate sense impression. This is true whether or not, as seems likely, some type of basic physical disposition, orientation, and awareness that is pre-linguistic informs language itself. What the vestiarian controversy demonstrates with particular force is the extent to which, and the historically shifting ways in which, material objects such as vestments, as well as the beliefs that inform these institutionalized objects, are subject to the manipulations of metaphor and to the encoding—the stabilizing or "fixing"—of metaphor in metonymy.

6.   Busirane's Place: The House of Abusive Rhetoric in The Faerie Queene

That the House of Busirane, culmination of the 1590 edition of Spenser's *Faerie Queene*, should be a "house" in the rhetorical sense—a rhetorical place or topos—came with the surprise of delayed recognition to me, as well as to the audiences with whom I have shared and explored this idea. The delay may testify to our distance from a deliberately, self-consciously rhetorical culture, even as its recognition suggests that this distance is not insurmountable. Erotic reality, a conception tottering on the brink of oxymoron, conspicuously and especially takes rhetorical forms, as it radically does in Busirane's House, precisely because it is so strongly imaginative and emotional. In this, it resembles religion. Civilized expression seeks containing forms, and Busirane's rule within his domain of rhetoric affords a striking and sadly abusive case in point.

The present chapter and the next one engage metaphor and catachresis—*translatio* and *abusio*, respectively—two rhetorical figures whose relationship has proved basic to post-structural conceptions of meaning and of its lack. In this chapter I shall argue that the first two rooms in the House of Busirane consist of rhetorical "places" or topoi familiar both to Spenser's heroine Britomart and to his contemporary readers. The third room, Busirane's inner sanctum, is all too familiar as well. Thomas Roche has glossed the enchanter Busirane as *abuse* or the archaic *abusion* (deceit, deception, delusion), to which I would now add *abusio*, a common Renaissance term for catachresis, understood either as a necessary use of metaphor, as a wrenched or extravagant use, or as both. In Busirane's House of Rhetoric in Book III, *abusio* reigns, or "ranes," supreme.[1] Busirane abuses figuration outrageously, fantasizing that metaphor is the same as reality; feigning and faining rape. While Britomart can *save* Amoret, thus ambiguously preserving her, she cannot destroy Busirane without killing the cultural object that Amoret is. It therefore makes sense that the poem should struggle with the figure of Amoret after Book III and that Busirane should survive his vanished art works, albeit bound by the rhetorical art he has abused. There is much to unpack here.

My argument in this chapter and the next one proceeds from the psychological and semantic working of metaphor and catachresis in the cultural context of Busirane's House to a broader discussion of metaphor and catachresis in the Roman rhetorics and their Renaissance legacies. I therefore move from examination of Spenser's complex reflection of and on Renaissance rhetoric at the end of Book III to what lies behind and informs it. In this way, I would avoid the impression, as the practice, of simply imposing traditional or current theory on the text at hand, while asserting the reciprocity—the continuing conversation—of this particular text with both.

Over the last three or four decades, the House of Busirane has variously been seen as Busirane's projection, as Amoret's, as Scudamour's, as Britomart's, and without regard for the niceties of mediating characters, as the narrator's. For this reason, I'll begin with the flat declaration that the House of Busirane, like the House of Holiness, the Bower of Bliss, The Gardens of Adonis, the Temple of Venus, or any other such place in *The Faerie Queene*, is a cultural site. Representation of this site is finally the poet's, as are all the figures within it, although by now it goes almost without saying that the poet's control of the site, his agency with respect to it, is mediated, limited, and compromised by his own position in language and history. Moreover, like other cultural sites in *The Faerie Queene*, the House of Busirane has special pertinence to the figures within it, especially to Britomart, the major figure in Book III, even as the House of Pride or the House of Holiness, for example, has special pertinence to Redcrosse but without being solely attributable to him.

Britomart, the knight of chaste love on whose quest Book III focuses, arrives at the culminating House of Busirane by chasing a Chaucerian allusion, namely, Ollyphant, the destructive fantasy that leads her to Scudamour. The image of Cupid on the shield (Italian: *scudo*) of Scudamour clearly identifies him as "*Cupids* man" and therefore as a kind of allegorical projection of Cupid, or *Amor/Amour* (III.xi.7, IV.x.54). Five cantos earlier in Book III, a heavenly Venus lost control of a wayward Cupid and descended to earth to seek him, only to find Diana, goddess of chastity and therefore traditionally her opposite. By herself, Diana represents the possibility of total, not to say repressive, control over Cupid's waywardness. After a temporary and symbolically promising reconciliation with Diana to search for Cupid, however, Venus then separates from Diana again, taking with her in *place* of Cupid the twin foundling she names Amoretta, or more commonly,

Amoret. The name she chooses "in her litle loues [Cupid's] stead [place]" makes it clear that *Amor(etta)*—diminutive, feminized love, hence beloved or love object—compensates and consoles her as a substitute in Cupid's absence and, given the cast of British and Faerie figures in Book III, as a supplement, or necessary extra, to the mythological Cupid (III.vi.28).

When Britomart, the virgin on an erotic love quest, finds Cupid's man Scudamour, then, a composite Venus-Diana might finally be said to have found Cupid. Symbolically, this confluence of figures seems another promising development, but Scudamour, the representative of Cupid Britomart finds, has been disabled by Busirane, who has abducted, and in this sense has ravished, Amoret, Scudamour's beloved, and, as it turns out, the very possibility of Scudamour's actualizing love. More pointedly, this Enchanter has "pend," or through his art confined, the Amor(et) principle—"*Venus* mayd," who is the necessary complement of Cupid's man (III.xi.10, IV.x.54). In short, the very possibility of true love has been arrested. Britomart's task is to enable this possibility by freeing Amoret from Busirane's House and malign control.

Although in recent years the enchanted House of Busirane has most often been discussed in Petrarchan terms, this site is surely no less classical and specifically Ovidian. It is also more broadly medieval than simply Petrarchan, and of course it is more exactly the composite of these forms in sixteenth-century guise. Once Britomart enters this enchanted site, the first room she finds seems to signal the inevitability of her arrival there. The tapestries on its walls share both their Ovidian source in the *Metamorphoses* and their sense of erotic compulsion with a number of Britomart's earliest experiences, for example, her beholding the tapestry in the House of Malecasta that depicts the fixated love of Venus for the boy Adonis and the discovery of her passion for Artegall to Glauce in terms that evoke specific comparison with the perverse loves of Myrrha, Byblis, Pasiphaë, and Narcissus (III.i.34–38, ii.41, 44). While Britomart's arrival in Busirane's "vtmost rowme" isn't exactly a homecoming, it is a familiar "place" or "house" in the rhetorical sense both to her and to Spenser's readers (III.xi.27). The *Metamorphoses* was a standard text in Elizabethan schools, excerpted for beginners and read in its entirety later on. It was memorized, its rhetoric extensively imitated, and its cultural message imbibed. Lynn Enterline has suggested how a figure like Ovid's suffering Hecuba could become "a 'mirror' or 'example' "—to which I'd add, a rhetorical "place"—"for pupils to imitate," ostensibly to develop their own styles but inevitably with further "social, imaginary, and personal" impact. Both Shakespeare's Lucrece and his Hamlet, she notes, use Ovid's Hecuba as just such a mirror "in and through which to understand and to express what they claim to be their 'own' emotions."[2]

The specific Ovidian passage on which the tapestries in the House of Busirane draw is the ecphrasis of Arachne's art in her ill-fated weaving contest with Pallas Athena. Immediately, there are ironies and crossings of gender in this situation, whose many complications discussion only gradually unlayers. When Britomart initially encounters Busirane's enchantments, she asks Scudamour in dismay, "What monstrous enmity prouoke we heare, / Foolhardy as th'Earthes children, the which made / Battell against the Gods? So we a God inuade" (III.xi.22). Then boldly invading this god, the female knight gazes at a tapestry that pointedly recalls the one woven by Ovid's Arachne, a woman bold—perhaps too bold?—in protesting the violent excesses of the gods' passions but also one whose protest is depicted sympathetically in many readers' eyes by the male Roman poet.[3] The tapestries Britomart views similarly show more than one sign of satiric protest: for example, in Mars' undignified "shreek" (rhyming with "eek") of passion, "With womanish teares, and with vnwarlike smarts," or in the sequence of Neptune's undying love only for Bisaltis in the alexandrine of one stanza— "Ne ought but deare *Bisaltis* ay could make him glad"—followed immediately in the next stanza by the laconic statement "He loued eke *Iphimedia* deare, / And *Aeolus* faire daughter *Arne* hight" (III.xi.41–42, 44).

But the cross-dressed knight Britomart finds her tapestry of female protest within the chambers of a male enchanter, who, like herself, is also the creation of a male poet. We might well stop at this point to ask, with Susanne Wofford, whose tapestry this is and through whose eyes we see, or more properly, "rede" it.[4] Arachne's, Ovid's, his narrator's, Britomart's, Busirane's, Spenser's, his narrator's, the interpretative tradition's, or our own? Going beyond the possibilities Wofford endorses, I would not exclude any of these, and the ecphrasis of the tapestry itself explicitly invites them in describing Jove's rape of Leda, breaking into apostrophe in the manner of Ovid to do so:

> O wondrous skill, and sweet wit of the man,
> That her in daffadillies sleeping made,
> From scorching heat her daintie limbes to shade:
> Whiles the proud Bird ruffing his fethers wyde,
> And brushing his faire brest, did her inuade;
> She slept, yet twixt her eyelids closely spyde,
> How towards her he rusht, and smiled at his pryde.
>
> (III.xi.32)

Considerable ambiguity of reference marks this much-discussed stanza. Is the skilled and sweet-witted man in the first line Busirane, the narrator, or Spenser himself? This time, the lines cited have no direct parallel in Ovid, hence no parallel in Arachne's tapestry, and they therefore belong to the three possibilities enumerated. But are we to forget that Britomart is our gazer and that these lines could also have something to do with her vision or her response to Arachne's?[5] In whose opinion is the man "sweet witted"? And what do the last two lines of the stanza mean: "She slept, yet twixt her eyelids closely spyde, / How towards her he rusht, and smiled at his pryde"? Leda sleeps, like Verdant in the Bower of Bliss, and yet, also to an extent like him, between her eyelids she seems to see—to spy—the swan rushing toward her. Is she awake or in a trance or in a daydream? Each of these possibilities would imply a different kind and degree of agency. The simple adverb "closely" could indicate that her eyes are indeed shut ("closely twixt") or that she spies with close attention an object close to her ("closely spyde"). The word "spy" itself carries an insistent association with stealth or closeness—intense, secretive observation. The final clause of the line, as Katharine Eggert has noted, is also ambiguous: does Leda smile in anticipation of rapture or does the swan smile in anticipation of ravishment?[6] And is the smile one of Jovian arrogance, of pure pleasure, his, hers, or theirs; or is it an ironic smile, a self-reflexive, deflating, Ovidian possibility that the availability of female perspectives enforces?

Another passage, even more frequently remarked, expresses ambiguity of reference as well. The walls of the Enchanter's House are clothed with arras,

> Wouen with gold and silke so close and nere,
> That the rich metall lurked priuily,
> As faining to be hid from enuious eye;
> Yet here, and there, and euery where vnwares
> It shewd it selfe, and shone vnwillingly;
> Like a discoloured snake, whose hidden snares
> Through the greene gras his long bright burnisht backe declares.
>
> (III.xi.28)

This time the inwoven threads of metal have an explicit precedent in Ovid, although it proves as striking in its difference as in its similarity: "There, too, they [Pallas and Arachne] weave in pliant threads of gold, and trace in the weft some ancient tale (illic et lentum filis inmittitur aurum / et vetus in tela deducitur argumentum.)."[7] In Ovid's version, the gold thread, belonging to Arachne and Pallas alike, lacks the last six lines of Spenserian description, which call attention—indeed, demand heightened attention—to the serpentine filaments. Rather than betraying the presence of art, they shout it by comparison to Ovid's text, unwilling as they may be, or rather, feign to be so. The participial pun "faining" as easily supports an exhibitionist impulse as it denies it, since the pun means either pretending or desiring: "As faining to be hid." The alternative of merely pretending to hide from but actually enticing the "enuious eye" would relate the serpentine threads to the gold grapes in Acrasia's Bower, which enfold themselves among the leaves "As lurking from the vew of couetous guest"—as if lurking but actually seducing (II.xii.55).

But art in the House of Busirane is not finally the same as in the Bower, where "The art, which all that wrought, appeared in no place" (II.xii.58).[8] Here, not unlike the rhetorical device *occupatio,* the sonneteer's topos of inarticulateness, or unlike the elaborate *declamatio* uttered in full erotic chase by Ovid's Apollo, art may want or pretend to hide but instead it displays itself, unwillingly or not. Like the pun "faining," the word "unwillingly," which specifically refers to shining, or conspicuousness—"It shewd it selfe, and shone vnwillingly"—again evokes the oscillating play of visual and interpretative perspectives. Moreover, it does so "vnwares," which is precisely the ambiguous way Malecasta sneaks up on Britomart and the way Busirane's knife wounds her and the knowing and not knowing way that Leda, in all her ambiguity, awaits the rush of the swan. This is an acute, incredibly telling way of realizing the combination of cultural exposure and innocence, knowing and not-knowing, that characterizes Britomart's condition and observation, as indeed her reading of Ovid. Once more, Britomart does not cause this place, whose meaning at once precedes and exceeds her role in it, but this place of rhetorical culture bears special pertinence to her condition and quest. Again as with Leda, she is mirrored to an extent in the object or site.

Before leaving the tapestries, I want to glance at some other relevant passages in which Spenser explicitly uses or more elusively recalls Ovid's tale of Arachne in order to suggest the nature and extent of Spenserian investment in this tale. I would speak of a genealogy of these uses, if the uncertainties of dating did not dissuade me from attempting it. In addition to the tapestries in the House of Busirane, Spenser uses Arachne's weaving contest with Pallas at length in "Muiopotmos." In this poem, Arachne's metamorphosis to a spider is the consequence of her "poysonous rancor" rather than of the spiteful temper of the goddess, as in Ovid (344). Thus Arachne is merely too bold an overreacher, rather than a courageous, if willful, exposer of divine predation. There is little here of the complication of an empathetic female observer's perspective, and the erotic depredations of the gods are reduced to the single instance of Jove and Europa, celebrated, according to Leonard Barkan, as "an intense orgasmic sea-triumph" (204). But one stanza describing Arachne's son, the spider Aragnoll, finds a curious refraction (or vice versa) in the Bower of Bliss. In it, the narrator describes the amazingly subtle net that Aragnoll spins to catch the joyous butterfly. This is "networke" so cunning and curious that neither damsel nor weaver, nor other skilled craftsmen dare compare their work to it, nor even, as the narrator continues,

> . . . doo I thinke, that that same subtil gin,
> The which the *Lemnian* God framde craftilie,
> *Mars* sleeping with his wife to compasse in,
> That all the Gods with common mockerie
> Might laugh at them, and scorne their shamefull sin,
> Was like to this.

> (368–74)

For a moment, Aragnoll, Arachne's malicious descendant, has a disconcerting resemblance to the Palmer in the Bower of Bliss, who captures Acrasia and Verdant in his "subtile net"—a latter day "*Lemnian* God," or Vulcan, netting his Mars and Venus. But another artist in the Bower, Acrasia herself, is also associated disconcertingly with Arachne's web-work, for she is "arayd, or rather disarayd, / All in a vele of silke and siluer thin . . . More subtile web *Arachne* can not spin, / Nor the fine nets, which oft we wouen see, / Of scorched deaw, do not in th'aire more lightly flee" (II.xii.77, 81). Artists both, Acrasia and the Palmer are also opposites, but here their oppositional status gets a bit blurry.[9]

Arachne is found as well in the Cave of Mammon, where her presence is associated with the fetishized eroticism of gold, on which, witness Marinell and Malbecco in Book III and in Book II Mammon himself, autoerotically feeding his eye and "couetous desire" on the "masse of coyne" in his lap (II.vii.4).[10] Entering the "house" of Mammon, Guyon first sees a vault from which "the ragged breaches hong,"

> Embost with massy gold of glorious gift,
> And with rich metall loaded euery rift,
>
> . . . .
>
> And ouer them *Arachne* high did lift
> Her cunning web, and spread her subtile net.

> (II.vii.28)

Perhaps it is not irrelevant to eroticism or, indeed, to poetry in the broader, Renaissance sense of eroticism that in a letter to Shelley, Keats used the second of these lines as a metaphor for the poet's art.[11] The wicked Mammon's House is a rhetorical "place," too, and in fact a biblical "place" (not to mention a parable), and it is also one insistently relevant to debate about the poet's craft—his seductive, "sensefull words"—and the value of his calling (VI.ix.26). Like Keats, Shakespeare and Milton remembered this House, the one for its verbal riches and the other for its moral worth, and Spenser's poet-figure in the October Eclogue, the shepherd Cuddie, has both words and wealth in mind when he dismisses poetry for its lack of "gayne" (10):

> So praysen babes the Peacoks spotted traine,
> And wondren at bright *Argus* blazing eye:
> But who rewards him [the poet] ere the more for thy?
> Or feedes him once the fuller by a graine? :
>
> (31–34)[12]

Not surprisingly, the poet also likens himself more than once in the *Amoretti* to a spider weaving courtship's web of words and bonds (XXIII, LXXI). Such weaving evokes an echo chamber of Ovidian ironies, including the courting poet's awareness of the woman's awareness of the game he is playing, an awareness he shows more openly elsewhere in the sequence and memorably in sonnets XVIII ("But when I pleade, she bids me play my part") and LIIII: "Of this worlds Theatre in which we stay, / My loue lyke the Spectator ydly sits / beholding me that all the pageants play." Aside from the obvious fact that Ovid's tale of Arachne engraved itself on Spenser's memory, these various occurrences of it in his work all bear on art and the role of the artist, and all occur in sinister or "daungerous," eroticized contexts—even in "Muiopotmos," when we recognize the full resonance of Clarion's "riotous excesse" amid "the pleasures of that Paradise" (168, 186). Taken together, they reinforce both the sense of multiple awarenesses playing over Arachne's tale and the correlative presence of Spenser's ambivalence toward it and personal investment in it, despite any number of mediating figures, that we also find in the multi-faceted rendering of Arachne's tapestry in the House of Busirane.

Britomart passes next from the tapestries to a Mammonic room overlaid with pure gold, in which the "monstrous formes" of false love are depicted, and on whose glittering walls hang the trophies of love's wars and conquests (xi.51–52). There she witnesses the procession of Cupid's masquers, figures that stage the very process of a false love, hardly distinguishable at moments from a true one. Ambiguity of origin characterizes the creations of this room, as before the tapestries described. As A. C. Hamilton conveniently summarizes, the masquers draw directly on the conventions of the medieval courts of love and of Renaissance triumphs, not least Petrarch's own, as well as on those of the Renaissance masque.[13] Again, these figures are hardly Britomart's creation, although they have special relevance to her condition and quest, as they do to Amoret's and Scudamour's, and to many another character's in Book III. The very fact, long recognized, that they can be read from either a male or a female point of view indicates their basically cultural, rather than exclusively personal, status. Their formal artificiality also proclaims their radical—indeed, their catachrestic—constructedness. Unlike the insidious art forms in Acrasia's Bower, they make no claims on nature. On reflection, who would want such mirrors of passion as these?

Their relation to Busirane is worth pursuing, however. Cupid's masquers are too close for comfort to the kind of form Malbecco becomes at the end of canto x, one that "Is woxen so deform'd, that he has quight / Forgot he was a man, and *Gealosie* is hight" (60). Malbecco's metamorphosis into a "passion . . . in the mind" introduces the first canto in which the House of Busirane figures centrally, and, in effect, it prepares for the masquers, whose humanity, like Malbecco's, has vanished. Like the fixed and fixated emblem "Gealosie," the masquers are impostors of the living and every bit as artificial, as "personified," hence metaphorized, as the "carkasse dead" of the False Florimell (III.viii.7, xi.1). Even though the masquers are in a procession—a kind of dead march—each pair in itself is a frozen stage of courtship, removed from the necessarily narrative process of allegory.[14] I am willing to call this Busirane's art and to consider the "inner roome" from which it emanates his as well. Years since, as already noted, Thomas Roche glossed Busirane as *abuse* in the sixteenth-century senses of "imposture, ill-usage, delusion," or as the archaic *abusion*, meaning a "perversion of the truth, deceit, deception, imposture" and, in the words of Book II, implying "fond . . . illusions" (xi., vs. 8–9).[15] Again, to these meanings I have added *abusio*, the familiar Renaissance word for catachresis, here understood as a wrenching of metaphor or an extravagant use of it, in any case, a violent (mis)use of language, of which the masquers' dead likenesses strike me as being a prime exhibit.[16] In this place, this house of rhetoric, *abusio* would indeed appear to reign, or "rane," supreme.

Another persistent association, if not alias, of *abusio* in the rhetorical tradition is *audacia*, or "boldness," and it offers a gloss for the strange, forward and backward, summoning and forbidding, aggressive and maidenly imperatives Britomart sees over the doors in the second, Mammonic chamber: "*Be bolde, be bolde . . . Be not too bolde*" (xi.54)[17] In a discussion of metaphor, including *catachresis/abusio,* in *De Oratore,* Cicero praises "paulo audaciores [translationes]," or, "somewhat bolder metaphors" that bring brilliance to a speech but do not violate "ratio"—reason, purpose, method, or indeed, the nature of things (*rerum natura*). Such figures are bold but not too bold.[18] Read through the lens of Ciceronian rhetoric, the writing Britomart sees above the doors in Busirane's rhetorical "place" has the Ciceronian quality of an invitation to use *audacia* and a caution against excess in doing so. In comparison to the alternatives in Cicero's discussion, however, the choice Britomart faces is edged with anxiety and real danger. Britomart or any reader, it would seem, would do well carefully and cautiously to heed the originally balanced Ciceronian warnings about rhetoric, now seen as elusive and treacherous to the unwary in the message they send.

With Britomart and her acceptance of the challenge of being bold, but not too bold, I am finally led to the third chamber of the House of Busirane, where its patron, the figure or at least the first figure behind the curtains, Busirane himself, primarily represents the radical constructedness of the entire place. Again, this art-full place simply doesn't make the same claims as Acrasia's Bower about its nearness to or indistinguishability from nature. This is art in capital letters, and alarmingly, Amoret's life in some sense depends on Busirane. Thus "the Lady [Amoret], which by him stood bound, / *Dernely* vnto her [Britomart] called to abstaine, / From doing him to dy" (xii.3: my emphasis). Once in Busirane's clutches at least, Amoret recognizes herself, and is recognized, as his creation, pleading for his life in order to preserve her own. Her identity as love, which is her life, depends on loving. She is, after all, "*Venus* mayd" (Venus made?) and the complement of "*Cupids* man," as she is described by Scudamour in Book IV (x.54).

The adverb "dernely," which conveys the tone or manner in which Amoret calls on Britomart to spare Busirane's life, means "secretly" or "privately, confidentially"; it also carries the sense "inwardly." *Dernely* is a strange but suggestive word in this context, one that in the past has often been glossed too casually in the derived senses "dismally" or "direly." More significantly, it intimates a special appeal or relationship, perhaps something understood between the two women. Yet *derne* means also "dark" and "secret" in the sense "done in the dark" often has associations with craft, deceit, or evil.[19] Conceivably, if disturbingly, it could further connect Amoret with her captor, at least while in his power. By way of association, the "dark secret life" that destroys Blake's rose comes to mind.

Clearly, however, Britomart cannot now destroy Busirane without destroying what Amoret is, the cultural object par excellence. Again, as I have suggested, this is the reason the poem has so much culturally significant trouble with the figure of Amoret after Book III, and it is also the reason that, although Busirane's art works vanish, he still survives, bound by the very chain or, in terms of traditional iconography, by the rhetorical art that he has abused.[20] Without him there is only a vacuum, and this vacuum might also have something to do with the fact that Spenser's own *Amoretti*, written and published between Book III and its sequel, cannot wholly escape the available conventions of erotic discourse but indeed must use and try to reshape them. The furnishings of Busirane's rooms may indeed vanish, but this is hardly the last we see of their kind in Spenser's poetry. What I earlier described as an alternative meaning of catachresis/*abusio*, namely a *necessary* extension of the signification of a word to something for which any other word is lacking, rather than a merely willful wrenching of language, could well bear both on the emptiness apparent with the vanishing of Busirane's furnishings and the persistence of Ovidian, Petrarchan, or otherwise "Busiranic" forms in Spenser's poetry. Abusive as these are, perhaps they are currently and culturally inescapable. Perhaps.

Busirane also represents a fantasy and, perhaps, additionally a culture of rape, as others have argued without qualification, but it should be noted as well that he is not successful. His fantasy remains exactly that, and Amoret remains a virgin: "Die had she leuer with Enchanters knife, / Then to be false in loue, profest a virgine wife" (IV.i.6). If it were otherwise, Busirane's whole significance as a peculiarly rhetorical form of abuse, an art with the power in actuality to arrest love, would be lost and with it the real cultural critique of the Book. Busirane abuses figuration and the perception based on it to feign that metaphor is the same as reality, that it IS absolutely rather than is and is not, as Paul Ricoeur would gloss this figure of perverse predication—"perverse" (from *pervetere*), "turned away, around, about"or "athwart," hence "tropic."[21] It is Busirane who *feigns* (and fains) rape. And his ideological legacy is the reading that believes him.

Britomart herself is wounded, although not deeply, by Busirane and is therefore vulnerable to him. Her heart is also pierced and her hair stood on end by his bloody verses, even while, her threatening sword above him, she controls him.[22] At one point in the description of his disenchanting verses—a rhetorical spell, which, like all spells, must be unbound—a truly ambiguous pronoun occurs, (con)fusing Britomart with Amoret. With "threatfull hand" unslackened, Britomart waits "[un]dismayd" (or un-dis-

maided) by the quaking of this House and undeterred by "daungers dout,"
a phrase offering to reassume the familiar form of an actual pair of the
masquers earlier seen (cf. xii.10–11, 37); thus she "abode," occupying and
inhabiting this "place,"

> . . . to weet what end would come of all.
> At last that mightie chaine, which round about
> Her tender waste was wound, adowne gan fall,
> And that great brasen pillour broke in peeces small.
> (III.xii.37)

The ambiguous referent of the pronoun "her" signals Britomart's *involvement*—literally her enwrapping, winding (Latin *involvere*)—in Busirane's
"mightie chaine," in the toils (and coils) of his rhetoric, thus invoking the
familiar iconographic identification of rhetoric with spellbound enchainment that I have earlier referenced. Arguably, the first seven lines in the next
stanza also encompass Britomart and Amoret, although my own awareness
of the situation described makes me think such a reading unlikely. Be that
as it may, what is significant about this momentary identification of Britomart with Amoret is that it comes only with Amoret's freeing at Britomart's
hand. It implicates Britomart in Amoret's predicament, and she could hardly
not be implicated, but again, like Britomart's superficial wounding, in doing
so it more tellingly exhibits the superiority *and* intimacy of her *derne*, or
dark, secret power.

But let us suppose that the stanza of whose identification with Britomart I
am skeptical, does indeed continue the identification of Britomart with
Amoret, since this stanza offers the best evidence for the actual raping of
Amoret and, in Susan Frye's argument, of Britomart as well:

> The cruell steele, which thrild her dying hart,
>> Fell softly forth, as of his own accord,
>> And the wyde wound, which lately did dispart
>> Her bleeding brest, and riuen bowels gor'd,
>> Was closed vp, as it had not bene bor'd,
>> And euery part to safety full sound,
>> As she were neuer hurt, was soone restor'd:
>> Tho when she felt herself to be vnbound,
> And perfect hole, prostrate she fell vnto the ground.
> (III.xii.38)

The crucial words occur in the lines: "Her bleeding brest, and riuen bowels gor'd, / Was closed vp, as it [the wound] had not bene bor'd." While these lines are about as transgressively suggestive as *The Faerie Queene* gets, I would reject a reading that swallows catachresis whole, actualizing the radical metaphors present here. The meaning of the lines depends heavily on that of the words "bowels" and "as" in them. Contrary to the popular twentieth-century understanding of *bowels* exclusively as "guts," in the sixteenth century this word commonly referred to "the seat of the tender and sympathetic emotions" or the "heart, centre," and in Spenser's writing it frequently, though not always, carries the latter meaning, as is also true of English translations of the Bible in this period.[23] Doublets, such as "bleeding brest" and "riuen bowels" in the first of the crucial lines quoted above, are rife in Spenser, and the prominence in canto xii of Amoret's transfixed heart would appear to favor the archaic meanings I have cited. Use of a singular verb and singular pronoun with reference to the wound in "brest" and "bowels" further enforces identification of this doublet as a single unit.

The other word, *as*, in the phrase "as it had not bene bor'd," could be read "as if," but it need not be. This word can also mean "inasmuch as" or "since," and that is what I take it to mean here: "inasmuch as it had not been bored."[24] Of course I would not reject the other possible reading out of hand, either, although in context I may find it a stretch—"far-fet" and, indeed, an *abusio*. Metaphor, after all, even abusive, catachrestic metaphor, *is*, as well as is not. As we have seen, Ricoeur insists on such metaphorical "split reference," a meaning that is there and not there, and Bourdieu similarly speaks of the ambivalence of sublation, of a lifting or raising that "simultaneously denies and maintains both the repression and the repressed" and thus "allows for a doubling of profits: the profit of saying and the profit of denying what is said by the way of saying it."[25] But in the Spenserian passage in question, the possibility of the counter-factual reading "as if," like the former possibility of reading *bowels* as "guts," hence "belly" or reproductive organs, would only return us to the multiple perspectives of the participants in this canto—here specifically those of Amoret, Britomart, Busirane, the sometimes unreliable narrator, and Spenser himself. The pun on "whole" in the final line of the stanza is equally undisturbed by the reading I have advanced or by the one that chooses Busirane's literalizing perspective on it: Amoret, representative object of love, is rendered "whole and wanting," at once perfect, or completed, for the passion of Cupid's man and both lacking and desiring him. Freely now, her responses, like Britomart's, are holistic in every sense of the hopeful or disheartening pun, as the reader will have it.

We hear or half hear what I would call submerged or, more graphically, *(im)possible* puns of the sort just addressed even when prolonged attention to syntax indicates that they are far-fetched and grammatically irrational. They are plentiful in the literature of the period, in Shakespeare and Donne for obvious instances, and notably in Spenser as well.[26] Studying the mental processes by which we select and comprehend words, the psycho-linguist Jean Aitchison has found evidence to support the viability of such puns: readers or listeners "briefly activate both meanings of a homonym, even in cases where one of them is inappropriate"; indeed, according to one model, "A whole army of words, it seems, marches up for consideration each time a word begins."[27] Aitchison's explanation of homonymic punning is readily extended to a syntactical construction or to the alternative significations of a single word.

Whatever the precise workings of our mental circuitry, a third Spenserian example of (im)possible punning is ready to hand slightly earlier in Britomart's confrontation with Busirane, and it raises similar issues of reading, thus contributing to this significant interpretative pattern. When Busirane's knife wounds Britomart, "Exceeding wroth therewith the virgin grew, / Albe the wound were nothing deepe imprest" (xii.33). In an examination of Spenser's puns on the word "nothing," Eggert has suggested that *nothing* here might be a noun and therefore a sexual pun, the familiar Shakespearean equivalent of "hole," or "vagina, genitalia": in this reading, "nothing [is] deepe imprest."[28] Once again, though surely prematurely, Britomart is presumed to have been raped. But, as Eggert has agreed, the concessive "Albe" (meaning albeit, although) preceding "nothing" syntactically negates such a pun and indicates instead that "nothing" is an adverb—that is, "nothing [or, not at all] deepe imprest," with the result that Britomart is far from having been violated except in a superficial sense. Once the grammatical reading dominates, the (im)possible pun spectrally present serves to insinuate a more threatening potential in the situation—one submerged and unrealized—and it may intimate as well the precariousness of Britomart's control at this early stage, a control that she maintains increasingly. Once again, the abusive reading is finally meaningful only as an expression of the threat and indeed of the projected fantasy of Busirane. The (im)possible pun would nominalize the word "nothing," insisting on its literal sense "no thing"; this is the sense that negates the male member, or "thing," in a common Elizabethan sense of the word *thing*, while also invoking it, and thus motivates the sexual pun. In this way, the "abusive" reader deconstructs the more abstractive adverb to find the material root that makes it a noun and a metaphor. Shades once again of that familiar debate between Derrida and Ricoeur about the viability of dead metaphors.

❧

I have earlier suggested that Amoret's significance as a cultural object illuminates why the poem has trouble with her figure after Book III, and I want to pursue the oddities of her role in Book IV in light of this suggestion. With others, I have tended previously to view Amoret as largely an idealized figure in Book IV, as one who has to be abandoned in the face of an ever-more nearly encroaching reality. While I'm not prepared to renounce this view, I would like to explore another one, which can be reconciled with it in the play of idealized and temporal perspectives that characterizes this book. Amoret, as Petrarchan love object, is something of an embarrassment to Britomart as they ride along together, sharing one horse and one saddle. If I allow myself a distracting thought about horses symbolizing passion, the imagistic possibilities are comic, as well as significant. Symbolically, Britomart and Amoret's combined silhouette recalls the hermaphrodite in the original ending of Book III. But more comically, in temporal, practical terms of narrative and character, we have reason to wonder what Britomart is to do with the bundle of predictable assumptions and expectations called Amoret that she has won in the House of Rhetoric. Her grumpiness itself is a qualification of her triumph, and it signals her discomfort: for an awkward moment, the darker memory of Redcrosse's Pyrrhic victory over Sans Foy, his trophies Duessa and the shield of Faithlessness, may even come to mind.

Whereas Redcrosse doesn't have, or at least doesn't grasp, a clue regarding the irony into which he is sinking, however, Britomart seems at least partly aware of a problem. She "maske[s] her wounded mind" from Amoret, who is in one sense the unfolded Venerian aspect of her own double-identity, but whether Britomart's is the love-wound of Artegall's image or the result of a scarring realization in the House of Busirane or the superimposition of the one on the other is left us to ponder, while Amoret's emotions are manipulated "Through fine abusion of that Briton mayd," namely, Britomart (IV.i.vii). Exploratory but surely cruel, Britomart's abusive playing with and upon Amoret's responses at once suggests curiosity and resentment—an openness to experience and a resistance to the stock-in-trade of conventional womanhood, to something of what Shakespeare's Angelo calls "the destined livery" of woman. It does not go without notice, of course,

that a measure of Busirane's own abusive masking has rubbed off on Britomart, his victorious enchainer, who is in this sense the apparent heiress of
his art, as well as of Amoret, its ultimate object. As a *figure* in an allegory,
Britomart, a young woman both vested and invested in male armor, has
herself more fully *become* a broad and complicated cultural signifier—a vehicle (*metaphora*) at once informative regarding, and potentially formative of,
cultural conceptions of gender.[29]

The addition of a real male, the unnamed knight whom Britomart claims
for herself on entering the nameless castle in the first canto of Book IV and
the devesting of her armor, subsequently allows her openly to assume an
unqualified and uncomplicated female identity and to achieve rapport with
Amoret, who becomes her emotional intimate and bedfellow. But when the
next morning Amoret and Britomart become an autonomous twosome
again in an exteriorized and less private landscape, they are not long on that
horse together before Blandamour challenges Britomart for possession of
Amoret. Now occurs the strange stanza that I've discussed at length elsewhere, in which perspectives oscillate between Britomart's and Blandamour's and between chivalric and erotic, outer and inner, and narrative
and symbolic values (i.36).[30] The only point needed here, however, is that
Amoret just does not fit smoothly or easily into Britomart's story (or vice
versa); or perhaps the point is that a form whose content accommodates
them both is persistently elusive and insistently problematical. Not entirely
unlike the disappearing Fool in *King Lear,* Amoret has to be vaporized into
symbolism, incorporated into and consumed by Britomart, or else to be separated from her to follow out the narrative logic of her own figure, "*Venus
mayd*"—Petrarchan object, fixated and predictable form. From the vantage
point of Amoret's figure, both her form and its content, it makes sense that
she should unwittingly stray from Britomart's side straight into Lust's preda-
tory arms and become the hot potato (unless it's the tar baby) that Timias
finds. It makes even more sense that she should have to withdraw from Britomart's company before Britomart can achieve loving "accord"—heartfelt
harmony—with Artegall (IV.vi.41).[31] Yet even in this "accord," Amoret's
presence lingers punningly: the word with which Spenser thus characterizes
it puns etymologically on Latin *ad,* "to, toward," and *cor/cordis,* "heart," and
phonologically on English *chord* and *cord.* While *chord* enriches the harmony
signaled by the word *accord* itself, is there not also a memory of Busirane's
chain in *cord?* Has the tie that binds been newly realized with this word
or is this transformation merely apparent? Could the tie that binds still be
enchainment?

Poor Amoret herself finally disappears from the story as an unregenerate regression in the memory of Scudamour, "*Cupids* man." Although freed from the immediate threat of Busirane, her figure is never truly reformed; instead, it is idealized in the poet's complaint in canto viii—stellified and transfigured and thus removed from the process of life—much as is Belphoebe's "ensample dead" in Book III.[32] In the poet's voice, her figure thus passes, if only momentarily, beyond sublation, which not only cancels to raise but also continues, to pure transcendence. In this ironic sense, the twinship of Amoret and Belphoebe is realized and thus fulfilled: "ensample[s] dead" both. To Britomart belong the actual possibilities, such as they might prove, of the living. But as we know, this, with the *Amoretti* as well, is another story—a subsequent, if also a related, one. Rather than to this story, a good part of which I have told elsewhere, however, I would turn in the next chapter to an earlier one that concerns the nature and relation of catachresis and metaphor in Roman rhetorics and would look as well at their legacy both in Spenser's time and our own. This story very much re-engages the question of *boldness* that is treated so pointedly in Busirane's House of Rhetoric.

7. Catachresis and Metaphor: "Be Bold, Be Bold, Be Not Too Bold" in the Latin Rhetorical Tradition and Its Renaissance Adaptors

Twice in recent chapters, I have invoked Richard Lanham's definition of catachresis as a wrenching of metaphor or an extravagant use of it, in any case, as a violent (mis)use of language. Qualifying Lanham's definition, I have also observed the appreciation of traditional rhetoric for the necessity, and not merely the extravagance, of catachresis in the absence of any other suitable words. Lanham's definition is a cogent synthesis abstracted from classical and Renaissance sources, and I have annotated it as such, along with reference to Patricia Parker's provocative analysis of definitions of metaphor and catachresis from classical times to the twentieth century. Here, I would additionally reference a similar, briefer, and more recent discussion of catachresis by Lisa Freinkel in connection with her reading of Shakespeare's sonnets.[1] Both Parker's and Freinkel's interpretations bear on issues that have been evident in the present volume from the start. Both identify classical conceptions of catachresis with what Freinkel describes as "the ultimately catachrestic structure of all metaphor" for which Derrida argues in "White Mythology" and thus as "the lack/rupture at the center of signification itself: the rupture that signals the 'differance' within sameness."[2] Asking what "is at stake in the distinction between catachresis and metaphor," Parker similarly responds with Derrida's view that "catachresis threatens the very distinction between proper and figurative on which the understanding of metaphor as something secondary and deviational—in relation to a 'proper' meaning—characteristically relied" ("Metaphor," 65). Parker reaches her conclusion, however, only after first employing the responses of eighteenth- and nineteenth-century rhetoricians to illuminate and interpret earlier ones, whereas Freinkel finds hers full strength in the classical sources and Augustine, which would have been available—indeed, familiar—to Renaissance writers. While my differences from Parker and Freinkel mainly involve details of translation, selection, and emphasis, these do mount up and finally suggest a different understanding of propriety, of metaphor, and necessarily of the latter's relation to catachresis. They therefore bear on the role of cultural history in interpretative readings, whether of classical rhetoricians, the House of Busirane, or Shakespeare's sonnets.

I hardly need observe at this point that translation has inherently not merely an interpretative but also a metaphorical dimension. The translation of classical and Augustinian sources is about as fundamental to the history of metaphor (*translatio*) and catachresis as it gets, and thus, fundamental to any interpretation of these figures. Often I have found respected Loeb translations of the relevant rhetorical texts of Cicero and Quintilian "loaded" from a historico-cultural point of view informed by late twentieth-century theory, particularly of the post-structural variety.[3] This is a point of view with legitimate claims, as evident in my initial chapter, and it is the one adopted by Freinkel and more complexly by Parker. But it is also a point of view to be questioned with respect to its totalizing claims, and it is challenged fundamentally by biases of translation in this instance.

Not surprisingly, then, such bias is enmeshed in the very questions of translation and history, sublation and origin, and synchrony and diachrony, with which I began. For example, the Sutton/Rackham translation of Cicero's *De Oratore* renders the phrase describing metaphors *quasi alieno in loco collocantur* "placed in a connection not belonging to them" and thereby introduces a notion of ownership dubiously expressed in the original, even while dropping the qualifying adverb *quasi*, "as if," that indicates figurality or a counter-factual condition. I am not suggesting that the Sutton/Rackham translation of "alieno loco" is inaccurate in terms of bilingual dictionary definitions (which, we do well to remember, are doubly interpretative), because it is certainly not so. I am only saying that it is a misleading definition for present readers and that from a contemporary perspective it is inappropriate to the Ciceronian context.[4] In the context of relevant linguistic discussion in *De Oratore*, *alienus* carries a stronger notion of being "strange"—that is, "foreign," as in early modern English reference to the merchant stranger or the Protestant stranger who finds religious asylum in England—than it carries a sense of dispossession or invasion.[5] In the Ciceronian treatment of metaphor, such strangeness conveys at moments an accompanying positive sense of *admiratio* or *ingenium*. Moreover, this is a sense of *alienus* available in classical Latin. In contrast, *alienum verbum* as Sutton/Rackham's "word that does not belong" variously sounds lonely and pathetic, morally judgmental and jingoistic, or else simply "pushy" in contemporary English. This is not the way the most influential Roman rhetoricians saw metaphor. Above all, the Sutton/Rackham translation is hard to square with Cicero's (or later with Quintilian's) relatively hospitable notion of linguistic propriety or his sense that metaphor is "natural" in human language.[6]

For another example, Sutton/Rackham and Butler's Quintilian translate *similitudo* or *simile* as English "simile"—the term in current dictionaries meaning a comparison employing *like* or *as*—where the context either does not call for so narrow a reading or, more often, resists it.[7] In passages affected, I have rendered these words "likeness," "similitude," or another equivalent. These translations have misled readers who have relied on them without sufficiently weighing the risks of translation. But "the devil is in the details," as the adage goes, and to them, a good many of them, I must now more specifically repair.

The oldest of the relevant Latin sources, the pseudo-Ciceronian *Ad C. Herennium*, proved greatly influential in the Middle Ages, and it influenced the Renaissance as well. While its author was still widely assumed to be Cicero in the latter period, the fact that as important a figure as Lorenzo Valla had cast doubt on its Ciceronian authorship by the mid-fifteenth century should be noted, along with the fact that in 1491, one Raphael Regius "positively divorced the work from [the authority of] Cicero's name."[8] To Harry Caplan, translator of the Loeb edition, the treatise exhibits a number of "puerilities" that give an experienced Latinist pause, and it appears to be based in good part on notes of a Latin teacher's lectures (xxi, xxiii).

The author of *Ad Herennium* writes that "Catachresis is the inexact use of a like and kindred word in place of the precise and proper one (Abusio est quae verbo simili et propinquo pro certo et proprio abutitur)." His adjectival examples of *abusio* look like simple forms of misuse—"short powers, slight stature, long wisdom (Vires hominis breves, parva statura, longum in homine consilium)"—something akin to linguistic tone deafness and effectually not far removed from malapropism (IV.xxxiii.45)[9] In metaphor, however, he thinks the tropic transference of meaning (*translatio/transfero*) justified by similarity between the "things," the objects or ideas, involved. Thus, in both metaphor and catachresis, similarity or likeness underwrites the trope, but in the one transference is grounded in things and in the other it is unidiomatic verbal slippage that appears to be based on a contradiction between physical, quantitative "things" (e.g. "long") and more conceptual, qualitative "things" (e.g., "wisdom"). His conclusion reenforces a fundamental commitment of metaphor to like things, as well as to restraint: "a metaphor ought to be restrained (pudentem: 'modest'), so as to be a transition with good reason (ratione) to a kindred thing, and not seem an indiscriminate, reckless, and precipitate leap to an unlike thing" (IV.xxxiv.45).[10] Notably, not to say metaphorically, abusively, and ironically, he also uses the same word that designates metaphor—*translatio/transfero*—repeatedly in legal contexts, for example, to refer to a strategic shift in a charge from theft to embezzlement. If only to enable legal maneuvering, his use of the word in this customary way affords a nice contrast—or perhaps a complement—to the rhetorical conservatism evident in his desire to regulate figurative meaning: "*Translatio* criminis est cum ab reo facti causa in aliorum peccatum transfertur (Shifting of the Question of Guilt takes place when the defendant refers the reason for his act to the crime committed by others)."[11] In sum, *Ad Herennium* affords a small measure of support for later associations, like Lanham's, of catachresis primarily with wrenched, far-fetched, or far-out metaphors and, of course, with the insensitive "abusio" that is simply misuse.

Cicero's *De Oratore*, finished in 55 B.C., exhibits a more relaxed, sophisticated, and synthesized understanding of metaphor, catachresis, and the relation between them.[12] This understanding is expressed by Cicero's nominally dialogic character and spokesman Lucius Licinius Crassus, and its *development* is vital for a properly contextualized interpretation. Crassus' account in Book III begins with basics: "words . . . are either the proper and definite (propria . . . et certa) designations of things, which were *almost* (paene) born at the same time as the things themselves; or terms used metaphorically (quae transferentur) and . . . [quasi alieno in loco collocantur: 'set as if in a strange place']; or new coinages invented by ourselves (aut eis quae novamus et facimus ipsi)."[13] I note that Crassus' qualifying *almost* (*paene*) stops just short, but still short, of linguistic realism.[14] The qualifying adverb *quasi*, earlier noted, contributes a provisional, open quality to the *locus alienus*, which partly defines and, in its own counter factual figurality, partly illustrates what metaphor is. The figure of "a strange place" could put us in the old blind alley of tautology, at the end of which awaits the rhetorical question, "Can you ever explain metaphor by metaphor, figuration by figure?" But this question itself—more precisely this negative assertion—is willfully half-seeing, since it posits an impossible, nonexistent criterion of pure literalness and assumes only the deficiency of metaphor, essentially overlooking its positive and creative significative force. In contrast, Cicero's Crassus sees something of both.

Focusing more explicitly on metaphor, Crassus finds its origin in "necessity (necessitas) due to the pressure of poverty (inopia) and deficiency (angustiis: 'limitations, difficulties')," and he elaborates on this origin in a little history that will resonate in the Renaissance and beyond: "For just as clothes were first invented to protect us against cold and afterwards began to be used for the sake of adornment and dignity as well, so the metaphorical employment of words was begun because of poverty, but was brought into common use for the sake of entertainment (delectationis: 'pleasure, delight')" (xxxviii.155). Here figuration seems to track the progress of civilization without the ontological anxiety that plagues writers in later Christian centuries, for whom the Fall is definitive. Incidentally, it also associates clothing with language as a needed addition—a desirable supplement—to an earlier and poorer condition.

Continuing, Crassus instances metaphor in the language of *rustici*, "country people," in order to suggest both the naturalness of using tropes and to show their basis in resemblance: thus "jewelled vines," "luxurious herbage," "joyful harvests." (One suspects that Crassus' *rustici,* or perhaps their translators, have read a pastoral or two.)[15] Metaphor, he then adds, is "a sort of borrowing (mutuationes: 'exchange')." Tropic borrowing, like resemblance, is another conception that contradicts Sutton/Rackham's persistence in rendering *alienum verbum* as "the word that does not belong," the intruder, rather than as the "strange" or "displaced word"—or, indeed, the "borrowed word" (xxxviii.155–56). Of course the word-concept "borrowing" is also loaded for modern readers not only with the recurrence of such terms as "usury," "excess," and "debt" in the Ricoeur-Derrida debate about dead metaphors and polysemy, but also with the long, complicated, economic history of borrowing, including usury, particularly in the Christian West. Here the Ciceronian word for borrowing, *mutuatio*, derives from *mutuor*, deriving in turn from *mutuum*, "reciprocity," whose cognate is *mutuus*, "given in exchange," and whose root is *muto*, "to change, exchange, barter." Elsewhere Cicero himself uses *muto* in combination with clothing, travel to another country, and metaphorical usage: respectively, "mutare vestem," "mutare terram," and "mutata verba."[16] The Indo-European root for all the pertinent cognate forms, namely **mei*, signifies "to change, go, move; with derivatives referring to the exchange of goods and services within a society, as regulated by custom or law," and also includes as English derivatives *communicate, remunerate,* and *emigrate.*"[17] Considering both this intertwining genealogy and the troubled history of borrowing, I have suggested for Crassus' *mutuationes* the translation "exchange," which makes more sense in the encompassing Ciceronian context because it suggests not simply need or taking but the positive advantage—even the "payoff"—that accrues in the transaction.[18] *Exchange* implies mutual benefit (*mutuus, mutuum*). Both sides get something, as happens in the enhancement of the word-concept *rose* by its notorious history as a metaphor or borrowed good in love poetry, and such metaphorical exchange therefore answers to Crassus' obvious admiration for the "rustic" metaphors he instances. My love may indeed be enhanced by a rose, but a rose is reciprocally so.

Crassus concludes his initial consideration of metaphor by remarking "somewhat bolder (paulo audaciores)" metaphors that do not originate in poverty but instead "[arcessunt: 'call into place, summon'] some degree of brilliance" to the speech (xxxviii.156).[19] Yet he cautions that metaphors still should be used to make the matter (*rem*) clearer through resemblance (xxxix.157). Brilliance, however exhilarating, bows to function and purpose.[20] That Cicero, the creator of Crassus' role in the dialogue, writes with his eyes primarily on an audience of lawyers and senators, not poets, is evident and relevant to our critical assessment. Context, like history, makes (or sometimes breaks) a difference.

Crassus' central statement concerning the use of metaphor consists of speculation as to why "everybody derives more pleasure from words used metaphorically" than from the proper names applied to objects (xxxix.159). The statement is rich and requires considerable quotation:

> if a thing has not got a proper name and designation of its own (suum nomen et proprium vocabulum), for example a "sheet" in a ship, a "bond" in the sense of a contract made with a pair of scales, a "separation" in the case of a wife, necessity compels one to borrow (sumere) what one has not got from somewhere else; but even in cases where there are plenty of specific words available, metaphorical terms give people much more pleasure, if the metaphor is a good one (si sunt ratione translata: i.e., 'if the words are translated in accordance with reason, purpose, method').[21] I suppose the cause of this is either that it is a mark of cleverness (ingenii specimen) of a kind to jump over things that are obvious (ante pedes posita: 'set before one's feet') and choose (sumere: alternatively, 'borrow') other things that are far-fetched (alia longe repetita);[22] or because the hearer's thoughts are led to something else and yet without going astray (aberrat), which is a very great pleasure; or because a single word in each case suggests the thing and a picture (simile: 'likeness')[23] of the whole; or because every metaphor, provided it be a good one (sumpta ratione est), has a direct appeal to the senses [xl.159–60].

Cicero's Crassus waxes still more enthusiastic regarding metaphor,

For there is nothing in the world (in rerum natura: 'in the nature of things') the name or designation of which cannot be used in connexion with other things; with anything that can supply a . . . [simile: 'likeness']—and a . . . [simile: 'likeness'] can be drawn from everything—[indidem verbum unum quod similitudinem continet translatum lumen affert orationi: 'a single word translated from that very place that contains the similarity (i.e., the source of the likeness) brings brilliance to the speech'].

For the bracketed part of the preceding passage, Sutton/Rackham reads, "with anything that can supply a simile—and a simile can be drawn from everything—a single word supplied by it that comprises the similarity, if used metaphorically, will give brilliance to the style."[24] Two points: in my own translation, whether the word or the place or both contain the similar-ity is unclear. That both do seems likely, given Crassus' fairly balanced sense of verbal propriety, which is pronounced but not constrictive. Perhaps "word-thing," as in Erasmian usage, would be an appropriate alternative to "place" here.[25] The second point again concerns the Sutton/Rackham translation "simile," where the text reads *similitudo* or, twice in the preced-ing passage and once in that before it, *simile*, which I render "likeness" or "similarity" (or, where suitable, a cognate term). Although Sutton/Rack-ham do not indicate, as does Caplan, the translator of *Ad Herennium*, that "rendering the names for . . . figures," they have, "abandoning strict consis-tency, used the English derivatives of the author's terms wherever possible, or the accepted English equivalents" (xxi), their use of the English term "simile" in passages that do not accord with its narrow sense in modern English, namely a comparison using *like* or *as*, is inappropriate and mislead-ing, as I have earlier suggested.

Cicero's Crassus typically follows his last surge of enthusiasm with a cau-tionary reminder to avoid, indeed to flee (*fugienda est*), a metaphor that lacks similitude or is *too* distant (*longe*), unseemly, disproportionate, or the like. He offers examples of each rhetorical offense, and most are persuasively clumsy, pretentious, tone deaf, or unidiomatic: for example, the far-fetched "Syrtis of his heritage" for a rock, the unseemly vision of Glaucia as "the excrement of the House of Lords" (*curiae*: 'Senate'), the disproportioned "hurricane of revelry" (xl.162–xli.163–64). While I could imagine an appropriate context for "a hurricane of revelry," I'm willing to assume that Cicero's Crassus, presumably less accustomed to hurricanes than I, has in mind an inappropri-ate one; anyway, the Latin word Sutton/Rackham translate as "hurricane" is "tempestas," which would make better Ciceronian sense here as "tem-

pest" or "fury." Cicero is nothing if not balanced. The keynote of his caution comes when his Crassus recommends toning down a metaphor that
appears "a little too harsh (paulo durior)" and then generalizes,

> etenim verecunda debet esse translatio, ut deducta esse in alienum locum,
> non irruisse atque ut precario, non vi venisse videatur ['indeed, a metaphor
> ought to be modest, as one taken to a strange place, not rushing in to take
> possession of it and as by permission present, not seeming to have come by
> force'].[26]

In letting Crassus' statements about metaphor have their say, I have resisted observing to this point that in fact, if not in name, he repeatedly describes catachresis as or under the rubric of metaphor, a practice that some,
assuming a later, problematical distinction between the two, have considered confused and confusing. Whether catachresis is understood as the borrowing of a related term to nominate a thing for which no term exists or as
a "far-fetched" or "brilliant" metaphor or as a "bold" one, I think it clear
by now that what a later rhetorical tradition has usually understood as catachresis can therefore be comfortably and smoothly subsumed under Ciceronian metaphor. To put this point another way, Crassus, Cicero's spokesman
on style, never gets exercised about catachresis in this sense or categorizes it
apart from other forms of metaphor, although at times modern interpreters
insist on doing this for him. Here the point is not that Crassus, or indeed
Cicero, is unable to maintain a stable notion of linguistic propriety but that
his sense of the proper is larger than that in some later centuries.

Moreover, Crassus later shows his awareness of catachresis as a separate
figure, understood more narrowly with the author of *Ad Herennium* as irregular or inferior usage, but he simultaneously expresses a measure of rhetorical relativism, irreverence, and large-mindedness of the sort I have earlier
observed in the Renaissance and especially in that good student of rhetoric
Zwingli, in effect conceiving of all the major tropes as forms of metaphor.[27]
In the words of James May and Jakob Wisse, recent translators of *De Oratore*,
it is "as a sort of appendix"[28] to the more extensive treatment of metaphor
that Crassus quickly and specifically reviews other major tropes, namely,
catachresis, metonymy, synecdoche, and allegory, back-referencing his earlier discussion of allegory as an extension of metaphor ("a chain of words
linked together: ex pluribus [verbis] continuatis connectitur") (xli.166).
"Often," Crassus explains as he turns explicitly to catachresis (*abusio*) and
effectually recalls the *Ad Herennium*, "we abuse (Abutimur saepe)" a word
"less elegantly (non tam elegante)" and more licentiously (*licentius*: 'more

boldly, unrestrainedly') in catachresis than in metaphor, although this figure is nonetheless "sometimes unobjectionable (interdum non impudenter)" (xliii.169). Distinguishing metaphor from metonymy (*neque translatum*), he defines metonymy as the substitution of one word for another, without "innovation (fabricationem)" or invention (*neque factum verbum est*), and he considers synecdoche related to it (*finitima*) as a subcategory might be. Yet "the figure of substitution or metonymy (traductio atque immutatio)" is itself also "metaphor of a sort (translata quodam modo)," as even the alternative names Crassus uses for metonymy indicate—*traductio*, "transference, a leading across," and *immutatio*, "change."[29] Indeed, if May and Wisse are right, as seems likely, in taking the conclusion of Crassus' brief, qualified venture into rhetorical taxonomy—in my own rendering of Crassus' words, into these 'trifling niceties' (*harum . . . minutarum rerum*)—to refer to catachresis as well as to metonymy/synecdoche, then all the major tropes are 'metaphors after a sort,' or "translata quodam modo."[30] Further, if we wish first to regard as Crassus' the earlier interpolated statement that a metaphor is a similitude contracted into one word and then with Sutton/Rackham to understand this statement as a modern reference to simile, we could have yet another instance of rhetorical inclusiveness to add to those of metaphor, metonymy, and catachresis in the preceding sentence (xxxix.157 and n. 301, above).

As for Crassus' awareness of the possibility of separating catachresis, broadly understood, from metaphor and his apparent lack of interest in doing so, a passage cited earlier is further pertinent. In it, Crassus mentions the bolder (*audaciores*) metaphors that call stylistic brilliance into place. If *audacia*, "boldness," is taken as another term for *abusio* or *catachresis*, alternative terminology the rhetorical tradition supports according to Parker and Lee Sonnino, the sentence following Crassus' praise of such "audaciores [translationes]," or, "bolder metaphors," would again indicate not only his awareness of the taxonomic and pedagogical alternative to his regarding metaphor as the all-encompassing arch-trope, but additionally his explicit awareness of such bolder metaphors as instances of catachresis in a broader sense than merely irregular or inferior usage: "However," as Crassus urbanely but pointedly observes to his interlocutors in the pertinent sentence, "there is no need for me to give you a lecture on the method of inventing these [figures] or on their classification"; thus, having raised the "trifling" taxonomic issue, he sidesteps it as a concern for beginners (xxxviii.156–57).[31] Yet as we have also seen, Crassus' praise for "audaciores [translationes]" is more precisely for "paulo audaciores," bolder figures that contribute brilliance but do not violate *ratio*, and it is therefore praise for figures that are bold yet not *too* bold, as Spenser puts it in the House of Busirane, and thus for figures, however brilliant, requiring judgment and assessment, or, in short, a sense of the nature of things (*rerum natura*).[32] Once again, it scarcely needs saying that such a sense, whether his, mine, or yours, is at once historical and ideological and, as such, especially sensitive to cross-cultural translation.

Further evidence for the association of unruly boldness with (unqualified) *audacia*, as distinct from a boldness that remains judicious, or "paulo audaciores," occurs dramatically, linguistically, and politically near the outset of Cicero's Book III when Crassus refers to his having suppressed Latin rhetoricians (teachers of speaking) during his term as censor. He explains that he was far from being opposed to the sharpening of young men's wits; rather, he objected to the encouragement of "shamelessness" (*impudentiam*)—"immodesty" in the rhetorical contexts hitherto examined—which, May and Wisse indicate, "may or may not have political overtones (reckless politics, demagogy)" (252, n. 115). Crassus adds that with the Greek teachers of rhetoric, "there was, apart from this exercise of the tongue, still some learning to be found and some knowledge worthy of humane culture. But these new teachers . . . were capable of teaching nothing but *boldness* [Sutton/Rackham: "nihil intellegebam posse docere nisi ut *auderent*"], certainly something that must be avoided in itself, even when combined with good qualities."[33] In this passage, among others to come, there is evident a basis for the association of unqualified *audacia*, "boldness," with the unruliness and thence with the aggressive *abusio* that were anathema to later periods and, for a case in point, another basis for its association with Spenser's House of Busirane.

Quintilian, writing in the first century A.D. and about a hundred years after Cicero, appears more willing than Cicero's Crassus to distinguish metaphor from catachresis, although on what grounds and to what end he finally does so are questionable. His apparent lack of consistency has provided the main basis for locating a deconstructive sense of linguistic rupture within the central Latin sources of the Western rhetorical tradition, a reading that must itself be recognized as a particular interpretation of his inconsistency. As before with Cicero's *De Oratore*, I shall try to let Quintilian's *Institutio Oratoria* have some say before intervening in it, although, given the necessity of translation, this is a more elusive goal than when the original text is in English. As in preceding pages, my effort to neutralize or else blatantly to display bias will avoid free translation, adhering as closely, not to say as doggedly, as possible to the original, except where flagged and argued. Freer translation tends to obscure both the connections between the Roman rhetorics and those of the Renaissance, my eventual goal, and the significance of them. To take a pertinent example, the Latin word *res*, "thing"—ambivalently material, immaterial, rhetorical, or linguistic "thing"—widely and repeatedly recurs simply as *thing* in relevant Renaissance texts, and not as the more illusively exact and limiting word or phrase often used to render it in modern translations.[34]

In Book VIII, on *elocutio*, or "style," Quintilian introduces his main treatment of metaphor and catachresis with a discussion of propriety vital to an understanding of his subsequent statements. He begins with the purpose or "end" of oratorical propriety, which is clarity, and immediately makes the related point that "*propriety* is capable of more than one interpretation" (VIII.ii.1). "In its primary sense," Quintilian continues, "it means calling things by their right names (sua . . . appellatio: 'by its own name')," although such forthrightness is "sometimes to be avoided" in the interest of social propriety, that is, to avoid obscenity, unseemliness (sordida: 'filthy things') or meanness. Immediately, however, he cautions that going to the other euphemistic or pretentious extreme is also to be shunned. Now, "tamen ['for all that']," he further adds, "everything that lacks appropriateness will not necessarily suffer from the fault of positive *impropriety* (protinus . . . improprii vitio: 'straightway . . . from the fault of impropriety'), because there are, in the first place, many things which have no proper term either in Greek or Latin" (ii.4). Clarifying examples follow, such as *lapidare*, "to stone," which must also be used for the throwing of clods or potsherds. Quintilian's next statement introduces the term catachresis for this extension of a term's signification but minimizes its distinction from metaphor in general:

> Hence abuse (abusio) or *catachresis* of words becomes necessary, while metaphor, also, which is the supreme ornament of oratory, applies words to things with which they have strictly no connexion (Translatio . . . verba non suis rebus accommodat: 'metaphor . . . does not fit words to things'). Consequently *propriety* (proprietas) turns not on the actual term, but on the meaning (vim significandi: 'the significative power'), and must be tested by . . . the understanding, not . . . the ear (refertur nec auditu, sed intellectu) [ii.6].[35]

Significantly here, metaphor is not based on strict likeness, and on the basis of the example *lapidare*, catachresis appears to be quite the opposite of the obvious misuse we get in *Ad Herennium*. Yet the line between metaphor and catachresis is obviously also thin, and it seems to matter less than a propriety that is more broadly representational, one not dependent on a strict connection of a specific word to a specific thing. Instead, propriety depends on the power or effect of the word, and it is a matter to be judged by the understanding, which is a measure that sounds rather like Crassus' *ratio*, with *vim significandi*, "significative power," taking Crassus' *audaciores*, "bolder," into account. Yet *vim significandi* is not paired with *paulo*, as is Crassus' *audaciores*, and the *intellectus* ("perception," "sensation," "understanding") with which he would test it, while including reason and even having a rational bias, also offers more range for a poet's wit. Translating to a Renaissance context, I think of the role of intellect in Castiglione's Ladder of Love or, for an example nearer to hand, of the dove-like flight of Donne's final prayer in *Devotion* XII.

Quintilian goes on to explain a second sense of the word *propriety* ("dicitur proprium") that "occurs when there are a number of things all called by the same name: in this case the original term from which the others are derived is styled the *proper* term," or what nowadays we often call the literal. As an example he gives the word *vertex*, meaning "a whirl of water, or of anything else that is whirled in a like manner: then, owing to the fashion of coiling the hair, it comes to mean the top of the head, while finally, from this sense it derives the meaning of the highest point of a mountain" (ii.7). Thus polysemous meanings or extended applications, which here are variously also catachrestic or metaphorical, are, depending on cultural usage, also live metaphors or dead ones—indeed, if dead, then coded metonyms, as is "the foot" of the mountain in our own time. Importantly, in either case, they are themselves considered proper by Quintilian ("*modo dicitur proprium*"), and if secondarily so, *proper* nonetheless (ii.7). Renaissance compilers of dictionaries would in time agree: Robert Estienne's extensively catachrestic definition of *gravis* in his *Thesaurus linguae Latinae*, which I cited in chapter 2, affords a prime example.

In the course of enumerating other kinds of linguistic *propriety*, Quintilian explicitly declares that this term "include[s] the appropriate use of words in metaphor (translata sunt propria dici)" (ii.11).[36] But his additional instances, which also include both idiomatic usage with a figurative basis and personified, hence metaphorical, epithets verging on metonymy, have lessening relevance to the present subject: for an example of the first, an instance in which "a thing which serves a number of purposes has a special name in some one particular context" (e.g., *augurale* as "the proper term for . . .

the general's *tent*"), and of the second, an instance in which "the salient characteristic of an individual comes to be attached to him as a *proper* name" (e.g., Fabius as *Cunctator*, "the Delayer": ii.8, 11).

Quintilian's remarkably broad sense of *propriety* both frames and influences his later discussion of metaphor and catachresis in the same book (VIII). Metaphor is "by far the most beautiful of *tropes* (longe pulcherrimus)" for Quintilian, and for him, as for Cicero's Crassus, it is natural in speech:

> Quae quidem cum ita *est ab ipsa nobis concessa natura*, ut indocti quoque ac *non sentientes* ea frequenter utantur, tum ita iucunda atque nitida, *ut in oratione quamlibet clara proprio tamen lumine eluceat* [vi.4: my emphasis].

> It is not merely so natural a turn of speech that it is often employed unconsciously or by uneducated persons, but it is in itself so attractive and elegant that however distinguished the language in which it is embedded it shines forth with a light that is all its own.

While this English rendering by Butler is helpful, parts of it obscure the significance of Quintilian's argument for my concerns. "Est ab ipsa nobis concessa natura," which Butler freely renders "so natural a turn of speech" actually reads, "It has been yielded—permitted—to us by nature herself."[37] Butler also renders "non sentientes" as "unconsciously," which may be a popular use of "unconsciously" in English but is also a misleading one here: "without noticing" would be more accurate.[38] The notion that nature has permitted or conceded (*est concessa*) the use of metaphor to us reflects Quintilian's awareness *both* that we naturally use metaphor *and* that metaphoric usage is out of the ordinary, or tropic, a turn away from the primitive natural meaning and in this sense therefore improper. A Renaissance (and Christian Neoplatonic) analogy to this view can be found in Sir Philip Sidney's argument that the poetic making (art, fiction) that exceeds Nature is not in a deeper sense unnatural since God made the poetic maker; indeed, in traditional terms, He did so through His agent Nature (101). Quintilian's semi-personified nature similarly grants metaphor, which is strictly speaking not natural, to us.[39]

Significantly, here so positively and constructively qualified an awareness of impropriety as Quintilian's also shares the same balanced sentence cited ("cum ita . . . tum ita") with this final clause: "tum ita iucunda atque nitida, ut in oratione quamlibet clara *proprio* tamen *lumine* eluceat," which I read, "then so delightfully and elegantly that however brilliant the speech, it [metaphor] still shines out with a light of its own" (my emphasis). "Proprio lumine"—these words incorporate Quintilian's conception of propriety into metaphor itself—a light of its own that is also an appropriate or proper light. Further, they reflect and intensify the notion of exchange and mutual gain, as distinct from that of one-sided benefit, which, I have suggested, is expressed in the Ciceronian use of the word *mutuatio* to describe tropology and preeminently metaphor, the arch-trope. This is a sense of metaphor and indeed of catachresis as *paulo audaciores* or *vim significandi* that is closer to Derrida's constructive conception of translation in "Des Tours de Babel," his reading of Walter Benjamin's essay on translation, than it is to his deconstructive sense of an irreparable "lack / rupture at the center of signification itself," with which my present chapter began.

This Derridean connection, again recalling my concerns in chapter 2, bears directly enough on immediate issues to invite brief expansion, which Eve Tavor Bannet's "Scene of Translation" economically provides. Discussing "Des Tours de Babel," Bannet finds in the idea of a surplus Derrida's conception of the translator's duty to the survival of the original. The survival "which the translator is engaged to give the original is not merely survival beyond the biological life and death of its author (*survivance*); it is a 'surplus of life [*un plus de vie*].' The original has not only to live longer, says Derrida, but also to 'live more [*plus*] and better, beyond the means of its author.'"[40] This surplus, also an expression of difference between author and translator, is also potentially as positive as that Gerald Bruns sees medieval writers discovering ("inventing") between the lines of a written source—as Chaucer discovered the *Troilus* between the lines of Boccaccio's *Il Filostrato*.[41] Tonally, such a surplus contrasts with the suggestions of deceptive masking or self-delusive idealization in "White Mythology," yet it confirms the substantiality of a surplus in this earlier text, even as it implies possibilities not fully realized there. This Derridean translational surplus, which is also metaphorical, reaches for the *mutuatio* and *proprium lumen*, the positive exchange and positive production, of Cicero's and Quintilian's conceptions of metaphor. It also challenges the exclusively negative emphasis on rupture with which my chapter began.

Quintilian's later, more explicit expounding of metaphor notes the condition that metaphor has to be used in the right way ("*recte modo*"), a way broadly comparable to the "*ratione*" of Cicero's Crassus, but again he emphasizes the benefits of metaphor, including catachresis, to human communication:

[Metaphor] adds to the copiousness of language (sermonis) by the interchange of words and by borrowing (permutando aut mutuando),[42] and
finally succeeds in accomplishing the supremely difficult task of providing a
name for everything. A noun or a verb is transferred (Transfertur) from the
place to which it properly belongs to another where there is either no *literal*
term (proprium deest: 'a proper term is lacking') or the *transferred* (translatum) is better than the *literal* (proprio melius). We do this either because it is
necessary or to make our meaning clearer or, as I have already said, to produce a decorative effect [vi.5–6].

Quintilian recalls Cicero in citing the catachrestic metaphors used by the
rustici ("country people" in the Sutton/Rackham Cicero, "peasants" in
Butler's Quintilian), such as calling "a vine bud *gemma*, a gem," and he asks
rhetorically, "What other term could they use?" He also offers examples of
enhancing and ornamental metaphors, even finding an instance in Cicero's
defense of Milo for the last, thereby further strengthening a Ciceronian
presence in the text at this point (vi.6–7).

Now Quintilian incorporates, develops, and clarifies the interpolated,
potentially limiting equivalence of metaphor to simile found in Cicero's *De
Oratore* and thereby unfortunately ensures that it will enter the subsequent
rhetorical tradition with his authority. Whereas today definitions of metaphor generally exclude explicit comparison, the equivalence at hand consists
of it. For example, Paul Ricoeur's and Jean Aitchison's definitions of metaphor are based on unconventionality: Ricoeur's might be encapsulated as
"a deviant predication," and Aitchison's is expressed as "the use of a word
with one or more of the 'typicality conditions' attached to it broken."[43]
Lakoff and Johnson and M. H. Abrams base their definitions on transference: on the one hand, metaphor is "a way of conceiving of one thing in
terms of another, . . . [whose] primary function is understanding" (*Metaphors*, 36); and on the other, a metaphor is "a word or expression which in
literal usage denotes one kind of thing or action [that] is applied to a distinctly different kind of thing or action, without asserting a comparison."
Notably, Abrams' definition, which is aimed at an undergraduate audience,
excludes comparison explicitly but appears to endorse a fallacy of transference unimpeded by deviation or difference. The definition in the enlarged,
first edition of *The Princeton Encyclopedia of Poetry and Poetics* focuses wholly
on the positive value of enhancement: here metaphor is "A condensed verbal relation in which an idea, image, or symbol may, by the presence of one
or more other ideas, images, or symbols, be enhanced in vividness, com-

plexity, or breadth of implication." Variant definitions seem, like metaphorical potency, endless.[44]

In Quintilian, however, this time a stronger case can be made for translating *similitudo* and even *comparatio* as "simile" in the customary modern English sense. But the case is far from airtight, since the Latin wording ("similitudo," "comparatio"), unlike Butler's translation, would still allow for analogy, comparison, exemplum, parable, or any other figurative likeness explicitly expressed—incidentally including that in an extensive epic simile, which is a far cry from the brief comparison Quintilian's example or a popular modern definition of *simile* would lead one to expect:

> On the whole *metaphor* is a shorter form of *simile* (metaphora brevio est similitudo), while there is this further difference, that in the latter we compare some object to the thing which we wish to describe, whereas in the former this object is actually substituted for the thing (haec pro ipsa re dicitur). It is a comparison (Comparatio est) when I say that a man did something *like a lion* (*ut leonem*), it is a metaphor (translatio) when I say of him, *He is a lion* [vi.8–9].[45]

Here, for several reasons, I would also pause over Butler's translation of *haec pro ipsa re dicitur* as "substituted for the thing."[46] First, this rendering participates in a pattern evident in the sentence immediately succeeding those I have cited, where "aliud pro alio ponitur" is rendered, "we substitute one for another"(vi.9). Second, there exists in Latin, but not in this passage, a verb *substituere*, meaning "to substitute," from which our own verb *substitute* derives.[47] Third, the English word *substitute* comes trailing clouds of coded metonyms in the context of late twentieth-century critical theory that threaten to close the text prematurely or to subject it to a one-sided emphasis on rupture and lack. Fourth, I doubt that *haec pro ipsa re dicitur* and *aliud pro alio ponitur* need carry the same signification for readers of Latin as the verb *substitute* for readers of English today.

Butler's translation is surely not impossible linguistically, but it is misleading in context and nowadays invites misinterpretation. I would translate the Latin expressions less freely—*haec pro ipsa re dicitur* as "this is said *for* the thing itself"—in an admittedly awkward effort to preserve the greater openness of the preposition *pro* in the clause, and I would translate *aliud pro alio ponitur* as "one is expressed [perhaps even better, 'placed there'] *for* another." Latin does not always translate—that is, "carry over"—gracefully to English, even though English is hugely indebted to it. *Pro* implies not only "in place of," but also the incredible openness of simple English "for," with translative possibilities including "in conformity with," "in accordance with," "in proportion to," "in relation to"; "in the capacity of"; "as" or "as if"; "in a degree or manner corresponding to"; "on behalf of," "for the sake of," "in the interests of."[48] Most of these—perhaps especially "on behalf of"— would convey the positive force of metaphorical translation, to which Cicero, Quintilian, and Derrida arguably subscribe. Conversely, the *sub* in *substituo* signifies only "under" or "in place of" and in modern English implies something more negative, secondary, and subordinated. The word "merely" or, in the same sense, the word "just" all too often accompanies a *substitute* in current English. The rest of *substituo* simply derives from *statuo* (whence modern English *statue*), meaning "to set up," "to put," or "to consider," and to my mind it offers no further complication, until and unless we enter an iconoclastic phase, as eventually happens, for example, in the English Renaissance.

Back in the text, Quintilian next praises "a bold and almost hazardous metaphor (*audaci et proxime periculum translatione*)," such as "'Araxes' flood that scorns a bridge'" and thereby again appears to associate significative force that is catachrestic with metaphor (vi.11).[49] Almost predictably given Quintilian's admiration of Cicero, there follows the Ciceronian caution against the misuse of metaphor (for similar reasons and examples: sordidness, disproportion, excess, etc.), and Quintilian sums up this section with his own version of the Ciceronian image of metaphor as a modest visitor in a strange place, as distinct from an aggressive, unruly intruder. Quintilian's version is relatively more forceful, however, and not without coincidence, it conspicuously combines catachresis—if understood as the occupier of a vacant place—with metaphor, understood as the occupier of another's: "For metaphor should always either occupy a place already vacant, or if it fills the room of something else, should be more impressive (*plus valere*: 'more meaningful,' 'more forcefully significant') than that which it displaces (*expellet*: 'expels')" (vi.18). Yet again there is nothing here that does not basically accord with what we have encountered earlier in Quintilian himself and in Cicero—in the former's *vim significandi*, "significative power," and the latter's *paulo audaciores*, "somewhat bolder."

Finally, both Cicero and Quintilian consider metaphor positively productive and even forceful or bold within some measure of restraint—*ratio*. Like the word-concept *logos*, however, *ratio* is the sign of the systemic restraint and in some contexts also of the disguise or misrecognition of metaphor within the Western cultural-philosophic tradition. It is the emergency brake, so to speak, on the metaphoric engine, suppressing or disguising the

uncanny and unruly and keeping language, especially the potency of metaphorical language, safely under rational control. Within Quintilian's, as before within Cicero's writing on metaphor, we would therefore expect to
find more distinct evidence of "lack" and "rupture" and might anticipate its
presence in Quintilian's most direct statements about catachresis, the figure
variously conceived as necessary, unavoidable, extreme, or "too bold," depending on the specifics in each occurrence of it. In these statements, both
Parker and Freinkel have found a crucial pressure point for the argument
that the presence of catachresis within metaphor disrupts a classical sense of
propriety, and to them I turn.

When, following a discussion of other figures—synecdoche, metonymy,
antonomasia, onomatopoeia—Quintilian addresses catachresis *explicitly* for
the first time, he does so immediately after expressing regret that onomatopoeia, here defined as "the creation of a word (*fictio nominis*)," too rarely
occurs in his own culture. "Although regarded with the highest approbation
by the Greeks, [it] is scarcely permissible to a Roman," he regrets, and he
urges "fresh creations" that will enrich the word-stock, especially since
"many of the words thus formed in antiquity (multa . . . ab antiquis ficta) are
daily becoming obsolete (moriantur)" (vi.31–32).[50] He next offers several
examples of neologisms (*pepoiēmena*)—"new derivatives . . . which are
formed in various ways from words in common use, such as *Sullaturit*, 'he
wishes to be a second Sulla,' or *proscripturit*, 'he wishes to have a proscrip-
tion' " or "*laureati postes*, 'laurelled door-posts,' for *lauru coronati*, 'crowned
with laurel' " (vi.32). Then there comes a passage of three to four lines that,
according to Butler, is "too corrupt to admit of emendation or translation"
(320, n. 1) and immediately after it this sentence: "These facts make *catachresis* (of which *abuse* is a correct translation) all the more necessary," since it
adapts "the nearest available term ['to something not having its own name':
quae non habentibus nomen suum accommodat]."[51] Here catachresis, of
which, he incidentally notes, *abusio* is the correct Latin translation, appears
desirably to help to compensate for a lack of creative growth in the Latin
tongue. Quintilian's examples of catachresis include the calling of all flasks
acetabula (narrowly, vinegar flasks) and all caskets *pyxides* (a flask made of
boxwood) and the murder of mother or brother a *parricide*. Each appears to
be merely an extension or a loosening of a narrower reference.

Now comes the statement whose inconsistency with Quintilian's earlier
discussion of catachresis, first as a "proper" term when needed and then as
a form of metaphor, has been taken to reveal the rupture at the heart of
signification and more specifically an internal contradiction in Quintilian's

view. I give Butler's English translation first, since it has provided evidence for this thinking:

> We must be careful to distinguish between *abuse* and *metaphor*, since the former is employed where there is no proper term available, and the latter when there is another term available. As for poets, they indulge in the abuse of words even in cases where proper terms do exist, and substitute words of somewhat similar meaning. But this is rare in prose. Some, indeed, would give the name of *catachresis* even to cases such as where we call temerity valour or prodigality liberality. I, however, cannot agree with them; for in these instances word is not substituted for word, but thing for thing, since no one regards prodigality and liberality as meaning the same, but one man calls certain actions liberal and another prodigal, although neither for a moment doubts the difference between the two qualitites [vi.35–36].

> Discernendumque est hoc totum a translatione genus, quod abusio est, ubi nomen defuit, translatio, ubi aliud fuit. Nam poetae solent abusive etiam in his rebus, quibus nomina sua sunt, vicinis potius uti; quod rarum in prosa est. Illa quoque quidam catachresis volunt esse, cum pro temeritate *virtus* aut pro luxuria *liberalitas* dicitur. A quibus ego quidem dissentio; namque in his non verbum pro verbo ponitur, sed res pro re. Neque enim quisdam putat luxuriam et liberalitatem idem significare; verum id quod fit alius luxuriam esse dicit, alius liberalitatem, quamvis neutri dubium sit haec esse diversa.

There is much to discuss in this passage, and I shall take what is said in the order of its saying, beginning with the first sentence. What the Latin actually states is "this whole family (hoc totum . . . genus) of catachrestic names (quod abusio est), in which the name has been lacking (defuit), is to be distinguished (discernendumque est) from metaphor, where there has been (fuit) another name." Butler's rendering of the opening Latin gerund *Discernendum* as "We must be careful to distinguish" amounts to importation of a moral and taxonomic imperative more appropriate to the nineteenth century than to Quintilian's context. Butler's deployment of the verbs "defuit" and "fuit" in the historical present rather than in the simple past or past perfect tense, while perfectly conventional, is also notable in this first sentence, since it cancels the suggestion, otherwise present in the Latin, that the newly imported term has adequately, beneficially, or indeed "properly" filled the former vacancy. The present tense also suggests identity between past lack and present condition and between stable meaning and metaphorical displacement, whereas, in contrast, Quintilian properly conceives catachrestic and metaphorical naming as retaining their tropic identity rather than blending into non-figurative usage. In other words, Quintilian's view, unlike his translator's, inclines toward the diachronic, as well as toward the beneficially developmental. This is not surprising, given Roman interest in etymology and its morphological salience in Latin.[52]

The next two sentences of the Latin citation differentiate the practice of poets from that of prose writers without making a qualitative judgment. Butler's rendering of the first of these is again biased, however, since it is a reinforcement of the obligation he imputes to us readers to keep catachresis and metaphor safely apart: "As for poets (Nam)," Butler's rendering begins, "they indulge in the abuse of words . . . and substitute words . . . ." The connector *nam*, "for" or even "and," which logically should function to tie poets to the "necessary" creativity of catachresis, becomes instead a dismissal of their practice. The verbal combination *solent . . . uti*, signifying "are accustomed to use," becomes the morally weighted "indulge," and the specific act of substitution, not named in the text, turns up there. In short, a fairly neutral observation regarding the prevalence of catachresis proper to poetry, as distinct from prose, one to the effect that poets, unlike prose writers, "customarily prefer to use (poetae solent . . . potius uti) neighboring words catachrestically (abusive)," becomes in Butler's translation an indictment of their preference that does not accord with Quintilian's receptivity to various forms of linguistic innovation throughout this whole section.[53] Again, while neither Quintilian nor Cicero before him takes the position that anything goes in a rhetorical *techne*, which is, after all, also the *art*, not the formlessness, of persuasion, neither of them exhibits an obsession with *ratio* narrowly conceived as inhibiting, constricting control. An emphasis on balance and moderation, as distinct from excess, with genuine gestures toward "brilliance" and "significative force" is typical of Roman intellectual culture and not peculiarly or anxiously or exceptionally associated with language.

The remainder of the passage in question trails off in the manner of taxonomies, seemingly in an afterthought to distinguish a category-slip from a properly linguistic trope. To call temerity valor is an act of (mis)judgment, not of tropology, in Quintilian's view here, and he would prefer not to disgrace the legitimate trope of catachresis by a confusion of the two. Yet even in this passage, his care to indicate that this is a personal judgment on his part again gestures toward a sensible degree of relativism regarding the appropriateness and application of rhetorical distinctions. This is a relativism lacking in recent centuries, where a more absolute, indeed more anxiously positivistic, sense of taxonomy develops and then, with significant consequences, gets read into the past.[54] In other words, the internal contradiction in Quintilian's discussion of metaphor and catachresis appears to be based first on a highly questionable translation of Latin and then on a second translation to a particularly negative version of the post-structural paradigm. Quintilian, like Cicero (or Crassus) before him, moves from a larger consideration—propriety in this case—to the traditional but more artificial mode of rhetorical taxonomy, a different thing with a different purpose: in a manner of speaking, he separates the spokes of the encompassing tropological umbrella (*verba translata*) for inspection and instruction. The difference between his earlier statement that metaphor catachrestically can provide a word where one has been lacking and his later statement that catachresis is separable ("is to be distinguished") from clarifying or enhancing metaphor signals a difference in explanatory purpose—in *ratio*—rather than a contradiction.[55]

One later passage in *The Institutio Oratoria* affords a definition of *trope* that bears helpfully on the status of metaphor as encompassing arch-trope.[56] In Book IX, Quintilian explains that a trope occurs when an expression is transferred from its "natural and principal signification to another (sermo a naturali et principali significatione translatus ad aliam), with a view to the embellishment of style or, as the majority of grammarians define it, the transference of . . . [dictio . . . translata: 'a word or saying'] from the place . . . [in quo propria est . . . in quo propria non est: 'in which it is proper to one in which it is not proper']" (i.4).[57] Within an appropriate context, a trope may thus be conceived as essentially a metaphorical act—a *sermo translatus* or *dictio translata*: other tropes, while susceptible of specification, are *also* conceivable as subsidiary versions of such an act and may (or may not) blend into it. Catachresis has throughout been a conspicuous case in point.[58]

Before proceeding, I want to comment on the derivations of *catachresis, abusio*, and *audacia*, since I shall turn next, via Augustine, Erasmus, Melanchthon, and Talon to the rhetorical tradition in the English Renaissance. There, occasionally in the presence, but even in the absence, of explicit etymological commentary, the roots of these non-native terms—"usurped" and therefore salient in common English usage—appear to influence the social reputation of this rhetorical trope. *Catachresis* derives from Greek *katachrēsthai*, "to misuse," which in turn derives from *chrēsthai*, "to use," and *kata*, perhaps most basically "down" (as in "catalogue," a descending order or "down-count") but here likely "against," or alternatively, "completely," "thoroughly," "degeneratively," or "excessively." Significantly and relevantly, however, *chrēsthai* in turn derives from *chrē*, "it is necessary" and therefore seems retrospectively to bear on a condition often associated with catachresis, namely its necessary use when a word is lacking[59] Within a linguistic context, the combination of the two Greek words *kata* and *chrēsthai* could and historically did suggest a wide range of nuances, as earlier parts of this chapter have indicated: on the positive side, "use polysemously," or "apply, extend"; "transfer" or "use tropically," "use completely or boldly or with significative force," and on the negative side most evident in the interpretative, culturally sensitive practice of modern lexicographers, "misuse," "use excessively (too boldly)," "use degeneratively" or, indeed, "use diachronously or literally," "use improperly." In these balanced but opposite nuances, Spenser's cumulative inscription in the House of Busirane "Be bold, be bold, be not too bold" seems to have come again, its wryly rhetorical distinctions, like those pertaining to metaphor, everywhere dependent on method, purpose, and judgment. The more abstract Derridean conceptions of deficiency *and* surplus, less fully narrativized than Spenser's, come to mind here again as well.

Abusio has etymologically a similarly checkered career. Derived from Latin *uti*, "to use," and *ab*, most basically "away from," *abusio* likewise carries positive and negative suggestions: on the one hand, polysemous use, transferred or tropic use, extended use; and on the other, misuse, excessive use, improper use. The very concept of use, it need scarcely be observed, implies both a broadly cultural linguistic context and one that is specific, actual, and agential. *Audacia*, "bold," in either a good or bad sense, is a word that is clearly associated with catachrestic use broadly conceived in *De Oratore*, if not actually employed there as a name for the trope; it derives from Latin *audere*, "to dare, venture, assert," which in turn descends from *avidus*, "vehemently desiring" or "greedy." Once again positive and negative suggestions are evident (and blatantly Spenserian)—everything from the Latin rhetorician's brilliance and force of meaning, to excess, impropriety, immorality, and other violations of *ratio*. Choice, context, and judgment or May and Wisse's "discrimination" again figure as the distinguishing features of use.

In *De Doctrina Christiana*, Augustine (354–430), like Cicero's Crassus, stops short of a linguistic realism that would make a fetish of propriety (*proprietas*) and such cognate conceptions as proper (*proprius*). While he comments at one point "that everyone seeks a certain . . . [similitudinem: 'similitude'] in making signs so that these signs, insofar as is possible, may resemble the things that they signify," he quickly adds, "since one thing may resemble another in a great variety of ways, signs are not valid (non constant: literally, 'do not stand firm') among men except by common consent."[60] Elsewhere his conventionalism is even stronger: for example, a sign variously graphic or verbal, such as *beta*, "means one thing among the Latins, another among the Greeks, not because of its nature, but because of agreement and consent to its significance (non natura, sed placito et consensione significandi)" (II.xxiv.37). Dropping Quintilian's third category of signs, the fictive, Augustine distinguishes proper ("propria") signs from figurative ("translata") ones and then continues, "They are called . . . [propria: 'proper'] when they are used to designate (cum . . . adhibentur: 'when they apply to') those things on account of which they were instituted (propter quas sunt instituta)" (II.x.15). "Figurative signs (Translata)," he continues, "occur when those things which we designate by literal signs are used (usurpantur) to signify something else;[61] thus we say 'ox' (bouem) . . . [and] understand an evangelist, as is signified in the Scripture, according to the interpretation of the Apostle, when it says, 'Thou shalt not muzzle the ox that treadeth out the corn' " (II.x.15).

Citing part of this passage, Freinkel offers the appropriate signification "taken up" for "usurpantur." But shortly after, "adopt[ing] Augustine's precise terminology," she explains and, indeed, *re-translates*, his final statement this way: "figures entail a 'usurpation,' a transfer of power and function. It is not the name that is appropriated, but the signifying power associated with the name; what is transferred or transported is the agency of the letter. In this way, the *res* originally designated by a name now becomes a *signum* of its own. A figure, then, is a second-order sign." (162). I would pause over this explanation for the issue it focuses with respect to *usurpantur*.[62] This issue again recalls the debate about dead metaphor treated in chapter 2. *Usurpo*, deriving from a combination of *usu*, "use," and *rapio*, "to snatch, seize," has one suspect parent with a pronounced history of violence. In classical times, however, its signification was variously positive or negative, ranging from "enjoy" or "cherish," at one extreme, to a neutral "take possession of" (e.g., of an inheritance), to an illicit possessing, and to the other extreme, "forcefully to usurp." To complicate matters further, to review the lengthy entry under *usurpo* in Lewis and Short's *Latin Dictionary* and in the *Oxford Latin Dictionary* is to get rather different impressions regarding dominant signification and lesser nuances. In both, however, *usurpo*, signifying

"to make (frequent) use (of a word, expression, etc.) in speech" is well doc-
umented as a common meaning.[63] The context in which Augustine's use of
the word occurs, specifically his instancing not just a biblical figure but one
apostolically authorized, surely argues for this signification of the word,
rather than for wrongful seizure or appropriation.

Yet we can just as surely argue that the shady side of *usurpo*'s past persists
and that Augustine's language speaks through and despite him, if we find
the argument credible here. Emphasizing the word *here*, I am shifting an
unqualified deconstructive imperative to a specific instance in a specific text
and asking it to answer to circumstance and historical moment. Deciding in
such an instance is an act of responsible agency, as well as of reading. That
language speaks the language-user is always already a possibility, but not always already a persuasive one in a given historical and textual context. For
my own part, I find Augustine's overall view of human language, as distinct
from the voice and the word within, sufficiently ambivalent that I could
easily imagine *usurpo*'s suspect past speaking through him in a discussion of
figurative usage; yet here, without a broader consideration of his complicated views on language answering to the Derridean requirement that the
etymological trace be systemic and in a passage in which this trace would
work against divinely sanctioned apostolic interpretation, such an argument
must be recognized as a hard, and by no means definitive, one.[64]

By analogy, a definition of English *usurp* current from the sixteenth to
nineteenth centuries and the *OED*'s telling sixteenth-century examples of
it can afford a fittingly open conclusion regarding Augustine's use of *usurpo*.
The definition reads, "To take (a word or words) into use; to borrow or
appropriate from another language, source, etc.; to employ, use," and examples include these: from Thomas Elyot in 1531, "Of them two [sc. 'celeritie'
and 'slownesse'] springeth an excellent vertue where unto we lacke a name
in englisshe. Wherfore I am constrained to usurpe a latine worde, callyng it
Maturitie"; and from a translator of Bullinger in 1573, "And these wordes
haue more grace in ours and other straunge languages, vsurped than translated. So haue remayned in the Church, Osanna, Amen [etc.]" (4.c). Interestingly, both *OED* examples are catachrestic: in the first a proper term is
lacking, and in the second there is a beneficial usurpation instead of a translation, or rather, there is a simple act of transference and appropriation.
Moreover, this is a usurpation that is said to move Hebrew words into
"straunge languages," or *alienae linguae*, like English. Combining these two
examples, we have Elyot's "lacke," or a minus, and the translator's "grace,"
a plus. I am inclined in conclusion to attribute their combined ambivalence

to Augustine's *usurpo*, as well. Certainly Erasmus, to whose rhetoric I next turn, employs the verb *usurpo* in *De Copia Rerum* simply to refer to usage within a historical context: "You will need to observe carefully the way usage varied at different periods (Diligenter itaque conueniet obseruare, quid in *vsurpandis* vocibus aetas variarit)." Presumably such "usurpation" or variations in usage afforded various gains and losses for the budding rhetorician whom Erasmus addresses to contemplate (319: I.xii; 52: I.xii: my emphasis).

Erasmus' *De Copia*, first published in 1512 and repeatedly revised and considerably expanded until 1534, was quickly "adopted as a textbook of rhetoric in schools and universities throughout northern Europe" (Knott, trans., 283). Defining the various tools of rhetoric, including tropes, Erasmus follows Cicero, Quintilian, and *Ad Herennium* in the main, often citing examples from Horace and other Latin or Greek writers, as well. His relatively brief, systematic presentations of each trope and of related topics, such as "harsh words," "obsolete words," and "indecent words," put a high premium on decorum and everywhere eschew violence. While these characteristic Erasmian emphases are anticipated in the Latin sources, concentration heightens them in *De Copia*, as do other Erasmian modifications. For example, both *Ad Herennium* and Erasmus censure a version of the following metaphor, which I cite here from *Ad Herennium*: "istum qui montis belli fabricatus est, campos sustulit pacis (this man, who hath builded mounts of war, destroyed the plains of peace)"; but *Ad Herennium* describes the creator of this metaphor as one "misled by the appearance of grandeur," who is unable to "perceive the tumidity (tumorem) of the style," whereas, Erasmus, having reversed the clauses and improved the first to read, "belli montes excitauit (raised the mountains of war)," observes that "The metaphor would have been . . . [Mollius erat: 'more graceful' or 'milder'] if the writer had used the image of a calm sea and a stormy one."[65] Here again is the excess accretively associated in the rhetorical tradition with catachrestic metaphor, and the same association pertains to misuse and the quality of being far-fetched, which are unexceptionally censured by Erasmus as well. Perhaps the core of the Erasmian view comes in his advice to teachers in another, closely related treatise, *De ratione studii*: "The nature and essence [vis: 'force'] of everything must be grasped, especially since it is from this source that they [i.e., poets] are accustomed to draw their similes [similia], epithets, comparisons, images, metaphors, and other rhetorical devices of that kind."[66] Here, we might say, Cicero's *ratio* and *rerum natura* are laid out for viewing—"opened," in a Renaissance idiom, or "exposed," in a more modern one. Erasmus' explicit pedagogical purpose is doubtless relevant.[67]

Interestingly, if puzzlingly, it is under the heading "catachresis" in *De Copia* that Erasmus also speaks of a "simile" ("similitudo") as "a metaphor that is made explicit and specifically related to the subject"; he adds, "Cicero's word for this is *collatio* 'comparison'" (337: I.19/7; 66: I.xix). At one point in discussing metaphor, he also finds it necessary to observe that "metaphor can sometimes lie simply in the use of a noun," that is, in a single word.[68] A trope is perhaps most commonly considered as a *verbum translatum*, the deviant use of a single word, although in Quintilian and elsewhere its reference is extended to a *sermo translatus*, a phrase or senténce (i.e., *sententia*), and therefore Erasmus' observation may register a cultural preference for narrative forms such as proverb, parable, and allegory (335: I.17; 64–65: I.xvii). Incidental observations such as these are notable chiefly for their bearing on patterns that emerge in subsequent rhetorics.

Like Cicero and Quintilian, Erasmus unsurprisingly considers catachresis, understood to be the figurative use of a word where no proper one exists, a subcategory of metaphor, the arch-trope. Treating "reciprocal metaphors," he notes, "sometimes metaphor is unavoidable (necessaria: 'necessary')," and he instances the language of "countrymen," the *rustici* ("gems" for buds, and the like), adding that "We [also] speak of a man as 'hard,' as 'rough,' for there is no other word" (335: I.17; 64, I.xvii). When Erasmus defines catachresis explicitly, he refers what his learned translator rightly expresses as its "force" back to that of allegory ("Eandem vim obtinet catachresis"); allegory has already been defined as "metaphora perpetua"—continuous metaphor—which the translator renders interpretatively as "a metaphor carried on *beyond the bounds* of a single word," i.e., beyond the bounds of a metaphorical trope, properly speaking (336: I,18/6; 66: I.xviii; my emphasis):

> Similar in force (vim) is catachresis, for which the Latin word is *abusio* . . . and it differs from metaphor in that we resort to . . . [*abusio*] where a . . . word does not exist, to metaphor where . . . [vbi aliud fuit: 'where one has existed'];[69] for example, we use the word 'parricide,' that is, 'father-killer,' for one who kills his brother, because 'fratricide' is not used; and *piscina* 'fish-pond' for a bathing pool, although there are no fish (*pisces*) in it. Other examples are: *short* powers of [a] man, the *long* wisdom of the man, *diminished* courage (for 'little') [336–37: I:19/7, 66: I.xix].

We first met the final examples in *Ad Herennium*. Here, as in that earlier pedagogical text, emphasis at the end falls on simple misuse. The earlier examples, found in Cicero and Quintilian, merely instance the catachrestic extension of a word when a proper one does not (yet?) exist.[70] Nothing is novel here, except at the outset of the definition that hint of a connection of catachresis with forcefulness and, if Knott's translation is justified, with an exceeding of bounds, or limits, that is found also in allegory.

The rhetoric of Philipp Melanchthon (1519), which was the main source (via an unauthorized version) of Leonard Cox's *The Arte or Crafte of Rhetoryke* (1524), first of its kind in English, contains even briefer synoptic definitions of various tropes than Erasmus' does.[71] Unexceptionally, Melanchthon gives *trope* and the arch-trope *metaphor* virtually identical definitions, defining the latter as "the transference of a word from its proper signification to something similar (*Μεταφορά* est, cum propter similitudinem transfertur vocabulum a propria significatione)" and offering "an iron heart (ferreum pectus)" as an example of it.[72] Yet his use of the word *similitudo* in this definition is worth noting, since he quickly adds that Cicero heaps "extraordinary praises (miris laudibus)" on the type of figure he calls a "brief likeness (brevem similitudinem)" (463).[73] Melanchthon's next sentence makes clearer that he now refers to what some modern editors of Cicero and Quintilian have translated as a "simile," "for a likeness declares that thing outright that a metaphor signifies less explicitly (Nam similitudine declaratur ea res, quae per metaphoram significatur)." This section presumably on metaphor then concludes with further praise of "omnis collatio," which, we have just seen, Erasmus, too, considers an explicit comparison. Thus, with the exception of the first sentence defining *metaphora*, the section treating this trope focuses entirely on the *brevis similitudo* and effectively indicates a near subsumption of the one in the other—seemingly another instance of rhetorical blending.

A brief section on *Κατάχρησις* follows, giving as much space to this trope as to *metaphor/similitudo*. Melanchthon defines catachresis as *abusus verbi*, the improper use of a word, and instances it by the familiar *parricide* applied more broadly to internecine killers, since it is a word as close to the real thing as we are said to find available. The rest of his comments, which include use of the ambivalent *usurpo*, sound neutral but looked at more closely could sound ambiguous as well. Further instancing catachresis, for example, he observes that "theologians use the word 'grace' not only for good will, but in Greek or Hebrew also for a favorable ruling or a financial reward (Gratiam dicunt Theologi, non tantum pro favore, sed etiam Graeco aut Ebraico more pro beneficio aut munere)" (466). But Melanchthon next observes that there are many similar examples existing in Scripture, because the Greek and Hebrew words and phrases cannot always be exchanged with (*mutare*: i.e., 'translated into') another language.[74] He then rings a change on Quintilian's objection to confusing a category-slip with catachresis, indicating that he is willing to consider such slippage catachrestic, although not to countenance it. Where for Quintilian, calling temerity valor is an act of (mis)judgment, *not* of tropology, for Melanchthon catachresis occurs when, in an act of singular (mis)judgment, we assert (*usurpamus*) that vices are virtues, or, conversely, we claim that severity is cruelty, or parsimony avarice.[75] Here we see catachresis' unruly reputation emerging, and notably in *usurpo*'s company.[76]

Omer Talon (1510–62), or Talaeus, a colleague and popularizer of Ramus (Pierre de la Ramée), largely follows Cicero and Quintilian with respect to metaphor and catachresis. In a section treating metaphor specifically, he first identifies it as a similitude compressed into one word ("ad vnum verbum contracta similitudo"), and then, compactly combining his two major Roman sources, he recalls Quintilian's view that metaphor brings "more light (plus luminis)"—more distinction—to a speech than does any other trope, yet he quickly adds the characteristic Ciceronian proviso, "especially if it is chosen in accordance with reason and judgment (si ratione sumpta est)." He ends on another familiar but more expansive Ciceronian note, observing that there is nothing in the "nature of things (in rerum natura)" whence a likeness (*simile*) cannot be drawn (11).[77]

In a more general discussion of tropology, Talon sees a trope shifting a word from its natural signification, the one it was born with (*à natiua significatione*), to another (*aliam*) (2). His phrasing recalls Cicero's statement that proper words were "almost (*paene*)" born with their referents but subtly shifts its force still closer to linguistic realism. Introducing a significantly related connection between tropology and concealment, he thinks Aristotle right in teaching that a trope is sometimes *alienus*, "strange" or "alien" because in it "a certain hiding or indirection (*latebra*) occurs through ambiguity and obscurity (quia . . . ambiguitatis & obscuritatis . . . quaedam sit)," and he observes the greater frequency of tropic speech in Plato. Such veiled tropes appear to be less to Talon's taste than those more clearly based on similarity, which he especially and repeatedly praises. Following Cicero closely, he now explains the (broadly or indirectly catachrestic) origin of tropes out of necessity owing to the poverty of language and their subsequent appeal because of their charm, distinction, and worth (*delectatio, ornatus, dignitas*). Then, having repeated Cicero's (and Quintilian's) caution that a trope ought to be modest ("verecundus debet esse tropus"), as if entering a strange place by permission rather than with disruptive force, he turns briefly and directly to catachresis, adding that "if the trope is harsher or more unfitting (dissimilar, disproportionate)" than modest "it is called *catachresis* [or] *abusio* (Quod si durior vel inaequalior fuerit, κατάχρησις, abusio dicitur)" (3). This is the first time in the texts I have treated that immodesty—excess, immoderation, violence—is *explicitly* labeled catachresis.

With implications for English Renaissance rhetorics, Talon continues, "As a trope, moreover, *audacia*, 'boldness,' is called *hyperbole*, 'excess,' or else *superlatio*, 'exaggeration' (Audacia autem tropi, ὑπερβολὴ [or] *superlatio*)" (3: sic). Among the English rhetoricians, Dudley Fenner will similarly speak of catachresis and hyperbole together, the one as harshness and the other as excess and, again like Talon, will do so right after recalling Cicero's recommendation of tropic *verecundia*, "modesty" (sig. D1v: Fenner's "maydenly"). Moreover, George Puttenham will describe "*Hiperbole*, or the Ouer reacher, otherwise called the loud lyer" as having "a spice of the same *false semblant* [as allegory, or continued metaphor]," since it occurs "when we speak in the superlatiue and beyond the limites of credit" (202). Talon, who follows Ramus in recognizing metaphor, metonymy, synecdoche, and irony as the four master tropes, also refers to hyperbole and allegory as metaphors (12). Taking Talon, Fenner, and Puttenham together, catachresis, hyperbole, *audacia*, and metaphor are thus all closely related and are typically under the umbrella of metaphor, the arch-trope *translatio*.

While I do not intend an exhaustive survey of statements about metaphor and catachresis in the rhetorical tradition, I want to consider roughly in chronological order a number representative of the English Renaissance, namely, those in the rhetorics of Thomas Wilson, Henry Peacham, Fenner, Angel Day, Puttenham, and John Hoskins, all of whom write in the second half of the sixteenth century, although Hoskins (1599) barely within it. My interest lies mainly in relevant changes of emphasis or meaning from those of the Roman rhetorics that are not simply attributable to the pedagogical purpose of any given rhetoric or handbook. Throughout, it will be my assumption that *Ad Herennium* and the rhetorical writings of Cicero and Quintilian, neither of whom wrote for beginners, were widely read during the Renaissance period and were therefore available for independent interpretation.[78] I should add that in my view the best interpreters of these earlier texts are finally the poets and playwrights, who read them: Spenser's House of Busirane, the House of Abuse, offers the example nearest to hand. Yet the rhetorics usefully afford fairly straightforward samples of normative contemporary readings, which fictive and imaginative writings in the period may complicate and exceed.[79]

Thomas Wilson elaborates on Cicero's story about the origin of tropes, notably associating it with the advancement of learning and wisdom: "When learned and wisemen gan first to inlarge their tongue, and sought with great vtterance of speech to commende causes: They founde ful oft much want of words to set out their meaning. And therfore remembring thinges of like nature vnto those whereof they speake: They vsed such wordes to expresse their mynde, as were most like vnto other" (170). Then the rest of the usual story unfolds: need gives way to pleasure and perspicuity—"light"—when "an apt and meete worde" "can not" express the "thing." Like Cicero and Quintilian, Wilson recognizes the positive advantage—the *proprium lumen*—of tropic translation (171). Indeed, "Neither can any one perswade effectuously . . . without the helpe of wordes [metaphorically] altered and translated" (172–73). Within this context, he defines metaphor unexceptionally as "an alteration of a worde, from the proper and naturall meaning, to that which is not proper, and yet agreeth thereunto by some likenesse, that appereth to be in it" (172). "Abusion, called of the Grecians *Catachresis*," occurs, he tells us, "when *for a certaine proper worde*, we vse that which is most nigh vnto it" (174–75: my emphasis), and familiar examples follow: the fish pond for any small pond, or "long talke, and small matter . . . for wee cannot measure, either talke, or matter by length, or breadth" (175). Of the rhetoricians treated so far, Wilson is the first actually to explain why the latter examples are improper. In this and in his extension of Cicero's story of tropic origin, his characteristic commitment to the rational "cause" of language is evident. Looking closely at his diction, I am also struck by his closeness to the Latin phrasing *pro proprio verbo* (see my emphasis just above) and by his correlative avoidance of the word *lack* or *substitute* in describing catachresis. Interestingly, Wilson's phrasing "for a certain proper worde" thus captures something of the ambiguous potential of Latin *pro*—"in place of" or "in behalf of." Wilson is a more careful reader of the Latin sources than many of his successors in this line.

Henry Peacham's version of tropic origin, which I discussed in chapter 2, is more troubled or confused than is the learned Wilson's. Comparatively, Peacham's account is notable for his characterization of the shift from necessity to pleasure in the use of tropes as a *refusal* to use proper words, although he soon alters this to a desire for greater "sweetnesse" and truth, the latter understood as a preference for a more perspicuous declaration of "the nature of the thing."[80] Peacham's definition of metaphor is so familiar as hardly to warrant repetition: in short, a word translated for necessity or pleasantness, which is also his definition of tropology in general. His definition of catachresis has two parts—"a necessary abuse of like words, for the proper, or when to that, that hath not his proper name, we lend the next or lykest vnto it": the second part is conventional, and where the first conceivably intends misuse in the manner of *Ad Herennium*, its calling such misuse "necessary" *despite* the existence of proper terms suggests the conflation of catachresis with metaphor. The example of catachresis from Deuteronomy 3 that Peacham gives and then glosses—"Drincke of the most pure blood of the Grapes, here likewyse blood is put for iuyce"—is, strictly speaking, by his own gloss metaphorical rather than catachrestic.[81] The reason he considers it catachrestic, I imagine, is that it is bold, perhaps too bold, or unnatural, excessive, abusive. It is hard not to think that Peacham chose this eucharistic translation of blood for the juice of grapes with more than merely rhetorical motivation, a cultural surplus that emerges ever more clearly as characteristic of Renaissance rhetorics.

In another rhetoric, Dudley Fenner, having expressed the customary origin of tropes (from necessity to delight) is notable first for his rendition of Cicero's memorably tropic caution about metaphor and second for his application of it. Fenner renders the Ciceronian characterization of metaphor in significantly novel diction: "this chaunge of signification must be shamefest, and as it were maydenly [Cicero's *verecunda*], that it may seeme rather to be led by the hand to another signification then to be driuen by force vnto the same." In an original twist, Fenner's version of Cicero's *verecunda*, suggesting a maiden to be led, not forced, is gendered distinctly and *socially* feminine, a development the forcefulness of the rest of the similitude in Latin had earlier resisted. The rest of Fenner's similitude, adjusted to his maidenly image, clearly gives abuse a moral dimension as well. Fenner adds, "yet sometime this fine manner of speech swarueth from this perfection [of unforced maidenliness], and then it is Eyther The abuse of this fine speeche, called Katachresis, or The excesse of this finenesse, called Hyperbole." He concludes, "The abuse of speeche is, when the chaunge is hard, strange, and vnwonted" (sig. D1v). Here catachresis is forced, wrenched, far-fetched, alien. Like Busirane, moreover, it is also abusive of maidens. Notable in connection with Fenner's version is the earlier English rhetoric by Richard Sherry, who gives a variation on the conventional example of catachresis, *parricide* for *fratricide*, that is similarly eye-catching for a reader attuned to the adventures of Britomart and Amoret: "vt quum paricidam [thus] appellamus, qui vxorem occidit ('as when we call a wife-killer a parricide')" (sig. xxir).

Angel Day's *English Secretary*, also discussed in chapter 2, is notable here only for its conflation of trope with metaphor and then with catachresis as well, all the while trying to distinguish among them by elusively various diction. A trope is "a variation of a worde or sentence from the proper & apt signification, vnto another neere vnto the same"; metaphor occurs "when a worde from the proper and right signification is transferred to another neere vnto the meaning"; and catachresis exists "where wee accommodate a name to a thing that is not proper."[82] Day avoids the calculated overlap of *trans-latio/transfero* for a trope and a metaphor that is characteristic of the Roman rhetorics, but in doing so he reduces a trope to a loose, undifferentiated "variation" from the "proper and apt." Transferring signification from the "proper and right" to mere proximity, metaphor is perhaps more transgressive, although not convincingly so. As an "accommodation," catachresis sounds eminently reasonable, but it becomes less so when instanced by conventional examples, namely, "*lend me your hand*," an expression "more proper" to money or borrowing, Day explains, or "*mens powers are short, . . . their counsels long*, when in neither . . . is anie such measure" (sig. Kk2r). Day sounds like someone trying hard to reconcile a pedagogically simplified taxonomy he once learned with a practice that fails neatly to conform to it.

George Puttenham and John Hoskins are two of the later and more interesting of the English writers of rhetorics. Puttenham positions metaphor and catachresis first and second at the start of a chapter whose title begins, "Of the figures which we call Sensable, because they alter and affect the minde" (188). Present in the rhetorical tradition from the outset, such affect and especially such specifically mental affect are emphatically renewed and highlighted in the sixteenth century. While Puttenham has little substantively new to say about the figures in question, the words he uses to characterize them are remarkably significant. Metaphor is decidedly forceful: "a kinde of *wresting* of a single word from his owne right signification, to another not so naturall, but yet of some affinitie or conueniencie with it, as to say, *I cannot digest your vnkinde* [i.e., 'unnatural'] *words*" (189: my emphasis on "wresting"). Puttenham enumerates three motivating "causes" of metaphor: first, "necessitie or want of a better word" that is "apter and more naturall"; second, "pleasure and ornament," and third, "to enforce a sence and make the word more significatiue"—Quintilian's *vim significandi*, "significative power" (189–90). Puttenham has his eye on a courtly audience for whom "wresting" and forcefulness have more appeal, one might suppose, than Cicero's *verecundia*, "modesty," or Fenner's feminized rendering of it—"maidenliness." Reading Puttenham's translation of *metaphora*, namely, "the Figure of transporte," with the flippancy it invites, one might further translate it "the figure of ambition," or more literally, "of carriage from one 'place' to another"—*place* heard not simply in the rhetorical sense but also in that Donne intends in "The Canonization": "get you a place," or, in Puttenham's treatise, a higher place, in the court.

When Puttenham turns next to catachresis, his morally weighted words and socially contextualized examples suggest a measure of difficulty in coming to terms with this "Figure of abuse":

> But if for lacke of a naturall and proper terme or worde we take another, neither naturall nor proper and do vntruly applie it to the thing which we would seeme to expresse, and without any iust inconuenience, it is not then spoken by this figure *Metaphore* or of *inuersion* [another term for metaphor][83] as before, but by plaine abuse, as he that bad his man go into his library and fet him his bowe and arrowes, for in deede there was neuer a booke there to be found, or as one should in reproch say to a poore man, thou raskall knaue, where *raskall* is properly the hunters terme giuen to young deere, leane and out of season, and not to people [190–91].

Untruthful application for lack of a proper term yet "without any iust[ifying] inconuenience" (i.e., real need or reason, or by inversion, suitability, aptness) is itself a hard nut to swallow, and Puttenham's examples ensure further trouble. The first (the "library"of the unlearned master) is abusive enough, although so "inconuenient" as to be silly, and the second ("raskall," a term misapplied but ironically applicable to a needy poacher) looks properly metaphorical. But perhaps it is the feint of social criticism in both examples, a criticism that remains diffused and unfulfilled, that troubles their aim and flattens their effect.

Puttenham's third example of catachresis makes matters worse, since by its end he has rationalized it sufficiently to persuade himself of its commendability and has probably persuaded a careful reader of its legitimate metaphoricity as well. Having cited the "very pretty" saying "*I lent my loue to losse, and gaged my life in vaine*," Puttenham continues,

> Whereas this worde *lent* is properly of mony or some such other thing, as men do commonly borrow, for vse to be repayed againe, and being applied to loue is vtterly abused, and yet very commendably spoken by vertue of this figure [catachresis]. For he that loueth and is not beloued againe, hath no lesse wrong, than he that lendeth and is neuer repayde [191].

What we are observing can as readily be interpreted as Puttenham's struggle with the fluidity of language use [*parole*], which resists division into a neat

rhetorical taxonomy, as it can his struggle with a rift at the base of signification. There may well be such a rift, and I have been inclined to suppose so.
As earlier indicated, however, recent neo-cognitivist arguments, backed by
persuasive neurological and developmental evidence, have led me to suspect
that any rift or rupture is to be found less in the grounding of language, to
which the afterlife of physically based "dead" metaphor attests, than at the
level of linguistic abstraction and conceptualization.[84] Be that as it may, *here*,
in the Roman rhetorics and on the other evidence examined to this point,
the artificial distinctions of taxonomy themselves appear to be the real problem rather than the symptom of epistemological rupture. As we have seen,
Cicero's Crassus moves smoothly and easily from a larger discussion of tropology, or Quintilian from a flexible consideration of propriety, to taxonomy as merely a different *modus operandi*, useful but more constricted, a
different kind of thing for a more limited purpose rather than a contradiction. For these writers, taxonomy is an orienting device or a guide to a series
of techniques rather than a finished whole. In contrast to them, Puttenham,
like most other Renaissance rhetoricians, struggles harder to impose the
technical distinctions of taxonomy. In this, he is, indeed, an early modern.
Or is he, finally? Does he really struggle so? The openness with which he
surrenders catachresis to metaphor at the end could also be his ironic,
courtly way of making just the same point about taxonomic niceties. The
resemblance of Puttenham's deployment of taxonomy to Foucault's distinction between a premodern allegiance to correspondence and analogy and a
modern fascination with mathematically precise taxonomic grids of identity
and difference may thus be more superficial than the resemblance between
Puttenham's irony, or doubleness, and other visions of difference/*différance*,
such as Derrida's.[85]

John Hoskins' statements about similitude, metaphor, and catachresis exhibit both a considerable grasp of the Roman rhetoricians and the play of an
active intelligence over them. Although Hoskins addresses similitude after
metaphor and before catachresis, I shall deal with it first. Hoskins has a very
definite idea of what it is, and this is certainly not just "ut leonem," to recall
Quintilian's thumbnail example of it. Rather, "a *Similitude* hath two sentences, of several proper terms compared; a *Fable* is a similitude acted by
fiction in beasts; a *Poet's Tale*, for the most part, by gods and men."[86] If
Hoskins remembers or cares about Quintilian's statement that metaphor is a
brief similitude, his idea of similitude would lead us to anticipate a richer
definition of metaphor than has been the Renaissance norm to this point,
and we get one. He explains that

A *Metaphor,* or *Translation,* is the friendly and neighborly borrowing of one word to express a thing with more light and better note, though not so directly and properly as the natural name of the thing would signify. . . . The rule of a metaphor is that it be not too bold nor too far-fetched. And though all metaphors go beyond the signification of things, yet are they requisite to match the compassing sweetness of men's minds, that are not content to fix themselves upon one thing but they must wander into the confines; like the eye, that cannot choose but view the whole knot when it beholds but one flower in a garden of purpose; or like an archer that, knowing his bow will overcast or carry too short, takes an aim on this side or beyond his mark [8].

Various memories of earlier texts abound in this passage, whether by way of similarity or contrast. What for Sutton/Rackham is a hostile intrusion, for Freinkel's Augustine a usurpation, and for Puttenham a wresting, is now "a friendly and neighborly borrowing" as if of a cup of flour. The greater light and better memorability ("note," or Latin *nota*) recall the special light— *proprium lumen*—Quintilian attributes to metaphor, and what I shall henceforth consider (with calculated ambiguity) *the rule of boldness* especially recalls Cicero, as for a moment does Hoskins' recognition of the mind's need to wander, which Cicero's Crassus described as "maxima est delectatio (a very great pleasure)" (III.xl.160). Yet even with all these memories, there is something special in Hoskins' characterization of metaphor: its creativity— its "go[ing] beyond," or exceeding, the proper and natural "signification of things." This is an excess or a plus required to match the comprehension of the mind, one reminiscent of Sidney's (or Shakespeare's) well known characterization of the poetic imagination and one that goes beyond the Roman sources.[87] To my mind, Hoskins' concluding similes do the work of metaphor, in retrospect perhaps casting a measure of justifying light on efforts to associate or even to conflate the two.[88] These similes are immensely suggestive: the hungry, associative eye or the archer who shoots fictively in order to get at a truth. As Hoskins subsequently adds, "a metaphor . . . enricheth our knowledge with two things at once, with the truth and with similitude" (8). This is a doubling, each having seemingly equal thingness. It is also cognitive, for it "enricheth," adds to, "our knowledge."

On catachresis, Hoskins is similarly suggestive: "*Catachresis* (in English *Abuse*) is now grown in fashion—as most abuses are. It is somewhat more *desperate* than a metaphor. It is the expressing of one matter by the name of another which is incompatible with it, and sometimes clean contrary" (11: my emphasis). Here at last is the culminating definition-cum-description that Spenser's Busirane merits: "desperate," which is easy to apply, whether we have Busirane himself, Amoret, or the nigh-suicidal Britomart of canto iv primarily in mind; "one matter," love, "by the name of an [incompatible or contrary] other" is easy as well, complicated only by whether the name in both instances is Busirane or whether in the former it is a combination of Ovid and Petrarch. Hoskins' linking of rhetorical form to social content is also notable, even if witty, and characteristic of the specifically moral significance of tropology we have been witnessing in the Renaissance rhetorics. "Somewhat more desperate" certainly resonates suggestively with Cicero's "paulo audaciores (somewhat bolder, 'more reckless, more audacious')" and puts the close association of *audacia* and catachresis again on the screen. Hoskins' sense that the catachrestic name is downright "incompatible" (disharmonious, incongruous, or antagonistic) with the matter to which it is applied is also a real shift from a sense of catachresis as the use of the nearest available word to describe something for which there is no proper word, although it is less of a shift from earlier, if subtler, associations of catachresis with immoderation. Hoskins' description of catachresis as the use of a name for something that is "clean contrary" to it goes even further, but it is tamed into irony by his examples, which follow:

> 'I gave order to some servants of mine, whom I thought as apt for such charities as myself, to lead him out into the forest and there to kill him,' where *charity* is used for *cruelty* (but this may also be by the figure *ironia*); and the abuse of a word from things far different [11].

Hoskins gives other examples of catachresis, which is "usual . . . with the fine conversants of our time, when they strain for an extraordinary phrase, as, 'I am not guilty of those phrases' [or] 'I am in danger of preferment'" (11). What I like about Hoskins is his connection with the current scene, but, like Puttenham, he, too, in his own way finally resolves catachresis into irony, another instance of blending or "rhetorical relativism" that is taxonomically irreverent in a rhetoric.

With Hoskins' rhetoric, as with others in the Renaissance, the extent to which rhetorical categories are fuzzy-edged or even fluid and the way they attract various contemporary social nuances are significant. Such *lived relativism* as Hoskins' lessens, if not ends, with the Renaissance and with the passing of the culturally dominant *awareness* of rhetoric as a viable epistemological form.[89] Insofar as formal rhetoric persists, later centuries will strive for more and better precision and with few exceptions will develop an illusive sense of propriety rigid enough to correlate with it. The rule of the monolingual dictionary will be a correlative development, as indicated in my second chapter. Reading backwards from later centuries to the lived and still modulating rhetoric of an earlier time will necessarily yield different conclusions. In contrast, my concern has first been to challenge an exclusively negative emphasis on deficiency, dissimulation, and rupture in the Roman rhetorics and instead to explore their broad sense of propriety and their balanced discussions of metaphor, even including forms of catachrestic metaphor, as productive and creative. My other concern has been to discover the fortunes of the rhetorical awareness that the English Renaissance inherits and modifies, often noticeably in the direction of current social application. Paradoxically, such modification could also already be a sign that rhetoric is becoming more self-consciously formal and less integrally a part of civic life, but this is to anticipate my next chapter.

Spenser's creative use of *boldness* (*audacia*) in Busirane's House of Rhetoric additionally affords my argument a concluding instance of lived relativism and expresses a measure of interpretative boldness itself, as well. In much of the present chapter, I have suggested that the cumulative motto "Be bold, be bold, be not too bold," which Britomart encounters perceptively and with which she must deal actively and morally in Busirane's House, is, like the rest of this rhetorical place, associated with metaphor and especially with striking, bold metaphor and the accompanying danger of its excess or abuse. This association is present in Cicero and thereafter in the rhetorical tradition, notably including its reception and development in Renaissance England. Rather than an explicit assertion or outright equation of an unqualified *audacia* with catachresis, however, this is precisely and persistently a traditional association that becomes available cumulatively, aggregately, and therefore interpretatively. My argument has been that this association, derived from rhetorical tradition, wryly informs the motto of Busirane's House, where it operates at once as a come-on and a caution. Its doubleness is similar in this respect to Acrasia's "jewelled vines," which likewise descend ironically from those of Cicero's *rustici* in his discussion of metaphor and catachresis.[90] *Be bold, be bold, be not too bold* teasingly, temptingly, instructively, and perversely encapsulates the etymological contradictions rooted in the conception of catachrestic metaphor itself and suspended (in both senses) in the larger concept of *ratio*. The House of Busirane may be about rhetorical technique and the making of meaning, but it is also about much else besides, as is rhetoric itself, which shapes and organizes rather than merely expresses "the nature of things," *rerum natura*.

8.   *Exchanging Values: The Economic and Rhetorical World Seen by Gerrard de Malynes, Merchant*

In 1622, Gerrard de Malynes, self-styled "Merchant," published his *magnum opus* entitled *Consuetudo, vel Lex Mercatoria, or The Antient Law-Merchant.* While concerned with mercantile law (and nowadays found in law libraries), *Lex Mercatoria* focuses primarily on mercantile custom. It fundamentally engages economic issues, as do Malynes' earlier writings, on which discussion of his historical significance has focused. *Lex Mercatoria* affords a broader context for these views than do his other writings, however, and it affords ways of looking at them that cast light on the curious fact of his also having composed an allegory about usury and exchange, complete with dragon and endangered maiden. It allows this allegory, *Saint George for England,* which is usually ignored or else discussed as if it were generically just another economic tract, to cast additional light on Malynes' understanding of signification and more generally of how the world works.[1]

The metaphoricity of this understanding is my central concern, and again, as especially in my chapters 2 and 7, it involves the intersection of rhetoric and finance, translation and investment, metaphor and currency exchange. Its comprehension is inseparable from Malynes' background and experience in the reigns of Elizabeth and James, from his socioeconomic views, and from the rhetorical forms and practices that shaped their expression. The first section that follows offers a general introduction to all of these. Subsequent sections focus on *Lex Mercatoria* more directly, at the end leading to the allegory of *St. George,* which dramatically brings to the fore the mutual reflection of Malynes' view of currency exchange and his problems with metaphor.

Malynes has contradictorily been described as sophisticated and forward looking or as pathetically tied to a medieval past.[2] Stylistically, he has been termed an Erasmian or a Ciceronian, although, despite one emotional sentence of thirty-eight lines about worldly inconstancy and debt, it would be hard to find a significant proportion of periodic sentences, the defining characteristic of a Ciceronian style, in the considerable bulk of his major volume *Lex Mercatoria*.³ He has also been characterized as one who relies on authority rather than experience, a description that is patently false, and as an inveterate invoker of Aristotelian categories.⁴ On the whole, Malynes is indeed an Aristotelian, yet his views are considerably more complicated than this assertion would suggest. In *Lex Mercatoria* he more than once observes that Aristotle knew nothing of the particular subject he is treating: for example, "Of the nature and diuersitie of Colours":

> for so experience hath taught vs in progresse of time, by long obseruation, wherein by Art I have found the truth by variation without the mysterie of dying, more certaine, than *Aristotle* or other Phylosophers by reason have conceiued, according to the Theoricke part by them described, which by the Practicke part I am assured of by experience as aforesaid [54].

Or, on exchange:

> The moneys in Christendome, which haue their ebbing and flowing doe shew their operation vpon commodities, maketh by plentie the price thereof deare, or by scarsitie better cheape, as hath beene noted: but Exchange hath a contrarie meane of working, for plentie of money maketh a low Exchange, and scarsity of money maketh a high Exchange and the price to rise, which is of great consideration; because it ouerruleth money and commodities, which neuer entred in the politicke studies of *Aristotle, Seneca,* or *Cicero,* who were but in the infancie of Trade [316].

Here Malynes is not only aware of what modern economists call a quantity theory of money—the effect of the money supply on price—but also of Aristotle's ignorance of it. His view indicates a degree of historical awareness, as well as an appreciation of the value of practical experience. While he might have thought that money should have either a fixed or pegged value—in his pragmatic similitude, that the yardstick measuring the cloth should not vary in length—he nonetheless clearly saw that this value fluctuated in his world: for "the benefit or profit of exchange is never known directly, but by the rechange thereof" (300; yard: 412, 423).

Elsewhere, as Glyn Davies observes, Malynes gives the *effect* of the quantity theory of money an amazingly more proto-Keynesian than backward-looking twist since he argues that " 'the more ready money' " merchants make, " 'the more employment would they make upon our home commodity, advancing the price thereof, which price would augment the quantity by setting more people on work.' "⁵ Higher prices would thus lead to expanded production and increase employment, bettering the lot of the poor—not exactly the conventional Elizabethan recipe for alleviating poverty. Still other economists have found in Malynes' writings either a "rudimentary form" of the purchasing-power-parity theory (incident on an exchange rate at which goods in different countries/currencies cost the same) or at least "all the ingredients for [it]."[6]

Malynes' own claim to authority rests essentially on his "fiftie yeeres obseruation, knowledge, and experience," to the last of which he refers tellingly and often: for example, to his experience with the freighting of ships, to his conversation with Archbishop Matthew and Lord Eure about the Copernican hypothesis, to his role as an arbitrator in a case of common law, to his direct acquaintance with an alchemist and his experiment, to his having worked to develop mines in England and Wales, to his instructive experience of a defective document of assurance (insurance), to an exemplary law "case of mine owne" against another merchant.[7] Malynes cites figures derived in part from his reading and in part from his experience, and he provides tables addressed directly to practical use throughout *Lex Mercatoria*. One of the more fascinating features of this book is, in fact, his effort to integrate the categories he inherits with those he has acquired from experience. That this comprehensive text was published at the height of a particularly severe economic depression, which urged explanation and redress, makes it a cultural register of further interest.

Although Malynes claims that his "ancestors and parents" were born in Lancashire, Raymond de Roover asserts on the basis of the name de Malynes and English records of the 1580s and 1590s that he was actually a Fleming who emigrated to England. These records list Malynes among resident aliens and show that he made a contribution to a "students' fund" of the " 'Dutch' church" and subscribed 200 pounds sterling to "a forced loan . . . levied on the merchant strangers" by Queen Elizabeth when England was threatened by the Armada. De Roover also suspects that Malynes might have been the scion of an aldermanic family in Antwerp.[8] In *Lex Mercatoria*, Malynes identifies his father as a mint master, and he was himself conspicuously involved with a whole spectrum of money matters throughout his life. He was an assay master of the mint and especially concerned about the functioning of the foreign currency exchanges.

Variously on record from 1586–1626, Malynes appears first to have been an active and reasonably successful merchant (apparently in the staple trade).[9] *Lex Mercatoria* indicates that he was also a diamond dealer at some point and clearly an inveterate projector, for example, proposing the establishment of a centralized house of commerce, expansion of apiculture and the revitalization of the fishing and mining industries, and the institution of non-usurious financial societies and pawn houses to help the poor, for whom he was a long-standing and moving advocate. He was fluent enough in several languages besides English—at least Dutch, Latin, French, Portuguese, and Spanish—to translate for the King and the Court.[10] Extant documents suggest that he, like a number of other merchants, was part of Walsingham's spy network, and he offered similarly to assist Robert Cecil.[11] He was also imprisoned as an embezzler in the 1590s, although under murky circumstances that involved the dealings of a notorious financier.[12] He was imprisoned again around 1619 as an honest bankrupt, whose participation in a royally authorized project to alleviate a chronic shortage of coin led to his financial distress.[13] Apparently it did not lead to his ruin, however, since by 1622 he was again, with Sir Robert Cotton (and others), by invitation of the Lord President of the Privy Council, addressing a remonstrance on foreign currency exchange to the king.[14]

In the waning years of Elizabeth's reign and then under James, Malynes had himself been a member of two royal commissions on exchange and coinage—in 1600 and 1609—and evidently a person with "extraordinary access to royal advisers," whose extant petitions and memoranda to the Privy Council between 1600 and 1620 are more numerous than any other merchant's. Indeed, on their basis, Lynn Muchmore has suggested that Malynes is "the most likely candidate" among the mercantile writers to have "influenced policy during the Jacobean years" ("Malynes," 337). By Malynes' own testimony in *Lex Mercatoria*, he considered himself above all a merchant experienced in double-entry bookkeeping, international finance, and mercantile custom and law, and he defiantly flings in the face of his long-standing merchant antagonist Edward Misselden the fact that as early as 1623 his "much respected" *magnum opus* had already been "translated into Spanish and French" (*Center*, 136). The *Short Title Catalogue* lists five editions of *Lex Mercatoria* in England alone between its appearance in 1622 and 1686.

In *Lex Mercatoria*, Malynes is both an opinionated observer and an absorber—a virtual blotter—of the views and texts of others. He holds that since "no man can be perfect in any one Science, . . . it [is] not amisse for a man to have knowledge in most or in all things" (258). He is a reader of Galen, probably as mediated by such a rendering as Helkiah Crooke's, and of "all the Bookes of *Paracelsus*," as also of Aristotle, Plato, the Geneva Bible, Cicero, Cato, Seneca, Vergil, Horace, Ovid, Chaucer, Erasmus, Copernicus, Calvin, More's *Utopia*, John Dee on navigation and Thomas Wilson and Thomas Culpepper on usury, at least part of Francis Bacon's *Novum Organum*, colonial accounts (Guiana, Virginia, the Bermudas), Jean Bodin's *Response to Malestroit*, and such "chroniclers" as William of Malmesbury, Froissart, Grafton, Holinshed, John Hayward, and Francesco Guicciardini, to name only a representative few writers specifically identified or readily recognized in his text.[15]

In *The Circle of Commerce or The Ballance of Trade*, Malynes' antagonist Misselden scornfully but accurately identifies two more obscure sources on which Malynes drew in *Lex Mercatoria*, namely, Thomas Milles's *The Customers Alphabet and Primer* (apparent inspiration of Malynes' central comparison of body, soul, and spirit to commodities, money, and exchange) and Milles's *The Custumers Replie* (apparent source of Malynes' phrase "*by Nature admirable, and by Art made amiable*").[16] Milles, a customer (customs collector) in Sandwich, addressed the subjects of exchange, usury, and regulated companies, specifically the Merchant Adventurers, all of which engaged Misselden and Malynes, and his writings would likely have attracted them both. The demonstrable accuracy of Misselden's charge of borrowing suggests that we have here examples of the absorptive, appropriative way the mind of Malynes worked and the extent to which it reflected his culture. In combination with Malynes' learning and wide experience, his sources and borrowings actually make his writing more historically interesting for my purpose, namely, to comprehend the metaphoricity of his world view.

In every sense, Malynes' view is mixed. Like his life, it straddles the Elizabethan and Jacobean eras, the past and the present, as well as the principled and utopian and the politic, merely expedient, or even corrupt.[17] Malynes strives for stability and coherence, but contrarily also for inclusiveness, including pages and pages of comparative weights and other measures, foreign terms, rates, and coins, and such bits of practical advice as how to whiten yellowed pearls (79). There are enough of such bits and tables, in fact, for *Lex Mercatoria* to have been labeled an almanac by its modern editor. Malynes also seeks form and teleological direction, sometimes assuming and at other times struggling to fashion and refashion tropes that might capture or create them, yet he finds a digression, anecdote, or additional rhetorical flourish irresistible, even when paradoxical or problematic. He is well along in years when he writes the *Mercatoria* and sees more than his categories can accommodate, but he would adhere to them if he could.[18] In this respect, he is hardly King Lear, but at moments he resembles a number of Jonsonian characters, and he is easily imagined as a merchant, along with William Co-kayne, in the audience of Donne, the Dean of St. Paul's.[19]

As earlier noted, discussion of Malynes customarily focuses on economic theory, nearly always in comparison to the theories of Misselden and Thomas Mun. Although I do not want to rehearse this comparison once again, some sense of it and, more importantly, of the economy of the period to which it pertains is needed. Usually comparison has worked to Malynes' disadvantage, since Misselden and Mun grasped the governing effect over time of the balance of trade on the functioning of the monetary system and the primary importance of a favorable balance, whereas Malynes, whose view was apparently more short-term (and arguably more acutely sensitive to immediate effects on the poor), thought monetary policy and especially the exchange rate to be the truly critical factor. Economic historians have chorically praised Mun in particular for anticipating one of their basic principles regarding trade (not irrelevantly coincident with Mun's atypically early-modern clean and lean prose). Some have even attributed to him an awareness of the self-regulating mechanism of specie flow (sequentially responsive to a positive balance of trade, inflowing specie, rising prices, a negative balance, outflowing specie, falling prices, and then a recurrence of the cycle) *and* his suppression of this awareness in favor of a seemingly endless expansion of trade modeled on the practice of the Netherlands.[20] As B. E. Supple has argued, however, such an expansion was problematic at best, and Mun's discounting of the monetary impact was a gross oversimplification.[21] Whereas economics in our own time has emphasized "the impact of money on economic activity," Rudolph Blitz has observed that neoclassical economics "conceived of money as a veil and as being more or less neutral in its effect."[22] While Mun's writing is full of contradictions, as Andrea Finkelstein has demonstrated, logically his propounding the absolute primacy of trade is on its way to this later neoclassical view.

In an extensive analysis, Supple stresses that a radical decline in export of cloth ultimately caused England's economic crisis in the early 1620s and that "a purely monetary explanation" must therefore be "inadequate." Yet his major argument is that this decline and the resulting unfavorable balance of trade occurred "*primarily* because monetary manipulations in Europe [accompanying the outbreak of the Thirty Years War] amounted to a virtual devaluation of foreign currencies and induced highly unfavorable terms of trade for English goods." In language that is notable for its relevance to Malynes' monetary emphasis, he further reenforces this point: "the *effective* and *immediate* cause of the depression . . . was a series of currency manipulations in some of the principal European markets for English textiles." Subsequently he adds, "The mechanism which *transmuted* an unfavourable balance of trade into an outflow of bullion was, of course, *the rate of exchange*. A heavier demand for foreign currency would drive the rate down until, if it continued long enough, it became cheaper to export specie [from England] than to buy a bill of exchange [an instrument of credit to transfer money abroad]."[23]

Recalling my earlier discussion of Cicero's *De Oratore*, I note that Supple's "transmuted" is as much as to say "translated" or, indeed, "exchanged" in a Ciceronian description of the workings of metaphor. While making this connection, however, I want to resist a premature leap to structural homologies of the sort Jean Joseph Goux and Marc Shell have theorized.[24] Their theories would level what is ambivalent and historically significant in Malynes' mixed view and thus cancel its value as a "specific instance . . . that might produce [the] surprising or overdetermined result" for which Mark Osteen and Martha Woodmansee have called in *New Economic Criticism* (34). Moreover, my conception of metaphor as an exchange that is transactive and productive is not the same as the mirroring structures Goux and Shell envision. Extending this observation to basic terminology, I note that the wing of a bat and the foreleg of a mouse are homologous, properly speaking; the wing of a bird and the wing of an insect, although visually more similar, are not; instead, they are analogically, apparently, and, indeed, perceptually related. In this, they are closer to metaphor than to biological (or chemical) science, on which the current definition of the term *homology* is based. While the fascinating and seductive "homologies" of Goux and Shell (Osteen and Woodmansee, 15–18) are cultural rather than biological, they are necessarily also metaphorized unless, of course, they are essentially metonymic, as in fact they appear to be: Goux's first move, for example is to assert that exchange—semiotic, economic, and psychoanalytical—is substitution, that is, metonymy (*Symbolic Economies*, 2). To follow Goux in translating a passively reduplicating historical structure or a unidirectional series of structures (e.g., Marxist, Freudian, Lacanian, or all three) to an earlier structure (e.g., Renaissance) outside this series may be a valid and interesting operation, but it is also an additionally tropic one. Goux's homologies are actually fictions. Shell, as earlier noted, refers to supposedly homologous structures as "tropic interactions," which are therefore at least potentially creative, but elsewhere he, too, identifies exchange with substitution.[25] For either of these theorists, an axis of substitution can be accessed from either metonymy or metaphor, the latter conceived to be passive or inert. In sum, I hope to examine the metaphoricity of Malynes' worldview, among whose components the economy looms large, without simply plugging in a series of predetermined homologous fictions, even as I interpret the connections of economic with other cultural expressions.

Fredric Jameson's critique of homologism, which he glosses as isomorphism or structural parallelism, and identifies as "The true target of the Althusserian critique" of expressive causality, or mediation among various structural levels of reality, is additionally useful as a point of reference here. Its immediate relevance is evident in another, more modern term for mediation that Jameson offers, namely, *transcoding*, or, in terms of my present argument, substitution—the metonymic shell game. Jameson explains homologism as a "simplistic and mechanical model" of relationship among various zones or sectors of social and cultural life, insofar as at "some level of abstraction," it renders differences among these "the same."[26] Jameson's own critique is difficult, however, since he is concerned both to honor Althusser's understanding that manifestly different superstructural levels are not "mere reflexes, epiphenomenal projections of infrastructural realities" and also to preserve mediation in some form. Accepting such Althusserian difference, Jameson also acknowledges straightforwardly, though again "At some level," that it "is certainly true" that the levels are reflexes and projections, and he further corrects Althusser by affirming that the very differences among levels are paradoxically themselves mediatory: thus "the distinguishing of two phenomena from each other, their structural separation, the affirmation that they are not the same . . . is *also* a form of mediation." This is so, because "one cannot enumerate the differences between things except against the background of some more general identity" (41–42).

Difference cannot be originary, then, and "at some level" it must be an appearance. Interaction and exchange between and among levels at this underlying and material, but also abstract and conceptual, level are the substantial froth on a fundamental unity. In light of my second and third chapters, distantly recognizable here is the tension between nominalism and realism, manifestation and essence, difference and oneness. Jameson's position also recalls the crux of the Ricoeur-Derrida debate about dead metaphor and sublation: Derrida reasserts the claim of the material base that puts in question the status of the sublating scaffold, which at once rests on the base and rises above it. Or perhaps Jameson's theory is more likely a *translation* of these tensions, that is, a genuinely productive and creative revision, and, in reality, itself another metaphor for them. As in Ricoeur's theory of metaphorical signification, examined in chapter two, where the word's difference, though strongly defended, is ultimately subsumed by the sentence, so in Jameson's version of mediation, in the name of reason and more precisely of *ratio*, the differentiating structural level at some point bows to the underlying identity. My *analogy* between these very different arguments, Ricoeur's position on the structure of metaphorical meaning and Jameson's position on the structure of culture and society, would recognize the possibility of a dynamic exchange, indeed a true conversation about metaphor, or translation, between them. I endeavor to do so without prematurely turning the one into the other "at some level," however, and, more exactly, without turning linguistic and rhetorical phenomena into economic and fully material ones, or vice versa. This would be to turn language *into* history and history *into* language, rather than to expose and to examine their productive, conceptual interaction, as I seek to do now.

Supple's argument, as recounted to this point, is that "the effective and immediate cause" of the economic crisis in the 1620s was monetary manipulation and that the rate of exchange "transmuted" this—carried it in modified, or indeed exchanged, form—to an unfavorable balance of trade and thence to a loss of bullion. This chain of causation has more detailed links. In the monetary anarchy that raged on the Continent in the early 1620s, enhancement or debasement had an immediate effect on the money of account, and lagging inflation in the countries enhancing *or* debasing currency (either to the same effect: less silver represented per unit of money) meant that an English merchant had to accept less or take a loss when he returned home the proceeds by exchange or else he had to raise his prices, with the result that he was priced out of the market.[27] Market conditions would also have encouraged him to return the proceeds in commodities, since these had become cheaper in terms of silver, and thus to try to recoup his profits. These alternatives all meant less inflow of specie to England and further pressure on the coinage there.

Additionally, the higher valuation of gold than silver in the mint par of England meant, by Gresham's Law, the less valued metal would flow out, or, as Malynes put it, "you cannot advance or inhance the one, but you abate and diminish the other. . . . whereas England by continuance of eleven to one hath beene a great looser of gold; so now by advancing the same not onely to twelve to one, but to $13^{1/5}$ for one, there hath followed a verie great losse of our silver which is over much abated [undervalued]" in exchange (310). An oft-cited passage in Rice Vaughan's contemporaneous *Discourse of Coin and Coinage* efficiently sums up the interrelated excess of imports over exports and the desperate shortage of coin in England:

When your Money is richer in substance, and lower in price than that of your Neighbour Nations, as our Silver is, than the Silver in the *Low-Countries*, how can you expect that the Merchant, who only seeketh his profit, will ever bring hither any Silver, when he can sell it in the *Low-Countries* at a higher Rate, and make more Money of it here by returning of it from thence hither, or by Exchange, or by Commodities? or, if any Merchant do bring Silver hither, it is to sell it to such who will have a higher rate for it, than can be produced at the Mint, . . . And again, . . . if our Silver be so rich, as the Merchant by transporting it into the *Low-Countries*, or elsewhere, can make profit by returning it in Commodities, or by Exchange; or that, which is yet more clear and evident, by returning it in Gold, must not our Silver be inevitably exhausted?" [144–45, cf. 42–43, 148]

Supple provides another apposite yet more alarming quotation from a contemporary manuscript that denies even the gold to England, for " 'The gold shall go for France, the silver for Holland, the commodities for England' " (92).

Economic historians have marshaled any number of reasons why classical economic models do not apply to the period in question. Among these are speed (or rather its lack) and tradition:

Economic pressures which, in the perfect models of classical economics, lowered monetary values while maintaining full employment of resources, were likely, in Stuart society, to provoke chronic unemployment or underemployment as they met the relatively rigid line of prices and costs. For an economy whose market values contained a significant traditional element *and which depended so much on the availability of metallic coin for its continuing activity*, fluctuations in the physical supply of liquid assets could impose longterm strains which cannot be measured by an exercise in formal logic. . . . [The fact is that] *men could not pay their debts, or borrow money, or buy goods, or sell them at profitable prices* [Supple, 177: my emphasis].

Describing "chronic long-run [economic] problems" that preclude singleminded reliance on the balance of trade as a corrective, Blitz adds to Supple's reasons for the extraordinarily protracted working of the automatic adjustment of the specie flow "the inflow of bullion from the Americas into Europe and its substantial subsequent outflow to the Orient [effectually a form of demonetization]," plus "demand [in]elasticities for oriental imports," the [systemic] limits to foreign investment, and the workings of bimetallism.[28]

Contemporary impediments to the working of a true bimetallic standard (proportion of silver to gold), which would otherwise have tended to adjust and perhaps to stabilize ratios, included a charge for minting, seigniorage (the king's cut),[29] and legal restrictions on export of specie or on exchange (Blitz, 162). Perhaps the most basic problem of all, as Supple suggests, was that the nations of Europe were unable to move together in altering the official prices of gold and silver (165). This is a problem that Malynes perceived at some level, as when he conceived (or dreamed) of an exchange based on "iust proportions"; when he spoke of trade as a way to build international community, as "a communication and entercourse betweene all nations . . . whetby [*sic:* whereby] one Common-weale should liue with another," as God intended in distributing "his seueral and distinct [material] Blessings to diuers Climats"; and when he decried William Cokayne's notorious scheme to corner the European market for finished, as well as undressed, cloth, because it violated such "common entercourse and mutual[ity]."[30] Unfortunately, however, Malynes' desperate solution to the inability of the nations of Europe to co-operate, namely, a unilateral fixing of monetary value, was unrealistic. His vision of economic co-operation was also fitful. He did not object if the balance of trade or the rate of exchange tipped in England's favor and, like his mercantile contemporaries, sought ways to make it do so.[31]

In the Jacobean economy a drain of silver could become catastrophic whether or not it coincided with a net drain of bullion because it meant that "the *effective* quantity of money" was significantly reduced. For most daily purposes, silver simply "*was* 'money'" (Supple, 172–73). No contemporary writer suggests that England offered merchants an attractive destination for silver, yet silver was effectively the medium of domestic exchange, as well as of foreign trade: "the greatest part of the Commerce of the Kingdom, and almost all the Inland Commerce, is made in *Silver,* the want whereof doth greatly prejudice the same" (Vaughan, 72). Its lack could mean severe economic hardship even if the specie flow were neutral. Additionally, in an economy that was not well monetized (as in this period) and in a market for precious metals that was still thin, it took little to trigger instability, and correction was slow to come (Blitz, 155, 160–61). In such an economy, the desire to amass bullion or "treasure," which has been considered a defining feature of the period, credibly accords with Supple's diagnosis that in fact it was "really a fear concerning the supply" of coinage, or as Malynes saw it, the "causes of the decay of Trade in England, are almost all of them comprised in one, which is the *want* [lack] of money."[32] Such a fear, related fundamentally to the chronic threat of unrest among unemployed subsistence workers in the cloth industry, characterized government concern and action in the period, ineffectual as they often proved to be. The basis of this fear was pragmatic, material, and very real.[33] Moralizing it simply as greed, whether then or now, is economically naive. Again, when set against Jacobean economic realities, Gerrard de Malynes' preoccupation with the primacy of monetary issues makes considerable sense, as does his correlative and striking sympathy for the poor.

In *A History of the Modern Fact*, Mary Poovey suggests that Thomas Mun's "antipathy to [i.e., his avoidance of] figurative language seems to echo his antibullionist position," and she adds gingerly, "Figurative language might have seemed like money to Mun: a medium of exchange that too frequently seemed valuable for its own sake rather than for what it could signify (or purchase)."[34] The chief antithesis to Mun she intends is Malynes, in whose writing she finds that "ornamental [i.e., figurative] language dominates every page"—or seems to (79). This was my impression of *Lex Mercatoria* too when I first met it, independent of Poovey's view. On closer examination, however, I found surprisingly fewer figures in its more than 500 pages than my impression had led me to expect. Of course there is the central metaphor of body, soul, and spirit for commodities, money, and exchange, "the three Essentiall Parts of Trafficke," and it accounts for the organization of the volume into three corresponding parts, although it is otherwise fitfully maintained (58).[35] Other bodily images, usually normative but occasionally diseased,[36] occur, as sometimes do natural images of sea, stars, and the like; a few images of navigation, such as the compass and rudder; and also of manufacture: a ship, a clock, a press, a scale, a sundial. Slightly better than a half dozen mythological references, largely monstrous, also occur: Scylla and Charybdis, Phaeton's horses, Hercules' foot, Momus, the Hydra. Nearly all the similitudes are explicit comparisons whose function appears to be largely illustrative rather than deliberately expansive or creative.[37] They evoke a shared world and most often a familiarly coded one. Not unlike the denser figures in Busirane's tapestry or procession, they are culturally paradigmatic, encapsulating perception, response, judgment, or a combination of these. While they would have been familiar to an Elizabethan, they would have been equally so to Jonson, Donne, Bacon, or, indeed, to any Jacobean with a grammar school education.[38]

Malynes' is a world of physical things, but, as earlier noted, it is also one of stories, hence noticeably of narrative voice, and of digressions, although his frequent self-consciousness regarding the latter paradoxically reflects a significant concern with structure: for example, he might note that an anecdote is a recreative diversion amidst factual detail, offer it as an aid to memory, or as a witness to experience. He observes in a chapter about plantations (colonies), that its inclusion at first "may seeme strange to the Law of Merchants," but that it really is not, since merchants undertake such ventures; in his chapter on alchemy, he hopes not to have given "offence to the Reader of this Booke, seeing it is but in one Chapter (accidentally) handled." He also apologizes for a literally, or rather, an etymologically "exorbitant [outside the orbit] chapter" regarding the division of commodities by lots and lotteries, insofar as these belong in his book as a form of "vendition," or selling and buying, engaged in by "adventurers," a term which also doubles for merchants and insurers.[39]

Again, Malynes' world, besides being full of things, is shaped by theory—especially but not exclusively Aristotelian—whose very estrangement from modern readers signals construction, fictiveness, and metaphor, not least because juxtaposed to so many intractably material, practical things. Yet some of these things are themselves infused with value. Coming as if by tour to the fifth chapter in the second part of the *Mercatoria*, which concerns the making of coinage, Malynes reviews topical ground covered in the preceding four chapters: "From the transcendent contemplatiue studie of [natural] Philosophers, of vapours and exhalations, to the Essence of Sulphur and Mercury generated into Ores of Mettalls, Wee have produced [Latin *producere*: "to bring forth, to lead"], Gold, Siluer, and Copper to the Mint to be conuerted into Moneys" (274). The actual conversion is delayed until the sixth chapter, however, with the fifth mainly devoted to the nature of the materials—gold, silver, and copper—that are ordinarily used for coin. Malynes' description of the qualities of gold is memorable for its insistent infusion of value:

> Such is the qualitie of fine Gold (by reason of the equall proportion of the foure Elements therein, that none is predominant ouer the other) that the fire doth not consume it, being also hot and drie of nature, neither is it subject to any other Element, for there is no rust or scurfe that doth diminish the goodnesse, or wasteth the substance; it doth abide the fretting and liquors of salt and vinegre without damage, which weareth any other thing; it needs no fire to be made Gold, as other mettals do, for it is gold as soone as it is

found; it draweth without wooll, as it were wooll; it is easily spread in leaues
of marvellous thinnesse; you may adorne or guild any other mettall with it;
it is not inferiour for making of any vessells; in colour it resembleth the
Celestiall bodies; it defileth not the thing it toucheth, as Siluer and other
mettals; it is not stinking in smell; the spirit of it can by art be extracted, and
the bodie (being as red earth) can neuer be moulten without the spirit be
againe added thereunto, as it were infusing life: and lastly, it is medicinable
and maketh glad the heart of man [275].

In no way can we consider this a literal or neutral description. Even if largely
conventional, it is strange, fanciful, and symbolic to modern eyes. Yet the
qualities Malynes values in gold are chiefly natural and material, with glances
at the more specifically aesthetic, the supernatural ("as it were infusing
life"), and the medicinal.[40] The jarring reminder that gold does not
"stink"—its tone here borrowed from Bottom the Weaver—in itself testifies to the infusion of otherwise overwhelmingly refined value. The whole
description sorts oddly with Malynes' abrupt, businesslike approach right
after it—"But for our purpose . . . it requireth to make Crowne Gold fit for
moneys" to have $1/12$ part alloy of silver and copper—and with his later,
hard-headed assertion that England's "losse of silver farre exceedeth the gold
in [economic] value" or, indeed, with his knowingly futile wish "that we
were of the Scithians mind, who contemned siluer and gold."[41]

In the next chapter, the sixth, Malynes is also at pains to demystify another assay master's supposition that the "Mysterie" of the fineness of Gold
and Silver is as "intricate" (perplexed and perplexing) as "the Transubstantiation of the Papists Sacrament," a comparison that will return later in this
chapter. To do so, he offers several reasonably clear pages to explain the
minting process, which are matter-of-factly based on what "I had obserued
and knowne aboue fortie yeares, my father also hauing beene a Mint-master."[42] Such contrasting perspectives between essential value and the practical business at hand abound in Malynes' book, and they mutually heighten
one another. As in the instance of his description of gold, they contribute
to an impression of metaphorical construction as well.

Discussing Malynes' concern for structure three paragraphs above, I
characterized as both "literal" and "etymological" his use of the word "exorbitant" to describe an apparently digressive chapter; more precisely, his
use recurs to the material roots of the word: Latin *ex*, "outside, away from,"
and *orbita*, "path, orbit." Thus it is actually figurative, whether in itself or as
indicated by the outset of his book where he draws an *analogy* between the

"*Globe of the World . . . composed of Earth and Waters* and "*the Bodie of* Lex Mercatoria, *made and framed of the Merchants Customes, and the Sea-Lawes*" (sig. A6v). Like Malynes' description of gold, even his "literal" language can carry a figurative charge that is not explicit and probably not deliberate, although in this instance it might well be, since he returns to an explicit analogy between the Globe and his book a second time, some eighty-six pages before the apology for exorbitance occurs (119, 205).

Another figurative pun in the *Mercatoria* whose deliberation is uncertain occurs more than once on the word *commonwealth*, as when Malynes refers to the "merchandizing" (commodification) of monetary exchange as "the canker of Englands Common-wealth," incidentally also the title of the earliest of his economic tracts (408). The monetary context of Malynes' statement ensures that "Common-wealth" will carry the sense "wealth, riches," now obsolete, as well as the larger, less exclusively material sense "welfare, well-being,"or sound "body politic."[43] Such figurative charges are often active in *Lex Mercatoria*, and they further contribute to our impression—and likely to Mun's—that Malynes' world, or rather his outlook on it, is distinctly metaphoric.

In an explicit analogy, Malynes uses the word *symbolization* in a more physically embedded way than is now current. Wise merchants, he tells us, have observed "that as the elements are ioined by Symbolization, the aire to the fire by warmenesse, the water to the aire by moysture, the earth to the water by coldnesse; So is Exchange ioyned to Monyes, and Monys to Commodities by their proper qualities and effects" (65). Offering the first part of Malynes' analogy as an example, the *OED* defines *symbolization*, a technical conception in early physics, as "the fact of 'symbolizing' in nature or quality; agreement or participation in qualities" (1.a)[44] In Malynes' analogy, although the elements may thus be joined, this working of nature merely affords a model for that of the economy; that is, Malynes does not explicitly assert that the economy participates in—or "symbolizes"—nature (or vice versa). Yet within the familiar analogical universe structurally present in the parallelism of his sentence, he certainly seems to. In other words, it is difficult to read the analogy as merely an analogy. Its linguistic and syntactical elements, like its natural ones, interrelate, implying that its natural and economic ones do as well. Its rhetoric thus evokes as economic reality what is actually a translation of physical reality to it. Here indeed is the content of form. Once again, the transmutation—the metaphorical crossover—is implicit and seemingly the result of perceptual habit embedded in language. Aristotle affords an additional explanation of this habit when he describes the metaphorical transference resulting from analogy as being "possible whenever there are four terms so related that the second is to the first, as the fourth to the third; for one may then put the fourth in place of the second, and the second in place of the fourth."[45] This transference of fourth to second or vice versa goes beyond merely associative relation to participation and *virtual* identity. It invites substitution. Moreover, with these observations, we are momentarily transported back to my discussion of proprietary participation and virtualism in chapter 3 on the Sacrament.

In addition to the analogically conceived universe and Aristotelian analogy, however, the emphasis in the education of merchants on the study of proportion (a/b = c/d) is also suggestive in relation to Malynes' conspicuous penchant for analogy. A trained eye for proportion was needed for the employment of methods for gauging the volume of non-stardardized containers, and many other commercial problems similarly involved proportion, such as bimetallism (ratio of silver to gold), "exchange rates, brokerage, [and] division of profits." Bruce Carruthers and Wendy Espeland recount the "cognitive aspects" of such skills and the special training merchants were likely to acquire. They also cite Michael Baxandall's demonstration of how Italian painters engaged the "gauging skills" of such (educated) viewers, an appeal we might easily extend to contemporary architecture (59, cf. 50–52). Malynes' proportional rhetoric, like so much in *Lex Mercatoria*, thus has the ambivalent capacity to look cognitively up-to-date, as well as Aristotelian or traditional. This capacity provides an unusual glimpse of the workings— specifically of the simultaneity, ambiguity, and overdetermination—of vestigial and emergent perceptions and thus of perceptual change.

The leisurely beginning of *Lex Mercatoria* is crucial in conveying other perceptual habits of Malynes. The first chapter opens with a little history of "the Law-Merchant" intended to exhibit its antiquity, authority, and value. Malynes finds this "Law" to be grounded in the "sociable" nature of human beings as God created them and in their need for the "mutuall contribution of offices" to live civilly and well. Then he carefully lays out the initiation and development of commerce as barter, "according to number, weight, and measure, and after, to auoid confusion, by *a commune pignus* [common token] currant mutuall, which we call money." The most ancient evidence of this last development, he tells us, is Abraham's "purchasing for money a field for buriall." With commerce came "the beginning of the Law-Merchant," which is older than any written law, including the "very morall Law it selfe, as written by *Moses*," and which actually turns out to be "the Custome of Merchants" (1–2). Malynes explains that Cicero's definition of true

law as "*Recta Ratio, naturae congruens, diffusa in omnes, Constans sempiterna . . .*
[or] right Reason, agreeable to Nature in all points, diffused and spread in
all Nations, consisting perpetually without abrogation" belongs even "more
naturally and properly" to this Custom of Merchants than to the "*ius gen-
tium,* or the Law of Nations" (3). Now comes a distinction between law and
custom, the definition of a merchant, and a layout of "the methode" of his
book, which is also an epitome of "what a compleate merchant ought to
know" (4–7). Comparison of this epitome with the 86 additional chapters
of the book in toto that follow again shows both Malynes' planning and his
penchant for amplification, extension, and digression. Although the topics
he enumerates include arithmetic, weights and measures, and the "daies and
times . . . and the beginnings of the yeare in all countries," few modern
readers are likely to be prepared for the next three chapters treating these
subjects, which, with chapter 1, provide the essential context for his first
major conceptual chapter, the fifth, which in due course follows (6).

The first of these conceptualizing chapters, which is on "Time," understandably, if expansively, cautions merchants carefully to observe

> the yeeres, moneths, weekes, and dayes, and (sometimes) the houres of their
> negotiation[s], with the course of the Moone, and the ebbing and flowing
> of waters, the variation of windes, and alterations of weathers, for stormes at
> the seas, and vnseasonable Times on land, whereby the haruests doe faile,
> and commodities become to be plentifull or scarce, and the prices thereof
> deere or good cheape [I.ii.8–9].

The rhythm of this passage certainly makes an impression, and it even responds suggestively to old-fashioned scanning: if nothing else, Malynes,
who appears to have been only conventionally religious, is to an extent the
product of what produced the prose of the King James Bible. If form has
content, this passage, with its combination of Ecclesiastes and the bottom
line, those prices "deere or good cheape," conveys—indeed, translates or
carries across to us—some sense of a biblical rhythm in our existence, even
our economic existence, and in this sense it is metaphorical. Biblical language, as well as rhythm, often permeates Renaissance texts, and not
uniquely Malynes' with metaphorical resonance. In a commercial context,
however, this resonance is both surprising and significant.[46] Functionally, it
again intimates a larger pattern.

Malynes turns next to a definition of time, which he declares "verie difficult, if we consider, that Time is inseperably conioyned with Eternitie,"
but he quickly adds that "if we obserue the attribute[s] of Time, and doe

distinguish things orderly, we shall easily perceiue what Time is, and make vse thereof." Ever practical, he lists these attributes, which are likely derived from relevant proverbs or "sayings" in a commonplace book and ultimately from a published collection, one or more by Erasmus being obvious candidates.[47] Malynes' long list, which resonates with memories of many a Renaissance drama or sonnet sequence, as well as with those of Roman sources, is worth quoting:

Time is the consumer of all things, *Tempus edax rerum.*
Time is the discouerer of all things, *Veritas filia Temporis.*
Time is vncertaine and wanteth bounds, *Tempora mutantur &c.*
Times minutes past, no treasure can restore, *Irrevocabile Tempus.*
Time doth pierce the hardest flint, *Gutta cavat lapidem, non vi sed sepe cadendo.*
Time hath a salue for all extremities, and yet begetteth vsurie.
Times office is to end the hate of foes.
Times glorie is to calme contending kings.
Time is a tutor both to good and bad, and doth discouer the affections of the mind.
Time offers still each houre to do amisse.
Time breedeth griefe, and heales when Art doth faile.
By Time and Wisdome passions are supprest.
In Time finall wedges cleaue the hardest oakes.
Time is the Anchor both of Trueth and Right.
Time hath set downe the compasse of his course.
Times motions do equall the reeling Sunne.
Time measureth our actions.
Time is the best gouernour of all our councells.
Time on the weariest wretch bestoweth rest.
Both Life and Loue in time must have an end [9].

Shakespeare's Polonius or William Cecil, Lord Burghley, could hardly have done better. Nor, perhaps, could have Lakoff and Johnson. "Time is money" is one of the two sayings with which Lakoff and Johnson's popular first book initiates evidence for their theory that human conceptualization is basically metaphorical.[48] They would likely have been much taken with Malynes' list of the metaphorical attributes that define time, had they known it, since it provides a historico-cultural dimension otherwise lacking in their evidence and relevant to its theorization.

Malynes' typically summary conclusion after considering his list is that "we shall find upon due consideration, that Time is but a distinction and measure of all things and betweene all things." His definition is not much different, in fact, from Lakoff and Johnson's "Time is money," since Malynes will soon show us that money measures value (yardstick-like) and coheres in a single system with time. While clearly aware of the ascribed quality of time's various definitions, he simply opts for the definition he thinks most pertinent to merchants' practical affairs. In his own culturally stated way, however, he seems dimly aware, since appreciative, of the metaphoricity of the various attributes he instances, even as he exercises his *ratio*—his "reason, discrimination, and judgment"—to choose his own.

Malynes proceeds from his proverbs and sayings to an equally large argument about the "reuolution of Time . . . wherein things returne to the same, or like estate wherein they were before" (9). The motions of the heavens, the seasons of the year, the sun, the moon, all are instanced. Then come the ages of the world (at length and from various sources), the various beginnings of the year (with explanations), and the better to explain the basis for these views, a great deal about the zodiac, eclipses, and the like. He records further variations in the measuring of time (again at length), which might incidentally be noted to have carried a very substantial element of cultural awareness, if not relativism, within a narrowly economic sphere. This chapter concludes with his proposal for reforming the Julian calendar, a reasoned alternative to Pope Gregory's, likely sparked by the commercial inconvenience of England's refusal to adopt what was well on its way to becoming standard calendrical time.

Malynes' next, brief chapter (I.iii) focuses on number. Mainly it treats numerology, pointing to the "mysteries and vertues . . . contained in numbers," as observed in Scripture, for example, by "the ancient Fathers," such as "*Ierome, Augustine, Origen, Ambrose Basil, Athanasius, Hilarius, Rabanus, Beda*, and others; amongst whom Doctor *Rabanus* hath made a booke of the[se] vertues" (17). Malynes, probably having consulted such a numerological compendium as Rabanus', is fascinated by the significant coincidence of numbers in the Bible and in nature and notably by patterned markers of time: seven sabbaths, the seventh month, seven-day feasts and fasts, "To say nothing of the Seuen Planets running their courses" (18). Guided sequentially by the numbers one to twelve, however, his eye roves from the unity of the Godhead, through the elements and human sensorium, to the Law and the prophets. His enumeration ends with everything from the twelve tribes of Israel or twelve stones in the Jordan River, to twelve apostles, twelve baskets of bread gathered, and twelve signs of the zodiac. This is the kind of performance that impresses readers with his medievalism. It should be noted, however, that his numerological interests were hardly anomalous in the reigns of the Tudors and first two Stuarts. In some quarters, they are still on the perceptual map today.

This chapter concludes with Malynes' report of "some Indians and Heathen[s]" in Guiana who lack a "diuision or account of Times and Number," by which he means "just like ours," for he proceeds to explain how they reckon time by the moons and employ a numeric system from one to ten, then ten plus one, ten plus two, and so on—presumably implying some coincidence with ours. He also reports how they mark the passage of time by subtracting sticks from little bundles of them, a method that enables them to keep track of the time of an appointment, when they "performe their promise, which may be a president to many Christians" (19). This account from the frontier may seem (but really isn't) an odd appendage to medieval numerology, as well as an instance of the mixture of past and present found in Malynes' text. The reason for its inclusion is not far to seek, however. Right after it, Malynes ties up this third chapter by remarking the "coherence" of number with time and thus of this chapter with the preceding one, and then, insofar as a providential God has made all things subject to "*Number, Weight,* and *Measure*," he leads us forward to the next chapter (I.iv) concerning the latter two of these (19). The account of the heathen, whose non-European practices might have been supposed to challenge the universality of God's providential nature, has been shown instead to support it. In chapter 1, Malynes declared his subject to be "not the spirituall but the civill life of man and the meanes thereto conducing": now basic constructs of civil life, time and number, have been shown to have a natural correspondence with one another—indeed, a true symbolization (1–2). They participate in a single, unified system and rhythm, as do the merchants whose traffic employs and depends on them.

Where the chapter on number is brief, chapter 4, concerning weights and measure, amounts to thirty-nine pages. Much of it catalogues the daunting variety of weights and measures for the different countries of Europe and for their commodities (wine, corn, beer, salt, wood, sea-coal, cloth, and the like). This chapter also includes measures for land and a discussion of dyeing, the latter of which he incorporates for three reasons: first, "because the quantitie of the stuffe wherby things are dyed, are done by weight"; second, in order to enable merchants better to judge colors, "knowing the nature thereof"; and third, in order to avoid practices of dyeing that fraudulently render cloth heavier than it is in fact (54). Incidental advice and tips are scattered throughout the chapter: warm water sooner runs through a hole than cold water, for example, or how to test and evaluate a scale, or the need to check a measure of corn against its weight.

The framing of chapter 4 manages simultaneously to be both moral and material. Malynes notes at its outset that weights and measure are necessary "to giue euerie man his owne" and, of course, "to buy and sell by" (19). They are the means "to distinguish *Meum* and *Tuum*" in accordance with law and the common consent of nations. Near chapter's end, he emphasizes that if English cloth is again, as formerly, "truely made, [it] will be more vendible beyond the Seas, where many complaints are daily made of the false making thereof." The keynote of his final advice is, by informed experience, "to distinguish truth from falshood, and . . . to know the goodnesse of things" (57–58). Here, each keynoted noun is materially referential, but these nouns are not the ones we would be likely to use nowadays to describe a shipment of cloth or spices. Repeatedly Malynes' language evokes echoes of other and larger contexts: "all *Substantiall* things . . . are by Diuine providence *subject* and gouerned by Number, Weight, and Measure"; "Weight and Measure doe controle each other, and . . . Number giueth *denomination* [distinction] to them both, to discerne *truth* from *falshood*"; "the weight of a Cloth is more to be regarded than the Measure, because the weight containeth *substance*, which is *abused* by stretching it in measure" (57: my emphasis). A near pun enforces the fact that "Substantiall things" are even by definition naturally "subject," since they "stand under" (Latin *substo*) something higher. Weight itself also has substance, the reality of material being in this instance. The abstracted conception of "weight" becomes tangible, and the container blends with the contained in casebook examples of conventional metaphor, as described by Lakoff and Johnson.[49] What is going on here is again weirdly, irrationally reminiscent of the language of debate about the Sacrament, as I have earlier described it, which Malynes could not be further from intending to recall at this point. But his very language is just a step away from an invitation to allegory: the "abuse" of Substance by stretching is against Nature and deceives Measure herself. I would add that Malynes is not unique among his mercantile contemporaries in using such language. What we have been looking at for some time now is a world view, and it does not belong singularly to Malynes. This view differs enough from ours to be at once more visible and more visibly metaphoric. In this respect, it resembles the lunch-counter code discussed in my fourth chapter that we, as outsiders, hear metaphorically. We hear it in a way we do not hear our own.

⤴

Malynes, thus having laid the ideological groundwork for his fifth chapter even more carefully than he could have realized, proceeds to its central economic conceptions. Here he expounds the three "Essentiall parts of Trafficke: Namely *Commodities, Money, and Exchange for Money by Billes of Exchanges*: which is effected by Number, Weight, and Measure." Respectively, these three parts are "the *Bodie, Soule, and Spirit of Commerce*," and function accordingly (58–59). So far so good, but he has trouble with his central metaphor the moment he imposes a history on it, since the commodious body, as primitive barter, appears to be operating with neither its soul nor its spirit. Happily, however, the monetary soul soon "did infuse life to trafficke, by the means of Equalitie and Equitie, preuenting aduantage between buyers and sellers." Now "the *Spirite* and facultie of the Soule (being seated euerywhere) corroborateth the vitall Spirit of trafficke, directing and controlling (by iust proportions) the prices and values of Commodities and Moneys." The phrase "by iust proportions," though slipped parenthetically into the metaphor, is crucial to the representation of the healthy body economic Malynes envisions and has so carefully anticipated in the preceding chapters. He then tries further to clarify the role of the directorial spirit of exchange, explaining that this spirit and faculty "taketh his originall from the Soule," as does the exchange from money, but he becomes concerned enough about his metaphor to add, "that is to say, The exchange . . . is grounded upon Moneys" (59). "Grounded" may well have been as moribund an architectural metaphor in Malynes' time as in ours, but here, in conjunction with soul and spirit, it stirs incongruously to life.[50] And, whereas money is the "publicke measure between man and man," exchange is next declared to be the "*Publica Mensura*" between nations, according to which all commodities are traded. To Malynes, I suspect, the *Publica Mensura* is not a figure but a fact, but to a disbeliever like Misselden (or a modern reader), for whom exchange is a passive, reflective mechanism rather than an active, controlling valuation, the substantializing Latin phrase is a "(dis)similitude."[51] All in all, Malynes' metaphors so far are mixed and somewhat unstable.

In a later chapter, Malynes finds it typical of the obtuseness of his opponents, notably Misselden, that they cannot grasp the distinction of spirit from body and soul that he draws in his central metaphor, insofar as they think spirit "is comprized vnder the name Soule" and originates in or derives from it.[52] But Malynes' distinction is based on traditional Renaissance medicine and makes sense by reference to it. As Galen and other ancient and more recent authorities are contemporaneously conveyed, augmented,

and updated by Helkiah Crooke, spirit is an "exhalation" of the blood that
ties the divine soul to the earthly body "as it were by a strong though not
indissoluble bonde."[53] It is corporeal: "*A subtle and thinne body always moou-
able . . . and the vehicle or carriage of the Faculties of the soule*," ideas Malynes
clearly echoes. Subtlest of all substances, "as the winde" the spirit "passeth
and repasseth at his pleasure, vnseene, but not vnfelt; for the force and in-
cursion thereof is not without a kinde of violence"—again a biblically resonant description suggestive in relation to Malynes' sense of the insidious yet
forceful effect of contemporary currency exchanges.[54] The description that
follows is further suggestive in light of Malynes' economic sophistication—
his awareness of the impacts of supply and demand, the quantity of money,
and the balance of payments—yet his insistence on the ultimately controlling impact of exchange: spirit is "always in motion, for the spirits [ex-
changes] are continually moued, not by another onely . . . but also by
themselues, that is, by an inbred principle of their owne," either "Vpward"
or "downe-ward—"*ultro-citroque*," to borrow Calvin's phrase.[55]

I remarked earlier that Malynes' figures are largely illustrative, but examined more closely, his central metaphor—in particular this independent
principle of movement up or down—now appears to have had a shaping
influence on his thought about currency exchange, which lies at the very
core of his economic theory. Modern economists such as Arjo Klamer and
Donald McCloskey have shown that the way things are expressed "matters
in economics" and affects both theories and policies, and Blitz's work on
Mercantilism provides another case in point. Invoking Hume's analogy
"between contiguous price levels in different countries and the scientific
principle that 'All water, wherever it communicates, remains always at a
level,'" Blitz replaces it with one better suited to the monetary turbulence
of the period in question, namely, "two mighty waterfalls, one pouring into
the pond and the other flowing out."[56] Both these analogies are conceptual
and constructive rather than merely illustrative.

At various later stages in the *Mercatoria*, Malynes rings changes on his central, tripartite metaphor of body, soul, and spirit, and Crooke's text again
indicates something of their figural logic. Recording controversy as to
whether there is one spirit or several, Crooke endorses the traditional Galenic view that there are "three manner[s] of spirites, because there are three
faculties of the soule, the Naturall, the Vitall, and the Animall; three principles, the Braine, the Heart, and the Liuer; and three kinde[s] of Vessels,
Veines, Arteries, and Sinnewes." When moved by an external principle, the
spirits "are Drawn hither or Driuen thither. They are driuen, the Naturall

from the Liuer, the Vitall from the heart . . . the Animall from the Braine.
. . . They are drawne, the naturall by the veines, the vitall by the particular
parts together with the Arteriall blood; the Animall verie rarely, vnless a part
be affected either with paine or pleasure."[57] Similarly, Malynes equates his
"three Essential Parts of Trafficke" to the three anatomical "principles"
Crooke enumerates: thus "as the Liuer (*Money*) ministreth spirits to the
heart (*Commodities*) and the Heart to the Braine (*Exchange*) so doth the
Braine (*Exchange*) minister to the whole *Microcosme*, or the whole Bodie of
trafficke."[58] Malynes' need to gloss his little allegory so openly with parenthetical equivalents, however, signals its forcing here. Its terms are aligned
and fixed, not tropically transferred or, indeed, creatively exchanged. Thus
merely coupled, their rhetorical effect seems far-fetched and improper—
even abusive.

Two other instances of Malynes' use of his central metaphor ask for a
broader, more synthetic gloss. In the first, Malynes argues that "Money then
(as the Bloud in the bodie) containeth the Soule which infuseth life; for if
Money be wanting, Trafficke doth decrease"; in the second, he characterizes the "Valuation of Moneys" as "the Spirit which giueth life vnto coynes,
for without it, weight and finenesse are in the nature of Bullion or Materi-
alls" (II.Pro.253, II.ix.307). Since he has already established in his introduction of the tripartite metaphor (I.v.58–59) that money is soul and that spirit
arises from blood, these similitudes could cause confusion and justify Misselden's charge of inept ignorance. But as Katherine Park explains in her account of "The Organic Soul," which draws on Melanchthon's *Liber de
anima* and additional sources, the *spiritus*, vaporized or exhaled from blood
and "disseminated throughout the body by the arteries and nerves . . . [is]
The source of all activity in the living body" and is often called "the 'first
instrument' of the [organic] soul."[59] Here again is Malynes' distinction between soul and spirit, as well as another clear indication that the soul in his
central metaphor, as in the first quotation above, is corporeal. That spirit is
the source of all activity in the body also corresponds to his otherwise odd
argument that in his time "Commodities and Money are Passiue," and the
exchange "is only Actiue" (60). Again the shaping influence of conceptually
significant metaphor on Malynes' economic thought is evident.

The likening of the *valuation* of moneys (internally by states, externally
by exchange) to life-giving spirit in the second quotation also makes sense
insofar as exchange has its "originall from the Soule," or organic soul-blood.
Subsequently, however, Malynes complicates this metaphorical conception
still further by locating will in the spirit. He explains that those philosophers

who place the soul in the blood—phrasing that indicates an awareness of alternative views—also place the will "in the spirit, residing in the heart of man, which the Anatomists demonstrateth [*sic*] to be a little concauitie" (III.Pro.377–78). This "little concauitie" sounds like Crooke's location of the seat of the vital spirit "in the Left caue or denne of the heart," which is "the cauity" of the left—"spirituall," "spongie," or "ayry"—ventricle, whence the spirit is "distributed" (elsewhere "diffused") by the arteries (373, 410). Further basis for Malynes' view, which assumes an Aristotelian analogy or working relationship between the activity of the inorganic will and the organic one, can be found in Melanchthon's *Liber de Anima*, where the heart, seat of the organic soul and source of the affections or feelings, sends these forth with the blood as voluntary, motivating spirit. More exactly, "with the earnest will is joined the heart. . . . [The] awareness [i.e., perception] of Julius is in the brain. But goodwill and hatred are in the heart."[60]

The expansive and progressive complication of Malynes' anatomical figure simultaneously encounters two related difficulties, one rhetorical and one conceptual. The first is what I'm tempted to term the too literal, too material extension of figuration and the consequent betrayal of it—the collapse of scaffolding by its own weight, so to speak. The second is that in the Renaissance, a "growing number of philosophers," such as Melanchthon himself, actually identified the organic soul with the spirit instead of distinguishing spirit as its instrument.[61] In other words, Malynes' conflation might well include confusion. On the one hand, then, the rhetorical problem—or since form has content, perhaps the more rhetorical problem—is an overelaboration of likeness in the interest of the certainty and substantial proof that will stabilize Malynes' theory. To his credit, this elaboration at least corresponds to the complexity of the economic system he perceives and wants to naturalize in anatomical terms, but its excess only exposes its artificiality and undermines his effort. On the other hand, the conceptual (or more conceptual) problem might actually be the reader's, that is, a problem of interpretation, since it involves the employment of contemporary medical beliefs that are themselves in question or evolving. If the vehicle of a metaphor is unstable or confusing, its tenor is bound to be so as well. Aside from the increasing tendency in the period to identify soul with spirit, Galenic views of the heart and arteries and of the liver and veins, which were conceived as separate systems, were "under frequent criticism," and as early as 1616, not least in the lectures of William Harvey, who in 1628 was to publish his discovery of the circulation of the blood.[62] The historical context of Malynes' anatomical metaphor suggests the extent to which and the palpable way in which the fabric of shared belief is beginning to fray and (catching the spirit of mixed metaphor from Malynes) the extent to which its material aspects are becoming more intransigently resistant to allegorical form. This is also to say the extent to which Malynes' world view is threatened.

Mixed metaphor is in fact an underlying issue in the *Mercatoria* if we return from the extension of Malynes' central metaphor to its origin within the fifth chapter of his first section, where my discussion of it also began.[63] There, within roughly a page of this origin, Malynes describes exchange metaphorically as "the Rudder of the ship of Trafficke, fastened vpon the Paralell of the keele of Equitie, which doth rule and direct the said ship vpon all the variations of the Commodities of all countries." This, too, is a metaphor and, as developed, a tripartite one to which he will return. Like the spirit, the rudder is the efficient cause of the ship's direction and government in his eyes, and "no man is so foolish as to attribute that power vnto the sailes . . . or to the maine bodie of it called the hull of the ship. Great is the error therfore of those that will ascribe any effectuall operation to the quantitie of Commodities [or balance of trade], . . . when the course of it" is "like a ship sailing without Rudder or Compasse."[64] The hull of the ship apparently represents commodities, and Money is comparable to the compass,

> hauing so manie variations upon the seuerall standards of the coines of all contries, and changing continually from time to time in valuation; Princes and Common-weales taking aduantage one against another, either to draw treasure into their Kingdomes and territories, or to aduance the price of their countrie Commodities. And Exchange may properly be compared to the Rudder of a Ship, which commandeth the directions of the Compasse accordingly, and so doth the Exchange command the course of Money: for let the standards of Moneys be altered either in weight, finenesse, or valuation, the Exchange by altering the price (with great facilitie) *according to equity* is able to meet and ouer-rule them all [I.v.61: my emphasis].

Malynes is not an enemy of exchange per se, which his image renders favorably, but an enemy of its abuse through inequitable, unreasonable exchange. Still, from a rhetorical *and* diagnostic point of view, as suggested above, his house is divided against itself. Even while he argues that monetary exchange is dominant, the extension, mixing, and content of his own similitudes short-circuit figural exchange on more than merely a surface level. His analogies, allegories, metaphors, and the like have a strange correspondence to his sense that exchange, as actually practiced in his time and opposed to his ideal of equity and just proportion, is badly out of joint. Equity and just proportion, of course, are another version of propriety, and "badly" means also "abusively" here.[65] The strange correspondence of Malynes' form to his content is, in sum, catachrestic, and my own explanatory metaphors (as has been noted) begin to mimic its mixing.

Malynes' major figures aim more for a consistency of functional relationship than for one of surface: more for the depiction of efficient causality (early seventeenth-century style) than of a living body and a sailing ship, although it is not irrelevant to his purpose and its comprehension (in both senses) that the body should be natural, and the ship artificial.[66] The aim of these figures is philosophical, abstract, and principled, yet, as we have already seen to an extent, their phenomenal elements are insistently and sometimes incongruously present. They create a sense of excess, whether arising from uneasiness, uncontrol, or sheer indulgence. Again, this is a sense recognized by Misselden, for one, and not just by a modern reading: "See another Simile, . . . See yet another dissimilitude," Misselden cries on reading *Lex Mercatoria*, and he concludes that Malynes has "abused the termes of Art . . . and improperly compared his *Par of Exchange* like a *Parret*, to *Clocks*, and *Shippes*, and *Dialls*, and *Actiue*, and *Passiue*, and what hee list himselfe" (*Circle*, 20–21, 23). This outcry against alleged impropriety (Misselden's "improperly") comes despite the pronounced figuration of Misselden's own tracts and highlights the variety and insistence of Malynes'.

"The interdiction of mixed metaphor," according to Dale Pesmen, "suggests that certain expectations of reality are implied." These expectations are at issue between the contemporaries Misselden and Malynes, despite their both being Aristotelian in orientation and either's supposing the other merely ignorant or obtuse. We might also say that a sense of propriety—a certain expectation of reality—obtains not only within a single metaphor but also among several of them, as we have seen, for example, within Malynes' central metaphor of the body and between this metaphor and his metaphor of the sailing ship. Pesmen observes that the mixing of metaphors makes us uneasily conscious of figuration and its designs on us. The mix is as likely to disenchant as to persuade us, since it not only violates our expectation of coherence but also highlights the constructedness of this expectation. Pesmen marshalls a host of past and present authorities to characterize the perpetrators of mixed metaphor as "the inspired, the impassioned, the unifiers," and those whose minds are "in confused states," or, more positively and with reference to Pepper's *World Hypotheses*, whose minds are "in process."[67] Excepting inspiration and simple confusion, there is something of all these states to be seen in Malynes' historically and culturally revealing deployment of figuration.

Before leaving the foundational fifth chapter of Part 1 for Malynes' sections on money and exchange (originative soul and active spirit), I want to touch on two additional features of this chapter, namely, kingship and imaginary, as distinct from substantial, existence. Both bear on assertions of Malynes' ideological conservatism—political on the one hand and on the other intellectual and perceptual. Much has been made of Malynes' reliance on royal power to maintain the health of the body economic, and true to expectations, in chapter 5 he not only depicts the king as "father of the common-wealth," but also argues that monarchy is the best form of government, since "one person (imitating nature) doth gouerne (as the head) all the parts and members of the bodie" (I.v.60, 63). Unquestioning acceptance of such statements seems to me the result of inattentive reading, however. Every one of them is conditional or qualified in some way, and in this book dedicated to King James, there are enough other signs of doubt, distance, or disappointment in the monarchy to give one pause. For instance, a prince "(as the father of the common-wealth) ought to be a seller and not a buyer," and he is so "when the expences of his common-wealth do not exceed his incomes and reuenues" (60). Only a reader unaware of James's extravagance could fail to recognize Malynes' statement as corrective advice. Three pages later, again utilizing humanist convention, Malynes holds up the mirror of the ideal prince to his not-necessarily-ideal king and follows it with a narrative about how a king, finding food dear, yet no dearth in his land, began to examine husbandmen, landowners, merchants, and artificers to determine the cause. Finding the role of merchants key, the king examines their views further, and the narrative becomes an exposition of the "wiser view" among them, which of course accords with Malynes' and which this idealized fantasy-king embraces. Any reading of this chapter is misleading that does not recognize convention, clearly signaled fiction, the advertisement of the writer's qualifications, and consequently what Malynes is actually doing.

In this chapter and others, Malynes rehearses a critical opinion of Henry VIII's radically inflationary tampering with the coinage during the preceding century, although, as ever, he turns from the long-term effects of such tampering to the pernicious impacts of current exchange rates. Elsewhere he comes closer to criticizing the reigning monarch. Of patents, among the Jacobean Crown's favorite sources of income, he observes that those are useful whose effect is to set people to work, to recompense the inventor, or to make things "(in some measure) . . . better cheape" for subjects. But, he asks indignantly, "What shall we say then, of those Graunts which make the commoditie good cheap to forraine Nations, and dearer to the subiects? Surely," he adds, "this cannot be without some great abuse."[68] Discussing such monopolies at length, he finally settles on a highly critical definition of them: "A kind of commerce in buying, selling, changing, or bartering, vsurped by a few, and sometimes, but by one person, and forestalled from all others to his or their priuate gaine, and to the hurt and detriment of other men; whereby of course or by authoritie, the libertie of Trade is restrained from others, whereby the Monopolist is inabled to set a price of commodities at his pleasure."[69] As earlier mentioned, he also criticizes the Cokayne project, which James pushed through his reluctant Council; he refers disdainfully to the practices of "late yeares, since the Customes were taken to farme"; and he holds up, as a model of which his own sovereign so far falls short, monarchs who have controlled the nefarious practices of bankers.[70] Malynes may subscribe to an ideal of kingship, and his motives in doing so may range from conviction to pragmatism, to expediency, to desperation, but his ideal does not stop him from seeing, recording, and unmistakably criticizing the actual world around him.

In the same fifth chapter, Malynes uses the word *imaginary* repeatedly and significantly, as he will do in later chapters, particularly in reference to money. His use often suggests the antithesis *substantial*, but it does not indicate the kind of outright hostility to the imagination that iconoclasm exhibits in this period.[71] The imaginary may indeed be a vain "conceit," as in the example he gives of a man who advised another to get rid of his trash by digging a hole to bury it, only to be asked what then should be done with the excavated dirt and to hear in response that he should dig a hole large enough to accommodate it, too. This is Malynes' example of the stubbornness of those (like Misselden) who deny principles indisputable "by reason and common consent" (I.v.61). Also imaginary, however, is the Copernican hypothesis, which Malynes uneasily thinks worth considering in this same chapter, as he will again later, only to report (not quite to endorse) Aristotle's view of the earth's centrality "generally approued" on the grounds of gravity and levity. Yet he moves by contrast ("But") from this general approval of Aristotelian theory to the *indisputable fact* that as surely as the index of a sundial, as opposed to the dial's passive numbers, indicates motion, so exchange (money) is active and commodities (trade) passive (61–62). Just what *imaginary* means to Malynes is hard to pin down from these examples.

One is delusive and the other, while speculative, is taken seriously enough to engage his attention not once but twice in the *Mercatoria* (cf. I.xxxiv.184). In another chapter, he refers in a positive way to a projected or hypothetical commonwealth that might attract productive colonists as an "imaginarie" one and an "Idea" worth pursuing (1622 edition: I.xlvi.234). Yet at the end of the fifth chapter of Part I, he also describes a gain of 25 percent through exchange as one that "would otherwise bee but imaginarie" (65). While this profit appears to be real, in some sense it apparently also is not real in his eyes. Rereadings of *Lex Mercatoria* suggest to me that such various usage is more in process than confused, and that this text, difficult as it can be on first reading, is a valuable early modern example of informed response to *changing* paradigms.

Elsewhere in the *Mercatoria*, Malynes refers to the credits and payments of banks, "without that any money is touched," as "almost or rather altogether imaginairie," that is, intangible, or as we might say, "only on paper" (132). Yet he is ahead of English law in favoring transferable bills of credit and exchange in accord with Continental practice—in effect a limited precursor of circulating paper money (97–100, 395). The headings in a written ledger of double-entry accounts, whose use Malynes recommends strongly, are also imaginary: for example, merchants are to designate their warehouses or commodities Debitor and their capital or stock Creditor, and "In the like manner (because their moneys are layed vp . . . in a chest, which they call Cash) they will therefore *imagine* . . . the said Cash a Debitor for the money they put into it, and when they pay out that money, . . . they will make Cash Creditor, and that partie to whom it was payed shall be made the Debitor."[72] Goods, coins, persons, and actions are thus translated to, and personified in, categories that realize only their financial, numerical equivalents. Merchants' foreign accounts are also to be kept according to the imaginary monies of the currency exchanges, and these are called "Imaginarie . . . because there is not any peculiar or proper money to be found *in Specie*, whereupon the Exchanges are grounded, as it was [grounded] in times past in many places" on "our Angell Noble" coin (386). Imaginary money is intangible, fictionalized, and ungrounded (insecurely fastened). Neither fixed nor pegged, it floats and is therefore insubstantial. The problem, in sum, is not the imaginary representation of substance but the lack of substance in the imaginary representation of money. I hardly dare add that, as in my third chapter on the Sacrament, the problem is *substantial*. The question of what matters (in both senses), like the question of what is real, hinges on a definition of this conceptual word.

❧

Malynes' introduction to the second Part of *Lex Mercatoria*, on money, specifies three properties money has, of which substantial value is the culmination. The first property expresses the quantity theory (the inverse response
of the price of money to its abundance or lack), and the second proceeds
from the operation of usury on money, with the result that "the rate of
Vsurie is become the ['ingrossed,' 'falsified'] measure whereby all men trade,
purchase, build, plant, or any other waies bargaine."[73] Both these properties
are wholly relational, rather than fixed. The third "propertie of Money, is
to have an internall value in substance, . . . for Moneys will haue substantiall
value" (254). That the first two conditions should have the same status as
properties of money that substantial value has is puzzling. Substance is
clearly material here, and if value is essential in some sense, then at most it
is an essence embedded in matter and materially manifest. Internal value, or
measure, is a property of money, and yet it is also (maddeningly) substantial
as Malynes describes it.

The problem here, as with the slippery concept *substance* in debate about
the Sacrament, involves various definitions: "A property is essential to an
entity if, necessarily, the entity cannot exist without being an instance of the
property"; otherwise, the property is accidental to the entity. At the same
time, "However, it is controversial whether every property that is essential
to something must be essential [versus accidental] by nature."[74] In short, the
status of properties is itself puzzling, as we have often seen in earlier chapters, and again, Malynes is more a mirror of his time than an originative
thinker. He would like money to have an intrinsic, substantial, and definitive value; this is his stabilizing ideal. At the same time, however, he recognizes that money *really* is not *functioning* this way in exchange, whether
domestic or foreign. He asserts the substantiality of its value, even as he acknowledges the apparent, accidental status of this. Reading his text is again
strangely to exist between two kinds of realities, one ideal and one actual,
and to see cultural change at enough distance to render it visible. Imagine a
merchant, even one with varying shades of gray in his career, who discovers
his principles when they are challenged by the reality he sees around him.
Perhaps my glance at King Lear earlier in this chapter is not quite as far
fetched as I supposed: can "they . . . touch me for [coining,]" when "I am
the King himself?" (IV.vi.83–84). Enhancement and debasement, and not
merely counterfeiting, come quickly to mind.

Malynes pursues the valuation of money in the ninth chapter of Part 2,
which opens with the statement earlier examined that valuation gives life

to coins, which are merely bullion or the material for coinage without it. Domestically, the authority of a prince or state (e.g., the Netherlands) determines the price, or value, at which coins will "go currant" within the kingdom. Between countries, "Merchants Valuation" determines this.[75] The prince can enhance (inflate) or debase the currency or alter the bimetallic ratio of gold to silver. Merchants' valuation, Malynes adds, can also raise or lower the prices of a currency by means of the official exchanges, by private exchanges at other than official rates, and by private financial dealings with mint-masters. While the domestic valuation can be enhanced or debased, however, it is nonetheless assayed, or assessed, and therefore grounded on intrinsic value, which, to awaken a sleeping metaphor, flatly contradicts such tampering.

As Malynes' contemporary Rice Vaughan similarly explains, "Money is said to have an Intrinsical value so much as there is Gold & Silver in it in fineness & weight." This is the "universal value of Gold and Silver." In contrast, "the local value . . . [is] call[ed] Extrinsical, as depending upon the impression of the mark and ordinance of the State." The latter "retaineth the Money . . . within his proper Limits and natural form"—strong, if not ambivalent, language for merely local value, I would note. Vaughan also cautions, however, "let any particular Prince or State raise [enhance] the price of Gold and Silver as they list, yet they will still hold the same proportion towards other things valued by them."[76] Manipulate the local value of money upward, and your just reward will be domestic inflation, not to mention (eventual) adjustment in the foreign exchanges. Thus a local valuation *does* carry value, if only ironically.

In addition, Malynes explains, the English valuation derives from the number of pieces (or pence, pennies) into which the Troy pound of twelve ounces sterling is divided, and he attributes some degree of rationality to this standard, as well. What really disturbs him is less that the King might "value a peece of sterling siluer weighing about foure pennie weight at twelve pence, [and] it wil be currant so within the realm," but that "Merchants in exchange wil value the same at $11\frac{1}{2}$ pence, and commonly at eleuen pence, and so it will be transported *in specie* by a low exchange, and the commodities of the realme will be sold accordingly" (311). In other words, its foreign valuation is irrational in Malynes' eyes not only because it is not founded on "iust proportion," but also because it will lead both to a drain of silver currency from England and to an undercutting of the *true value* of English commodities. Yet, as we have seen, money has ambivalent properties: on the one hand its value varies and floats; on the other, it possesses intrinsic, substantial value. Either tendency is ambivalently "proper" to it. Slipping into a Saussurean metaphor of coinage for linguistic value, we could also say that its significance (*signum/ficans*: "sign/making") as what Malynes calls the "*commune pignus* currant mutuall," a token "which we call money," is disturbingly ambivalent as well.[77] Yet metaphor, it is worth remembering, is but also is not. Saussurean analogy notwithstanding, Saussure's *langue* and *parole* are not the same as intrinsic and extrinsic valuation; linguistic sublation, or "raising," is not monetary enhancement; and a deconstructive exposure of origin is not monetary debasement. Such analogies *hypothesize* illuminating patterns of cultural perception; that is, they both create *and* reveal them. Basically, they are metaphoric, and their specific terms vary significantly—historically, culturally, and textually.

In view of Malynes' awareness of the ambivalence of monetary value, his extensive consideration of usury in the second section of *Lex Mercatoria*, in which money is focal, makes organizational and associative sense. The oft-repeated view that Malynes expresses a medieval hostility to usury does not make much sense, however. Characteristically, his view is more sensitive to conflicting considerations, and it is more unsettled. As commonly noted, the very notion of "usury" derives from what the nature of money is conceived to be. Instead of reverting to his discussion of this nature, however, Malynes offers a chapter enumerating various historical prohibitions of usury: the Bible, Saints Jerome, Ambrose, and Bernard, canon and civilian lawyers, various Popes, Aristotle, Plato, Tacitus, Lucullus, Cato, the Emperor Charles the fifth, and more (II.x). Notably, he tells us only that Aristotle thought usury an unnatural monster but not why, namely, that money is by nature barren, not productive, and, as understood by the Middle Ages, a consumptible entity (like bread), not a fungible entity for rental or hire— that is, for lending at interest.[78]

Malynes begins the next chapter in this section, namely II.xi, with a reminder that he has rehearsed prohibitions against usury but then quickly adds, "neuerthelesse the practice of it is most vsuall in many Kingdomes and Common-weales, and the Lawes are also made accordingly." He genuinely worries the moral and ethical issues further, however: "this sinne [usury] is rather in the conscience, than in the act"; "the Law of England doth tollerate tenne vpon the hundreth [10%]"; "But the intent and not the rigour thereof [of the rate], is to bee weighed for the cleering of iustice." His statements sound like an examination of conscience or, alternatively, like a balancing act. After all those prohibitions in the preceding chapter, he unaccountably adds that "The word Vsurie was not so odious in times past."

At last his destination comes into view: although his "meaning is not to maintaine Vsurie Politike [in exchange, systemic] in all respects, contrarie to the opinion of Diuines," he concludes that "ouer-precisenes" regarding it "may breed a great inconuenience to the Common-wealth" (II.xi.329). His view here is not unlike that of his mercantile contemporaries, including Mun, or his own regarding the importation of luxury goods, namely, that this should not be excessive, "alwaies admitting ciuilite," however. It assumes of a kind of balance or *ratio*, for "reason must rule herein" (84).

But the economic inconvenience from over-preciseness of which Malynes speaks in excusing "reasonable" usury is serious. *Inconvenience* is a much stronger term in his time than in ours—one that could even underwrite charges of treason—and "preciseness" is a coded reference to the scruples of puritans, whom Malynes heartily dislikes.[79] His final observations in chapter 11 about usury take refuge in the generalizing effect of proverbial wisdom: "time and occasions do alter things; as the case for the present standeth with England and forraine Nations, we haue Vsurie like a Woolfe by the eares, dangerous to be kept, and more dangerous to abandone the same"; or again, "simply to disallow it [usury/interest] is to cut off all trade and commerce, or reparation of damages, and to goe about to remedie a mischiefe with a greater inconuenience."[80] One proverb, about the wolf, invokes nature; the other—"better a mischief than an inconvenience"— invokes law: thus *physis* and *nomos*, both bases, are covered. The upshot is Malynes' nervous, qualified endorsement of usury, which will have complicating ramifications for his views on bills of exchange, themselves a veiled and sometimes not-so-veiled form of usury, or interest, or indeed, of speculative investment.

Ultimately, Malynes defines his mixed position regarding usury more carefully. For example, usury is "neuer hurtfull but where it biteth; and the matter of conscience consisteth in the not getting of your debtor, and not in the taking of much or little interest" (II.xi.329). More precisely, he posits three kinds of financial dealings: gift, bargain, and loan. To these, in his view, correspond the beggar, the needy householder, and the rich merchant, and his advice is to give freely to the first, to lend freely or mercifully to the second, and to profit from the third, using in all cases, "conscience with discretion" (336). His view, which is not original, combines comfortably with Calvin's, of which Tawney has written that Calvin treated usury "as a particular case of the general problem of the social relationships of a Christian community, which must be solved in the light of existing circumstances." Tawney added, of course, that the practical effect of Calvin's position "was to weaken the whole body of opposition to usury."[81] Otherwise, Malynes' remedy is a lowering of the legally allowed rate of usury in England of 10 percent to 6 percent, the procurement of "plentie of money really *in specie* within the Realme, together with the meanes vsed in other countreys in the lieu of moneys; as the transferring or setting over of Billes betweene man and man, the [imaginary] paiments by assignement in Banke without handling of moneys, and Letters of Credit, or Billes of Exchanges" (335). All the latter are forms of paper money, the way of the future.

Malynes reserves particular venom for the "intollerable Vsurie" of (pawn) brokers, who *exchange* money for household and other goods, extorting rates of 30, 50, 80, up to 400 percent that are enough "to stupifie a mans senses." He depicts a chain of extortion in which "the poore housholder and mechanicall man" are devoured and consumed, for most "Brokers haue their money masters [bawds, metaphorically][82] to whom they pay" 15 or 20 percent and some of these masters pay 10 percent to others, "so that one thing driueth or inforceth another. Like as in a clocke where there be many wheeles, the first wheele being stirred driueth the next, and that the third, and so forth . . . or like as in a presse going in at a straight, where the formost is driuen by him that is next him, and the next by him that followes him, and the third by some violent and strong thing that drives him forward. . . ." (II.xi.337–38). Malynes does not always use mechanical imagery in negative contexts, but he does so strikingly and reiteratively enough here with these wheels within wheels for us to take notice. The clock and press that image such relentless cruelty are peculiarly the products of human invention. For a moment, they are proto-Dickensian.[83] Although they are technically similes (in a modern classification), they do the re-conceptualizing work of metaphor.

A footnote in de Roover's essay on Malynes inadvertently and ironically reinforces the *prospective* impact of Malynes' clock wheels. De Roover takes Malynes' image "Comparing the economic system to clockwork" positively, acknowledging in his note that he found the image attributed to Malynes in Tawney's *Religion and the Rise of Capitalism* but that he has been unable to locate it in Malynes' own writing. Lacking Malynes' context, he instances the image of clock wheels as a positive sign that the Mercantilists were "blazing new trails" and "tak[ing] apart the [economic] mechanism in order to find out how it worked and how the cogs fitted together" (358 and n. 62). His misperception without benefit of context is revealing. The effect of Malynes' image is more complex: its mechanism *does* look forward and it reflects his awareness of the changing world around him; but it also belongs to a context in which he decries, "This intollerable Usurie . . . by the Brokers," and looks back nostalgically to an earlier vision of social harmony among the several "estates," or social classes.[84] And yet it is not long after this chapter (II.xii) that Malynes also details and commends the double-entry method of bookkeeping, in which a merchant makes his warehouse Debitor and Cash Creditor in his ledger and thereby indistinguishable from the creditor or debitor who is (or once was) a real person, one, to adapt Levinas' dictum, with a face.[85] *Lex Mercatoria* is a text written near a social, economic, and political watershed, and sequential reading of it can produce ironic effects unintended by its author, as well as emergent and regressive ones. The hindsight enabled by nearly four centuries, moreover, is itself a tropic trans-action.

Part 3 of the *Mercatoria* focuses on "Exchanges for Moneys by Billes of Exchanges," the controlling spirit of traffic and commerce in Malynes' tripartite scheme (377). Here, in the conception of the foreign currency exchanges—in the transfer and transmutation of funds—rather than in the more inert conception of quantity or even of substance, is where the connection between verbal and metal tokens is most vital and suggestive. Predictably, it intersects with religion as well, to provide the sort of "coherence," or structure, that Andy Clark associates with cultural scaffolding. Malynes begins discussion of exchange, as he begins most topics, with a history. Although he does not invoke Aristotle specifically, his history is Aristotelian in spirit. Aristotle thought barter natural and exchange a natural outgrowth of it but also thought that the use of coin led, via retail trade, to wealth-getting and therefore to a need to distinguish between a natural art of wealth-getting, whose end is the good life, and an unnatural one in which profit becomes an end in itself.[86] Malynes' version of this view makes conspicuous use of analogy, or proportion. As money was invented to avoid the problems of carting commodities around, he reemphasizes, so, when other nations imitated the Romans in coining moneys, "Exchange by Bills for moneys was deuised," to avoid the danger and trouble of carrying money from country to country. Therefore, he continues, there was appointed "a certaine Exchange, . . . giuing *Par pro Pari*, or value for value, with a certaine allowance to accomodate the Merchant" (377). The allowance is the fee or percentage and thus the moderate usury (so to speak) *for* accommodation. *Par pro pari*, plus reasonable allowance, will become Malynes' mantra in criticizing the exchange of his day. As earlier indicated, whether by *par pro pari* Malynes means intrinsic or pegged value has been questioned, but what he clearly does not mean is the exchange rate of his day, a value he considers merely arbitrary or floating.

In Part 3 Malynes distinguishes four kinds of exchange, of which the first two, *Cambio Commune* and *Cambio Reall*, involve simple changes from one kind of coin or currency to another, "without any transportation of the coyne, but giving *Par pro Pari*, or value for value, with a certaine allowance"—that is, the mantra (378). Malynes considers exchanges in this pure form indispensable to trade: for "as Ships cannot saile without water, no more can trafficke subsist without Exchange in the accustomed places [cities, markets, fairs]."[87] The other two kinds of exchange, *Cambio Sicco* (Dry Exchange) and *Cambio Fictitio* (Fictitious Exchange), he considers fundamentally pernicious and, indeed, abusive. They are merely subterfuges to avoid the laws against usury. According to de Roover, both were basically loans from which the lender expected a profit, or interest, that "was not stipulated beforehand by agreement between the parties but was determined afterward by the unpredictable course of the exchange." The transaction was therefore speculative, and "windfall profits or losses due to exchange fluctuations" were possible for either party to it.[88]

De Roover defines dry exchange more specifically "as a transaction involving exchange and re-exchange in which no money payments were made abroad." It was considered dry because it did "not feed the current of foreign trade" ("Dry Exchange," 264–65). Malynes intends this meaning sarcastically when he details such a loan, ostensibly from London to Stoad, "wherein they [bankers] will be sure to make him [the merchant] pay verie great vse or interest, of fifteene or twentie in the hundreth for the taking vp of this Money, and to make it more drier Exchange, they will be contented to take no Bill at all, but the Merchants promise to pay it as other men doe at the same [length of] time, dealing in Exchange for the said place of Stoad." The merchant is not only to pay the unpredictable charges for exchange to Stoad and rechange back to London but also "charges of Factoridge and Brokeridge"—use of the bank's factor at Stoad and a broker's commission—apparently without the merchant's ever having left London (380). To borrow Malynes' central anatomical image, thus the merchant would be bled dry by extortionary rates.

De Roover explains fictitious exchange as "merely a form of dry exchange" in which the bills of exchange were "made out *pro forma*, often under fictitious names," but without even going through the motions of sending them abroad, although interest "was still computed on the basis of the [foreign] exchange rates" ("Dry Exchange," 264–65). Malynes illustrates such a transaction with the example of a merchant whose need to raise cash to save his credit drives him to buy goods that he presumably hopes to sell at a profit. But instead of getting his goods on credit from those "hauing store of commodities at all times," the merchant is forced to get them at the rate of a fictitious exchange: for when he comes to the bankers or their brokers, "they faine that they haue need of Money, and must sell their commodities for readie Money; Prouided alwaies (say they with louing protestations) we will pleasure you thus far, looke what the goods come vnto, we will take it vp for you by Exchange for Venice, Lyons, or some other place, so as you will pay vs for Exchange, Rechange, or any other incident charges: whereunto the merchant agreeing, then shall he be sure to pay soundly for the vse of the Money, and loose exceedingly vpon the wares."[89]

The extremes of dry and fictitious exchange aside, Malynes is exercised about the misuse of the fundamental concept of exchange itself. Again, his basic belief is that a "true" exchange "is grounded vpon the weight, finenesse, and valuation of the Money of each countrie, according to the *Par*, which is, value for value." Here, by "valuation" he means the "severall standards proportionable" of the various countries, or in England the sterling standard: this is the "proportionable valuation relatiue within [the countries] themselues, according to their seuerall standards for weight and finenesse," and thus, it would seem, a stable structure firmly based on the bimetallic mint par of each country. In London, he would even like to see a central "royall Exchange" reestablished and employing official rates (382, 385).

In contrast, what he opposes vigorously is "this course of Exchange . . . of late yeares abused, and (as it were) made a merchandise, [which] doth ouerrule the course of Commodities and Moneys by rising and falling in price, according to plentie and scarcitie of Money, and in regard of discrepaunce and distance of time and place."[90] Made a merchandise itself to be traded for profit or let out to hire, money is no longer the stable measure or yardstick of value. In ethical, if not in purely economic, terms, it has become a very un-Aristotelian end in itself.[91] The discrepancy of time in Malynes' objection refers to the custom of specifying that bills of exchange be paid "at sight," "usance," or "double usance," each term referring to a different length of time and costing more or less interest accordingly. Place is simply another such variable, and even these variables he would apparently avoid.

Malynes'opposition to the working of the quantity theory of money in Part 3 of *Lex Mercatoria* clearly has its basis in intrinsic value. In significant accord with the rhetorical categories of his world, he labels the view that attributes the cause of monetary value to the relative supply of money *histeron proteron*, the rhetorical figure signifying "backwards." "If moneys be [valued] here low and elsewhere high," he then asks rhetorically, "how is this knowne but by the valuation of Exchange?"—that is, by the yardstick, or a stable measure of value. Assay master himself, he responds by comparing the exchange to "the Assay, whereby the finesse of gold and siluer [or intrinsic value] is knowne" (III.x.422). Conversely, the valuation in exchange is *merely* extrinsic and "by *denomination* [in name only], for the name of a thing doth not alter the value really, but the substance doth . . . , if it be altred; much lesse doth plenty or scarcity of monie cause their values, it being contrary to the *nature and propertie* of money; the yeard doth measure the cloth, but the cloth doth not measure the yeard" (422–23: my emphasis).

When Rice Vaughan wrote of the "proper Limits and natural form" of money, he yoked it to the extrinsic value given currency by the prince or state. Earlier, in the ninth chapter of Part 2, Malynes himself has characterized the "Valuation of Moneys" by the prince as the spirit that gives life to coins, without which they are mere bullion and according to which they are "esteemed at a price certaine . . . to go currant" within the kingdom, that is, in certain denominations (307). Even if enhanced, they are grounded in the par, albeit paradoxically.[92] There is still a substantial reality out there, although it can also be an equivocal one—a reassuring contradiction, so to speak. Malynes has described the valuation in exchange as working similarly in theory. Now, however, in Part 3, since valuation in exchange is in fact insecurely grounded and therefore not working as it should, it is *merely* denominative, or nominal, and not true.[93]

In light of Malynes' metaphoric cast of mind, his penchant for continued metaphor, and his having actually written an allegory, another exchange in another century returns ironically to mind, namely, Archbishop Thomas Cranmer's reply to a disputant at Oxford regarding the Sacrament: "*Substantia* [substance] may be predicated denominatiuely in an allegory, or in a metaphore, or in a figurative locution," to be followed by Cranmer's next retort to his antagonist, "You know not what tropes are."[94] Cranmer's language has almost incredible resonance within Malynes' very different text. With it, the whole unsettled, ambiguous matter of denomination as metaphor, exchange or mutation, or else as metonymy, mere naming or substitution, is back. This is certainly not to say that Malynes now means by denomination, or naming, the virtual, derivative reality Cranmer intended or vice versa, although mere "naming" was one of several meanings historically available in Cranmer's time, too. What "goes current" as a token is coded and in some sense metonymic. In contrast, what Malynes is reluctantly facing and resisting is real, unsecured, or ungrounded, and (if you will) creative exchange. Real *metaphor*—as distinct from metaphorical reality or philosophically *real* metaphor—is not what he wants. But who are we to say the alternative to the stability he desperately desires is not nothing? King Lear (perversely but persistently) comes again to mind, as does Ricoeur's definition of metaphor as deviant, or perverse, predication.

Briefly, I would pursue this cultural connection among rhetorical figure, sacrament, and finance that is implicit in the conceptual language, specifically including the metaphorical language, of Tudor-Stuart culture to another text that I earlier identified as the inspiration and source of Malynes' central metaphor of body, soul, and spirit. In *The Custumers Alphabet*, Thomas Milles equates merchants' valuation in exchange with counterfeiting the King's coin and excoriates certain "Vndertakers," who are variously characterized as farmers of customs (Crown patentees) and "*Marchants*, that (Tradelesse themselues) liue by buying and selling[,] . . . raysing all their profits from others Trades and paynes" (sigs. F2v, K2r):

> If *Exchange* of *Goodes* by Gold & Siluer, the BODY & BLOOD of *Kings* and *Kingdomes* (represented to vs in CURRANT COYNE,) be the Spirit of *Trafficke*, and mysticall Cyment that glewes so fast together the mutuall coniunction betweene Soueraignes & Subjects, by *Lawe* and *Grace*, as religious Iustice hath taught us to beleeue, Then drawe these *Vndertakers* their Methods all from ROME, where first was taught the doctrine that enchaunts and transubstantiates our *Eucheristicke Sacraments*, (representing to vs the BODY and BLOOD of CHRIST, by BREAD and WINE,) to *Idolatrous Masses*, and our Christian *Exchange* into Iewish Vsury.[95]

Ironically in Milles's accusations, metaphor now belongs to Rome rather than to the Reformation, but not without an occasional anticipatory protest in the sixteenth century, as we have earlier seen, for example, from Peter Martyr: the Roman Catholics "dooe muche abuse the latine verbe substantif, *Est,* and muche contrarie to the propre significacion that [*est*]" should have cause it "to signifie *transubstanciatur*[,] is chaunged in substaunce, or to stand for *conuertitur* . . . or for *transmutatur*," instead of for its "true and propre significacioun" (fol. 15r).

More immediately, interest and extortion are one for Milles, and the metaphorical, or proportional, interchangeability of figure, body, and coin is also complete. Malynes is a more interesting and complex case: he does not express these equations and prejudices as directly or as extremely, but more subtly they inform his views.[96] Earlier in the *Mercatoria*, Malynes was at pains to demystify another assay master's supposition that the "Mysterie" of the fineness of Gold and Silver is as "intricate" (perplexed and perplexing) as "the Transubstantiation of the Papists Sacrament." Malynes' rational distinctions are better than Milles's, but he is at the very least on the same cultural frequency. Engaged and informed observers of their society, Milles and Malynes present a snapshot of the intermixtures of the old and the new. Reformed in religion, one that depends heavily on metaphor, but lagging in the socioeconomic sphere, they are both nonetheless metaphorizers in the one but not in the other. Cultural change is ever uneven.

Bankers, long synonymous with "exchangers" and "cambists" (Italian *cambiare*, "to exchange, to change") on the Continent, are a particular abomination to Malynes, as his views of dry and fictitious exchange might have led us to suspect and as he is not shy to inform us: "Some men of iudgement haue found my writings to be inuective and patheticall against Bankers, wherein they are not mistaken." He alleges that the "Banker doth make the price of Exchanges, with the correspondence of other Bankes elsewhere at his pleasure and most aduantage" (408–09). The international money market, he claims, manipulates and, in the final analysis, really controls the exchanges. Milles makes the same point more extremely when he describes "that *Labyrinth* of Errors, (*Marchandizing Exchange*,)" as "the yeerely, monthly, and daily deuouring Iawes of that Monster of *Creete*, and Bawde of *Bankers* (VSURY,)" that is, usurious interest.[97] Putting the matter as I have, however, I am not supposing an equivalence between an international money market that does not deserve the name and a modern one. But rather than fashionably disdaining Malynes' theory of financial conspiracy by bankers, which is shared by Misselden and even by Mun to an extent, I *am* suggesting that it not only has some element of credibility in his time but is also all too currently familiar.[98] If someone or some identifiable collective body can be held responsible, the situation seems somehow rational, remediable, subject to control.

Rice Vaughan's assessment of Malynes' desire for *par pro pari* exchange is *contemporarily* more reliable than Misselden's or Mun's, both because it concentrates directly on this issue as a way of addressing the immediate, paralyzing problem of the silver drain and because Vaughan lacks the conspicuous self-interest of these two co-operating merchants.[99] Moreover, he even-handedly recognizes that for want of sufficient information about the workings of the monetary system, "the wisest States and the greatest Councils . . . have been abused by misterious names [terms], and perplexed subtilties of *Mint-men, Gold-Smiths* and *Exchangers*" (227). Vaughan devotes a separate chapter to Malynes' proposal "Of equalizing the Exchange," abstracting this as follows:

> if it be effectually ordained, That no man shall give his Money here, to receive less in intrinsical value there by Exchange; and that no man shall give his Money there, to receive more in *intrinsical* value here by Exchange: it is plain, That no man shall have his Advantage to carry his Money thither in *specie*, nor no man shall have his Disadvantage to bring his Money thence in *specie*: and if the same course be observed in all places and at all times, let other Nations use what they please to raise or abase the values of their Moneys, they shall never prejudice the Kingdom by it [185–86].

Vaughan proceeds to a closer examination of this proposition and lays out "the *Impossibility* of putting it in Execution," although not without first observing that "the *intrinsical* value be the principal Rule by which Exchanges are squared ['equalized, balanced, justified']."[100] Vaughan's observation is precisely what Malynes has desired but has argued a de facto reality denies.

But Vaughan does not stop with this observation in principle. Instead, he adds as his main objection to Malynes' proposal that variable circumstances "alter the Exchange" and recites the working of the quantity theory consequent on them, which if disabled, he adds, will simply lead to an increased reliance on specie and aggravate the problem of its export (187). "But suppose this *Difficulty* could be overcome," he continues, hypothesizing an above-par valuation of English money: "he then which at these times would have made over Money by Exchange into . . . [Continental countries with lower valuations] should have had but the *intrinsical* value in Money of these Countries," whereas the exporter of specie "would have had more than the *intrinsical* value" (187–88). Having scored one point, he then applies the principle of equality to a different situation to score another: "If the Equality of Exchange will give impediment to export *Silver* out of *England* into *Holland*, will not the same equality of Exchange give the same degree of Impediment to import Silver out of *Spain* [still considered the fountain of silver] into *England*?" (189). In other words, if England is ever to solve its shortage of coin or to increase its wealth, must not a perpetuation of stasis be avoided? To use the word *stasis* here, not to mention related terms such as *stability, balance,* and *equilibrium,* is to invoke basic issues in Elizabethan and early Stuart culture: for example, mutability in Spenser's writing, Jonson's complementary fascination with movement and stillness, and the vagaries of changing fortunes, virtually synonymous with the omnipresent sea, in Shakespeare's plays.[101]

In another instance of culturally loaded usage, Malynes uses the term *abuse* throughout *Lex Mercatoria,* but it occurs with particular frequency when he decries the current practice of the exchanges. While not examining his every use of this favored term, I want to consider their significant variety, in some instances cited earlier. One such use even coincides explicitly with the word *usurpation* (*usurpo*), of interest in connection with metaphor and more specifically with *abusio,* or catachresis, in my seventh chapter. With such coincidence, language again participates noticeably in history, as did the copulative form of the verb of being, in which Reformation debate on the Sacrament lay dormant, as if in a Yeatsian version of Leda's egg.

In one instance of *abuse* seen earlier, Malynes refers to cloth whose substance is abused by deceptive stretching. In a second, the cloth is "abused," that is, increased in weight by fraudulent dyeing. A third "abuse" occurs in the use of straight lines in navigational charts when they should really be curved or "Helicall." The first two abuses directly involve material substance, but the common denominator for all three is the *misrepresentation* of material truth, as when money lacks, or fails to represent, substantial value (I.iv.55, 57; xxxiv.185).

When Malynes focuses his attention on abuses more specifically of the economic *system,* he speaks of wise merchants not driven by greed (or gain), who recognize foreign currency exchanges as the abusive cause of the silver drain from England (I.v.64). The forestalling or "buy[ing] up of all things" [i.e., cornering the market] by a Society or Company such as the Merchant Adventurers or East India Company is also an "odious" "abuse" and, like exploitative usury, "biting." On the same page, a monopoly is "usurped by a few . . . and forestalled from all others"; two pages later, patents are a "great abuse"; and elsewhere any evilly practiced custom, that is, a custom abused, is a "usurpation": "*Non est consuetudo, sed usurpatio.*"[102] In these last several instances, *abuse* and *usurpation* have virtual synonymy as "misuse," and it is clear that Malynes would have considered the exchanges of his day usurpations, as well as abuses. In the context of unequal exchanging, he also associates audacity (*audacia*), which is connected with "bold" metaphor in Cicero, somewhat cryptically with dishonest self-interest not based on *par pro pari*: thus our "Mint men" and much more "our Goldsmiths and Merchants . . . either are ignorant, or wise in their own conceits; . . . for wis-dome draweth backe, where blind Bayard is audatious" (310). Mint men bought gold and silver, and goldsmiths, like merchants, functioned as ex-changers. Despite what Malynes thinks the obvious truth about abusive ex-changes, the proverbially headstrong horse Bayard charges blindly but audaciously forward, as wisdom, whether that of Malynes himself or that of mint men, goldsmiths, and merchants or conceivably even that of the Crown, holds back, each presumably for different reasons. *Ratio* languishes; once again, as in my chapter on Spenser, although in a different sphere of activity, *abusio* reigns.

Denouncing unequal exchanges, Malynes employs *abuse* twice on a sin-gle page, and he reiterates this charge often, as when he declares "this course of Exchange . . . of late yeares abused, and (as it were) made a merchandise" (II.viii.291, III.ii.382). But "as it were"—this signal of figurality or a counter-factual condition—once again hovers between recognition and de-nial, between creative, conceptual metaphor and mere metaphor, between historical insight and empty flourish. Again, Malynes straddles two worlds, and they are rhetorical, as well as economic, ones. The way he thinks and the way he writes, his content and his form, overlap conspicuously and sig-nificantly.

To recognize this overlap, however, is not to accept the contrast with which I began between Mun's correlative antipathies to bullion and figura-tive language and Malynes' domination by both. Aside from the problem of Mun's own inconsistencies regarding the importance of money, Malynes' use of figuration is, as I have argued throughout, more complex, distinctive, and historically significant than a desire simply to amass treasure. While his belief in the economic dominance of money has been clear from the start, his commitment to monetary accumulation and expansion for their own sakes has not been. In view of his overriding desire for economic stability, substantively grounded, and his emphatic belief in the need of equitable monetary relations among nations, his interest in such accumulation and expansion is actually less pronounced than Mun's. His commitment to fig-urative language, if measured by the arch-trope metaphor, is similarly quali-fied by his distrust of exchange. His avowed preference is rather for "demonstratiue reasons and infallible arguments, *illustrated* by similies"—again, for rationality, assurance, substance, stability (*Center*, 6: my emphasis). Metaphor, understood as surplus and creative exchange, is what persistently threatens his vision.

❧

In the course of enumerating the traditional prohibitions against usury in *Lex Mercatoria*, just prior to the focal chapters on abusive exchanges, Malynes summarizes his allegory *Saint George for England*, first published in 1601 but, he firmly believes, still current and accurate in 1622.[103] For my purposes, *Saint George* affords a final instance of Malynes' thought and writing that has something to tell both about Malynes and about continued metaphor, or allegory, as his age defined it. His dedication of *Saint George* to Sir Thomas Egerton (for whose many favors he is grateful) opens with reference to the "*inuented* historie of S. *George*," which "howsoeuer heretofore *abused*, may *conueniently* be *applied*" to the matter at hand (sig. A2r, my emphasis). As the emphasized words indicate, he is fully aware of the constructed nature of his material, even as he asserts the "conuenience"—the aptness and rightness, indeed, the truth—of his application. The operative description of his subject matter comes in his address to the reader, which spells out the enormous threat to the commonwealth posed by a "*Dragon, a monster found out by couetousnesse the roote of all euill*" (sig. A6v).[104] This dragon, he is at pains to tell us, has a "*taile, wherein lyeth his greatest strength*," which he uses to deprive the Prince of his treasure and ready money "*by falsifying the valuation of mony*"; he causes the rule and measure of money "*to be made vncertaine, and as it were a merchandize*" (sig. A7r). This is quite a dragon's tail (and tale), if by now also a familiar Malynesian one.

But there is more to come: "*This dragon is called* Foenus politicum [politic exchange, based on extrinsic, "merchants" valuation], *his two wings are* Vsura palliata [veiled usury, hidden interest] *and* Vsura explicata [open usury], *and his taile inconstant* Cambium [exchange]." And it gets even better: "*The virgin is the kings treasure: the champion* Saint George *is the kings authoritie, armed with the right armor of a Christian*"; his sword is the spirit of God's word, and his piebald horse, various laws of the kingdom, and so on (sig. A8r). Even before getting to the allegory proper, any modern reader (and perhaps Sir Thomas?) is thinking, "Oh, no." But why?

As one who has spent a good deal of time with *The Faerie Queene*, I have found myself wondering just how Malynes' heavy hand differs from Spenser's in the Letter to Raleigh, published, I hasten to add, at the end of the 1590 edition and omitted from that of 1596.[105] Aside from placement, or emphasis, an obvious difference is *translatability*, in all its synonymity with metaphor. Spenser's Letter, or address to the reader, describes another generically Arthurian "*knight of the Redcrosse, in whom I* [Spenser] *expresse Holynes*," and when a fuller description comes, it involves narrative: "*Soone after entred a faire Ladye in mourning weedes, riding on a white Asse, with a dwarfe*" *behind her leading a warlike steed,*" and so on.[106] By shifting into narrative mode, Spenser's letter moves quickly away from merely stated equivalents to their more embodied and temporal forms, that is, toward a kind of human credibility or "realism"—if not in the documentary sense here, not in a purely Platonic sense, either. Spenser's abstract equivalents for his Arthurian protagonists, such as Holiness, Temperance, and Chastity, moreover, are "natural," by which I here mean cultural and traditional, whereas Malynes' scream their artificiality. Spenser's are also significantly spiritual and moral, whereas Malynes' are economic and material: with the latter's that old Cold War mock of an allegorical romance, Soviet style, comes to mind—"boy meets tractor; girl meets sewing machine." The resistance of matter at some basic level to human form and meaning—its stubbornness, its unreasonable rigidity, which is to say its seeming inhumanity—is again at issue.[107] Here the possibility of a primordial rift at the base of signification, whose expression in the Roman rhetorics my last chapter questioned, returns with a vengeance.

As an alternative to this primordial rift, Clark's notion of "scaffolding" (again, a metaphor with limits) from a fundamental physical orientation or grounding affords the first connection "upward" toward abstraction, conceptualization, and representation required, with subsequent and more problematical steps to come.[108] But these subsequent steps eventually have to confront directly the issue of limit, sublation, or transcendence so basically argued in the debate between Derrida and Ricoeur regarding dead metaphors and living ones. Implicit in this complex issue, while not limited to my present description of it, is the creative productivity of metaphor as an agent of sublation, whether creative metaphor is conceived as the breaking of an inherited or established code or, more likely and more often, as the exceeding of it.

Here, with the question of creativity and the relation of language and rhetoric to it, I return for a moment to the neo-cognitive totalizing of Lakoff and Johnson. Like Derrida or indeed Ricoeur, Lakoff and Johnson occasionally revert to the etymology of a word and more often to what they term the "metaphoricity" (physical foundation) of a clichéd, or coded, expression as evidence that concepts are basically metaphorical and essentially physical. They firmly assert that "not all conceptual metaphors are manifested in . . . words. . . . Some are manifested in grammar, others in gesture, art, or ritual." Perhaps one could take their repeated use of *manifest* to indicate that they assume language (understood broadly as a system of signs) to be a semiotic pre-condition—a kind of cultural brain wiring—within human society, but elsewhere they clearly resubscribe to their view that language merely expresses thought, which is somehow pre-existent. For example, "Metaphor is centrally a matter of thought, not just words. Metaphorical language is a reflection of metaphorical thought. Metaphorical thought, in the form of metaphorical, cross-domain mappings [e.g., transferring the idea of travel to love] is primary; metaphorical language is secondary." More baldly, "concepts must exist before there can be words for them."[109] Thus the signs don't really matter; only the metaphorical concept does. This conclusion seems to me oxymoronic: what is thought without language, and can a concept be thought without it? While most concepts are verbal, a phenomenon historically and culturally dictated itself, my questions do not exclude conceptual expression, refinement, extension, or full realization in plastic and somatic forms. As I have earlier suggested, Lakoff and Johnson's "concept" is either that of which an amoeba is capable or else it ignores the problems of abstraction, conceptualization, and sublation, as well as the more specific bearing of creative metaphor on history and human culture.[110]

When Malynes' allegorical *Saint George*, which repeatedly, if inadvertently, invites reflection on figuration and its relation to physical matter, actually gets under way, it begins, incredibly enough, with a virtual translation to prose of the opening of *The Canterbury Tales*:

> Aprill hauing with his sweete showers moystened the drought of March, bathing euery veine of the rootes of trees & ingendring floures, *Zephirus* with his pleasaunt breath prouoking tender crops by vertue of young *Phebus*, holding her course in *Aries*. Abstinence in Lent performing her accustomed race feeding on waterie creatures, the Moone being entred into the aquatike signe of *Pisces*, and my bloud increasing with the nource of digestion, caused me to slumber. . . . [1].

Increased interest in astronomical detail and then the attention to diet—those "waterie creatures," or fish—is the first sign, and further attention to the physiology of the digestive process the incontrovertible sign, that we are shifting from Chaucer (now via the Squire's Tale) to Malynes.[111] Again, what is it about these material and physical details that exceeds the mere fact of shifting from Chaucer? Concentration, extension, physicality, "realism"?

Malynes' slumber gives way to a dream vision, and he commits it to paper to ease his overburdened memory, which is as full as "a trammell [fish net] replenished with fish."[112] In this vision, he travels to a *locus amoenus*, "a most fruitfull Iland" called Niobla (Albion, i.e., England). Here savory and delicious fruits distill nectar, fair rivers run with silver streams, green fields display a variety of flowers, "easie high waies [are] set with fruite-trees on euery side," "stately hills" grace "their *Horizon* as the nose doth the face"; and there are also "liuely fountaines of refreshing water, and . . . the sweete and harmonious melodie of birds, whose warbling notes did penetrate my eares." In this setting, all his senses are "reduced to puritie," seeming "to haue obtained fruition of their wished desires" (2–3). While I have only half-quoted Malynes' description, it is pretty good, if variously conventional and derivative, until those hills rear their noses on the horizon. Recalling tonal touches in Shakespeare's *Venus and Adonis* (just for a Renaissance example), one wonders whether Malynes could be joking, trying to spoof George and his dragon, *loci amoeni*, dream visions—perhaps even the opening of *The Canterbury Tales*. Humor could be a way of getting attention, and his satire, if that is what it is, could still carry a serious economic point. But remembering the incongruity of gold's not stinking in Malynes' otherwise refined description in *Lex Mercatoria*, I am inclined to see another flicker of Bottom the Weaver: "Bottom, thou are translat[ing]"![113] Even so, what is so incongruous, so egregiously un-tropic, so stubbornly literal about a nose on the face of the horizon? Whatever happens here—and an invitation to visualization and cultural valuation are pertinent—a significant *exchange*, a dis-placement, between face and horizon fails to occur. Both hills and nose remain too much themselves and therefore simply incongruous.

Discussing the common Reformation characterization of the sacraments as visible words, I earlier had recourse to Ricoeur's view, synthesizing and extending others', that good metaphors—indeed, good tropes—enable something like visualization: "it is as though the tropes gave to discourse a quasi-bodily externalization," one that is there and not there. "By providing a kind of figurability to the message, the tropes [*figures*, after all, of speech] make discourse appear." "As though . . . a kind of," the visualization is itself metaphorical and approximate. This quasi-visualization, or more inclusively this quasi-sensuous realization, is largely what misfires (oops) in Malynes' nose on the horizon. The force of his failed figure is *mere* visualization, reduction to the physical or "literalization."[114]

As the dreaming Malynes basks in "felicitie . . . [among] these rare blessings," a "loathsome smell scale[s] the fortresse of . . . [his] nose" (what is it with him and noses?), and he soon meets an old man, whose face shines with "amiable reuerence" (4). The old man explains that the "pestiferous smell, as dangerous to the smelling as the cockatrice is to the sight," arises from the terrible, cruel dragon that daily devours the island's inhabitants and threatens the king and his daughter. This dragon is akin to the dragon that threatened the king's royal ancestor, whom St. George miraculously rescued from ruinous loss. At the dreamer's request, the old man then recounts a very long tale about the depredations of the dragon, with a brief flashback en route to recount St. George's defeat of the dragon's scaly predecessor.

He begins, however, with an idealized description of a city by the side of the river Semath (Thames) and of the life of inhabitants of this island kingdom that "ouerfloweth with milk and hony." Before the ravages of the dragon, "euery man [lived content,] vsing and enioying his own, & nothing but his own, which in regard of charity euery man possessing, yet seemed not to possesse at all." Here every man works for the good of the commonwealth, and trade proceeds "with an equalitie"; free lending occurs, hospitality is maintained, and commiseration for the poor is exercised (7–9,13,15). Unfortunately, the dragon now dwells in the midst of the city by the side of the river, though he also roams at pleasure throughout the island, where "he will gobble vp a whole towne, and there a goodly parke, here a Lordship or Manor, and there a most pleasant wood" (9, 36). He feeds on

> the most precious meate, which doth command all other meates and delicacies. And behold his cruelty by so much the greater, as most vsually this meate is prepared vnto him by the poorer sort, and vpon them he feedeth most greedily. And whether euer that *serpent* went skipping vpon his taile before the curse, I know not: but I am sure this beareth his taile aloft like a conquerer, riding in his triumphant chariot [11–12].

Again, this really isn't too bad for allegory, although the action is secondhand. The precious meat (archaic: food) is money, and the serpentine charioteer is not an insurmountable problem for anyone raised on animation, for which the seventeenth century had its imaginative equivalents.

As of about the seventeeth page, however, Malynes' allegorical impulse begins to flag. His allegory becomes the old man's oration, with extensive exempla of exploits simply incredible for a dragon whose tail is stronger than that of Gargantua's horse and who for recreative digestion fells elephants with this tail around their legs, bull-whip style.[115] Malynes does tell us, though only at the very end of his allegory, that he saw him "as if I had seene some *satire*, halfe a man & halfe a beast," but even with the possibility of a historically sanctioned, if mistaken, pun on *satire* (literary mode and satyr), this just doesn't compensate for fifty pages of sequential, formulaic statements regarding draconic accomplishments, which begin like the following: "Others he maketh to go loaden with gold and siluer"; "Others he maketh voide of all charity"; "Others he maketh to vse the Lawes like vnto cobwebs"; "Others haue ability giuen them by the multiplicities of sutes grounded vpon bonds and counterbonds, to accumulate riches and to incorporate farmes, and to make vnlawfull inclosures of grounds"; "Others he causeth to put the king in remembrance of certaine olde moath-eaten lawes, of euery man forgotten, as a way vnto him honorable and profitable, hauing a shew and colour of Iustice"; "By the meanes of his taile he maintaineth a league with forreine nations, and causeth them to serue his turne, by bringing in superfluous commodities at a deare rate"; "He doth falsifie our weight and measure, and bringeth thereby inequality, . . . making of money a merchandize" (19–21, 41–42, 73). Again, the constructive, creative metaphorical exchange that credible allegory requires is precisely what is lacking.

Malynes' enumeration of draconic effects lacks the active movement of narrative. Allegory as autonomous form, rather than as localized metaphor, is necessarily narrative, inhering in drama and narrative proper.[116] A freestanding allegory also requires material susceptible of sublation, something matter per se, including some material kinds of subject matter, simply resists, and it requires a manner of abstraction, conceptualization, scaffolding, or sublation that is constructed to be at least locally credible.[117] In strikingly analogous historical anecdotes, Rice Vaughan, who wrote of local valuation by the prince as ensuring the "proper Limits and natural form" of money, also recounts more than once how the people can refuse and thus disable princely valuation of the coinage, whether enhanced or debased: for example, in Ireland, at the end of Elizabeth's reign, "as soon as the Exchanges of *base* [debased] *Moneys* sent thither did cease in *England*, it [the money] was instantly rejected there, and would not pass currant [even] for so much as in the true intrinsical value it was worth."[118] The people simply had no faith in what Vaughan, like Malynes, elsewhere calls the "abstract and imaginary" valuation (or, irrelevantly for my purpose, no faith even in the intrinsic one). The English had similarly lacked faith in the value of Malynes' copper farthings, the coins meant to relieve England's shortage of circulating currency in the royally authorized project whose failure bankrupted Malynes and led to his temporary imprisonment in the Fleet in 1619. Apparently the people had the right to exchange their copper farthings for silver and promptly did so, thus translating Malynes into bankruptcy. The *credibility* of the token, vehicle, or sign, whether metal or verbal, or, indeed, financial or religious, is clearly crucial.[119]

But Malynes himself, whose writing features varieties of similitude from analogy and simile to metaphor and allegory, finally and ironically resists active, transforming exchange in rhetoric as in economics, in language as in money. Mixed as his view of the world may in fact have been, he is finally more committed to the fixed forms of his dreams than to the process he sees around him but paradoxically also to the grounding of these forms in a material world that he does not fully realize is, or is swiftly becoming, a fiction. Our own ability to recognize it as such rests on its strangeness, its alienation. For us, like Ptolemy's universe or like metaphor as Cicero so suggestively characterized it, Malynes' depiction of his world occupies a place no longer its own: *locus alienus*.

To examine the texts of earlier periods is to recognize how highly and variously metaphorical human culture, especially but not exclusively intellectual culture, has always been at its conceptual core. I have no doubt that it remains so, although the ways in which this is true may not be as fully evident to us as in the more estranged (*alienus*) and rhetorically oriented culture of Shakespeare or Cranmer, of Donne or Foxe, of Spenser, Hoskins, or Malynes. I have little trouble imagining scholarly readers at some distant future date finding copious documents to substantiate the analogous, but not identical, tropicality of our own culture. My imagined readers will find especially rich pickings in texts treating literary and cultural theory, as a number of my chapters have suggested, including the examination of homology in my last. My purpose throughout this book has not been simply to identify and examine metaphoricity, however. It has been more broadly and conceptually to identify what metaphor does, how it constructs and creates, provokes and produces, in cultural language and history. That it does so is to my mind profoundly, and perhaps definitively, characteristic of the scaffolding of human culture.

Notes

Chapter One

Renaissance Metaphor and the Dynamic of Cultural Change: An Introductory Road Map

1. Ricoeur, *The Rule of Metaphor: Multi-disciplinary Studies of the Creation of Meaning in Language*, trans. Robert Czerny (1977; rpt. Toronto: Univ. of Toronto Press, 1979), 285–86. Lexically, the German verb *aufheben,* cognate of the noun *Aufhebung,* signifies "lift," "raise," or "keep," "preserve," or "abolish," "suspend." As Harry Berger, Jr., notes in *Fictions of the Pose: Rembrandt Against the Italian Renaissance* (Stanford: Stanford Univ. Press, 2000; 429–30), Hegel's term has been rendered verbally in English both as "sublate" and as "supersede." Since *sublate,* a derivative of Latin *tollere/sublatus,* "to lift up," shares with the word *translate* (Latin *transferre/translatus*), a common Indo-European root, namely, *telə-,* it is germane to my concern with translation, or metaphor, as an agent of sublation in a way that *supersede* is not. Historically sublation, in its bearing on translation, is the more appropriate English term in the present context. See also my chap.2, n. 33, below.

2. *Being There: Putting Brain, Body, and World Together Again* (Cambridge, MA: MIT Press, 2001), 32–33.

3. Quotation from Clark, xi.

4. *Philosophy in the Flesh: The Embodied Mind and Its Challenge to Western Thought* (New York: Basic Books, 1999), 17; cf. 3, 344, 348. As Lakoff and Johnson's argument progresses, they increasingly invoke a more generalized cultural experience evident in folk theory and the like, rather than only a physical basis. Their comprehensive assertions are impressive, although often too general or based on evidence already in language or subject, as in the instance of the amoeba, to questions of definition and reduction. Not until page 431, incidentally, do they get around to defining a category as "a kind of thing . . . defined by a concept . . . that . . . characterizes the essence of the category."

5. "The Metaphorical Process as Cognition, Imagination, and Feeling," in *On Metaphor,* ed. Sheldon Sacks (1978; rpt. Chicago: Univ. of Chicago Press, 1979), 141–57, here 142.

6. Cf. Marc Shell, *Money, Language, and Thought: Literary and Philosophic Economies from the Medieval to the Modern Era* (1982; rpt. Baltimore: Johns Hopkins Univ. Press, 1993), 4: Shell refers to "the tropic interaction between economic and lin-

guistic symbolization and production." For Mark Osteen and Martha Woodmansee, "the most troubling problem for 'language and money' theorists concerns the viability of homologies": Introduction to *The New Economic Criticism: Studies at the Intersection of Literature and Economics*, ed. Woodmansee and Osteen (London: Routledge, 1999), 3–50, here 29. See also my chap. 8, 172–74, below.

7. Ricoeur, "Metaphorical Process," 141–57, here 151; also his *Rule*, 256. See also Wolfgang Iser, *The Fictive and the Imaginary: Charting Literary Anthropology* (Baltimore: Johns Hopkins Univ. Press, 1993), xiv–xv, whose language my description also invokes: like Ricoeur's Majorcan tales, Iser's category of the fictive is not tied to "the old dichotomy of fiction and reality." The fictive "keeps in view what has been overstepped," but it is nonetheless "an act of boundary-crossing" that at once "disrupts and doubles the referential world." In the simultaneity of Ricoeur's split reference, as in the pastoral narratives that Iser privileges, the crossing of boundaries, disruption of the everyday, and doubling of reference actually *trans-figure* the world that we know, rather than merely reflecting, refusing, or rising above it.

Chapter Two

Translating Investments: The Metaphoricity of Language, *Hamlet*, and *2 Henry IV*

1. *Shakespeare Verbatim: The Reproduction of Authenticity and the 1790 Apparatus* (Oxford: Clarendon, 1991).

2. Patricia Parker, *Literary Fat Ladies: Rhetoric, Gender, Property* (London: Methuen, 1987), chap. 3, is a notable exception, as is the impressive chapter on translation in her *Shakespeare from the Margins: Language, Culture, Context* (Chicago: Univ. of Chicago Press, 1996). In both chapters, Parker invokes George Puttenham's treatment of metaphor under the translative heading "the figure of transporte": see *The Arte of English Poesie* 1589 (facsimile 1906; rpt. Kent, OH: Kent State Univ. Press, 1988), 188–90. On *translatio studii*, see Douglas Kelly "*Translatio Studii*: Translation, Adaptation, and Allegory in Medieval French Literature," *Philological Quarterly*, 57 (1978), 287–310; and on translation from one language to another, see Glyn P. Norton, *The Ideology and Language of Translation in Renaissance France and Their Humanist Antecedents* (Genève, Droz, 1984).

3. *OED*, s.v. *translate, translation*; the *MED*, s.v. *translation*, notes meanings that are in most cases still available at least to the sixteenth century: e.g., the glorious transformation of a person into a constellation, the transfer of power or prerogatives from one person to another, the alienation of a kingdom from its ruler, the capture or exile of a people. On translation among companies, see Steve Rappaport, *Worlds within Worlds: Structures of Life in Sixteenth-Century London* (Cambridge: Cambridge Univ. Press, 1989), 110.

4. *Women, Fire, and Dangerous Things: What Categories Reveal about the Mind* (Chicago: Univ. of Chicago Press, 1987), 12–14, 334, 378, 534–40; cf. also George Lakoff and Mark Johnson, *Metaphors We Live By* (Chicago: Univ. of Chicago Press, 1980), e.g., chaps. 1–3, 12; and Mark Johnson, *The Body in the Mind* (Chicago: Univ. of Chicago Press, 1987), chaps. 2–3. It should be noted that Lakoff's radial category is essentially synchronic.

5. *The Rule of Metaphor*, chap. 2. Although Ricoeur does not explicitly critique early modern theories of metaphor, what he finds wrong with Fontanier's work applies to them.

6. See Ricoeur "Metaphorical Process," 142–43; and Jacques Derrida, "White Mythology: Metaphor in the Text of Philosophy," trans. F.C.T. Moore, *New Literary History*, 6 (1975), 5–74, here 55. Ricoeur observes the metaphoricity of the term *metaphor* in a context indicating he has in mind the philosophical problem of the hermeneutic circle that Derrida makes crucial in "White Mythology," his best-known and basic analysis of metaphor.

7. Richards broaches the idea of metaphorical tenors and vehicles in *The Philosophy of Rhetoric*, although without specifically attributing his inspiration for this terminology to the literal meaning of *metaphora*: New York: Oxford Univ. Press, 1936, chap. 5, esp. 96–98. Accounts of the development of the literary theory of metaphor in the twentieth century frequently give foundational prominence to Richards' terminology. For relatively more recent and expansive wordplay with the coincidence of vehicle and trope, see Jacques Derrida, "The Retrait of Metaphor," trans. Eds., *Enclitic*, 2:2 (1978), 4–33, here 6–7.

8. Essentially, I accept Leah Marcus' arguments regarding the terms "early modern" and "Renaissance" and, like her, consider both useful and usually interchangeable: "Renaissance / Early Modern Studies," in *Redrawing the Boundaries*, ed. Stephen Greenblatt and Giles Gunn (New York: Modern Language Association, 1992), 41–63. In the present chapter, however, "early modern" implies a Tudor and pre-Restoration Stuart core with fuzzy chronological boundaries, which is particularly applicable to certain linguistic and rhetorical issues. "Renaissance" (e.g., Renaissance rhetoricians) implies the chronological core.

9. E.g., on resistance to Latin in the religious sphere, see, for example, William Perkins, *Workes*, 3 vols. (London: John Legatt, 1612–13), II, 670–71; John Foxe, *Actes and Monuments of matters most speciall and memorable, happenyng in the Church, with an Vniuersall history of the same* (London: John Day, 1583), 1890: subsequent reference is to this edition, unless otherwise specified; Harold Fisch, "The Puritans and the Reform of Prose-Style," *ELH*, 19 (1952), 229–48, here 232. By royal decree, Lily's Latin Grammar reigned supreme in English schools of the early modern period. Relevant to pedagogical resistance are ten elucidations of Lily in English between 1590 and 1660; such translations were a means of circumventing the reigning monopoly on basic instruction, with its presentation in English only of the rudiments: see G. A. Padley, *Grammatical Theory in Western Europe, 1500–1700: Trends in Vernacular Grammar*, 2 vols. (Cambridge: Cambridge Univ. Press, 1985), I, 147–53; also my second chapter in *Words That Matter: Linguistic Perception in Renaissance English* (Stanford: Stanford Univ. Press, 1996). Richard Helgerson explores the politics of Elizabethan views of language in *Forms of Nationhood: The Elizabethan Writing of England* (Chicago: Univ. of Chicago Press, 1992), chap. 1.

10. So-called hard-word dictionaries, which become available in the vernacular around the turn of the century, do not count in this sense. (On the teaching of grammar in Latin, see my preceding note.)

11. From "Directions for the Reader" in the 1589 edition (rpt. Menston, Eng: Scolar, 1970). Rider's dictionary was subsequently revised and enlarged by Francis Holyoke, and it saw 23 reissued and new editions in the first sixty years of the seventeenth century. *OED*, s.v. *travail v.*, 1.b, c; s.v. *travailer.* "One who travails or labours"; s.v. *travel v.*; s.v. *traveller.* The spellings of the words *traveler* and *travailer* were interchangeable. According to Rappaport (299), "most apprentices possessed basic literacy skills," and an appreciable number of them clearly possessed more, as the celebrated Merchants Taylors School would indicate. Cf. also Thomas Mun, *England's Treasure by Forraign Trade,* 1622–23 (written), 1664 (published) (Rpt. New York: Macmillan, 1928), 3: "although there be no necessity that . . . a Merchant [of foreign trade] should be a great Scholar; yet is it (at least) required that in his youth he learn the Latin tongue"; on the dating of Mun's tract, see my chap. 8, n. 21, below.

12. See DeWitt T. Starnes, *Robert Estienne's Influence on Lexicography* (Austin: Univ. of Texas Press, 1963), esp. chap. 7. Estienne's dictionary is fairly representative of that of Ambrogio Calepino ("Calepine"). In Starnes's words, it had a "far-reaching influence" on lexicography in England during the early modern period (v). All citations of Estienne's *Thesaurus* will be from *Dictionarium, seu Latinae linguae thesaurus* (Paris: Robert Estienne, 1543). Translations throughout this book are mine unless otherwise indicated.

13. Estienne draws on Varro's *De lingua Latina* for the derivation of *vestis* from *vellus* and, in the next example, for that of *monumentum* from *moneo.* Modern philology recognizes neither of Estienne's derivations of *vestis.*

14. Estienne's reasons for deriving *lex* from *lego* draw heavily on Cicero's argument in *De legibus*, I.15–17: *Cicero,* trans. Clinton Walker Keyes (London: Heinemann, 1977), XVI. His definition also relies on a traditional understanding of prudence (e.g., Aristotle, Aquinas).

15. Reference to Nashe's *Lenten Stuffe* is found in the *OED*, s.v. *locupleatly.* Neologisms, requiring some form of retranslation, were rife in the period; e.g., see my nn. 35–36, immediately below, and the statements they annotate.

16. The same is true of Thomas Cooper's *Thesaurus linguae Romanae et Britannicae* (1565; rpt. Menston, Eng.: Scolar, 1969). Cooper's comprehensive Latin-English dictionary was another standard lexicon in sixteenth-century England.

17. Since my discussion of the conditions of meaning in early modern England draws, as here, on several sources I cite in *Words that Matter,* there is some overlap of observation. For additional discussion of Estienne's definition of *gravis,* about which more can be said in other connections, see chap. 3 of my *Words.* Cf. also Mark Johnson, *Body in the Mind,* 80–84, on the metaphorical projection from a physical realm to a figurative and perceptual one that best illustrates his theory regarding the embodied basis of human understanding.

18. *Consuetudo* (1622; rpt. Amsterdam: Theatrum Orbis Terrarum, 1979), e.g., 325; *Circle* (1623; rpt. New York: Augustus M. Kelley, 1971), e.g., 44.

19. Attridge, "Language as History/History as Language: Saussure and the Romance of Etymology," in *Post-Structuralism and the Question of History,* ed. Derek

Attridge, Geoff Bennington, and Robert Young (Cambridge: Cambridge Univ. Press, 1987), 83–211, e.g., 200–203. Much of Attridge's essay is concerned with Saussure's *problematizing* history rather than denying it (e.g., see 186). More recently, neo-cognitivists have argued that language is ontologically based in physical experience. If this is true, then the signifier at some very basic level is not arbitrary: for a superb review of these theories, see the introduction to Mary Thomas Crane's *Shakespeare's Brain: Reading with Cognitive Theory* (Princeton: Princeton Univ. Press, 2001). What the neo-cognitivists have not accounted for, however, is the effect of language at a less physically oriented level on physical orientations (such as "up and down"). The problem of abstraction, not to say of conceptualization and sublation, thus arises again.

20. Henry Peacham, *The Garden of Eloquence* (1577, 1593; rpt. New York: Scholars' Facsimiles & Reprints, 1954), 1–2: citation from 1593, with my emphasis.

21. "Substitution theory" is the term employed by Ricoeur (*Rule*, 4, and passim), after Max Black's characterization of a view that holds "a metaphorical expression to be used in place of some equivalent *literal* expression": *Models and Metaphors: Studies in Language and Philosophy* (Ithaca: Cornell Univ. Press, 1962), 31.

22. *The English Secretary or Methods of Writing "Epistles" and "Letters"* (1599; rpt. Gainesville: Scholars' Facsimiles & Reprints, 1967), 77; cf. 78.

23. In a relevant discussion, Derek Attridge relates this logic to the nature-art tension in Puttenham's treatise on rhetoric: *Peculiar Language: Literature as Difference from the Renaissance to James Joyce* (Ithaca: Cornell Univ. Press, 1988), 17–45.

24. See G. A. Padley, *Grammatical Theory in Western Europe, 1500–1700: The Latin Tradition* (Cambridge: Cambridge Univ. Press, 1976), 32, 35, 39, and passim.

25. A distinction between the grammatical "séntence" and the semantic "senténce" (as in Middle English) enables sententious expressions, even when grammatically isolable or complete, to function as subsentential units like the other rhetorical figures of thought and speech with which they were classed during the Renaissance. Padley also distinguishes between the "sentence," or *oratio* (after Priscian), which is normally understood in the Renaissance as a semantically "complete thought," and the sentence understood formally or structurally (32). Concern focused on the former in the early modern period.

26. The difficulty modern students experience in reading texts written in a periodic style is perhaps instructive. Even with a master of this style like Richard Hooker, whose lengthy sentences achieve a complex unity, it is arguably the distinction and importance of the component parts, rather than the fact of final unity, that separates a periodic style from others simpler in structure but grasped more readily as wholes.

27. Ian Hacking, *Why Does Language Matter to Philosophy?* (Cambridge: Cambridge Univ. Press, 1975), 187; also 19, 29, 161–62, 166.

28. *Philosophical Papers* (Oxford: Clarendon, 1961), 24.

29. To the tangle of tropic roots Derrida discovers in Aristotle, cf. the rhizome of Gilles Deleuze and Felix Guattari, as cited and invoked by Harry Berger, Jr.,

"Hydra and Rhizome," in *Shakespeare Reread: The Text in New Contexts*, ed. Russ McDonald (Ithaca: Cornell Univ. Press, 1994), 79–104, here, 95:

> In a rhizome . . . semiotic chains of every kind are connected . . . according to very diverse modes of encoding, chains that are biological, political, economic, etc., and that put into play not only regimes of different signs, but also different states of affairs. . . . A semiotic chain is like a tuber gathering up very diverse acts—linguistic, but also perceptual, mimetic, gestural, and cognitive. . . . Language stabilizes around a parish, a diocese, a capital. It forms a bulb. It evolves by means of stems and underground flows. . . . Language can always be broken down into its internal structural components, an activity not fundamentally different from a search for roots [*On the Line*, trans. John Johnston (New York: Semiotext[e], 1983), 11–13].

Fertile as is this liberating rhizome, its conception, which typically experiences dynamic stabilizers—elsewhere temporary blockages—does not engage the constructive, creative dimension of form (or context, individuated time, history, etc.) as fully as does the Ricoeur-Derrida dispute, treated below.

30. Derrida's French is cited here and elsewhere from "La mythologie blanche (la métaphore dans le texte philosophique)," *Poétique*, 5 (1971), 1–52, here 39. The French cited two sentences below in my text is from the same page.

31. Ricoeur is not alone in seeing etymology as the central issue: e.g., David E. Cooper, *Metaphor* (Oxford: Basil Blackwell, 1986), 23–27. Quotations from Ricoeur's original French are from *La métaphore vive* (Paris: Seuil, 1975); subsequent reference to the French will be to *Vive*.

32. "White Mythology," 7, and "La mythologie blanche," 2: "de plus value linguistique"; I take Derrida's view to be in assent with (indeed merging here with) that of Anatole France. (See also 26, cited in the note immediately below this one.) Cf. as well Jacques Derrida, "Des Tours de Babel," trans. Joseph F. Graham, in *Difference in Translation*, ed. Joseph F. Graham (Ithaca: Cornell Univ. Press, 1985), English translation, 165–207; original French, 209–48. I discuss Derrida's understanding of translation in "Tours de Babel" in chap. 7, below; this understanding contrasts tonally with the suggestions of deceptive masking or self-delusive idealization in "White Mythology." It also confirms the substantiality of a surplus in this earlier text, even as it implies possibilities as yet uninvented there.

33. Ricoeur's charge is not without justification, although it takes a statement by Derrida out of its larger context: 25 of "White Mythology" reads, "metaphorization . . . is nothing but a movement of idealization . . . namely *sublation (Aufhebung)*." Derrida adds that *Aufhebung* is "that memory which produces signs and interiorizes them (*Erinnerung*) by raising up, suppressing and conserving sensible exteriority" (25). Ricoeur's "only" is hardly what the two Derridean passages quoted above in my text suggest, however; on pages 13–14, Derrida also expresses serious reservations about the uninterrupted continuity—rational process?—implied by the idea of "wearing away" itself as a translation of metaphorical process. He reiterates his view that the process of wearing away includes the production of surplus value and

extends his opposition to (simple) etymologism in "The Retrait of Metaphor," 13–16, esp. 15. As Dominick LaCapra observes in "Who Rules Metaphor?" Derrida's emphasis in "Retrait" shifts somewhat from that in "White Mythology"—"perhaps because of Ricoeur's 'critique' ": *Diacritics*, 10, winter (1980), 15–28, here 27. Since my interest is less in the evolution of Derrida's thought than in the radical opposition to it of Ricoeur's view of the etymological trace, I rely on "White Mythology," the text that Ricoeur specifically engages and the one in which the basic issues are sharply etched. For another revealing variant in the argument, however, cf. J. F. Ross, *Portraying Analogy* (Cambridge: Cambridge Univ. Press, 1981), 51, whose lack of interest in what he calls "diachronic manifestations" manages simultaneously and proleptically to dismiss Derrida's metaphorical trace and Lakoff's metaphorical grounding in experience: Ross asks, why a person would "want to trace 'force' [magnetic fields] back through actual differentiations to 'force' used experientially in observations like 'He ought not to force that stone into place.' " With notable emphasis on continuity, he suggests that "A *constructed* series of [synchronic] stepwise adaptations from the one use to the other ought to be sufficient to display the continuity of meaning" (51). Although Ross's theory, too, is synchronic, other statements he makes about the diachrony of language are suggestive, and I will adapt them to my purposes later in this essay.

34. *Rule*, 133; cf. 129–30, where Ricoeur incorporates the word—but the synchronic word—into his sentential metaphorics. Ricoeur's theorizing acknowledges many debts, among the most important of which is to Max Black's groundbreaking essay on metaphor in *Models and Metaphors*. Writing (in the French edition) at virtually the same time as Ricoeur, Christian Metz has a view of the relation and relative importance of the word to the sentence that is similar to Ricoeur's: *The Imaginary Signifier: Psychoanalysis and the Cinema*, trans. Celia Britton, Annwyl Williams, Ben Brewster, and Alfred Guezzetti (Bloomington: Indiana Univ. Press, 1982), 225–26. Metz's view of polysemy is fairly pedestrian, yet based on inadequacy or lack as distinct from association and extension in creative or constructive senses (237–39). His orientation is primarily synchronic, fundamentally homological, and finally psychoanalytical. On homology, see chap. 8, 172–74, below.

35. F. W. Bateson, *English Poetry and the English Language* (1934; rpt. New York: Russell and Russell, 1961), 31, n. 2.

36. *The Cambridge History of the English Language*, ed. Roger Lass (Cambridge: Cambridge Univ. Press, 1992), III, 341.

37. For Ricoeur's consideration of polysemy, see *Rule*, 113–33; the statement cited is found on 115; on 113, 115, and esp. 131, Ricoeur asserts the centrality of an understanding of polysemy to his study. Unlike Ricoeur, many theorists use the term *polysemy* without attempting to define it responsibly. In *From Etymology to Pragmatics: Metaphorical and Cultural Aspects of Semantic Structure* (1990; rpt. Cambridge: Cambridge Univ. Press, 1997), the linguist Eve E. Sweetser, finding no "adequate account" of semantic change and its relation to polysemy to exist, attempts one with similarities to that at which I have arrived independently via literary theory and criticism (1–3, 47, 50, chaps. 1–3, and passim). Interestingly, what a literary specialist

regards as "context," Sweetser calls "cognition" or sometimes even "cognitive science" (e.g., 55). *Vive la translation!*

38. My calling economic terminology Derrida's in this encounter may be somewhat unfair; in *Rule*, 130, Ricoeur writes, "The word preserves the semantic capital constituted by . . . contextual values deposited in its semantic treasury." In this acknowledgment of the word's "identity," however, Ricoeur seems to be anticipating his treatment of Derrida's arguments, which will occupy him directly at a later stage.

39. A similar point could be made about the metaphorics of Jean-Joseph Goux's *Symbolic Economies: After Marx and Freud*, trans. Jennifer Curtiss Gage (Ithaca: Cornell Univ. Press, 1990). Goux's essay "Numismatics" (chap. 1), whose earlier publication Derrida cites approvingly in "White Mythology," opens with the assumption of a replacement (i.e., substitution) theory of metaphor and thus with a word-centered or symbol-centered one (9–10). For further consideration of Goux, see chap. 8, below.

40. Since Lakoff and Johnson have more to say specifically about the nature of metaphor in *Metaphors We Live By* than in their more recent *Philosophy in the Flesh: The Embodied Mind and its Challenge to Western Thought* (New York: Basic Books, 1999), I have concentrated on the former. Other writings by them are relevant. Lakoff's *Women, Fire, and Dangerous Things* is a theory of categorization in which metaphor plays a significant but not dominant role. In Mark Johnson's *Body in the Mind*, however, not only "the issue of the cognitive reality of image schemata" but also of "their metaphorical extensions is central" to the argument (101). None of these volumes by Lakoff, Johnson, or both of them specifically addresses the treatment of metaphor by Ricoeur or Derrida, although Johnson shows a positive interest in Ricoeur's theorizing of imagination in his own substantial introduction to *Philosophical Perspectives on Metaphor*, ed. Mark Johnson (Minneapolis: University of Minnesota Press, 1981). In *Philosophy in the Flesh*, Lakoff and Johnson summarily dismiss radical relativism (i.e., post-structuralism, Derrideanism), as well as the view that "metaphorical *language* is deviant," instead asserting that "Metaphorical *thought* is normal" (124: my emphases). The latter view generally rejects rationalist positions, and implicitly Ricoeur's.

41. *MED*, s.v. *investiture*; *OED*, s.v. *vest v.*, I.1, 2; *vestment*[1], 1, 2.

42. *OED*, s.v. *invest v.*, I.1.a–b, 2.a; 3.a, 4–8; II and II.9.a; *investment*, 1, 5.

43. John Florio, *A Worlde of Wordes, or Most Copious Dictionarie in Italian and English* (London: A. Hatfield for E. Blount, 1598). Jean-Christophe Agnew, *Worlds Apart: The Market and the Theater in Anglo-American Thought, 1550–1750* (Cambridge: Cambridge Univ. Press, 1986), 85, 116, 146, notes but may underestimate a play of meanings in the use of *invest/ment* in the period. He does not mention the fact that the financial meaning of *investment* exists in Italian from the fourteenth century.

44. Quotation from *The Oxford Dictionary of English Etymology*, ed. C. T. Onions (Oxford: Clarendon, 1966), s.v. *invest*. See also *OED*, s.v. *invest*, II and II.9.

45. Of particular interest on the exporting of cloth and wool are William Robert Scott, *The Constitution and Finance of English, Scottish and Irish Joint-Stock Companies*

to 1720, 3 vols. (1912: rpt. New York: Peter Smith, 1951), esp. I; George Burton Hotchkiss, ed., *A Treatise of Commerce*, 1601, by John Wheeler (New York: New York Univ. Press, 1931); also suggestive is Frances Elizabeth Baldwin, *Sumptuary Legislation and Personal Regulation in England* (Baltimore: Johns Hopkins Press, 1926). In 1569, James Peele, a self-described teacher of the "art of Italian merchants' accounts," attempted to introduce Italian methods (and vocabulary) to England in *The Pathe way to Perfectnes, in th' accomptes of Debitour, and Creditour*; according to Scott, however, the attempt was unsuccessful (I, 60, n. 1; 158–59). The only version of Peele that I have examined—fragmentary and on film—did not include the word *invest/ment*. Raymond de Roover reports, however, that double-entry bookkeeping "was spreading fast among the English merchants [ca. 1600], although it had been practiced assiduously by the Italian banking houses in Lombard Street [central London] ever since the fifteenth century, if not earlier": "Gerard de Malynes as an Economic Writer: From Scholasticism to Mercantilism," in *Business, Banking, and Economic Thought in Late Medieval and Early Modern Europe: Selected Studies of Raymond de Roover*, ed. Julius Kirshner (Chicago: Univ. of Chicago Press, 1974), 346–66, here 362. Andrea Finkelstein reports that Luca Pacioli's instructions for double-entry bookkeeping (1494) had been translated into English, Dutch, and French manuals by 1543: *Harmony and the Balance: An Intellectual History of Seventeenth-Century English Economic Thought* (Ann Arbor: Univ. of Michigan Press, 2000), 20.

46. See *OED* s.v. *wear, v.*[1] and s.v. *ware, v.*[2]: etymological histories and primary definitions. First recorded in 1417, *ware* occurs throughout the early modern period and well into the nineteenth century. An example is found in Roger Ascham's *Toxophilus*: "They shall fynde it bothe lesse charge and more pleasure to ware at any tyme a couple of shyllynges of a newe bowe"; another example in Heywood's *I Edward IV*: "I have wared all my money in cow-hides at Coleshill Market."

47. See Baldwin, *Sumptuary Legislation*, 131, 140–49, 152, 220, 248. Also Wilfred Hooper, "The Tudor Sumptuary Laws," *English Historical Review*, 30 (1915), 433–49, esp. 437–46 (Elizabeth's reign). Finkelstein cites contemporary instances in which the tailor's measure becomes a metaphor for "the need to keep each rank in its place" (23).

48. For a recent example, Richard Waswo argues against Marjorie O'Rourke Boyle's claim that Erasmus' conception of language is innovative by asserting that Erasmus "states the standard formula—'what clothing is to our body, style is to thoughts'": *Language and Meaning in the Renaissance* (Princeton: Princeton Univ. Press, 1987), 217. With Waswo's elaboration, namely, that Erasmus even "amplifies" the formula "at great length in terms of cleanliness, propriety, and so forth," compare the more complex implications of Jacques Revel's "Uses of Civility," in *A History of Private Life*, ed. Philippe Ariès and Georges Duby (Cambridge, MA: Harvard Univ. Press, 1989), III, ed. Roger Chartier, 167–205.

49. *Works*, ed. Edwin Greenlaw et al, *A View of the Present State of Ireland*, ed. Rudolf Gottfried (1949; rpt. Baltimore: Johns Hopkins Press, 1966), X, 121. Cf. Ann Rosalind Jones and Peter Stallybrass, "Dismantling Irena: The Sexualizing of Ireland in Early Modern England," in *Nationalism & Sexualities*, ed. Andrew Parker,

Mary Russo, Doris Sommer, and Patricia Yaeger (New York: Routledge, 1992), 157–71; also Peter Stallybrass' "Worn Worlds: Clothes and Identity on the Renaissance Stage," in *Subject and Object in Renaissance Culture*, ed. Margreta de Grazia, Maureen Quilligan, and Peter Stallybrass (Cambridge: Cambridge Univ. Press, 1996), 289–320.

50. Cf. Gramsci: "Every time that the language question appears, in one mode or another, it signifies that a series of other problems are beginning to impose themselves": cited by Jonathan Steinberg, "The Historian and the *Questione della Lingua*," in *The Social History of Language*, ed. Peter Burke and Roy Porter (Cambridge: Cambridge Univ. Press, 1987), 198–209, here 206. Similarly, on clothing, cf. Marjorie Garber, *Vested Interests: Cross-Dressing and Cultural Anxiety* (New York: Routledge, 1992), 10, 16–17; Claire Sponsler, "Narrating the Social Order: Medieval Clothing Laws," *Clio*, 21 (1992), 265–83, esp. 275–82; Jean Howard, "Cross-dressing, The Theater, and Gender Struggle in Early Modern England," *Shakespeare Quarterly*, 3 (1988), 418–40, esp. 422. Further suggestive in regard to the symbolic dimension of clothing is Anne Hollander's *Seeing through Clothes* (1975; rpt. New York: Viking, 1978), e.g., xiii, 85.

51. On such categories, see Lakoff, *Women, Fire, and Dangerous Things*, and also Lakoff and Johnson, *Metaphors We Live By*. See also Baldwin, 194 (Elizabeth's dresses), 36, 162 (clothing and the symbolism of national identity), 81 (clothing and the symbolism of power), 33–34 (nobility and wealth), 167 (extravagance). Also relevant are the now-classic treatments of Elizabeth's use of symbolic dress by Frances Yates, *Astraea: The Imperial Theme in the Sixteenth Century* (London: Routledge and Kegan Paul, 1975), 29–87, 215–19; and Roy Strong, *The Cult of Elizabeth: Elizabethan Portraiture and Pageantry* (London: Thames and Hudson, 1977), esp. 46–54. See also chap. 5, below, on vestments and the vestiarian controversy.

52. Cognate forms of *invest* occur seventeen times in Shakespeare.

53. Max Black's final revision of his theory of metaphor in *Models and Metaphors* describes a "so-called dead metaphor" as "an expression that no longer has a pregnant use," and he suggests the sliding categories "extinct," "dormant," and "active" to replace the less discriminating categories "living" and "dead": "More about Metaphor," in *Metaphor and Thought*, ed. Andrew Ortony, 2nd ed. (Cambridge: Cambridge Univ. Press, 1993), 20–41, here 25.

54. *The Riverside Shakespeare*, ed. G. Blakemore Evans et al, 2nd ed. (Boston: Houghton Mifflin, 1997): *As You Like It*, II.vii.58. Subsequent reference to Shakespeare will be to this edition unless otherwise specified. In *2 Henry IV*, *Riverside* observes the spelling Westmerland, rather than Westmoreland.

55. "Vagueness" is actually Stephen Ullmann's term, which Ricoeur adopts but which subsequently becomes "openness" in his discussion (*Rule*, 113, 116, 126, 127). Perhaps "openness" might be more appropriately described as accepting rather than as enduring meaning. Ricoeur cites Nelson Goodman's description of metaphor approvingly, however—"the application of an unusual and impertinent predicate to a subject that 'yields while protesting' "—a fact suggesting the validity of endurance at best: the gendered, indeed sexual, nuances of Goodman's metaphorical

description are notable (132). Considering the influence of social forces (earlier psychological forces) on the word, Ricoeur worries about formlessness: there is a persistent tendency in his discussion for the sentence effectually to become form, and the word matter or, perhaps more exactly, an entity of inferior form, whose "identity" is dangerously inclined to mutable expression (e.g., 127, despite 130; 118–199 for psychological forces). The "openness" to which he refers is actually translated an "opening towards" sentential form (127), a phrasing that suggests desire more specifically and substantially than the French "ouverture . . . en direction" does (*Vive*, 163). See also *Rule*, 113–33 passim, however.

56. The *OED* gives the same line from *Othello* as the first occurrence of *invest* with the meaning "To clothe or endue with attributes, qualities, or a character" (I.3.a). That Shakespeare's use of the word is likely innovative suggests his interest in it, here as elsewhere. It should also be noted, however, that *OED* definitions are readings—indeed translations—of words in their contexts and therefore, like other interpretations, subject to rereadings and retranslations.

57. Puttenham's rhetoric frequently refers to metaphor as an "inversion" of proper sense: "what els is your *Metaphor* but an inuersion of sence by transport"? (166, cf. 190). Mark Johnson, *Body in the Mind*, 107, declares polysemy, understood as "multiple *related* meanings" that are metaphorically elaborated, some of the best evidence for his theory of human cognition; he also believes that any adequate theory of meaning "should be able to explain semantic change over time" (193). Johnson is especially interested in "metaphor as a pervasive principle of human understanding that underlies our vast network of interrelated literal meanings" (65). While I am not sure what Johnson means by "literal," it seems to amount to "not-traditionally-figurative" (as in figure of speech). I would differ from him in *stressing* the cultural rather than the physical grounding of metaphoric clusters (or systems). Although I certainly agree that there are many instances in which a bodily grounding is active, in others it proves reductive.

58. Where I have used the phrase the "expressive capacity" of language, Ricoeur employs the phrase "cumulative capability" (*le caractère cumulatif, cette aptitude à la cumulation*): mine suggests a culturally activated etymological potential, a process that is historical, human, and linguistic; Ricoeur's suggests a massing of verbal senses that is inexplicable even after the fact. The difference in nuance is significant: we accumulate things but express meaning (*Rule*, 116; *Vive*, 149–50). Cf. also Sweetser, who, having defined polysemy synchronically, observes refreshingly that "we cannot rigidly separate synchronic from diachronic analysis" (1, 9).

59. Attridge, "Language as History," 200. On Saussure's inconsistencies, see, for example, 190–93, 196–99, 204. Also Ferdinand de Saussure, *Course in General Linguistics*, trans. Wade Baskin, ed. Charles Bally and Albert Sechehaye, in collaboration with Albert Reidlinger (1959; rpt. New York: McGraw-Hill, 1966), e.g., 10, 28–31, 98–101, 173–76, 189–90, 225, 212–14, 231–32. As this paragraph attests, I have profited from Attridge's richly suggestive discussion of etymology.

60. Attridge, "Language as History," 200 (my emphasis on "popular and scholarly"); cf. 193, 198. Folk etymology is an obvious example of a popular theory or

story about language; in the early modern period scholarly theories of etymology blended fluidly with popular ones. Cf. Mark Johnson, *Body in the Mind*, 171–72 (narrative structure as a necessary component of human reason and imagination). Suggestive in this regard for my own thinking about narrative has been Jean-François Lyotard's connection of narrative with customary knowledge (vs. modern technology): *The Postmodern Condition: A Report on Knowledge*, trans. Geoff Bennington and Brian Massumi (Minneapolis: Univ. of Minnesota Press, 1984), 19, and passim.

61. Richard Abrams describes a "network of substitutions" among the characters of *2 Henry IV*; he also sees the play as "a study in decomposition," in which "Henry like Hal exists on the plane of rumor": "Rumor's Reign," *English Literary Renaissance*, 16 (1986), 467–95, here 491, 481, 477. Cf. Harry Berger, Jr., "Hydra and Rhizome," 86–87, and "Sneak's Noise or Rumor and Detextualization in *2 Henry IV*, *The Kenyon Review*, n.s. 6 (1984), 58–78; Berger's theoretical observations on pages 59–61 parallel those I make about *Hamlet* at a later stage of this essay.

62. John Calvin, *Institutes of the Christian Religion*, trans. Ford Lewis Battles, ed. John T. McNeill, 2 vols. (London: S.C.M., 1961), II, 1385: Bk. IV.xvii.21. A caveat, however: the word "humanly," whose emphasis is mine, should be noted, along with the fact that Renaissance rhetoricians were not, by and large, a profound lot. Their views would be hard-pressed to accommodate (let alone explain) Sidney's notion of the poetic imagination—or Shakespeare's, in another mood. Most writers of imaginative literature in the period were able to go back directly to the Latin classics, as I do in a subsequent chapter on metaphor and catachresis. Additionally, the "older," more Catholic views of language and symbolization were also available and much debated in the period.

63. About to kill Hotspur at Shrewsbury, Hal tells him, "all the budding honors on thy crest / I'll crop to make a garland for my head": *1 Henry IV*, V.iv.72–73.

64. E.g., Frank Kermode, ed., in the 2nd Riverside edition, glosses *invests* "besieges," a gloss that goes back to Theobald. Similarly, Harold Jenkins, ed., *Hamlet* (London: Methuen, 1982) adopts the Quarto's *invests* in the sense "besieges, hence presses upon" as "a Shakespearean metaphor . . . not easily attributable to the Q₂ compositor"; cf. note 73, below. For a contrasting example, Philip Edwards, ed., *Hamlet, Prince of Denmark* (Cambridge: Cambridge Univ. Press, 1985) prefers the Folio's *invites*, while acknowledging *invests* to be an "odd misreading" and preferable on the grounds of its being the more difficult alternative or *durior lectio*.

65. I have replaced the editorially intrusive semicolon after "vows" in the first line with a grammatically more accurate comma.

66. Perhaps more properly, *dura lectio*, since Theobald's emendation (based on a presumed but plausible mistaking of *bauds*, i.e., *bawds*, for *bonds*) is not a Quarto or Folio reading. See Clayton's "Quibbling Polonii and the Pious Bonds: The Rhetoric of *Hamlet* I.iii," *Shakespeare Studies*, 2 (1966), 59–94; also M.M. Mahood, *Shakespeare's Wordplay* (London: Methuen, 1957), 119–20; Ann and John O. Thompson, *Shakespeare: Meaning and Metaphor* (Iowa City: Univ. of Iowa Press, 1987), 115–16; and Sandra K. Fischer, *Econolingua: A Glossary of Coins and Economic Language in Renaissance Drama* (Newark: Univ. of Delaware Press, 1985), s.v. *investment*, 88. My

subsequent comments necessarily overlap with these descriptions and particularly with Clayton's, which is not only first-rate but nearly exhaustive. Unlike him, however, I regard the imagery of beggary as simply a subset to that of clothing and take the three major images in the passage to be clothes, commerce, and religion: cf. Clayton, 77. Also cf. J.J.M. Tobin's more recent argument for " 'Bawds' not 'Bonds' " (*Hamlet Studies*, 4:1–2 [1982], 94–95) on the basis of echoes of Apuleis' *Golden Asse* here and elsewhere in *Hamlet*; similarly, consider my ch. 8, n. 82, below, and in my text, 200.

67. The sense "sieges" has been assumed for *investments* in this passage, for example, by Mahood, 119–20, and Jenkins, ed. The first record of the verb *invest* in this sense that the *OED* cites is in 1600.

68. On bonds/bands as clerical collars, see Clayton, 80–81; Mahood, 119–20.

69. In *Shakespeare Reread*, the provocative essays by Helen Vendler, Stephen Booth, and George T. Wright are, in toto, quite relevant: respectively, "Reading, Stage by Stage: Shakespeare's Sonnets," 23–41; "Close Reading without Readings," 42–55; "Troubles of a Professional Meter Reader," 56–76. More immediately, the perceptive essay of Louise D. Cary treats "the infinitely decomposible and recomposible nature of language" in *Hamlet* and remarks how "the word, the sentence, . . . [and] the plot," like the grave in Act V.i, "ultimately fail . . . to contain" it: "*Hamlet* Recycled, or the Tragical History of the Prince's Prints," *ELH*, 61 (1994), 783–805, here 784, 799. Cf. P. K. Ayers, "Reading, Writing, and *Hamlet*," *Shakespeare Quarterly*, 44 (1993), 423–39; Jonathan Goldberg, "Hamlet's Hand," *Shakespeare Quarterly*, 39 (1988), 307–27.

70. *Language and Symbolic Power*, ed. John B. Thompson, trans. Gino Raymond and Matthew Adamson (Cambridge, MA: Harvard Univ. Press, 1991), 142–43; *Ce que parler veut dire: l'économie des échanges linguistiques* (Paris: Fayard, 1982), 175–76. Subsequent reference is to these editions: cited as *Power* and *Parler*.

71. Still referring to Heideggerian practices, Bourdieu writes as follows of the etymological trace: "By using ordinary words in other ways, by reviving the subtle truth, the *etumon*, which has been lost by routine usage, one turns the correct relation between words into the principle by which philological/philosophical alchemy stands or falls" (146).

72. The linguistic system of Heidegger's writing, as Bourdieu describes it, succeeds because of the complicity of qualified, or initiated, readers (i.e., readers within the system) in Weimar Germany: 150–51.

73. Bourdieu writes informatively about the complex ambiguity of the term "popular speech" (90–102), the communication characteristic of diverse classes of linguistic habitus and markets, but he does not engage popular practices such as wordplay and folk etymology.

74. *Power*, 256, n. 3; *Parler*, 17, n. 3.

75. In the early modern period, reissues and new editions of bi-lingual lexicons frequently number in the double digits: see Gabriele Stein, *The English Dictionary before Cawdrey* (Tübingen: Max Niemeyer, 1985), 410–31.

76. *Rule*, 133: my emphasis; *Vive*, 171, reads, "entre les mots et les phrases." Insofar as this French phrase amplifies "entre *prédication* et *dénomination*," "between predication and naming," the translator's rendering "sentences" for French "phrases" is justified. It is further justified by the larger context of Ricoeur's discussion. The translator notes that Ricoeur has checked the translation (viii).

Chapter Three

Language and History in the Reformation: Translating Matter to Metaphor in the Sacrament

1. Diarmaid MacCulloch, *Thomas Cranmer: A Life* (New Haven: Yale Univ. Press, 1996), 379.

2. Huldrich [Huldrych] Zwingli, *Friendly Exegesis, that is, Exposition of the Matter of the Eucharist to Martin Luther*, trans. Henry Preble, in *Writings of Huldrich Zwingli*, ed. H. Wayne Pipkin, 2 vols. (Allison Park, PA: Pickwick Publications, 1984), II, 239–385, here 356–57.

3. Gordon Rupp, *Patterns of Reformation*, (Philadephia: Fortress, 1969), 25–27; Johannes Oecolampadius, *Briefe und Akten zum Leben Oekolampads*, ed. Ernst Staehelin (Leipzig: M. Heinsius Nachfolger, Eger and Sievers, 1927), I, 337 (#235); *Tertullian adversus Marcionem*, ed. and trans. Ernest Evans, 2 vols. (Oxford: Clarendon, 1972), II, 492–93. See also Martin Luther, *Confession Concerning Christ's Supper 1528*, in *Word and Sacrament*, III, ed. and trans. Robert H. Fischer, 151–372, here 176: vol. XXXVII of *Luther's Works*, ed. Jaroslav Pelikan and Helmut T. Lehmann. 55 vols. (Philadelphia: Concordia Publishing and Muhlenberg Press), 1961). Also "Marburg Colloquy, 1529" in *Great Debates of the Reformation*, ed. Donald J. Ziegler (New York: Random House, 1969), 71–107.

4. Stephen Gardiner, *An Explication and assertion of the true Catholique fayth, touchyng the most blessed Sacrament of the aulter* (Rouen: Robert Caly, 1551), sig. G4r (accurately citing Cranmer); cf. Nicholas Ridley, *A Brief Declaration of the Lord's Supper*, otherwise entitled *A Treatise against the Error of Transubstantiation*, in *The Works of Nicholas Ridley*, ed. Henry Christmas (Cambridge: Cambridge Univ. Press, 1843), 5–45: "after a certain manner of speech" (41).

5. Desiderius Erasmus of Rotterdam, *Annotationes*, in *Opera Omnia*, ed. Jean Le Clerc, 10 vols. (Leiden: Petrus Van der Aa, 1703–06), VI, 715–16; also *Erasmus' Annotations on the New Testament: The Gospels* (facsimile of the 1535 text, with all earlier variants), ed. Anne Reeve (London: Duckworth, 1986); and Erika Rummel, *Erasmus' "Annotations" on the New Testament: From Philologist to Theologian* (Toronto: Univ. of Toronto Press, 1986), 156–57.

6. Emile Benveniste, *Problems in General Linguistics*, trans. Mary Elizabeth Meek (Coral Gables: Univ.of Miami Press, 1971), 131.

7. Benveniste, 165: "Ancient Semitic did not have a verb *to be*." It should be observed that Benveniste writes within the context of his discussion of the copula. An exception to his statement taken literally or absolutely would be Hebrew *hoveh*, the verb *to be* in its existential sense, which is customarily restricted to God: e.g., "God was, God is, God will be."

8. Huldrych Zwingli, *On the Lord's Supper*, in *Zwingli and Bullinger*, trans. G. W. Bromiley (Philadelphia: Westminster, 1953), 185–347, here 224. Also "Ad Theobaldi Billicani et Urbani Rhegii epistolas responsio," *Huldreich Zwinglis Sämtliche Werke*, IV, ed. Emil Egli, Georg Finsler, Walther Köhler, and Oskar Farner, in *Corpus Reformatorum*, XCI (Leipzig: M. Heinsius Nachfolger, 1927), 893–941, here 918–20: "*Causa huius est, quia Hebraeus sermo non est Latinus; nam si Hebraeus esset Latinus, indubie esset in his locis verbum 'est.'*"

9. The word *mou*, "my," is unrelated to the "temporal or modal localization" and "the subjectivity of the speaker" of which Benveniste writes and does not affect his argument regarding the absent verb and the implications of its absence. The meaning of the phrase *mou sōma* is more complicated, however, since its referent is variously thought to be Christ's natural body born of the Virgin, his glorified body, his mystical body, or a combination of these. *Mou sōma* invokes the problem of the materiality, the localization, and even the singularity of the body of Christ in a way susceptible either of symbolic or of physical interpretations—of impersonality or of its opposite. In other words, it settles nothing.

10. Charles H. Kahn, *The Verb 'Be' in Ancient Greek*, part 6 of *The Verb 'Be' and Its Synonyms: Philosophical and Grammatical Studies*, ed. John W. M. Verhaar (Dordrecht: D. Reidel, 1973), 436.

11. Kahn, 199–201, 373–75, 386. But see also my note 7, immediately above.

12. Ernst Cassirer, *The Philosophy of Symbolic Forms*, trans. Ralph Mannheim, 4 vols. (New Haven: Yale Univ. Press, 1953), I, 314–15.

13. Benveniste, 135, for instance, cites as a nominal assertion the Ilocano adjective *mabisin*, "hungry," which expresses the utterance "he is hungry" without a verb or even a pronominal sign.

14. Brian Byron, "From Essence to Presence: A Shift in Eucharistic Expression Illustrated from the Apologetic of St. Thomas More," in *Miscellanea Moreana: Essays for Germain Marc'hadour*, ed. Clare M. Murphy, Henri Gibaud, and Mario A. Di Cesare (Binghamton, NY: Medieval and Renaissance Texts and Studies, 1989), 429–41, here 430.

15. Byron, 432 (sic); Gardiner, *Explication*, sigs. B1r–v, G7r.

16. Thomas Cranmer, *An Answer unto a Crafty and Sophistical Cavillation Devised by Stephen Gardiner*, in *Writings and Disputations*, ed. John Edmund Cox (Cambridge: Cambridge Univ. Press, 1844), 1–367, here 32, 103.

17. Richard A. Lanham, *A Handlist of Rhetorical Terms* (Berkeley: Univ. of California Press, 1968), 73.

18. Peter Martyr Vermigli, *A Discourse or traictise of Petur Martyr Vermilla Florentine, the publyque reader of diuinitee in the Vniuersitee of Oxford wherein he openly declared his whole and determinate iudgemente concernynge the Sacrament of the Lordes supper*, trans. Nicholas Udall (London: Nycolas Udall, [1550?]), fol. 42r (my emphasis). On Martyr's considerable influence in England and specifically on Cranmer, see Marvin Anderson, "Rhetoric and Reality: Peter Martyr and the English Reformation," *Sixteenth Century Journal*, 19 (1988), 451–69; for a contrary assessment, which nonetheless grudgingly admits some degree of influence, see Basil Hall's learned and forceful

essay, "Cranmer, the Eucharist and the Foreign Divines in the Reign of Edward VI," in *Thomas Cranmer: Churchman and Scholar*, ed. Paul Ayris and David Selwyn (Woodbridge, Suffolk, Eng.: Boydell, 1993), 217–58, here 227–34. But a number of passages Hall cites can be debated, either through context or a less narrow or less literal reading; the same is true of his rendering of many passages in Cranmer's published writing. Stephen Greenblatt, "Remnants of the Sacred in Early Modern England," in *Subject and Object in Renaissance Culture*, ed. Margreta de Grazia, et al, 337–45, here 342, suggests that the primary literary importance of Reformation debates about the sacrament lies in "*the problem of the leftover*, that is, the status of the material remainder"—the bread and, even more, the body. The problem of the sign, the verb of being, which is inseparable from the question of figuration, is, to my mind, of equal import: "To be or not to be," moreover, is the focal question.

19. Stephen Gardiner, *A Detection of the Devils Sophistrie* (London: John Herforde, 1546), sigs. D8v–D9r. I have not used a capital letter for the term "reformers" in an effort to distinguish those MacCulloch, 2–3, calls "evangelicals" from the reformers later in the century. (MacCulloch's term "evangelicals" is unsuitable in an American context, since it suggests fundamentalism.) Generally, I have also used the term "conservative," instead of "Catholic," to refer to Catholics like Stephen Gardiner, who assented to Henry's break with Rome but drew the line at real (bodily) presence. Glyn Redworth's biography of Gardiner can be useful in locating Gardiner's position: Redworth observes that lawyer-bishops such as Gardiner were likely to accept the Royal Supremacy, trading one authority for another, and that Gardiner preached "the very presence," rather than "real presence," in order to satisfy the more radical reformers under Somerset's protectorate: *In Defence of the Church Catholic: The Life of Stephen Gardiner* (Oxford: Basil Blackwell, 1990), 10, 266.

20. Cf. Peter Newman Brooks, *Thomas Cranmer's Doctrine of the Eucharist: An Essay in Historical Development*, 2nd ed. (London: Macmillan, 1992), 70: "By the middle of the century, Zwinglianism is an outmoded and unhistorical term (although, of course, the 'Reformed' school undoubtedly owed much to the clarity of Zwingli's theology)." At least in England at mid-century, where all the leading controversialists acknowledged their reading of Zwingli, they owed a debt explicitly and openly. His name often appears in their writings, although more as an important point of reference than as an authority to be embraced without modification. See n. 42, below.

21. Gardiner, *Explication*, sig. G6v: Gardiner cites Philipp Melanchthon's warning to Oecolampadius.

22. *Answer to the Bishop of Winchester's Book*, in *Early Writings of John Hooper*, ed. Samuel Carr (Cambridge: Cambridge Univ. Press, 1843), 97–247, here 120, cf. 221.

23. Thomas Cranmer, *A Defence of the True and Catholic Doctrine of the Sacrament of the Body and Blood of Our Saviour Christ*, ed. G. E. Duffield (Philadelphia: Fortress, 1965), 71; Foxe, *Actes and Monuments*, 1583, 1434 (the Catholic Hugh Weston to Cranmer, ventriloquizing the latter's argument); Calvin, *Institutes*, II, 1362: IV.xvii.3.

24. Cf. a particularly clear instance of the same technique in Foxe, who cites Cranmer: "Christ is seene here in earth euery day, is touched, is torne wyth the teeth, that our tongue is red with his bloud: which no man hauing any iudgement will say or thinke to be spoken without trope or figure" (1434). For a less sympathetic and less political response to Cranmer's appropriation of realist language than Foxe's, see MacCulloch, 491–92. For a moving passage about spiritual hunger, see Cranmer, *Defence*, 66–68.

25. As seen in my previous chapter, apparently "dead" metaphors have active metaphorical roots for Derrida; for Ricoeur, dead metaphors do not affect the sublated concepts that etymologically and, in Derrida's argument, systemically build on them.

26. The doctrine of transubstantiation had certainly encountered its skeptics over the centuries, and, with striking relevance, in the fourteenth-century heresiarch John Wyclif, who believed that the bread remained on the altar after the words of consecration had been spoken: see Anne Hudson, *The Premature Reformation: Wycliffite Texts and Lollard History* (Oxford: Clarendon, 1988), 281–90, esp. 281–82; also Miri Rubin, *Corpus Christi: The Eucharist in Late Medieval Culture* (Cambridge: Cambridge Univ. Press, 1991), chap. 1 and 320–34. Most of the Reformation was anticipated by the later Middle Ages. Nonetheless, there was a radical and widespread development of attitudes, ideas, and institutions in the early modern period that brought these earlier, less normative signs of change to fulfillment.

27. Cf. Michel de Certeau's realistic balance regarding resistance, which he describes as "tricky and stubborn procedures that elude discipline without being outside the field in which it is exercised" and, I would elucidate, without being outside the categories and consequences of this dominant field: *The Practice of Everyday Life*, trans. Steven Randall (Berkeley: Univ. of California Press, 1984), 96. See Caroline Walker Bynum, *Fragmentation and Redemption: Essays on Gender and the Human Body in Medieval Religion* (New York: Zone, 1991), chap 6; *Holy Feast and Holy Fast: The Religious Significance of Food to Medieval Women* (Berkeley: Univ. of California Press, 1987), chaps. 6–7; *The Resurrection of the Body in Western Christianity, 200–1336* (New York: Columbia Univ. Press, 1995), chap. 6.

28. The type is both unclear and likely erroneous here: it reads "in in," which I take to be a mistake for "do in," as I have indicated. "Deade," the reading I consider probable, instances a word and spelling that recur in the text, but another possible reading is "steade."

29. Gardiner, *Explication*, sig. O4v–O5r–v. On *iugle*, see *OED*, s.v. *juggle v.*: 2. "To conjure," 3. "To play tricks so as to cheat or deceive," 4. "To deceive by jugglery [legerdemain, trickery, deception]; to deceive, trick, cheat, beguile." To Gardiner's exposition of matter, compare Martyr, fol. 19r–v: Catholics "put and hold the quantitee that is in the Sacrament to bee a quantitee in manier onely *Mathematicall*, that is to saie, not reall nor materiall in dede, but separated and deuided from all materiall substaunce, that maie bee seen or felte, and consisting in our imagination onely and in our understandyng, which quantitee if it be diuided or broken in pieces, it is onely so conceiued in our reason, & by vertue of our understandyng."

30. Derrida, "White Mythology," 48, 50; also chap. 2, 15, above.

31. On Cranmer's nominalism, see Eugene K. McGee, "Cranmer and Nominalism," *Harvard Theological Review*, 57 (1964), 189–216; the challenge to McGee's essay by William J. Courtenay, "Cranmer as Nominalist," *Harvard Theological Review*, 57 (1964), 367–80; and McGee's response, "Cranmer's Nominalism Reaffirmed," *Harvard Theological Review*, 59 (1968), 192–96. Also, on the sacramental bread and wine as "self-enclosed, empirical objects of the Nominalist tradition," see Cyril C. Richardson, "Cranmer and the Analysis of Eucharistic Doctrine," *Journal of Theological Studies*, 16 (1965), 421–37, here 427. While MacCulloch acknowledges a "nominalist element" in Cranmer's training at Cambridge, he is skeptical about attempts to show that Cranmer's thinking is nominalist in a comprehensive sense (491).

32. *Encyclopedia of Philosophy*, ed. Paul Edwards, 8 vols. (London: Collier-Macmillan, 1967), III, s.v. *Essence*; VIII, s.v. *Substance*.

33. Ibid., VIII, s.v. *Substance*.

34. Cranmer's *Defence* affords a specific gloss on "sacramentally": "for he is not in it, neither spiritually, as he is in man; nor corporally, as he is in heaven; but only sacramentally, as a thing may be said to be in the figure, whereby it is signified" (214). In one sense "sacramentally" is a redundant word in Cranmer's response to Ogelthorpe, but it also looks like an effort to signal something more than a "mere" symbol.

35. *The Complete Works of Aristotle*, ed. Jonathan Barnes, 2 vols. (Princeton: Princeton Univ. Press, 1984), *Sophistical Refutations* 167a1–20 (example of the Ethiopian who can be denominated "black," although he has white teeth). I am much indebted to Paul Spade for my explanation of derivation. Subsequent reference is to this edition of Aristotle.

36. Aristotle, *Categories*, 1a13–15, 10a 27–10b1–11.

37. Harry Berger, Jr., "Metaphor and Metonymy, and the End of the Middle Ages," on *Summa Theologica*, I.67, 1, resp.: unpublished essay. See also Ralph McInerny, *Aquinas and Analogy* (Washington, DC: Catholic Univ. of America Press, 1996), 131–33; St. Thomas Aquinas, *Summa Theologiae*, Blackfriars Edition, 60 vols. (London: Eyre and Spottiswoode, 1964–76), I.13, 5–6, resp, I.67, 1, resp.

38. My emphasis. For "denominating form," see McInerny, 133; Aquinas, I.13, 11, resp.: "unumquodque enim denominatur a sua forma."

39. Charlton T. Lewis and Charles Short, *A Latin Dictionary* (1879; rpt. Oxford: Clarendon, 1966), s.v. *denominatio*. See also *William of Auxerre's Theology of the Hypostatic Union*, ed. Walter Henry Principe (Toronto: Pontifical Institute of Medieval Studies, 1963), 212, n. 14.

40. Discussing the validity of the statements "Deus est homo" and "Verbum est homo," Scotus concludes, "For the supposit subsisting in any nature, as the supposit of the nature, expresses [something that is] formally such according to that nature; now that [hypostatic] union is believed to be of such a kind, that through it the Word subsists in human nature, as a supposit does in a nature; therefore through it the Word is formally man. . . . But 'god' signifies a name that is both common [to several Persons, i.e., the Trinity] and that in any one hypostasis, that is person, is

ordered *denominatively,* just as is the case with [the name] 'man'. For it is God who
has divine nature, and man who has human nature. The minor premise is proved
by Augustine . . . *That assumption was of such a kind that it would make God man, and
man, God"*: John Duns Scotus, *Opus Oxoniense,* in *Opera Omnia,* 26 vols. (Paris: L.
Vivès, 1891–95), Bk. III, d.vii, q. i, n. 3 (my trans. and emphasis on *denominatively*).

41. On Scotus' view of the hypostatic union and particularly of the role of the
human will in salvation, see my *Growth of a Personal Voice: "Piers Plowman" and "The
Faerie Queene"* (New Haven: Yale Univ. Press, 1976), 133–34, 136–40.

42. Cranmer, *Defence,* 227: my emphasis on the rhetoric relevant. Cranmer, by
his own testimony, had read "almost everything that has been written and published
either by Oecolampadius or Zwingli" (MacCulloch, 180). On Cranmer's various
views, see MacCulloch, 181–83 and chap. 9; also Peter Newman Brooks, e.g., 37,
43–44, and passim. Cranmer (*Answer,* 225) compares Bucer to Oecolampadius and
Zwingli; Gardiner (*Explication,* sig. N7r) cites Zwingli, as he does elsewhere. Peter
Martyr's *Discourse* on the Sacrament specifically examines and compares the doc-
trines of the Lutherans and Zwinglians: e.g., fols. 91v–107r. My own use of the term
Zwinglian is also meant to signal a *kind* of influence through other, more mixed and
moderate channels such as Martin Bucer, Peter Martyr, and at a greater distance,
Johann Heinrich Bullinger and Philipp Melanchthon.

43. As Cranmer acknowledged at his trial in 1555, Ridley was the agent by
whom his views on the Eucharist changed from real presence to a more decidedly
reformed position that rejected real (corporeal) presence (MacCulloch, 355).

44. Foxe, 1378: my emphasis; 1386, erroneously marked 1374 in the edition
cited.

45. Cf. Cranmer's indignant response to Gardiner: "I declare, in my book, virtue
to be in them that godly receive bread and wine, and not in the bread and wine.
And I take virtue there to signify might and strength, or force, as I name it (which
in the Greek is called δύναμις, after which sense we say, that there is virtue in herbs,
in words, and in stones), and not to signify virtue in holiness, (which in Greek is
called ἀρετή), whereof a person is called virtuous, whose faith and conversation is
godly" (*Answer,* 181). In the passage at issue between Cranmer and Gardiner, the
Archbishop actually writes "to [not 'in'] them that worthily eat and drink" the
bread and wine, these elements "be turned not into the corporal presence, but into
the virtue of Christ's flesh and blood" (*Defence,* 187). Whereas holiness is not substantial, the "virtue" he seems to have in mind appears similar to the *substantialis
vigor* that Calvin sees flowing from Christ the head to the members: B. A. Gerrish,
Grace and Gratitude: The Eucharistic Theology of John Calvin (Minneapolis: Fortress,
1993), 179–80, n. 72. Cranmer's response to Gardiner is also sensitive to the distinction between what the receptor or worthy recipient of the sacrament initiates and
what belongs to grace and God.

46. This systematic connection might be conceived as an *abstract* one and aligned
with Calvin's use of the phrase "*abstractum aliquid a substantia*" to characterize "the
vital power we receive . . . *from* the substance" of Christ in the Supper, a phrase that
Gerrish finds "unfortunate" and puzzling, since Christ himself is supposed to be the

eucharistic gift in Calvin's theology of the sacrament (*Grace and Gratitude*, 179–180n72). Ridley's explanation perhaps clarifies Calvin's. Hall, 253, takes a Calvinist statement regarding the substance of Christ's body to mean "the fundamental reality": such a translation is hardly unambiguous. Cf. also Robert Whalen, *The Poetry of Immanence: Sacrament in Donne and Herbert* (Toronto: Univ. of Toronto Press, 2002), 10–12.

47. Gerrish's treatment of Calvin's concern with and for the object (*Grace and Gratitude*, 167–68, 177–80) is more nuanced and convincing than Waswo's identification of Calvin's concept of symbolism with Coleridge's: "a mystical participation of the sign in the thing, of the temporal, material symbol in the eternal, spiritual signified," 255.

48. Heiko Augustinus Obermann, *The Harvest of Medieval Theology: Gabriel Biel and Late Medieval Nominalism* (Cambridge, MA: Harvard Univ. Press, 1963), passim, esp. 1–9, 249–80.

49. John Hooper, *Answer*, 128, 190–91. Hooper's *Answer* was originally published in Zurich (1547).

50. See, in addition to Gerrish's *Grace and Gratitude*, his *The Old Protestantism and the New: Essays on the Reformation Heritage* (Chicago: University of Chicago Press, 1982), esp. chaps. 6–7; and his "Discerning the Body: Sign and Reality in Luther's Controversy with the Swiss," *Continuing the Reformation: Essays on Modern Religious Thought* (Chicago: Univ. of Chicago Press, 1993), chap. 3.

51. Hall does acknowledge that Cranmer refers in his *Commonplaces* to Calvin's first edition of the *Institutes* but hastens to add that Cranmer omits Calvin in his later *De Re Sacramentaria*. Having discounted Calvin's influence, Hall urges instead that of Melanchthon and Bucer (54).

52. Cf. MacCulloch: Cranmer "would not have enjoyed the language which Calvin in self-assertive mood could use, that the sacraments 'confer' or 'contain' grace" (616). Also, cf. Calvin, *Institutes*, II, 1403: IV.xvii.32, regarding the nature of true presence in the sacrament: "it is a secret too lofty for either my mind to comprehend or my words to declare. And, to speak more plainly, I rather experience than understand it."

53. Although Cranmer's *Answer* was first published in 1551, he revised and thereby reauthorized the text while in prison.

54. Gerrish, *Grace and Gratitude*, 177–80. Cf. John Calvin, *A Treatise on the Sacrament of the Body and Blood of Christ*, in *Writings and Translations of Myles Coverdale*, ed. George Pearson (Cambridge: Cambridge Univ. Press, 1844), 425–66: "the inward substance of the sacrament is annexed to the visible signs" (441); the figure is "joined unto his verity and substance" (440); "he refresheth us with his own proper substance" (442).

55. Gardiner, *Explication*, sigs. F4v–F5r; Cranmer, *Answer*, 90.

56. When confronted by Bucer's use of the analogy of sunbeams and substance, Cranmer hotly objects that Bucer "denieth utterly that Christ is really and substantially present in the bread, either by conversion or inclusion, but in the ministration he affirmeth Christ to be present; and so do I also" (*Answer*, 225). Cf. also Martyr's

distinction between the eye and its eyesight, which Martyr compares to that between the sun and its sunbeams in order to illustrate a non-corporeal extension of virtue or power (fol. 95r).

57. In connection with the yearning of the English people for the corporeal presence, see the impressive historical studies of Rubin and of Eamon Duffy, *The Stripping of the Altars: Traditional Religion in England 1400–1580* (New Haven: Yale Univ. Press, 1992). Also relevant is chap. 1 of David Aers and Lynn Staley, *The Powers of the Holy: Religion, Politics, and Gender in Late Medieval English Culture* (University Park: Pennsylvania State Univ. Press, 1996).

58. Martyr, fol. 106v–07v. Cf. Martin Bucer, *Censura,* in *Martin Bucer and The Book of Common Prayer,* ed. and trans. E. C. Whitaker (Great Wakering, Essex, Eng.: Mayhew-McCrimmon, 1974), 56–57: "Certainly the Holy Fathers understood . . . no other change in the elements than one by which the bread and wine, in their own nature and in the permanence in all circumstances of their natural characteristics, were changed from their usual and ordinary use and were, as we might say, 'transelemented,' so that they became symbols of body and blood and thus of the whole Christ, both God and man [ex vulgari communique usu, eo mutarentur, & quasi transelementarentur, ut iam essent eiusmodi corporis, & sanguinis, adeoque Christi ipsius totius, Dei & hominis . . . symbola]." At Cranmer's request (according to the original printed edition of 1577), Bucer offered in the *Censura* detailed suggestions for revision of the 1549 prayer book: see Whitaker, ed., *Martin Bucer,* 2–3.

59. Cranmer's *Answer,* 181, reads, "in them."

60. Martyr, fol. 105r. In the *Friendly Exegesis* of the sacrament that Zwingli addresses to Luther, he comments on the use by earlier apologists of the image of a hot iron or blade as an analogy for the two natures of Christ, and he twits his German opponent for applying it, as Cranmer does, to the Eucharist: "This metaphor you took from them if you confess it. If you deny it, you pilfered it and twisted it to support the notion of the flesh in the bread, Luther" (320–21). On *realist language*: MacCulloch interprets (or to my mind, misinterprets) Cranmer's use of realist language as merely resulting from rhetorical insensitivity (491–92).

61. See MacCulloch, 630–32. Stella Brook's discussion of language in the Book of Common Prayer is pertinent as well: *The Language of the Book of Common Prayer* (New York: Oxford Univ. Press, 1965).

62. Ricoeur, "Metaphorical Process," 142.

63. E.g., Martyr, fols. 48v, 104v; cf. Gardiner, *Explication,* sig. L4r: "the sacrament is [to the reformers] but a visible preachyng." That it is arguably *also* more than "merely" (as Gardiner's reductive "but" implies) this for Cranmer and Ridley does not negate the point at hand. But cf. Hall, 232–33, who distinguishes between sacraments as visible words and a presentation or exhibition of "the Presence."

64. Julia Houston, "Transubstantiation and the Sign: Cranmer's Drama of the Last Supper," *Journal of Medieval and Renaissance Studies,* 24 (1994), 115–30; Ricoeur, "Metaphorical Process," 147–48; Paul Henle, "Metaphor," in *Philosophical Perspectives,* 83–104, esp. 87–88; Charles Sanders Pierce, *Pierce On Signs,* ed. James Hoopes (Chapel Hill: University of North Carolina Press, 1991), e.g., 251–52.

65. Houston, 125–26; Ricoeur, "Metaphorical Process," 148–49: subsequent parenthetical reference to Ricoeur in this chapter is also to "Metaphorical Process."

Chapter Four

Donne's Tropic Awareness: Metaphor, Metonymy, and *Devotions upon Emergent Occasions*

1. My example of metonymy is a variant of one in Lakoff and Johnson, *Metaphors We Live By*, 35.

2. Umberto Eco, *A Theory of Semiotics* (Bloomington: Indiana Univ. Press, 1979), 280; also 155, 133–42. Cf. John R. Taylor, *Linguistic Categorization: Prototypes in Linguistic Theory*, 2nd ed. (Oxford: Clarendon, 1995), 122, 139.

3. Roman Jakobson's discussions of these differences have been especially influential: *Studies on Child Language and Aphasia* (The Hague: Mouton, 1971), 41–42, 54–55, 67–68; Jakobson and Morris Halle, *Fundamentals of Language*, 2nd ed., rev. (1971; rpt. The Hague: Mouton, 1980), 69–96. Christian Metz, 180–82, offers a useful critique of Jakobson. In another helpful review of rhetorical categorization in the last two centuries, Gérard Genette criticizes the reduction of figuration to metaphor and metonymy: *Figures of Literary Discourse*, trans. Alan Sheridan (New York: Columbia Univ. Press, 1982), 103–26, especially 105–12. Neither Jakobson nor Genette attends to shifts in audience and correlative shifts in ideology—faith, for an example inescapably pertinent to Donne—that bear directly on interpretation; Metz, a film theorist, is very much attuned to the audience but synchronically. Kenneth Burke describes the reactivation of dead metaphor as a metaphoric " 'archaicizing' device we call 'metonymy,' " or in his lexicon, " 'reduction.' " Thus Burke conceives of an exchangeability of the two figures, although despite the promising word "archaicizing," this is not conceived, as mine is, to be contingent on a difference between codes and cultures: *A Grammar of Motives* (1945; rpt. Berkeley: Univ. of California Press, 1969), 506. Metz (e.g., 190, 199–200) perceptively treats the complementarity and interchange of metaphor and metonymy in film and to an extent in language, but his observation that metaphor never gives rise to metonymy is historically insensitive, unless he either has in mind exclusively the origin rather than the subsequent fate of metaphor or refers exclusively to film (201). John Taylor puts emphasis on the cultural role of metonymy and comes tantalizingly close to seeing a dynamic relation between it and metaphor without directly engaging his apparent intuition (chap. 7, esp 139).

4. Luther, *Confession Concerning Christ's Supper 1528*, 210. Also Bernhard Erling, "*Communicatio Idiomatum* Re-examined," *Dialog*, 2 (1963), 139–45; Joseph N. Tylenda, "Calvin's Understanding of the Communication of Properties," *The Westminster Theological Journal*, 38 (1975), 54–65; Alasdair Heron, "*Communicatio Idiomatum* and *Deificatio* of Human Nature: A Reformed Perspective," *The Greek Orthodox Theological Review*, 43 (1998), 367–76.

5. Zwingli, *Friendly Exegesis*, 320: I have moved a misplaced comma after "when," instead putting it after "which."

6. Older writers in the Catholic tradition had also used *denominatio* or meton-ymy to describe the *communicatio idiomatum*, as indicated in chap. 3, 53–54, above. Synecdoche can be considered merely a category within the larger term metonymy, although Luther clearly thinks it has a more integral, inherent meaning.

7. *The Complete Poetry of John Donne*, ed. John T. Shawcross (Garden City, NY: Doubleday, 1967), 105–06.

8. Helen Gardner, ed., *The Elegies and the Songs and Sonnets of John Donne* (1965; rpt. Oxford: Clarendon, 1970), 205, calls attention to the interesting but less perti-nent "old saying, 'By this fire, that's God's angel.'" The saying could have origi-nated in a memory of the Psalm.

9. An essential point of reference for any discussion of "Aire and Angels" is the issue of the *John Donne Journal*, 9 (1990), which consists of seven rich and varying interpretations devoted entirely to this poem. For example, while R. V. Young holds that the male speaker's love is presented as being purer than the woman's, Michael C. Schoenfeldt thinks that the opposite could be the case but finally takes the position that the poem "assert[s] simultaneously the superiority of male and of female love, and in so doing installs a space for the imagination of sexual equality within a discourse of masculine hierarchy": respectively, "Angels in 'Aire and Angels,'" 1–14, and "Patriarchal Assumptions and Egalitarian Designs," 23–26, here 26.

10. For related views, see the following in volume 9 (1990) of the *John Donne Journal*: Schoenfeldt, 23, 26; John R. Roberts, "'Just such disparitie': The Critical Debate about 'Aire and Angels,'" 43–64, esp. 43–44, 61; Albert C. Labriola, "'This Dialogue of One': Rational Argument and Affective Discourse in Donne's 'Aire and Angels,'" 77–83, here 79, 81; Achsah Guibbory, "Donne, the Idea of Woman, and the Experience of Love," 105–12, here 108–09, 111.

11. Jacques Courvoisier in effect interprets Zwingli's doctrine of the Eucharist as incorporation into the body, or visible church, of Christ: *Zwingli: A Reformed Theo-logian* (Richmond, VA: John Knox Press, 1963), 74–76. In this influential reading, there is "a transubstantiation of the gathered community into the body of Christ," which "is not localized in the bread but in the church gathered about the bread" (76). Herein lies Zwingli's real presence—one with an emphasis on community that is Donnean, debated as the basis of this emphasis might be. See also Gerrish, *The Old Protestantism and the New*, 121: Gerrish downplays the ecclesiological element in Zwingli's thinking on the Eucharist, observing that "even where Zwingli inter-prets" the body "ecclesiologically, he interprets it christologically also in the self-same sentence." He notes, however, that this interpretative duality might be "for polemical reasons."

12. On catachresis, see Lanham, 21. Lanham's handbook is primarily based on classical and Renaissance terms and usage. Patricia Parker at first seems skeptical about Lanham's synthetic definition, but her discussion of Cicero and Quintilian supports it, as more obviously does her reference to the views of the Renaissance rhetoricians Dudley Fenner and John Hoskins; for the former catachresis is "'the [violent] abuse'" of metaphor and for the latter the "'somewhat *more desperate*'"

form of it: "Metaphor and Catachresis," in *The Ends of Rhetoric: History, Theory, Practice*, ed. John Bender and David E. Wellbery (Stanford: Stanford Univ. Press, 1990), 60–73, here 61, 66–67.

13. Calvin, *Institutes*, ed. McNeill, II, 1402: IV.xvii.30; see also Calvin's *Institutio Christianae Religionis 1559*, in *Corpus Reformatorum*, ed. Guilielmus Baum, Eduardus Cunitz, and Eduardus Reuss (Braunschweig: C. A. Schwetschke et filium, 1864), XXX, 1031: "quod discrimine inter naturas sublato, personae unitatem urgens, ex Deo hominem faceret, et ex homine Deum." When I cite Calvin's Latin (hence-forth *Corpus*), I do not follow the conventions of italicization in the edition by Baum et al. Relevantly and comparatively, I would also cite an English churchman contemporary with Donne, namely Lancelot Andrewes: "Ea nempe conjunctio inter Sacramentum visibile, et rem Sacramenti invisibilem, quae inter humanitatem et divinitatem Christi, ubi, nisi Eutychen sapere vultis, humanitas in divinitatem non transubstantiatur"; somewhat freely, "Truly there is the same union between the visible bread and wine of the sacrament and its invisible reality that exists between the humanity and divinity of Christ, where, unless you wish to smell of Eutyches, the humanity is not changed into the divinity" (*Responsio ad apologiam Cardinalis Bellarmini*, in *Works*, 11 vols. [1854; rpt. New York: AMS, 1967], VIII, 265).

14. *Institutes*, ed. McNeill, II, 1385: IV.17.21; *Corpus*, XXX, 1019: "nomen ipsum rei fatemur attributum fuisse symbolo; figurate id quidem, sed non sine aptissima analogia. Allegorias et parabolas omitto, ne quis subterfugia me quaerere, et extra praesentem causam egredi causetur."

15. *Institutes*, ed. McNeill, II, 1385: IV.xvii.21; *Corpus*, XXX, 1019: "Dico met-onymicum esse hunc sermonem, qui usitatus est passim in scriptura, ubi de mysteriis agitur. Neque enim aliter accipere possis quod dicitur, circumcisionem esse foedus, agnum esse transitum, . . . denique petram, ex qua in deserto aqua profluebat, fuisse Christum, *nisi translatitie* dictum accipias" (my emphasis).

16. *Institutes*, ed. McNeill, II, 1386: IV.xvii.21; *Corpus*, XXX, 1020.

17. *Institutes*, ed. McNeill, II. 1385: IV.xvii.21; *Corpus*, XXX, 1019–20: "Nec modo a superiore ad inferius nomen transfertur; sed contra, etiam rei signatae tri-buitur nomen signi visibilis. . . . Nam etsi essentia symbolum a re signata differt, quod haec spiritualis est et coelestis, illud corporeum et visible, quia tamen rem cui repraesentandae consecratum est, non figurat tantum ceu nuda et inanis tessera, sed vere etiam exhibet: cur non eius appellatio in ipsum iure competat?"

18. On the conflation of essence and substance in the Western philosophic tradi-tion, see my chap. 3, 49–50, above. Eucharistic debate in the sixteenth and seven-teenth centuries is significantly involved in this conflation.

19. *Institutes*, ed. McNeill, II, 1385–86: IV.xvii.21; *Corpus*, XXX, 1020: "quae a Deo sunt instituta, multo maiori ratione rerum nomina mutuantur, quarum et cer-tam minimeque fallacem significationem semper gerunt, et adiunctam habent secum veritatem."

20. Waswo, 254–56: as indicated in my third chapter, Waswo's deriving Calvin's theory of language from his discussion of the sacrament, an exceptional instance in

which action and effect are psychological and spiritual, seems dubious to me. One of the sticking points between the reformers and the conservatives (or Catholics) involved the efficacy of language, but the reformers insisted that language as such lacks efficacy: words do not effect a transformation of the object. Such a change occurs within the subject: see chap. 3, 43–45, 56, 58, 60, above.

21. *Institutes*, ed. McNeill, II, 1386: IV.xvii.21; *Corpus*, XXX, 1020.

22. For further discussion of the Spenserian passage, see my essay "The July Eclogue and the House of Holiness," *Studies in English Literature*, 10 (1970), 17–32, here 30–31.

23. *Devotions upon Emergent Occasions*, ed. Anthony Raspa (1975; rpt. New York: Oxford Univ. Press, 1987), 62. David Sullivan, among others, has suggested that Donne's use of the word "stationes" for the various stages of his *Devotions* affiliates them with the stations of the cross: "The Structure of Self-Revelation in Donne's *Devotions*," *Prose Studies*, 11 (1988), 49–59, here 53. Accepting this possibility, I also use the word "stations" to emphasize the status of each station as a stage, at once a performance and post (literally, a "standing": from Latin *stare*), in a progressive linear sequence. Whether Mary Arshagouni Papazian's view that Donne considers himself irrevocably "elect" is on target or not, her essay persuasively conveys a sense of the *Devotions* having at once a circular and linear structure: "Donne, Election, and the *Devotions upon Emergent Occasions*," *Huntington Library Quarterly*, 55 (1992), 603–19.

24. Sharon Cadman Seelig speaks of the *Devotions* rising "to its climax at its mid-point" in Station XII: *Generating Texts: The Progeny of Seventeenth-Century Prose* (Charlottesville: University of Virginia Press, 1996), 20.

25. Raspa, ed., 162. Lewis and Short, s.v. *spiro*, record an instance in which *spirans* means "boiling," hence hot or warm, as well as the more common and obviously relevant meaning "breathing, living." Evelyn M. Simpson, *A Study of the Prose Works of John Donne*, 2nd ed. (Oxford: Clarendon, 1948), 243, glosses Donne's pigeon(s) by reference to "the fashionable remedy of applying pigeons cut in half 'to draw the vapors from the Head.'" She also cites Samuel Pepys's entry for 19 October 1663, when the Queen "was so ill as to be shaved and pigeons put to her feet": *The Diary of Samuel Pepys*, ed. Robert Latham and William Matthews (Berkeley: Univ. of California Press, 1971), IV, 339. In a footnote to the same passage, Pepys's editors report that the Queen's treatment was "a medieval remedy used well into the 18th century, mainly for fevers." Pepys's report here, as elsewhere in the *Diary*, suggests that the remedy is reserved for desperate cases: e.g., "his breath rattled in his throate and they did lay pigeons to his feet . . . and all despair of him, and with good reason" (IX, 32). Another of Raspa's references, Thomas Coghan (or Cogan) conversely writes that "Pigeons are very hoat and moyst, wherefore they are not good [f]or those that be cholericke, or enclined to any feuers, but to them which be flemmaticke & pure melancholie, they are very wholesome, and be easily digested"; the reference to Coghan is thus misleading, since he has ingested pigeon, not pigeon poultice, in mind: *The Haven of Health* (Henrie Midleton for William Norton, 1584), 134. Confirmation of Simpson's undocumented statement that the pigeons are halved, as well as the additional information that they are halved while

living and an instance of this practice contemporary with Donne, can be found in *A Dictionary of Superstitions*, ed. Iona Opie and Moira Tatem (Oxford: Oxford Univ. Press, 1989), 308. For contemporary refences, see Francis Bacon, *The Works of Francis Bacon*, ed. James Spedding, Robert Leslie Ellis, and Douglas Denon Heath (Boston: Brown and Taggard [imprint varies; vols. 6–10: Taggard and Thompson], 1860–64), IV, 218: "It is received and confirmed by daily experience, that the soles of the feet have great affinity with the head and the mouth of the stomach; . . . Likewise pigeons bleeding, applied to the soles of the feet, ease the head" (I.96). Also, Jeremy Taylor, *The Whole Works of Jeremy Taylor*, ed. Alexander Taylor (London: Longman, Green, Longman, and Roberts, 1862), IX, 357.

26. On the Donnean nature of this correspondence, see Jeffrey Johnson's reading of Donne's communal emphasis: *The Theology of John Donne* (Woodbridge, Suffolk, Eng.: Boydell and Brewer, 1999), passim, e.g., 32: "'Almighty God ever loved *unity*. . . .'" See also my note 11, immediately above, regarding Zwingli's communal emphasis, which is to a provocative *extent* analogous to Donne's.

27. By reference to *Pseudo-Martyr*, Raspa, ed., suggests that Donne gives spiritual primacy to the heart as the seal of the conscience and notes the customary physiological primacy of the brain (161–62). In the context of Meditation XII, designation of the heart/conscience as the moral center makes the best sense. The traditional designation of both heart and head as sites of the soul may also facilitate the associative movement of Donne's figures between them. Relevant contextually as well is the attribution by Aristotle of motive primacy to the heart and by Galen to the brain, a contradiction for which "the usual solution [in Renaissance medicine] was to introduce a conceptual hierarchy in which the heart ruled the brain in some ultimate or philosophical sense and the brain ruled the nervous system directly": Nancy G. Siraisi, *Medieval and Early Renaissance Medicine: An Introduction to Knowledge and Practice* (Chicago: Univ. of Chicago Press, 1990), 81–82. See also my discussion of Melanchthon on the heart in chap. 8, 189–90, below.

28. On the interest in hieroglyphs in Donne's time, see Martin Elsky, *Authorizing Words: Speech, Writing, and Print in the English Renaissance* (Ithaca: Cornell Univ. Press, 1989), 146–68; and for a different view, Andrew M. Cooper, "The Collapse of the Religious Hieroglyph: Typology and Natural Language in Herbert and Bacon," *Renaissance Quarterly*, 45 (1992), 96–118; and my *Words That Matter*, chap. 1.

29. In a chapter on orientational metaphors, Lakoff and Johnson argue that up and down are physically experiential; they are thus "intuitive orientations," to use another traditional way of describing them (*Metaphors We Live By*, 14–21). Donne's metaphorizing here qualifies, if not counters, their theory that metaphor, hence cognition, has primarily a physical basis.

30. Jeremy Taylor's remarks on the use of pigeons to cure fever are peculiarly relevant to the blood guilt of living sacrifices. Taylor observes of the prohibition of such cruelty to beasts in the Old Testament, that "even this very precept is by all the world taught to yield to necessity and to charity, and cruelty to beasts is innocent when it is charity to men: and therefore though we do not eat them, yet we cut

living pigeons in halves and apply them to the feet of men in fevers": *Works*, IX, 357.

31. Although less literally than I, Seelig suggests that the purgative pigeons are "clearly emblems for the expiation of Christ" (20). See also Sullivan's argument that Donne personalizes Loyola's *Spiritual Exercises*, making them autobiographical; the result is "a kind of self-portraiture in the *Devotions* similar to Dürer's portrait of himself as Christ" (53); see also Joan Webber's extensive discussion of Donne's personalized focus in the *Devotions: The Eloquent "I": Style and Self in Seventeenth-Century Prose* (Madison: Univ. of Wisconsin Press, 1968), chap. 2.

32. *Philosophy in the Flesh*, 555–57: Lakoff and Johnson also embrace the empathy of *panentheism*.

33. Clark, 32–33; on "scaffolding," see also 179–92 and 194–218, esp. 209. Also my chap. 8, 211–12, below.

34. "The Circus Animals' Desertion," *The Collected Poems of W. B. Yeats* (1956; rpt. New York: Macmillan, 1959): my emphasis.

Chapter Five

Vesting Significance and Authority: The Vestiarian Controversy under Cranmer and Its Treatment by Foxe

1. For relevant discussion of Bacon's historiography and actual practice of history in *Henry VII*, see my *Biographical Truth: The Representation of Historical Persons in Tudor-Stuart Writing* (New Haven: Yale Univ. Press, 1984), chaps. 9–10, esp. 164, 178 ff. A caveat, however: I would not now use the possibly misleading phrase "strictly historical" to distinguish a more naively "objective" practice from a more interpretative—indeed a more truly "historical"—one, which in 1984 I called an "interpretative authenticity," terminology that is now dated (178).

2. *Tudor Puritanism: A Chapter in the History of Idealism* (Chicago: Univ, of Chicago Press, 1939), 84. My use of the word "magisterial" reflects the judgment of Patrick Collinson, *The Elizabethan Puritan Movement* (1967; rpt. Oxford: Clarendon, 2000), 12. In adopting the term "puritan," I am guided by Collinson's caution against a rigid sense of this term in the Elizabethan period (13–14, 22–28). In the main, the puritans sought to complete reform of the established church by purifying its practices and beliefs in accord with the Bible. The term "puritanism" postdates the vestiarian controversy of 1550–51, but its roots do not (60).

3. "A Demonstration of the trueth of that Discipline which Christ hath prescribed in his worde for the gouernment of his Church, in all times and places, vntill the end of the world," in *A parte of a register: contayninge sundrie memorable matters, written by diuers godly and learned in our time, which stand for, and desire the reformation of our Church, in discipline and ceremonies, according to the pure worde of God, and the lawe of our lande* (Middleburg: Richard Schilders, [1593?]), 10 (sig. B1v). By Udall's time, the issue of discipline, which continued explicitly to include vestments, had mushroomed into more direct questioning of the entire structure of the church. See also the numerous references under "Vestments" in *The Seconde parte of a register*, ed. Albert Peel, 2 vols. (Cambridge: Cambridge Univ. Press, 1915), II.

4. On the persistence of the controversy, see especially part 1, part 2, chaps. 1–2, and part 8, chaps. 4–5, of Collinson's *Puritan Movement*; also Knappen, chap. 10; and Kenneth Fincham, "Clerical Conformity from Whitgift to Laud," in *Conformity and Orthodoxy in the English Church, c. 1560–1660*, ed. Peter Lake and Michael Questier (Woodbridge, Suffolk, Eng.: Boydell, 2000), 125–58.

5. Cf. Roland Barthes' discussion of a uniform as participating in a metalanguage in *Mythologies*, selected and trans. Annette Lavers (New York: Hill and Wang, 1972), 116–27.

6. Meg Twycross and Sarah Carpenter offer a number of observations that are provocative when connected with the language the reformers repeatedly used to describe their more conservative opponents: for example, hypocrites, maskers, stage-players, actors in pageants: *Masks and Masking in Medieval and Early Tudor England* (Aldershot, Hants, Eng.: Ashgate, 2002). They note that "the Middle Ages gradually established masks as literary and visual symbols of hypocrisy and doubleness" and that hypocrisy is often personified as a religious or a wolf in sheep's clothing (281, 289). The Scribes and Pharisees in the Bible, of course, are labeled "hypocrites," and both the Fathers and later biblical commentators assumed that a theatrical metaphor was implicit in this word (288).

7. Quotations from E. W. Hunt, *The Life and Times of John Hooper (c.1500–1555) Bishop of Gloucester* (Lewiston, NY: Edwin Mellen, 1992), 115, 119–20; John Hooper, *An Oversight and Deliberation upon the Holy Prophet Jonas*, in *Early Writings*, 431–558, here 440 (two printings give the variant "fathers" rather than the preferred reading "feathers"), 479; Nicholas Ridley, "Reply of Bishop Ridley to Bishop Hooper on the Vestment Controversy, 1550," in *The Writings of John Bradford, M. A., Fellow of Pembroke Hall, Cambridge, and Prebendary of St. Paul's, Martyr, 1555*, ed. Aubrey Townsend (Cambridge: Cambridge Univ. Press, 1853), 375–95, here 392; *Original Letters Relative to the English Reformation*, ed. Hastings Robinson, 2 vols. (Cambridge: Cambridge Univ. Press, 1846–47): Letter 194 (John Ab Ulmis to Henry Bullinger, 1550), II, 408–10, here 410, and Letter 99 (Christopher Hales to Rodolph Gualter, 1550), I, 186–88, here 187. Also, Anthony Gilby, *A Pleasaunt Dialogue betweene a Souldior of Barwicke and an English Chaplaine* (n. p., 1581), sigs. A3r, E5r, F8v.

8. Ann Rosalind Jones and Peter Stallybrass want to have the vestiarian controversy two ways—to keep attention first on the cloth and second to interpret it as the marking of bodies: *Renaissance Clothing and the Materials of Memory* (Cambridge: Cambridge Univ. Press, 2000), 4–5, 59. Both ways are wonderfully provocative, but they also tend to circumvent the basic religious and political issues and to make this controversy, which is actually a symptom, more "central" and self-sufficient than in fact it was. Symptoms, it should be noted, inhere in the disease.

9. Gilbert Cope, "Vestments," in *A Dictionary of Liturgy and Worship*, ed. J. G. Davies (New York: Macmillan, 1972), 366; Aidan Kavanagh, "Liturgical Vesture in the Roman Catholic Tradition," in *Raiment for the Lord's Service: A Thousand Years of Western Vestments*, by Christa C. Mayer-Thurman (Chicago: Art Institute of Chi-

cago, 1975), 13; Joseph Braun, "Vestments" (origin), in *The Catholic Encyclopedia*: 7 July 2002 (http://www.newadvent.org/cathen/15388a.htm).

10. Wharton B. Marriott, *Vestiarivm Christianvm: The Origin and Gradual Development of the Dress of Holy Ministry in the Church* (London: Rivingtons, 1868), 53–54: when Jerome continues, he speaks more specifically of a bishop: "We see then that to one who is chief in priestly ministry to God the Gospels (laid upon his head) are a sign that he is under authority," namely, God's. Of course the rites of ordination existed in various versions and underwent change over the centuries: the English Sarum rite, for example, has the *codex evangeliorum* placed upon the neck of the candidate for episcopal consecration, rather than specifically on the head: William Maskell, *Monumenta Ritualia Ecclesiae Anglicanae*, 3 vols. (Oxford: Clarendon, 1882), II, 270–72.

11. Final quotation from Marriott, 20, n. 30. Mayer-Thurman adds that cotton grows on bushes; silk is the product of a worm, and wool or fur of animal origin. She also remarks another possible connection between linen and the shroud in which Christ was believed to have been wrapped for burial (25). She does not offer any explanation of why an origin directly from the ground, rather than from a bush, would be desirable, but the direct creation of earth by God and the formation of Adam ("red earth") from the "dust of the ground" in Genesis seem likely reasons.

12. The translation, except where bracketed, is that of H. B. Porter, Jr., *The Ordination Prayers of the Ancient Western Churches* (London: Society for Promoting Christian Knowledge, 1967), 19, 21; see also 91. Porter's English effectually renders the Sarum Latin found in Maskell, II, 275–76; because Porter does not claim to be following Sarum but the Gelasian rite as representative of the late composite rites of Western Christendom, however, I have checked his translation against the relevant text in Sarum, from which I cite the bracketed Latin with my own translation when a less free or more precise sense is needed for the purpose of my argument.

13. See Porter, 80, on provenance; also Paul F. Bradshaw, *The Anglican Ordinal: Its History and Development from the Reformation to the Present Day* (London: Society for Promoting Christian Knowledge, 1971), 4–5; Edward P. Echlin, *The Story of Anglican Ministry* (Slough, Eng.: St. Paul Publications, 1974), 1–22. On Hooper's life as a monk (possibly a Cistercian), see Hunt, 14–18.

14. Cope, 366–67; Braun (development).

15. According to the 1552 Ordinal, bishops were to wear a rochet for Communion, rather than the surplice worn by priests. As explained more fully in subsequent pages, however, the rochet is a form of the linen alb, of which the similarly linen surplice is also a version.

16. Citations above in this paragraph from Marriott, 69, 89, and here, 95: Isidore, Rabanus, Amalarius, respectively. The translations and paraphrases of Rabanus and Amalarius are mine.

17. Marriott, 116, 134: translations and paraphrases mine. The nature of Alcuin's emphasis on action is clearer by reference to some other remarks about the alb made by Jerome: the linen tunic "is closely fitted to the body, and is so scanty, and with sleeves so narrow, that there is no fold in this garment. It reaches a little below the

knee. For better understanding of what I say I may employ a somewhat common word of our own. Our soldiers, when on service, wear linen garments, which they call 'shirts,' fitting so closely, and so fastened about the body, as to leave them free for action, whether in running or in fighting, hurling the javelin, holding the shield, wielding the sword . . . as need may require. And so the priests [Levitical], standing prepared for the service of God, wear a tunic such as this, so that while they have their robes of beauty, they may hasten to and fro like men that stand stripped for speed" (Marriott, 13). Typically, Jerome proceeds to symbolism and contemporary application here.

18. Marriott, 165–66.

19. *The Praise of Folly*, trans. Betty Radice, ed. A.H.T. Levi, in *Collected Works of Erasmus: Literary and Educational Writings* (Toronto: Univ. of Toronto Press, 1986), XXVII, 77–153, here 137.

20. Marriott, 91, 117, 132 (Hugh), 155–56. Amalarius is an interesting exception: noting that the chasuble (*casula*) pertains to all clergy, he sees it signifying the works that pertain to them all, namely fasting, vigils, simplicity or truthfulness, reading, psalmody, prayer, physical labor, doctrine, silence, and others of this sort. (Quite freely, I have rendered as the various works "fames, sitis, vigiliae, nuditas, lectio, psalmodia, oratio, labor operandi, doctrina, silentium, et caetera hujusmodi"; Amalarius seems to have monks especially in mind.) He adds that when a clerk is dressed in a chasuble, he is clothed in all the works enumerated (Marriott, 98).

21. Maskell, II, 221: the deliberately literal translation is mine. Porter, 89, gives the following "later composite" variant to accompany bestowal of the chasuble: "The blessing of the Father and the Son and of the Holy Ghost descend upon thee, and mayst thou be blessed in the priestly order and offer acceptable sacrifices, for the sins and offences of the people, unto Almighty God, to whom be honour and glory."

22. E.g., see Braun (development) and Marriott, lxxxiii.

23. Marriott, 166–67: translations and paraphrases mine.

24. *The First and Second Prayer Books of Edward VI* (1549, 1552; rpt. London: Prayer Book Society, 1999), 291n: the "Ordinal was not printed as part of the first issues of the Prayer-Book of 1549, but as the colophons of some copies show, it was intended to be bound up with copies of the Prayer-Book." The 1552 Prayer Book, discussed subsequently, contained a re-revised Ordinal from the start. Bradshaw, 18–28, suggests that the revised Ordinal of 1550 is largely Cranmer's, although based on Martin Bucer's rite; see also my n. 41, immediately below. References to both Prayer Books will be to this edition, abbreviated as *PB*.

25. *PB*, 286–89; the explanation about ceremonies comes at the beginning of the second Prayer Book (324–26), rather than at the end.

26. Bradshaw, 12, citing Cranmer's rendering of the Lutheran catechism of Justus Jonas; preceding citation from page 9. Bradshaw notes that in 1540 the other bishops and divines thought ordination to consist of prayer and the imposition of hands (9), and this is a view expressed in the 1543 revision of *The Bishops' Book* known as *The King's Book* (10–11).

27. Cope, 376, glosses "vestement" as "chasuble, stole, and maniple," whereas J.R. Porter indicates only chasuble, albeit without suggesting that *only* the chasuble is intended: see *PB*, x, also the source for the next quotation.

28. MacCulloch, 486–87; also Collinson, *Puritan Movement*, 32.

29. For the Latin texts, see Maskell, II, 218–19, 221, 224–26; cf. 245–49. Echlin, 6–11, provides a fairly detailed rendering of the Sarum rite.

30. Bradshaw, 73, instances the conservative Bishop Edmund Bonner as one who thought the words of the *porrectio instrumentorum* crucial and a statement by Bishop Ridley implying that this belief was widely held. See Ridley, *A Brief Declaration of the Lord's Supper*, 19: "the order of the priesthood . . . (they say) is given by virtue of these words said by the Bishop, 'Take thou authority to sacrifice for the quick and the dead.'"

31. Quotation from "Reply of Bishop Ridley to Bishop Hooper," 387. On Ridley's relation to Cranmer, see MacCulloch, 355. Aside from the return of traditional vestments under Queen Mary, it should also be noted that the Elizabethan Parliament of 1559 reinstated (at least "on paper") the vestment rubrics of 1549—alb, cope, and chasuble: see J. H. Primus, *The Vestments Controversy* (Amsterdam: Kampen: J. H. Kok, 1960), 75; also Collinson, *Puritan Movement*, 30–34.

32. Describing Hooper's career, I draw mainly on Hunt, passim: for a fuller account of Hooper's clash with Cranmer and Ridley, see his chap. 7, as well as Primus, chap. 2, on which Hunt draws, and MacCulloch, 471–85.

33. Hooper, *An Oversight and Deliberation upon the Holy Prophet Jonas*, 554, cf. 534.

34. *PB*, 300, 308; Hunt, 119. Hooper appears to be mistaken here (as he discovered when appointed a bishop) in his statement that the oath of supremacy is not required of bishops: see *PB*, 314, 460.

35. C. Hopf, "Bishop Hooper's 'Notes' to the King's Council, 3 October 1550," *The Journal of Theological Studies*, 44 (1943), 194–99, here 196.

36. Primus, 17, works to rationalize the contradiction, which he first admits. His interpretation is based on Hooper's initial lack of clarity and ex post facto clarification. This strikes me as special pleading.

37. "Notes," 197–98. For Ridley's rendering, see his "Reply . . . to Bishop Hooper," 379.

38. On Ridley's earlier aberrations from church law, see Hunt, 124–25, and Primus, 12–14.

39. On Hooper's support for Mary Tudor, see Hunt, 188–89, and "An Apology against the untrue and slanderous reports made against me John Hooper, late bishop of Worceter and Gloceter, that I should be a maintainer and encourager of such as cursed the Queen's Majesty's highness," in *Later Writings of Bishop Hooper, Together with His Letters and Other Pieces*, ed. Charles Nevinson (Cambridge: Cambridge Univ. Press, 1852), 554–67, here 556–67: where significant, I cite the longer forms of Renaissance titles but otherwise the familiar and shorter modern form. Hunt points to Hooper's high regard for monarchy; it should be noted, however, that this regard now extends to all magistrates, indeed to all who "minister" divinely extended power: see, for example, Hooper's "Annotations on Romans XIII," in his

Later Writings, 93–116, here 101–08. On the implications of the clash between Hooper and Ridley, see Primus, 34.

40. *Works,* I, 21 (Bk. I.ii.11, cf. I.i.1).

41. Echlin, 2, describes the first Edwardine Ordinal as the work of Cranmer, Ridley, and Peter Martyr (the "learned men with him" of Ridley's reply) and also notes its resemblance in many respects to the Roman Pontificals and Bucer's draft Ordinal. According to Bradshaw, 20–21, Cranmer's major source for this Ordinal was Martin Bucer's rite, supplemented by the Roman Pontificals and some material of his own composition.

42. *Censura,* in *Martin Bucer and the Book of Common Prayer,* 18, 20. Also MacCulloch, 480–81.

43. *Later Writings,* 20–63, 65–92. In the absence of an extant 1550 edition, Nevinson, ed., prints two later editions, 1581 and 1584, which differ only in spelling. I have cited the 1584 edition, whose full title continues, *"made and set furth by Jhon* [sic] *Hooper, wherein is declared what a christian manne is bound to beleve of God, hys King, his neibour, and hymselfe.*

44. Hunt, 135. *PB,* 313, specifies that the newly "elected" (appointed) bishop shall have "upon hym a Surples and Cope," as will the consecrating bishops. Knappen, 83, indicates that a rochet could serve as a surplice. This is true in 1552 but does not accord with instructions in the 1550 Ordinal. Knappen also reports that in 1550 "bishops wore white linen sleeves on their street gown," whereas the historians of liturgy consider this shift of the wide sleeves from rochet to chimere an extravagant eighteenth-century development: see Cope, 379.

45. Sir Philip Sidney, *An Apology for Poetry or The Defence of Poesy,* ed. Geoffrey Shepherd (Manchester, Eng.: Manchester Univ. Press, 1973), 101, lines 35–36. Forrest G. Robinson, cited here on "speaking picture," earlier suggests that "by 'picture' Sidney means an abstraction, a concept made visible to the reader's mind": see *The Shape of Things Known: Sidney's Apology in Its Philosophical Tradition* (Cambridge, MA: Harvard Univ. Press, 1972), 99–100.

46. Collinson, *Puritan Movement,* part 2, chaps. 1–2, 4; part 5, chaps. 1–2. The references under "Vestments controversy of Elizabeth's reign" in Collinson's index provide a useful tour; see the more specific references under "Surplice," as well.

47. Collinson, *Puritan Movement,* 257. According to J. F. Mozley, Foxe himself "had scruples about wearing the clerical vestments laid down in the Queen's [Elizabeth's] injunctions of 1559": *John Foxe and His Books* (London: Society for Promoting Christian Knowledge, 1940), 63. These injunctions "ambiguously required the eucharistic vestments . . . in use in the second year of Edward VI," or 1549 (Collinson, *Puritan Movement,* 34). See my note 24, immediately above, on the dating of the first Edwardine Ordinal.

48. On Foxe's use of sources, see Mozley, chaps. 5–6; Warren W. Wooden, *John Foxe* (Boston: Twayne, 1983), 22–23; Patrick Collinson, *Elizabethan Essays* (London: Hambledon, 1994), 151–77; John King, "Fiction and Fact in Foxe's *Book of Martyrs," John Foxe and the English Reformation,* ed. David Loades (Aldershot, Hants,

Eng.: Scolar, 1997), 12–35, here 12–15; Thomas S. Freeman, "Fate, Faction, and Fiction in Foxe's *Book of Martyrs*," *The Historical Journal*, 43 (2000), 601–23.

49. On the political significance of Latin, cf. Timothy Rosendale, " 'Fiery Toungues': Language, Liturgy, and the Paradox of the English Reformation," *Renaissance Quarterly*, 54 (2001), 1142–64: "England's Reformers sensed that the Latin hegemony was part and parcel of the papal hegemony against which they struggled both theologically and politically" (1145). Also J. H. Anderson, *Words That Matter*, chap. 2.

50. On the medieval terms of discussion, see Bradshaw, 6 and n. 3 on the same page.

51. Referring to Cranmer's degradation (treated later in this chapter), John R. Knott similarly notices that Cranmer's dismissing the vestments as "this gear" highlights the ceremoniousness of the Latin formulae for removing them: *Discourses of Martyrdom in English Literature, 1563–1694* (Cambridge: Cambridge Univ. Press, 1993), 73.

52. The perceptive conception of a "fallacy of expressive, or imitative, form" is Yvor Winters'. Winters defines it as "the procedure in which the form succumbs to the raw material of the poem," to which I would add, "or of any other text, though especially in the instance of a text exhibiting a rhetorical consciousness, as decidedly is the case in Foxe's Martyrology." See Winters' *In Defense of Reason* (New York: Swallow and William Morrow, 1947), 41. Nowadays some of us would not use the term "fallacy," which assumes a non-fallacious stance, to describe such a form or might refer to a contaminating discourse rather than to a form.

53. The Catholic power does not recognize Hooper's consecration as a bishop, and so he is only degraded from the priesthood here.

54. My comma. (In a modern edition, the preceding comma and this one would be a parenthesis or at least a dash.)

55. Quotation from C. S. Lewis, *English Literature in the Sixteenth Century, Excluding Drama* (Oxford: Clarendon, 1954), 193. In an essay sensitive to Protestant theater, Laurie Shannon sees in Latimer's apparel "the costume of Humilitas": " 'His Apparel Was Done Upon Him': Rites of Personage in Foxe's *Book of Martyrs*," *Shakespeare Studies*, 28 (2000), 193–98, here 195. I take his apparel to be more complexly significant. While I would agree that Humilitas is one possible reading, this possibility is certainly qualified by mockery. Latimer's ironic attitude toward his examiners, evident in his verbal tactics, is not humble.

56. Most recent citation from 1883. Previous citation from Foxe's first English edition *Actes and Monuments of these latter and perillous dayes, touching matters of the Church* (London: Iohn Day, 1563), 1493. In the 1583 edition, Foxe references the Pope's Pontifical but refers us back to the 1563 edition for the actual content of it.

57. *Actes*, 1768: I have silently omitted a misleading comma after "garment."

58. The quoted phrase is from the final sentence of Alexander Pope's *Dunciad*: *The Poems of Alexander Pope*, ed. John Butt (New Haven: Yale Univ. Press, 1963), 800.

59. Although Ridley, like Cranmer, who goes to the stake in a ragged gown and old cap, was of gentlemanly birth, whereas Latimer was not, it is further notable that Foxe does not read the sartorial difference between Ridley and Latimer at the end in terms of inherited social class. Latimer's elevation to the episcopacy, even if eventually rejected by him, would render such a reading moot in any case.

60. *The Mirror for Magistrates* is a familiar sixteenth-century expression of the *de casibus* or Fall-of-Princes genre that is popular at least from Chaucer's time on (e.g., Chaucer's *Monk's Tale*, Lydgate's *Fall of Princes*, etc).

61. See Foxe, 1881; and for the Pope's bull, "Bulla Pauli papae mandans depositionem et degradationem Thomae Cranmer, archiep. Cantuar.," in *Concilia Magnae Britanniae et Hiberniae*, compiled by Davide Wilkins (1737; rpt. Brussels: Culture et Civilisation, 1964), IV, 132–36. Foxe tells his readers that he has expressed "the full tenour" of the "executory Letters of the Pope sent to the king and Queene" in his "first impression of Actes. Pag. 1490." Since the first edition of *Acts* is not readily available, I would note that Foxe's much-maligned nineteenth-century editor helpfully inserts the "full tenour" into the 1583 edition at this point: *The Actes and Monuments of John Foxe*, ed. Stephen Reed Cattley, 8 vols. (London: R. B. Seeley and W. Burnside, 1838), VIII, 69–71.

62. Knott, 31–35, discusses the extent to which Foxe's martyrs imitate biblical models. The practice is widespread in the sixteenth century and looks back to the saints' lives of earlier periods: see my *Biographical Truth*, part 1, esp. chaps. 1–3.

63. Thanks to Debora Shuger for hearing this additional echo.

64. Again, Cattley, ed., inserts Foxe's full text from the earlier edition into the 1583 one: VIII, 77–79. In the 1563 edition of *Acts* to which Foxe refers, pages 1493–95 give the entire text of the degradation from the Pontifical—what Foxe himself describes as "a ful and perfect description of all and singuler rites and ceremonies thereunto pertaining, taken out of the popes booke, called Pontificale" (1493).

65. The Pope's bull directs that the pall should be the first vestment to be removed: *Concilia Magnae*, IV, 135: "Primo, Pallium degradator aufert a degradando, dicendo, Praerogativa pontificalis dignitatis, quae in pallio designatur, te eximimus, quia male usus es ea."

66. After "doing," I have replaced a period with a comma. See *OED*, s.v. *Gear sb.*, I.1, II, 5.

67. Cited from Donne's "Satyre III," vs. 43–47, 50–54 (Shawcross, ed., 24). The quotations in the following sentence are from Donne's Holy Sonnet beginning "Show me deare Christ, thy spouse" (349), a poem probably written twenty years or more after "Satyre III," the latter dating from roughly the mid-1590s.

68. *Devotions*, 76. *The Sermons of John Donne*, ed. George R. Potter and Evelyn M. Simpson, 10 vols (1953; rpt. Berkeley: Univ. of California Press, 1984), VII, 70–71. For discussion of these words in the Second Prebend Sermon, see J. H. Anderson, *Words That Matter*, 212–13.

69. Calvin, *Institutes*, I, 499: II.xv.4–5. Also Victoria Silver's discussion of this covering in Luther and Calvin as justification: *Imperfect Sense: The Predicament of Milton's Irony* (Princeton: Princeton Univ. Press, 2001), chap. 1, esp. 67.

70. *The Works of George Herbert*, ed. F. E. Hutchinson (1941; rpt. Oxford: Clarendon, 1959), 174.

71. For a provocative discussion of related issues in *The Temple* and reference to further pertinent criticism of Herbert, see Robert Whalen, "George Herbert's Sacramental Puritanism," *Renaissance Quarterly*, 54 (2001), 1273–1307, esp. 1276, 1303. Whalen defines the "sacramental Puritanism" he finds in Herbert as a conformity between outward behavior and thought (1303–04). In this view he follows (and cites) Ramie Targoff: "The Performance of Prayer: Sincerity and Theatricality in Early Modern England," *Representations*, 60 (1997), 49–69, here 50–51; also Whalen's *Poetry of Immanence*, 112–14, 121, 175. In Herbert's poem, I am suggesting a shift inward and away from outward emphasis with respect to the vestiary symbol, not to prayer or to the power and authority of the eucharistic *bread* as such, and I am doing so in the context of its long history. For relevant discussion of the inconsistencies of conformity in the English Church, see esp. Fincham, passim, and Peter Lake, "Moving the Goal Posts? Modified Subscription and the Construction of Conformity in the Early Stuart Church," in *Conformity and Orthodoxy in the English Church, c. 1560–1660*, ed. Peter Lake and Michael Questier (Woodbridge, Suffolk, Eng.: Boydell, 2000), 179–205.

Chapter Six

Busirane's *Place*: The House of Abusive Rhetoric in *The Faerie Queene*

1. The pun on *reign* was first remarked by Harry Berger, Jr., *Revisionary Play: Studies in the Spenserian Dynamics* (Berkeley: Univ. of California Press, 1988), 173. Berger takes the first part of Busirane's name as a pun on "busy," which assumes a different pronunciation of the first vowel from that active in the pun on and allusion to *abusio*, "abuse," "catachresis."

2. Lynn Enterline, *The Rhetoric of the Body from Ovid to Shakespeare* (Cambridge: Cambridge Univ. Press, 2000), 19, 25–26. Also Jonathan Bate, *Shakespeare and Ovid* (Oxford: Oxford Univ. Press, 1993), 19–22, 28.

3. For example, see Leonard Barkan, *The Gods Made Flesh: Metamorphosis and the Pursuit of Paganism* (New Haven: Yale Univ. Press, 1986), 2–5; Jones and Stallybrass, chap. 4, esp. 89–97; Heather James, "Ovid and the Question of Politics in Early Modern England," *ELH*, 70 (2003), 343–73, here 358–63.

4. Wofford, remarking the frequent puns on *read* (or "rede") in III.xi and xii, focuses attention especially on Britomart's gazing. Our arguments share ground in distinguishing between Busirane's literalist perspective and Britomart's healthier responses: "Gendering Allegory: Spenser's Bold Reader and the Emergence of Character in *The Faerie Queene* III," *Criticism*, 30 (1988), 1–21. William Oram's remarks on the House of Busirane are current, succinct, and much to the point: "Spenserian Paralysis," *Studies in English Literature*, 41 (2001), 49–70, here 60.

5. Of particular interest in this regard is Jones and Stallybrass, chap. 6, which treats women's use of mythological sources in their needlework and their utilization of such work for protest, at times, as in the instance of Mary Stuart, whose needle-

works were even introduced as evidence by prosecutors at her trial. Or for a witty
case in point, see *Amoretti LXXI*:

> I joy to see how in your drawen work,
>   Your selfe vnto the Bee ye doe compare;
>   and me vnto the Spyder that doth lurke,
>   in close awayt to catch her vnaware.

6. Katherine Eggert, "Spenser's Ravishment: Rape and Rapture in *The Faerie
Queene*," *Representations*, 70 (2000), 1–26, here 11–12.

7. Ovid, *Metamorphoses*, trans. Frank Justus Miller, 2nd ed., 2 vols. (1921; rpt.
London: Heinemann, 1966), I, 292–93. James, 364, perceptively relates the erotic
pleasures of Busirane's tapestry to "tyrannical abuse," but without engaging rhetorical *abusio*.

8. For a useful, but on this point a differing, comparison of Bower and House,
see Sarah Annes Brown, *The Metamorphosis of Ovid: From Chaucer to Ted Hughes*
(New York: St. Martin's Press, 1999), 41–46, 50–56.

9. The Palmer is elsewhere in Book II an artist, a spinner of myth, as I have
argued long since in "The Knight and the Palmer in *The Faerie Queene*, Book II,"
Modern Language Quarterly, 31 (1970), 160–78.

10. Witness also Ben Jonson's *Volpone*, and see note 261, below. Morton W.
Bloomfield notes that John Wyclif refers to avarice as a spider in his *Tractatus de civili
dominio*: *The Seven Deadly Sins: An Introduction to the History of a Religious Concept,
with Special Reference to Medieval English Literature* (East Lansing: Michigan State College Press, 1952), 189.

11. Keats writes, "*an artist* must serve Mammon—he must have 'self concentration' selfishness perhaps." He continues, "you might . . . be more of an artist, and
'load every rift' of your subject with ore": From *The Letters of John Keats*, ed. Hyder
Edward Rollins (Cambridge, MA: Harvard Univ. Press, 1958), II, 322–23; cited by
Paul J. Alpers in *The Poetry of "The Faerie Queene"* (Princeton: Princeton Univ.
Press, 1967), 264. Provocative, too, in connection with a broader eroticism than a
post-Freudian one is Debora Kuller Shuger's assertion that "The identification of
the erotic with sexuality" and the privileged location of erotic desire in the genitals
"emerged sometime after 1650." She argues that in the Renaissance "sexual desire
is an inflection of erotic longing, not its origin or essence": *The Renaissance Bible:
Scholarship, Sacrifice, and Subjectivity* (Berkeley: Univ. of California Press, 1994), 178,
180.

12. On Shakespeare, see Harold F. Brooks, "*Richard III*: Antecedents of Clarence's Dream," *Shakespeare Survey*, 32 (1979), 145–50. Milton refers to the House
of Mammon in *Areopagitica* in *Complete Prose Works*, ed. Ernest Sirluck (New Haven:
Yale Univ. Press, 1959), II, 516.

13. A. C. Hamilton, ed., *The Faerie Qveene*, by Edmund Spenser (London: Longman, 1977), 413.

14. I disagree with the general tendency in recent criticism to reduce allegory to
abstraction and then to oppose it to narrative, not recognizing that allegory is itself

a narrative mode. See, for example, my reviews of otherwise admirable books by Gordon Teskey and Sayre Greenfield: the first in *Arthuriana*, 7 (1997), 125–28, and the second in the *Spenser Newsletter*, 30 (1999), 1–4.

15. Thomas Roche, *The Kindly Flame: A Study of the Third and Fourth Books of Spenser's "Faerie Queene"* (Princeton: Princeton Univ. Press, 1964), 82.

16. In addition to Hamlet's catachrestically resolving, "I will speak daggers to her," Lanham gives as another instance of extravagant (and implicitly emblematic) metaphor, "when a weeping woman's eyes become Niagra Falls" (21). See also my chap. 4, n. 12, above, and chap. 7, passim, below.

17. Lee A. Sonnino: *A Handbook to Sixteenth-Century Rhetoric* (New York: Barnes and Noble, 1968), 16, considers *audacia* an alternative name of catachresis, a point I treat further in the next chapter. For the translation "maidenly" (or "maydenly") of Cicero's "verecunda" in *De Oratore* (ed. G. P. Goold, trans. E. W. Sutton, completed by H. Rackham, 2 vols. [1942; rpt. London: Heinemann, 1988], Bk. III.xli.165), see Dudley Fenner, *The Artes of Logike and Rhetorike* (Middleburg: R. Schilders, 1584), sig. D1v. Unless otherwise noted, reference to *De Oratore* is to this edition.

18. *De Oratore*, Bk. III.xxxviii.156–xxxix.157. For a fuller discussion of implications, again, see my chapter on metaphor and catachresis, below. James, 358–65, ties the boldness in the House of Busirane to Ovid's political *audacia*. Her persuasive and congenial argument is complicated by Spenser's other uses of the Arachne myth, however.

19. *OED*, s.v. *derne, adv.*; *dern, a.* and *sb.*, 1–2, 5–6; *MED*, s.v. *derneli(che), adv.*, a–d. The spelling of the adverbial form in Spenser's text conceivably suggests familiarity with the medieval usage; the contextualized meaning does so more definitively. The editorial exception, published since the writing of this chapter, is A. C. Hamilton's new edition of *The Faerie Queene* (Harlow, Eng.: Longman, 2001), 404n: Hamilton still offers "earnestly or dismally" but now prefers "secretly." He rationalizes his preference on the grounds that Amoret does not want Busirane to hear her plea. His gloss, while moving in the right direction, perhaps oversimplifies what is at stake here. Busirane himself, after all, could tell Britomart about his power over Amoret in order to save his neck, or at least he could if he actually grasped its extent. In any event, Hamilton's explanation would not preclude my less innocent reading. My argument would also lend a more knowing or even more sinister cast to Lauren Silberman's view of Amoret as "the lady who says yes": *Transforming Desire: Erotic Knowledge in Books III and IV of "The Faerie Queene"* (Berkeley: Univ. of California Press, 1995), 63.

20. Rhetoric is often associated with a chain. Alciati's popular emblem book, for example, depicts Hercules, representative of eloquence, whose art is rhetoric, "as an old man, trailing after him a crowd of people fastened by the ears with chains issuing from his mouth." The description is Jean Bodin's in his *Six Books of the Commonwealth*, cited with further bibliographical references, by Jane Aptekar, *Icons of Justice: Iconography and Thematic Imagery in Book V of "The Faerie Queene"* (New York: Columbia Univ. Press, 1969), 229–30, n. 18. Thomas Wilson makes conspicuous

use of the same image of Hercules in the Preface to his rhetoric: *Wilson's Arte of Rhetorique 1560*, ed. G. H. Mair (Oxford: Clarendon, 1909).

21. "Metaphorical Process," 151. Also Ricoeur's *Rule of Metaphor*, 248, 254–56. I derive the suggestive term "perverse predication" from Jonathan Hillman's "deviant predication," derived in turn from Ricoeur. The word *trope* derives from Greek *tropos*, "turn."

22. For a radically different reading of this scene (or place), see Susan Frye, *Elizabeth I: The Competition for Representation* (Oxford: Oxford Univ. Press, 1993), 122–24, 129–30.

23. *OED*, s.v. *bowel, sb.*, 3–4, but also 1–2.

24. *OED*, s.v. *as, adv. (conj.,* and *rel. pro.)*, 18.

25. Ricoeur, "Metaphorical Process," 151; Bourdieu, 142–43. See also my chaps. 2 and 3, above.

26. E.g., see my discussion of the end of Donne's *Deaths Duel* in *Words That Matter*, 227–29; and of *Hamlet* in chap. 2, 30–32, above.

27. Jean Aitchison, *Words in the Mind*, 2nd ed. (Oxford: Blackwell, 1994), 215, 217, but all of chaps. 17–18 should be consulted: Aitchison favors an electrical model of selection and comprehension—a kind of electrical circuit board—to an army or "cohort" model. See also my chap. 2, 31–32, on punning in Shakespeare's *Hamlet.*.

28. Unpublished paper delivered July 7, 2001, at the International Spenser Society Conference in Cambridge, England, to which I refer with Katherine Eggert's kind permission.

29. More accurately, Britomart's armor is that of a Saxon queen (III.iii, 58–60), but armor itself is coded male in Spenser's culture, as is evident whenever Britomart meets a knight with her visor down. A second point: I have been concerned to insist that the House of Busirane is a cultural site rather than a single character's fantasy. A reader invested in psycho-analytic metaphor, might further wish to interpret Britomart's abuse of Amoret in the 1596 *Faerie Queene*, along with her participation in Amoret's plight as a victim in 1590, through the lens of Lacan's traversing (completing, experiencing both sides of) the fantasy. Reading Lacan, Slavoj Žižek translates cultural ideology to individual fantasy. In other words, he explains the psycho-analytic process, necessarily individualized, of its more culturally generalized Althusserian version in a way that is more relevant to my own view than is unmediated Lacan. Looking back from Spenser's Book IV with Žižek in hand, we might see Britomart turning from a transferred (hence metaphorized) identification of herself as the object of desire, or an identification with Amoret, to an identification of herself as the agent of desire, or Busirane. But this Lacanian-Žižekian reading, although interesting in itself, needlessly adds another layer of systemic metaphor to traditional allegorical projection, and this system brings with it an alien agenda, including the narrower conception of erotic desire that I have earlier referenced (my n.11, immediately above). The focus on an inclusive cultural problem also shifts to one that is more narrowly focused on the single character in whom it is internalized. Such an interpretation threatens to contain and to gender the problem of Busi-

rane specifically as Britomart's, whereas Spenser's poem, in my view, represents the breadth of Busirane's cultural basis, one from which even the Spenserian poet finds it difficult fully to escape. See Jeffrey Jerome Cohen, "On Saracen Enjoyment: Some Fantasies of Race in Late Medieval France and England," *Journal of Medieval and early Modern Studies*, 31 (2001), 113–46, here 128, 132–33; also Žižek, *The Sublime Object of Ideology* (London: Verso, 1989), 30–45; and his "Revisioning 'Lacanian' Social Criticism: The Law and Its Obscene Double," *The Journal for the Psychoanalysis of Culture and Society*, 1 (1996), 15–25. Thanks to Lowell Gallagher for asking about Lacan and to Patricia Ingham for the reference to "Saracen Enjoyment."

30. See "Whatever Happened to Amoret? The Poet's Role in Book IV of *The Faerie Queene*," *Criticism*, 13 (1971), 180–200, here 191.

31. I have discussed Artegall's martial engagement of Britomart, which ends in "accord," in *The Spenser Encyclopedia*, ed. A. C. Hamilton, et al (Toronto: Univ. of Toronto Press, 1990), partly s.v. *Artegall* and partly s.v. *Britomart*. See also A. C. Hamilton's notes on the battle in his second edition of *The Faerie Queene*.

32. *The Faerie Queene*, III.v.51–52, 54; IV.viii.29–33. See my essay " 'In liuing colours and right hew': The Queen of Spenser's Central Books," in *Critical Essays on Edmund Spenser*, ed. Mihoko Suzuki (New York: Simon and Schuster Macmillan, 1996), 168–82, here 171–76.

Chapter Seven

Catachresis and Metaphor: "Be Bold, Be Bold, Be Not Too Bold" in the Latin Rhetorical Tradition and Its Renaissance Adaptors

1. *Reading Shakespeare's Will: The Theology of Figure from Augustine to the Sonnets*. (New York: Columbia Univ. Press, 2002), 160–63: sic as cited. I reviewed Freinkel's book in *Yearbook of Comparative and General Literature*, 50 (2002–03), 189–94.

2. Freinkel, 161, 332–33, n. 13. Victoria Silver identifies catachresis with mixed metaphor, defined as "a conflating of two logically incompatible ideas" (83; cf. 127 and 366, n. 28) or as "manifest incompatibles" (152). Within modern interpretation of Renaissance theology and Lutheran theology in particular, a revisionist interpretation of catachresis is itself becoming something of a master trope.

3. Although more recent English translations of Cicero's *De Oratore* than the Loeb edition by Sutton/Rackham and of Quintilian's *Institutio Oratoria* than the Loeb version by Butler now exist, I am using Sutton/Rackham as my base text for Cicero, and Butler for Quintilian, as well as Caplan's still current Loeb translation for *Ad C. Herennium* (see respectively my chap 6, n 17, above, and my nn. 11, 8, immediately below, for the initial bibliographical citation of these texts). I do so for three reasons; first, these are the translations cited by the secondary criticism that I engage and seek to correct on the basis of the Latin text; second, these translations have been standard in English for Cicero and Quintilian until very recently, indeed, until 2001; third, these editions still provide the most conveniently available Latin texts for most readers, which I shall cross-reference, wherever relevant, with Donald

A. Russell's edition of Quintilian, namely, *The Orator's Education*, ed. and trans. Russell, 5 vols. (Cambridge, MA: Harvard Univ. Press, 2001): hereafter, Russell; and with the recent translation of *De Oratore* by James M. May and Jakob Wisse, namely, *Cicero: On the Ideal Orator* (New York: Oxford Univ. Press, 2001): hereafter, May/Wisse.

4. Examples cited in this paragraph and the next are numerous in the texts I use, and they will be discussed in specifically referenced detail below. I would also note here that if Sutton/Rackham, Butler, and even Caplan were translating today, they would likely choose different words in many passages. My purpose is not to criticize them but to assess use of their renderings in a current context, as well as the need to reinterpret the original language.

5. As Bruce R. Smith notes, "Overseas visitors were impressed with the number of foreign-speakers, primarily merchants and Protestant refugees, who made their homes in London": *The Acoustic World of Early Modern England: Attending to the O-Factor* (Chicago: Univ. of Chicago Press, 1999), 54. Among likely readers of Latin rhetorics, as distinct from subsistence workers and apprentices in the manual trades in times of dearth, xenophobia was uncommon as a rule.

6. Here I attribute to Cicero the views of his nominally dialogic character Lucius Licinius Crassus in *De Oratore*. On the validity of such attribution, see May/Wisse, 3 ("Cicero's own ideas are most often clear enough in the end"), 13, 16–17: "the ideas presented in the dialogue are clearly his [Cicero's] own, as is shown by the many correspondences with his later rhetorical works. . . . Moreover, from one of Cicero's letters it is clear that he spoke 'through the character' of his interlocutors" (17).

7. Dominance of the current, narrow meaning of *simile* is quite modern. A Renaissance rhetorician such as George Puttenham, for example, does not recognize *simile* as a figure. The *OED*, s.v. *simile*, 1, cites Langland (1393), for the meaning "A comparison of one thing with another, esp. as an ornament in poetry or rhetoric" as the first use of the word in English; Langland does not intend the narrow modern English meaning. The *OED*'s next citation is 1589, with another in 1602, still without the modern meaning. For a final example from the *OED*, in 1646 Thomas Browne writes, "Playing much upon the simile or illustrative argumentation"; Browne's is another testimony to the broad meaning of the term, whose narrowing evidently occurs sometime in the twentieth century. Consultation of two popular modern desk dictionaries produced the following results, s.v. *simile*: "A figure of speech in which two essentially unlike things are explicitly compared, usu. by means of *like* or *as*" (*The American Heritage College Dictionary*, 3rd ed. [1993; rpt. Boston: Houghton Mifflin, 1997]); "A figure of speech in which one thing is likened to another, dissimilar thing by the use of *like*, *as*, etc.": *Webster's New World College Dictionary*, 3rd ed. (New York: Macmillan, 1988]).

8. Harry Caplan, ed. and trans., *Ad C. Herennium* (1954; rpt. London: William Heinemann, 1981), ix. Caplan assigns the work to c. 86–82 B.C. (xxvi) and notes that its fourth book is "the oldest extant formal study of figures" (xx). Unless otherwise identified, translations are Caplan's. Gualtiero Calboli observes how novel and

tentative the whole notion of a category of tropes was when the *Ad Herennium* was written, a fact that bears on some degree of awkwardness evident in its treatment in the later Roman rhetorics: "From Aristotelian λέξις to *elocutio*," *Rhetorica*, 16 (1998), 47–80, esp. 57, 60.

9. The abbreviated translations are mine.

10. Cf. Horace's "Ars Poetica," vs. 48–51 (i.e., "The Epistle to the Pisones," or, Epistle, II.3): "si forte necesse est / indiciis monstrare recentibus abdita rerum, / fingere cinctutis non exaudita Cethegis / continget, dabiturque licentia sumpta pudenter ('If by chance it is necessary to explain obscure things by new terms, you will have the chance to frame words not heard of by the old-fashioned Cethegi, and a license will be given if used modestly [alternatively, 'with moderation,' or Rudd, 'with discretion'): *Horace: Epistles, Book II and Epistle to the Pisones*, ed. Niall Rudd (Cambridge: Cambridge Univ. Press, 1989). Subsequent reference is to this edition and translations of the Latin are mine, although with consultation of Rudd's notes: here, I adopt his translations of "abdita" and "continget." Rudd explains that the present passage applies to the "three main ways of inventing new terms": "to use an already-existing Latin word in a new, technical sense by analogy with its Greek equivalent" or "a new Latin word could be constructed on an existing root" or finally, "a Greek word could be imported" 157, n. 49.

11. *Ad Herennium*, II.xv.22: my emphasis; for other examples, see I.xii.22, cf. II.xii.18, I.xv.25. Quintilian makes the same recommendation: *The Institutio Oratoria of Quintilian*, ed. and trans. H. E. Butler, 4 vols. (1920; rpt. London: William Heinemann, 1980), III, Bk. VII.iv.13. Subsequent reference to Quintilian's Latin text is to this edition, as is reference to its English translation, unless otherwise indicated.

12. For the date, see H. Rackham's introduction in *De Oratore*, I, ix–x. Subsequent reference to Cicero's Latin text is to this edition, and except where otherwise indicated, to the Sutton/Rackham translation.

13. *De Oratore*, xxxvii.149–50: my emphasis; for "quasi alieno in loco collocantur" May/Wisse offer "as it were, put in a place that is not their own." Here, as elsewhere in this chapter, I use an ellipsis and then bracket the Latin original and my own translation, the latter in single quotation marks. Elsewhere, within quotation marks or indented citations, I have included a parenthesis with the original Latin, at times following the Latin with my alternative translation enclosed within single quotation marks. While these methods occasionally produce a complicated citation, the alternative would be repetitious citations and recitations of the same passage, which I find a greater obstacle to sustaining or following an argument.

14. With the exception of Plato's character Cratylus, a genuine linguistic realist is hard to find in classical times. Conventionalism is unquestionably the dominant view, and it is one more hospitable to a flexible sense of linguistic propriety than realism would be.

15. My classicist colleague Eleanor Winsor Leach confirms my impression that Crassus' *rustici* (rendered "farmers" by May/Wisse) might have been exposed to pastoral but more explicitly hears Lucretius in their diction. May/Wisse (270, n. 194)

report that Cicero's first example and probably his second are wrong, insofar as they are not tropic in origin according to modern scholarship.

16. Examples s.v. *muto*: *Cassell's Latin Dictionary*, rev. J.R.V. Marchant and Joseph F. Charles (New York: Funk and Wagnalls, 1956).

17. *The American Heritage College Dictionary*, appendix, s.v. *mei–*.

18. I can scarcely deny that "exchange," too, is a concept that becomes complicated in the late sixteenth and earlier seventeenth centuries, when it is related to, yet at one remove from, borrowing itself, and it also offers the more positive nuances I discuss. The question of "exchange" is exceedingly complex, and I shall deal with it further in my chapter on Malynes, below. For a perceptive, informative treatment of usury and borrowing, see David Hawkes, *Idols of the Market Place: Idolatry and Commodity Fetishism in English Literature, 1580–1680* (New York: Palgrave, 2001), chap. 4; chap. 1 is also relevant.

19. "Call into place, summon" is my rendering; Sutton/Rackham offer "convey," and May/Wisse "introduce," either of which is fine, but neither engages the idea of "place"—primarily rhetorical place—active throughout Crassus' discussion and elsewhere in both translations. In modern commentary, "place" plays a role: for example, Parker interprets its use in Cicero's and Quintilian's rhetorics in terms of a social hierarchy (e.g., "Metaphor," 63, 66–69).

20. Between Crassus' admiration of bolder metaphors and his cautionary reminder, there is an "irrelevant explanation of the difference between a simile [Is it technically a simile or is it just a likeness?] and a metaphor," which Sutton/Rackham consider "clearly an interpolation": "Similitudinis est ad verbum unum contracta brevitas, quod verbum in alieno loco tanquam in suo positum si agnoscitur, delectat, si simile nihil habet repudiatur ['The brevity of similitude is contracted into a single word, which, put in its strange place, pleases if it is recognized as true, or genuine, but is rejected if it bears no likeness']" (xxxix.157 and 122, n. a: my translation). Even though Sutton/Rackham reject this interpolation, their translation begins by covering over an initial non sequitur: "A metaphor is a short form of simile contracted into one word; this word is put in a position not belonging to it as if it were its own place, and if it is recognizable it gives pleasure, but if it contains no similarity it is rejected." May/Wisse simply delete the interpolation, noting that they have done so.

21. *Ratio* is about as difficult a word to translate into modern English as Greek *logos*, to which its range of meanings is related, and for a similar reason. In English, its various meanings have been dispersed in a way analogous in English itself to the separation of the meanings in medieval *trothe* into modern *truth* and *troth* (archaic except in a traditional wedding ceremony: "plight troth"), although this English analogy has fewer dimensions of significance than does *ratio*. Interestingly, May/Wisse offer "discrimination" as their translation of *ratio* here and elsewhere. On meanings of *ratio* and its relation to *logos*, as not irrelevantly understood by Erasmus, see Marjorie O'Rourke Boyle, *Erasmus on Language and Method in Theology* (Toronto: Toronto Univ. Press, 1977), 20–23.

22. I note here Crassus' (or Cicero's) making his own language embody and perform the cleverness, indeed the "genius," he is talking about. His awareness of the relation of form and content is evident, if *in nuce*.

23. May/Wisse translate *simile* as English "simile," in effect incorporating into the text at this point the gist of the interpolated passage (my n. 20, immediately above) that they have rejected. They also offer annotation identifying metaphor with simile (271, n. 201).

24. For the bracketed clause the May/Wisse translation reads, "For if something can be the source of a simile—and everything can—, then from this same source a single word containing the resemblance, when used as a metaphor, can lend brilliance to a speech." Their note on the passage turns it from a commentary on metaphor to one on metaphor as abbreviated (English) simile: 272, n. 202.

25. On Erasmian "word-things," see Terence Cave, *The Cornucopian Text: Problems of Writing in the French Renaissance* (Oxford: Clarendon, 1979), 21.

26. *De Oratore*, xli.165: translation mine, as indicated by the brackets, although I gratefully borrow Sutton/Rackham's translation of *precario* as "permission." To my mind (not to say, ear), however, other parts of the Sutton/Rackham translation contradict everything else Crassus has said: "in fact the metaphor ought to have an apologetic air, so as to look as if it had entered a place that does not belong to it with a proper introduction, not taken it by storm, and as if it had come with permission, not forced its way in." "Apologetic" is a far cry from "modest" or even "maidenly" (a Renaissance translation of *verecunda*); "a proper introduction" suggests the perspective of the butler belt; and "taken it by storm" is translative invention of a high order. Tone is not irrelevant to content, as citations of this passage in the history of Ciceronian reception make obvious. For the Renaissance translation "maidenly" (or "maydenly"), whose gendering ill fits the force the rest of the Latin sentence rules out, see Dudley Fenner, sig. D1v (discussed further below, 159). While my own translation has followed tradition in taking *verecunda* to be figuratively consonant with the distinctly personified similitude that ends the sentence, it would be possible not to do so and to translate it simply as "unforced," the sense *Cassell's Latin Dictionary* gives it in combination with *translatio*, citing Cicero. Doing so is a viable option that would enable a heightening of the violence eschewed in the figure ending the sentence. May/Wisse render the sentence, "In fact, a metaphor ought to be restrained [verecunda], and being in a place that is not its own, it must appear to have been escorted there, rather than to have burst in; it must seem to have come with permission, not by force."

27. May/Wisse in their introduction frequently suggest or explicitly remark Crassus' and Cicero's impatience with and even parody of traditional rhetorical taxonomy: see 11, 16, 36, 41. They translate as follows Crassus' response to the request of Sulpicius, another conversant, that Crassus address the particulars of style, such as tropes, that pertain to praise and brilliance in oratory: "Still, I will follow my conviction that in these matters, *petty though they may be*, we ought to go back to the authorities who invented them" (my emphasis); the Latin reads, "censebo tamen ad

eos qui auctores et inventores sunt harum sane minutarum rerum revertendum"
(Sutton/Rackham's Latin: *De Oratore*, III.xxxvii.148).

28. May/Wisse, 274, n. 213.

29. *De Oratore*, III.xlii.167, xliii.169. Cf. Lakoff and Johnson, *Metaphors We Live
By*, 29–32, on the container for the contained as a metaphor and Puttenham, 192,
on this trope as a metonymy.

30. *De Oratore*, III.xxxvii.148, xliii.169: as again signaled by the single quotation
marks, my translations in both instances. The May/Wisse translation of Crassus'
conclusion reads, "But surely you see that the other device [i.e., allegory], which is
made up, as I have explained, of a succession of several metaphors, is not a matter
of a single word, but of a continuous passage, while these devices, which are either
metonymies [i.e., synecdoche, as well as metonymy itself] or mean something other
than they literally do [e.g., catachresis], consist in words that are, in some way, metaphorical" (xliii.169).

31. Sonnino, 16, identifies *audacia* as an alternative name for *catachresis*. Also Parker, "Metaphor," 61. I have been unable to identify Sonnino's source, which she
does not specify, and suspect it to be her *interpretation* of the Ciceronian *audaciores*.
Parker does not specify a source.

32. For relevant instances of *audacia/audeo*, cf. Horace, "Ars Poetica," vs. 9–10
("'pictoribus atque poetis / quidlibet audendi semper fuit aequa potestas'"), and vs.
125–27 ("si quid inexpertum scaenae committis et audes / personam formare
nouam, seruetur ad imum / qualis ab incepto processerit, et sibi constet").

33. *De Oratore*, III.xxiv.94 (my emphasis in both the English and Latin). Here I
cite the May/Wisse translation in the interest of economy, since this passage is not
part of the critical debate in English.

34. On Latin *res* and English *thing*, see the pages listed under these entries in the
index of my *Words That Matter*.

35. Russell translates *vim significandi* "semantic value." This rendering, while useful, seems antiseptic to me; it is too narrowly rational. On an appropriate style, cf.
De Oratore, III.xxv.100: "in the case of writings and speeches faults of over-colour-
ing are detected not only by the verdict of the ears but even more by that of the
mind (in scriptis et in dictis non aurium solum sed animi iudicio etiam magis infu-
cata vitia noscuntur)."

36. Russell reads, "Good metaphors also are often regarded as instances of Propriety." Note his interpretative capitalization.

37. Russell reads, "This is . . . a gift which Nature herself confers on us."

38. Taken seriously, "unconsciously" would mean that Quintilian's *rustici*,
"country people," are either sleep-walking or expressing the uncanny when they
refer to "jewelled vines" and "joyful harvests." Likewise, his *rustici* when they refer
to vine buds as gems (see subsequent discussion). Russell also renders *non sentientes*
"unconsciously."

39. Cf. Wolfgang Iser's discussion of Aristotelian mimesis, 282–83. According to
Iser, the artist imitates "the things of Nature as they *ought* to *be*, at once completing

(or perfecting) and imitating the naturally given. Art and Nature are thus seen to be "'isomorphic in structure.'"

40. Bannet, "The Scene of Translation: After Jakobson, Benjamin, de Man, and Derrida," *New Literary History*, 24 (1993), 577–95, here 585. Also, Derrida, "Des Tours de Babel," in English, esp. 178–79, 182–83, 188–91; and in the original French, 221–23, 226–2, 232–35.

41. For Bruns's observation, see *Inventions: Writing, Textuality, and Understanding in Literary History* (New Haven: Yale Univ. Press, 1982), 55–56, 59.

42. Russell translates *permutando aut mutuando* "by exchanges or borrowings," phrasing that even more clearly supports the possibility of a sense of exchange in the discussion of metaphor by Cicero's Crassus. As Russell's translation continues, such exchanges and borrowings "supply its [language's] deficiencies (quae non habet)." Butler's rendering folds this last clause into the second half of the sentence.

43. Aitchison, 148; for Ricoeur, see *Rule*, chap. 5, n. 21.

44. Abrams' *A Glossary of Literary Terms*, 5th ed. (New York: Holt, Rinehart, and Winston, 1988), 65; *The Princeton Encyclopedia*, ed. Alex Preminger, enlarged edition (Princeton: Princeton Univ. Press, 1974), s.v. *Metaphor*.

45. See also the remarks in *De Oratore* concerning "resemblance (similitudine)," which involve *imago* or *collatio*, replete with examples utilizing *ut*: II.lxvi.265. Numerous pages of *Ad Herennium* are devoted to *similitudo*, variously termed *comparatio*, *simile*, and the like: IV.xlv.59–xlviii.61; cf. IV.xlix.62.

46. Russell similarly translates the Latin expression *haec pro ipsa* "*substituted*" (sic: italics) here.

47. While *substituere* occurs far less commonly than do expressions using *pro*, according to the *Oxford Latin Dictionary* and to Lewis and Short, examples of *substituere*, meaning "substitute," can be found in Cicero, Suetonius, Pliny, Quintilian, and a good number of less familiar writers. If we extend relevant usage to legal contexts, an arguably valid extension based on the linguistic proximity of legal applications, like monetary ones, to rhetoric, additional examples are to be found.

48. *Oxford Latin Dictionary*, s.v. *pro*.

49. Russell's translation, which reads, "a bold and hazardous metaphor," further strengthens the force of this description. Russell's Latin text, like Butler's, includes the adverb *proxime*, "nearly," however.

50. Cf. *De Oratore*, III.xxxvii.149–50: "new coinages invented by ourselves (eis [verbis] quae novamus et facimus ipsi)." Of course Quintilian admired Cicero's rhetoric and was influenced by it. On new coinages, cf. as well Horace, "Ars Poetica," vs. 46–72: e.g., "ut siluae foliis priuos mutantur in annos, / . . . prima cadunt, ita uerborum uetus interit aetas, / et iuuenum ritu florent modo nata uigentque" (60–63: I have omitted Rudd's line 61a, a nineteenth-century supplement); within the same passage, Horace also demands why he should not be able to invent a few words, as did Cato and Ennius, and he declares that it has always been licit to put into circulation words impressed with a current stamp (55–59). Here an observation about Cicero by Erasmus, including Erasmus' use of the word *ausus*, "bold" to characterize the Roman writer's neologising, also affords a provocative parallel to what

Quintilian urges: "The words *beatitudo, beatitas* 'blessedness,' and *mulierosus*, 'fond of women,' *mulierositas*, 'fondness for women' were bold inventions of Cicero's ('Beatitudinem' et 'beatitatem,' 'mulierosum' et 'mulierositatem' Cicero primus ausus est dicere)." Cited, respectively from "*Copia*": *Foundations of the Abundant Style*, trans. Betty I. Knott, in *Collected Works of Erasmus* (Toronto: Univ. of Toronto Press, 1978), XXIV, ed. Craig R. Thompson, 279–659, here 319: I.xii; and *De Copia Verborum ac Rerum*, ed. Betty I. Knott, in *Opera Omnia*, Vol. I, part 6 (Amsterdam: North-Holland, 1988), here 52: I.xii. Subsequent reference in English or in Latin is to these editions, unless otherwise noted.

51. *Institutio Oratoria*, VIII.vi.34. Freinkel, 161, interprets "These facts," which follow the garbled lines in the text, as referring to Quintilian's observation earlier in the preceding passage, or, as she modifies Butler's rendering, "that many neologisms and onomatopoeia are impermissible in Latin." Quintilian's "vix permittitur," or "scarcely permissible," thus becomes "non permittitur," and the nearer antecedent, his interest in new coinages, is neglected (VIII.vi.31). See also my n. 50, immediately above. Russell's recent edition unscrambles the garbled lines, which he translates as follows: "but it [the invention *laureati postes*, 'laurelled door-posts'] has successfully established itself (sed hoc feliciter evaluit). *Oinoio* and *bioio* ("wine," "life") are tolerable in Greek, and Ovid amuses himself with this *-oeo: vinoeo bonoeo*. Making *arquitenens* a single word or *septentriones* two also seems harsh (Dure)" (VIII.vi.33). These formerly inaccessible lines continue Quintilian's observations about linguistic invention in the same generally positive vein. The discussion of catachresis beginning "Eo magis necessaria catachresis" comes next, and Russell renders "Eo" ("These facts" in Butler) as "These limitations of Latin." In effect, then, he, too, understands catachresis, as described by Quintilian, to be a desirable antidote to linguistic stagnation.

52. Russell's Latin text differs a little from Butler's here, as necessarily does his translation: "Discernendumque est ab hoc totum tralationis [thus] istud genus, quod abusio est ubi nomen defuit, tralatio ubi aliud fuit (The whole genus of Metaphor must be distinguished from this [catachresis], because Catachresis is found where there was previously no word, Metaphor where there was a different word)" (vi.35). Russell, too, softens Butler's moral imperative, if less than I should wish, and he translates *defuit* and *fuit* in a past tense. His text might also be taken to suggest that metaphor in the broad sense (i.e., the whole genus thereof), which encompasses other tropes, might be distinguished from metaphor in the narrow sense, which excludes them. Cf. my nn. 56, 58, immediately below.

53. Russell translates Quintilian's observation about poets fairly neutrally, too, and thus offers further support for my argument: "The poets are in the habit of using closely related words catachrestically even for things which do have names of their own; this is rare in prose." Further relevant as well is Quintilian's commendation of poetry as a source of inspiration, verbal sublimity, and affect in *Institutio Oratoria*, X.i. 27–30; also 46–64, on specific poets.

54. See Parker, "Metaphor," 64–65, 68–69, 71–72. Parker's discussion of César Chesneau Dumarsais and Hugh Blair in the eighteenth century and Pierre Fontanier

in the nineteenth, which relies on the dubious Loeb translations of the Roman rhetoricians, explicitly argues for recurrent contradictions (or rifts) in their considerations of metaphor and catachresis; incidentally but effectively, however, it also suggests the significant extent to which these key, latter-day rhetoricians had a restrictive sense of propriety and taxonomy. Deconstruction thrives on such a sense, most often justifiably. Metz more than once also writes of the classifying impulse of these later centuries and of our own: e.g., 178–79.

55. Cf. Russell, introduction, volume I, 10, where he comments on various "split" discussions in the *Institutio*: "Looked at from this point of view [i.e., from the view of purpose], some features of its organization which at first sight seem surprising cease to matter very much." See also my n. 8, immediately above.

56. In Book VIII.vi.1, Quintilian earlier defines a trope without using *transfero* or a cognate term: "Tropus est verbi vel sermonis a propria significatione in aliam cum virtute mutatio (By a *trope* is meant the artistic alteration of a word or phrase from its proper meaning to another)." This definition, notably employing a cognate of *muto*, is also large enough to encompass metaphor and catachresis.

57. The omitted portion of Butler's rendering reads, "which is strictly theirs to another to which they do not properly belong." In the interest of consistency, I have again elided the unnecessary and potentially misleading language of (not) belonging.

58. Cf. Russell's introduction to Quintilian's Book VIII: catachresis "is a sort of compulsory Metaphor or Synecdoche" for Quintilian (306). See also the end of my n.56, immediately above.

59. Etymologies based on the *OED*, Lewis and Short, the *Oxford Latin Dictionary*, Henry George Liddell and Robert Scott, *A Greek-English Lexicon*, rev. Henry Stuart Jones et al. (Oxford: Clarendon, n.d.), and the *Oxford Dictionary of English Etymology*, ed. C. T. Onions (Oxford: Clarendon, 1966), s.v. *catachresis* in all of these and also s.v. *cata* in the *OED*. I have rationalized differences in transliteration (*ch* vs. *k*) in my sources.

60. *On Christian Doctrine*, trans. D. W. Robertson, Jr. (Indianapolis: Bobbs-Merrill, 1958), (II.xxv.38). For the Latin: *De Doctrina Christiana*, 1–167: Bk II.xxv.38, in *Sancti Aureli Augustini Opera*, Pt. IV, 1, ed. Joseph Martin, *Corpus Christianorum*, Series Latina, XXXII (Turnhout, Belg.: Brepols, 1962).

61. In this sentence I quote Robertson, but I have changed his use of the singular to the plural to accord with the Latin. Like Sutton/Rackham and Butler, Robertson often changes the Latin plural to an English singular: is this the translators' desire for a more abstract, exact, positivistic effect?

62. Aside from the problem of *usurpantur*, the penultimate sentence of Freinkel's statement, from which her conclusion follows, puzzles me: she explains that "the *res* originally designated by a name now becomes a *signum* of its own," and she concludes, "A figure, then, is a second-order sign." The word *res* in a context dealing with signification is notoriously ambiguous: simply put, is it the thing itself or the thing understood within language, the fleshly ox or its designation—or could it be both? Only God writes in "real" things, however. Human writers, even the

divinely sanctioned writers of the Bible, write in a human language of signs, as Augustine well (if somewhat unhappily) knew. Does Augustine really think that a fleshly ox signifies a preacher? Surely the ox-within-language, the name of the ox (*bos*), is what his *res* refers to: "thus we *say* 'ox,'" and Scripture "*says*, . . . 'the ox'" (II.x.15: my emphasis). The signified already within the sign merely gets redirected to another referent. All human language, then, not just tropic language, is second-order for him.

63. Quotation from the *Oxford Latin Dictionary*, s.v. *usurpo*, 4.

64. Freinkel, 36–37, has a more positive view of Augustine's position regarding human language than I. Her view fits oddly with her understanding of his use of *usurpantur*, to which my own ambivalent view is ironically better suited. For Augustine, as I understand him, the ineffable *verbum*, which is heard only by the inward ear, or the understanding that floods the spirit in a rapid flash, differs profoundly from actual speech, the sound of our mouth: see Augustine's "De catechizandis rudibus," in *Patrologia Latina*, ed. J. P. Migne (Paris: Garnier, 1887), XL, 311–12; and for a classic statement of Augustine's position, see *The Trinity*, trans. Stephen McKenna, in *The Fathers of the Church* (Washington, DC: Catholic Univ. of America Press, 1963), XLV, 475, 477–78, 487: Bk. XV.x.19, xi.20, xiv.24: e.g., the "word cannot be uttered in sound nor thought in the likeness of sound, such as must be done with the word of any language; it precedes all the signs by which it is signified" (xi.20, 478). In Augustine's epistemology, in contrast to Freinkel's evaluation of speech and even more to her valuation of the greater materiality of writing, true understanding is pre-verbal with reference to ordinary human language, and the relation of the truth that shines within to the words we speak remains at best obscure: see the classic essay by R. A. Markus, "St. Augustine on Signs," *Phronesis*, 2 (1957), 60–83, esp. 77, and Margaret Ferguson, "Saint Augustine's Region of Unlikeness: The Crossing of Exile and Language," *Georgia Review*, 29 (1975), 842–64. While such views are debated in the secondary literature on Augustine, I do not see how any reading of his works can avoid confronting them.

65. *Ad Herennium*, IV.x.15, *De Copia*, 314: I.11; 46: I.xi. Knott translates *Mollius erat* as "less violent," a rendering much to my purpose but slightly freer than the one I have offered in the text.

66. The full title is *De Ratione Studii ac Legendi Interpretandique Auctores*. Present reference is to *On the Method of Study*, trans. Brian McGregor, in *Collected Works of Erasmus* (1978), XXIV, ed. Craig R. Thompson, 660–91, here 674–75. For the Latin, see *De Ratione Studii*, in *Opera Omnia* (1703–06), I, 517–30, here 523 E. I have used brackets rather than parentheses for the Latin insertions because they are not taken from the Latin text on which McGregor bases his translation.

67. From this point on, with an occasional exception, I have found it too cumbersome to refer to Cicero's nominally dialogic character Crassus, rather than directly to Cicero himself, as do Renaissance rhetorics.

68. Perhaps Knott (335: I.17/29–31) translates too simply from her Latin text, which reads, "in simplici nomine" (64–65: I.xvii). Two observations: first, within an Aristotelian logic, which presumably influenced Erasmus, a verb in and by itself

may be termed a noun or a name and regarded as substantival; it is, strictly speaking, only a verb when used in a proposition. An infinitive, lacking person, number, tense, and functioning substantivally (e.g., "To run is natural"), further straddles the grammatical line between noun and verb. See Aristotle, *De interpretatione*, 16b19–22; and M. T. Larkin, *Language in the Philosophy of Aristotle* (The Hague: Mouton, 1971), 31–32, which I follow here. Larkin explains that the term *name* or *noun* ("ὄνομα") includes not only verbs, but also "all the declinable parts of speech except perhaps the relatives" and speculates that "the reason for this is that 'case' as used by Aristotle is broader than the present grammatical usage" and comprises "tense, number, and voice of verbs," "genders and cases of nouns," "adjectives derived from the noun and the adverb derived from the adjective," and "the singular and plural forms of nouns." In addition, of course, "adjectives and adverbs are reduced to the noun and the verb," a practice with ramifications for grammatical categories themselves throughout antiquity, the Middle Ages, and the Renaissance. My second observation is that in an earlier *Opera Omnia* of Erasmus, the phrase in question reads, for whatever reason, "in verbo simplici"—in a single word: I refer to volume I of the 1703–06 edition, 18: I.xvii.

69. Without ellipses, Knott's translation reads, "Similar in force is catachresis, for which the Latin word is *abusio* 'abuse' or 'misapplication,' and it differs from metaphor in that we resort to misapplication where a proper word does not exist, to metaphor where we substitute something for the proper word."

70. Cf. Johann Susenbrotus (d. 1543), Σὺν δε θεοι μάκαρες [*Syn de theoi makares*] *Epitome troporum ac schematum et grammaticorum & rhetorum* (London: Gerard Dewes, 1562), 10: Susenbrotus similarly instances the familiar *piscina*, "fish pond," but then, virtually quoting Quintilian, he goes on both to distinguish between metaphor as displacement of an existing word and catachresis as the provision of a word where one does not exist and further notes the relatively more frequent occurrence of catachresis in poetry than in prose. The explicit sense of catachresis his rhetoric represents is therefore more complex than simple misuse.

71. On the influence of Melanchthon's rhetoric in the sixteenth century, see Quirinus Breen, "The Subordination of Philosophy to Rhetoric in Melanchthon," *Archiv für Reformationsgeschichte*, 43 (1952), 13–27; Manfred P. Fleischer, "Melanchthon as Praeceptor of Late-Humanist Poetry," *Sixteenth Century Journal*, 20 (1989), 559–80, here 573; Daniel M. Gross, "Melanchthon's Rhetoric and the Practical Origins of Reformation Human Science," *History of the Human Sciences*, 13 (2000), 5–22, here 5–7.

72. Philippi Melanthonis, *Elementorum Rhetorices*, in *Opera*, ed. Carolus Gottlieb Bretschneider, 28 vols. (Braunschweig, Ger.: C. A. Swetschke et Filium, 1834–59), XIII, 413–506, here 463: citing Demosthenes, Melanchthon says that a trope occurs "when a word is turned from its proper signification to something similar or close (cum vox a propria significatione ad rem similem aut vicinam vertitur)."

73. Melanchthon is likely thinking of the "Cicero" of *Ad Herennium* (see my n. 45, immediately above).

74. "Sed in sacris literis multa similia exempla extant, quia interpretibus non licuit ubique Graecam aut Ebraicam phrasin mutare" (464). See my earlier discussion of Cicero's *mutuatio* as "exchange" and of its relationship to such cognate terms as *muto/-are*, 133–34, immediately above.

75. Here I have paraphrased Melanchthon's "Est et *καταχρησις* quam singulari consilio interdum usurpamus, ut cum pro virtutibus vicina vicia, aut econtra tradimus, ut pro crudelitate severitatem, pro avaricia parsimoniam."

76. Cf. Richard Sherry's similar association of catachresis with *usurpo* in *A Treatise of the Figures of Grammar and Rhetorike* (London: Richard Tottell, 1555), sig. xxi-verso: "Catachresis est necessaria nominis alieni vsurpatio pro proprio (Catachresis is the necessary use of an improper term for a proper one)."

77. *Audomari Talaei rhetorica, e [P.] Rami, regii professoris praelectionibus observata* (London: Society of Stationers, 1620), 11. Subsequent reference is to this edition, and translations are mine. Talon's rhetoric dates from 1545.

78. E.g., *De Oratore*, III.xxxviii.156–57: "However there is no need for me to give you a lecture on the method of inventing these [somewhat bolder metaphors] or on their classification"; *Institutio Oratore*, VIII.vi.13: "But I am not now teaching boys." See also Russell's general introduction, *Institutio*, vol. I, 9: "as Quintilian often makes clear (e.g., 1.4.17), the *Institutio* is a handbook for teachers and parents, and contains far more than it is wise to tell the average student."

79. Cf. Edgar Wind, *Pagan Mysteries in the Renaissance*, rev. ed. (Harmondsworth, Middlesex, Eng.: Penguin, 1967), 238: "it seems to be a lesson of history that the commonplace may be understood as a reduction of the exceptional, but the exceptional cannot be understood [merely] by amplifying the commonplace. Both logically and causally the exception is crucial, because it introduces the more comprehensive category." My phrasing "fictive and imaginative" alludes to Iser's theorizing of the fictive and imaginary.

80. *The Garden of Eloquence* (1577, 1593; rpt. New York: Scholars' Facsimiles and Reprints, 1954), 1–2 (1593 edition).

81. *The Garden of Eloquence* (London: H. Jackson, 1577), sig. C4r. The example offered in 1577 remains in the edition of 1593, where it is offered along with others.

82. (London: C. Burbie, 1599), sigs. Kk1r, Kk2r: I have silently corrected the spelling of "transferred," which reads "tanasferred" in the text.

83. Cf. Talaeus (Talon), 3: "continued metaphor (continuatio) is called allegory [or] inversion (*ἀλληγορία*, inuersio nominetur)." Also Susenbrotus, 5: a trope "changes and transposes (*inuertas* [thus] atque commutet)" the signification of "a word or speech (dictionis vel orationis)." My emphasis on *inuertas*, which is clearly an error for *invertat*, whence English *invert* and, via *inversio*, English *inversion*. Talon's identification of allegory as inversion is based on Quintilian, VIII.vi.44.

84. For a review of relevant work in neo-cognitivism, see especially Mary Thomas Crane, *Shakespeare's Brain*, 3–35; and Crane and Alan Richardson, "Literary Studies and Cognitive Science: Toward a New Interdisciplinarity," *Mosaic*, 32 (1999), 123–40. The following are also of particular interest: F. Elizabeth Hart, "Cognitive Linguistics: The Experiential Dynamics of Metaphor," *Mosaic*, 28

(1995), 1–23, and "Matter, System, and Early Modern Studies: Outlines for a Materialist Linguistics," *Configurations*, 6 (1998), 311–43; Antonio R. Damasio, *Descartes' Error: Emotion, Reason, and the Human Brain* (New York: Avon, 1994); and Andy Clark, chap. 8, also 220, and passim. On the basis of neo-cognitivist embodiment, Hart and Crane challenge the autonomy and arbitrariness of the sign. The implications of this fundamental challenge for the entire post-structural and postmodern enterprise are enormous.

85. Cf. Derek Attridge's discussion of the nature-art tension in Puttenham's treatise as an instance of the Derridean logic of the supplement: *Peculiar Language*, 17–45. Michel Foucault's well-known distinction is found in *The Order of Things: An Archeology of the Human Sciences* (1971; rpt New York: Random House, 1973), esp. chaps 1–2. I am grateful to Lowell Gallagher for suggesting a connection with Foucault here. As Foucault does not recognize sufficiently in the oversimplicities of *The Order of Things* (and Gallagher does), however, the foundation for modern distinctions is to be found in Galileo, as well as in Descartes.

86. *Directions for Speech and Style*, ed. Hoyt H. Hudson (Princeton: Princeton Univ. Press, 1935), 10. The text capitalizes the entirety of the terms I have emphasized.

87. *Apology for Poetry*, 100–101; and *Midsummer Night's Dream*, V.i.12–17.

88. Cf. Aristotle, *Rhetoric*, 1406b20: "the simile is also a metaphor." For discussion, see 1413a1–14.

89. On the passing of rhetoric (as distinct from "rhetoricality" or discursivity), see John Bender and David E. Wellbery, eds., *The Ends of Rhetoric*, 3–39, esp. 15, 25, 38; and Mary Poovey, *A History of the Modern Fact: Problems of Knowledge in the Sciences of Wealth and Society* (Chicago: Univ. of Chicago Press, 1998), 7 and chap. 2, esp. 41, 85, 91–92. What Poovey calls "historical epistemology" includes rhetoric (as *copia*) conspicuously in the Renaissance. Her contention that rhetoric "upheld the status and epistemological hierarchies of the classical world" is provocative, but it needs a good deal of qualification (91). The extent to which the categories of Renaissance rhetorics are fuzzy-edged or even fluid and the way they attract various contemporary social nuances are pertinent qualifiers.

90. The phrase "jewelled vines" occurs in both Cicero and Quintilian as an example of the "natural" metaphor the *rustici* ("rustics") speak, and it has earlier recurred in my discussion. Its relevance to the art of Acrasia's grapes is evident, as more generally is that of the treatment of metaphor in the Roman rhetorics.

Chapter Eight

Exchanging Values: The Economic and Rhetorical World Seen by Gerrard de Malynes, Merchant

1. E.A.J. Johnson, "Gerard de Malynes and the Theory of the Foreign Exchanges," *The American Economic Review*, 23 (1933), 441–55, here 446, n. 28, makes the point that *Lex Mercatoria* fairly epitomizes Malynes' many publications on economics. In the same spirit, de Roover describes it as Malynes' "great" and most

inclusive work, "his major contribution to economic literature": "Gerard de Malynes," 346–366, here, 350, 365.

2. For a helpful, recent synopsis of opinion about Malynes' place in economic history, see Finkelstein, 29.

3. Gerard Malynes, *Consuetudo, vel Lex Mercatoria, or The Ancient Law-Merchant* (London: Adam Islip, 1629), 221–22: "The mutabilitie and inconstancie . . . neerest to his losse." Subsequent reference is to this edition, except when otherwise indicated. Occasionally, I shall refer to the 1622 edition, also published by Adam Islip, since a number of pages were missing in the copy of the 1629 edition to which I had access as my base text. Pagination in the 1622 edition appears to be the same as in 1629, with differences limited to accidentals and the rare addition or omission of a single word. Since *Lex Mercatoria* has not been easily available in recent times, I want to mention an inexpensive modern copy of it, the text of which I have checked against 1622/1629 and have found impressively accurate in the main: *The Merchant's Almanac of 1622, or Lex Mercatoria, the Ancient Law-Merchant*, reissued by Katie F. Hamilton (Phoenix, AZ: Metheglin Press, 1996). As explained more fully below (n. 35), when situating my discussion of *Lex Mercatoria*, at times I shall refer parenthetically to section and chapter, as well as to page. Malynes dropped "de" from his name in his later publications; in the interest of consistency, I have retained "de" for bibliographical reference, although I otherwise refer to him simply as "Malynes." Like Malynes' surname, his first name is variously spelled in the secondary literature: "Gerard" or "Gerrard."

4. E.g., Poovey, 79, 82; also 66–67, 83–84.

5. *A History of Money: From Ancient Times to the Present Day*, 3rd rev. ed. (Cardiff: University of Wales Press, 2002), 232: here Davies follows E[li]. F[ilip]. Heckscher, *Mercantilism*, rev. [2nd] ed., trans. Mendel Shapiro, ed. E. F. Söderlund, 2 vols. (London: Allen and Unwin, 1955), II, 227–28. Malynes' observation, cited by Heckscher and Davies, comes from *A Treatise of the Canker of Englands Common Wealth* (London: W. Johnes, 1601). For a partial parallel—one without the higher prices—cf. Rice Vaughan, *A Discourse of Coin and Coinage* (London: Th. Basset, 1675), 61–62: "plenty of Money doth help to encrease Manufactures"; he accords primacy to manufactures, however, for they "do breed Money, and Money again doth breed Manufactures." Vaughan's treatise was written in the mid-1620s, although not published until 1675: on dating, see B. E. Supple, *Commercial Crisis and Change in England 1600–1642: A Study in the Instability of a Mercantile Economy* (Cambridge: Cambridge Univ. Press, 1959), 219, n. 3.

6. According to the PPP theory, a hamburger costing 4 U.S. dollars and 3 pounds British would indicate a PPP ratio of 4:3. Lawrence H. Officer finds the ingredients of the PPP theory in Malynes' writings but concludes that Malynes never completes the argument: "The purchasing-power-parity theory of Gerrard de Malynes," *History of Political Economy*, 14 (1982), 256–59, here 258. Officer cites Joseph Alois Schumpeter, *History of Economic Analysis* (New York: Oxford Univ. Press, 1954), 737: "This Purchasing-Power Parity theory [sic], or some rudimentary form of it, goes far back and can . . . certainly be attributed to Malynes."

7. *Lex Mercatoria*, 8, 136, 155–56, 184, 212, 257–58, 262–63, 425.

8. I follow de Roover's "Malynes," 346–48, closely here. It has gone unnoticed that in *The Maintenance of Free Trade* (1622; rpt. New York: Augustus M. Kelley, 1971), 48–49, Malynes takes personally Misselden's reference in *Free Trade or The Meanes to Make Trade Florish* (1622; rpt. New York: Augustus M. Kelley, 1971), 14–15, to Belisarius' blinding because of envy, not guilt, and his begging as an insulting allusion to Malynes' copper farthing project (see n. 13, below). On the same pages, Malynes appears to refer to his status as a foreigner when he writes, "Wise men haue noted, that the due obseruation of vertue, maketh a Stranger grow naturall in a strange Countrie, and the vicious a meere Stranger in his owne natiue Soile"; Misselden's provocation for this reflection, also unremarked by others, can be found in his *Free Trade*, 105, where Misselden cites Malynes' *Canker of Englands Common Wealth* and adds immediately afterward, "Which seemes to haue in it much more *Dutch* then *English*." Yet in view of the personal slurs and accusations in which writers of tracts indulged in Malynes' time, it seems odd that his opponents did not fault him less obliquely for his claims about his parentage, for personal dishonesty, or for his imprisonments: see also n. 11, below. For the rest of Malynes' biography, unless otherwise noted, I follow de Roover, "Malynes"; E.A.J. Johnson, Lynn Muchmore, "Gerrard de Malynes and Mercantile Economics," *History of Political Economy*, I (1969), 336–58, and *Lex Mercatoria*, here 263. I have consulted the *DNB* currently available (still 1917), s.v. *Malynes*, as well, although much of its account is out of date.

9. Finkelstein, I, gives the dates 1586–1626. De Roover, in "Malynes," 346, gives the dates 1583–1623, deriving them from Muchmore's in his "Malynes," 356–57. Finkelstein refers to Malynes as the scion of a trading family, but without indicating her basis for doing so (6). She accepts Malynes' claims about his ancestry and suggests that he might have been the son of a denizated alien, who was in England in 1562 (26–27, 273, n. 4). If so, the Elizabethan recoinage would have been an obvious reason for Malynes senior's presence, as *DNB* hypothesizes, since Malynes junior tells us his father was a mint-master.

10. I offer de Roover's conservative estimate of Malynes' linguistic skills, plus Portuguese: "Malynes," 349. On Malynes' linguistic skills, see Katie Hamilton, ed., *Lex Mercatoria*, 1–4, where she asserts (presumably on the basis of evidence in the text) that besides English, Malynes had French, German, Italian, Spanish, Portuguese, and Latin; and for an instance of Malynes' service as interpreter of Portuguese for King James, see *Lex Mercatoria*, 262.

11. Muchmore, "Malynes," 339: Historical Manuscripts Commission, *Calendar of the Manuscripts of the Most Hon. the Marquis of Salisbury* (London: Eyre and Spottiswoode, 1892–95), Part VI, 262–63, 455–56. In addition to suggesting the connection with Walsingham noted by Muchmore, these entries indicate that Malynes offered intelligence to Robert Cecil in the 1590s. Of course they also show that his offer came under the duress of imprisonment. E.A.J. Johnson, 454, n. 79, remarks the unethical dealings of Edward Misselden, Malynes' inveterate opponent in economic tracts. Finkelstein, 55, records that Misselden was also accused by the Dutch

of spying for England and by the English ambassador of working for the Dutch. Many merchants were in a position to furnish "intelligence" to their governments.

12. Muchmore, "Malynes," 338–39; but also *Calendar of the Manuscripts of the Most Hon. the Marquis of Salisbury*, Part VI, 15–16. Cf. de Roover, "Malynes," 349; Finkelstein, 27, 274 n. 9.

13. See E.A.J. Johnson, 444–45, for the story about Malynes' patent for copper farthings, a project that can either be seen as purely for gain or as also for the relief of the poor. In either case, "Malynes appears to have sought diligently to meet his responsibility" under the patent, an effort that bankrupted him (445). The patent required him to honor the exchange of the copper farthings for silver. In *Maintenance*, Malynes observes that the copper farthings were and indeed "are" necessary and commodious tokens, "whereby the waste of much Siluer is preuented, the meere poore releeued, and many of their liues saued" (48–49). Finkelstein notes that Mun also went bankrupt in 1607 as a result of his speculative schemes (75).

14. For the remonstrance of Malynes, Cotton, Sir Ralph Madison, John Williams (goldsmith), and William Sanderson (merchant), see Malynes' *The Center of the Circle of Commerce* (London: William Jones, 1623), 75–77; also his Epistle Dedicatory in *Maintenance*.

15. *Lex Mercatoria*, 258. For additional readings, especially in law, see de Roover, "Malynes," 350; and see Finkelstein, 30–33, for an even more extensive list based on all Malynes' published works. Also nn. 105, 111, below.

16. *The Circle of Commerce or The Ballance of Trade* (1623; rpt. New York: Augustus M. Kelley, 1971), 29; *The Custumers Alphabet and Primer* (London: William Jaggard[?], 1608), sig. E2r; and Milles's *The Customers Replie* (London: James Roberts, 1604): sig. A6r for the phrase quoted. Bruce G. Carruthers and Wendy Nelson Espeland note that overseas merchants, among the more sophisticated of early modern businessmen, often accumulated large professional libraries: "Accounting for Rationality: Double-Entry Bookkeeping and the Rhetoric of Economic Rationality," *American Journal of Sociology*, 97 (1991), 31–69, here 50–51, 54. Malynes' taste may be more eclectic (typical of the "Renaissance" man) than professional, but it certainly includes a number of professional books. On the education of merchants, see also Finkelstein, 57.

17. De Roover, an authority on medieval and Renaissance business and banking institutions, flatly declares, "That Malynes, more than any other economic writer of his time, represents the transition from Scholasticism to mercantilism is not a debatable statement" ("Malynes," 350–51). Finkelstein, while at one point describing Malynes as straddling an old world and a new one, does not maintain a balance between these sides of Malynes in her discussion of his writing (50, cf. 1–2, 25). She argues overwhelmingly for his moral conservatism. My view of *Lex Mercatoria* is considerably more mixed.

18. Although *mercatoria* is an adjective, I am nominalizing and objectifying it to avoid the awkward repetition of Malynes' longer title and the ambiguity in some contexts of *Lex* alone. *Mercatoria* also invokes the title by which Malynes' book is

generally known, as *Consuetudo* does not. There is Renaissance precedent for such nominalization.

19. Donne preached William Cokayne's funeral sermon. Malynes was briefly associated with Cokayne in the copper farthing project, from which Cokayne, not liking the terms, strategically withdrew but which bankrupted Malynes. As later noted, Malynes criticizes the notorious Cokayne project to corner the export market on finished cloth and less openly on unfinished cloth as well, which played a significant role in precipitating the great depression of the early 1620s in England.

20. See in particular pages 22–23 of Mun's tract *England's Treasure by Forraign Trade* (1664; rpt. New York: Macmillan, 1895); also J. D. Gould, "The Trade Depression of the Early 1620s," *Economic History Review*, 2nd series, 7 (1954), 81–90, here 83; and Gould's "The Trade Crisis of the Early 1620s and English Economic Thought," *The Journal of Economic History*, 15 (1955), 121–33, here 130–31: "Mun thought as far as the self-regulating principle, but . . . rejected it," recommending instead that any increase in the stock of bullion be used "as liquid capital to finance a greater volume of trade" (my emphasis). As Gould observes, the early seventeenth century would have found a Humean theory of specie equilibrium hard to square with "the facts of contemporary Dutch economic development." Cf. also Hawkes, 43–44.

21. Supple, 215, 217–18: "one of the major theoretical flaws in his [Mun's] system is precisely that he did not acknowledge the ultimate tendency to equilibrium which derived from the repercussions of specie flows on trade balances through international prices. . . . there was a basic invalidity in his approach, . . . for it is entirely misleading to view the balance of trade as a 'cause' of the movement of treasure." See also Muchmore, "Malynes," 353–54: "Mun's analysis should be considered a retardation of economic doctrine. . . . Mun chose to rule out all monetary considerations and to rely . . . solely upon the balance of trade. . . . this rigid view . . . ignores capital movements or international borrowing or lending, excludes the bimetallic flows which had substantial influence upon the domestic money supply, and fails to recognize that the organization and integrity of the monetary sector can have an impact upon conditions of trade." Also, Muchmore, "A Note on Thomas Mun's *England's Treasure by Forraign Trade*," in *The Early Mercantilists*, ed. Mark Blaug (Aldershot, Hants, Eng.: Edward Elgar, 1991), 187–92: Muchmore analyzes Mun's shift from the account he published in 1621 of a shortage of silver in England, which posited mainly a monetary cause, to his account in *England's Treasure* [published posthumously in 1664 but deriving from the controversy about treasure and exchanges in 1622–23: Supple, 211], which argued that the balance of trade alone was the cause. Muchmore relates both publications to Mun's role as member and director of, as well as spokesman for, the East India Company, whose very existence was threatened because of its reliance on the export of specie to the East. Misselden, a friend of Mun, had a similar role in the Merchant Adventurers, in which he served as the Company's Deputy-Governor at Delft from 1623–33, and also as a commissioner for the East India Company. His writings, like Mun's, exhibit a conspicuous element of commercial self-interest. See also the quite different interpretations of

Finkelstein, chaps. 3 (Misselden) and 4 (Mun): she considers Mun as much a moralist as a proponent of trade.

22. "Mercantilist Policies and the Pattern of World Trade, 1500–1750," in Blaug, ed., 147–63, here 158–59. It is not just coincidence that even Adam Smith cites *England's Treasure* by name (Finkelstein, 74). Mun's economic views are contradictory and confused in Finkelstein's judgment, however, and she argues effectively that Mun is torn between the intrinsic value of money and the balance of trade (80–88). For a recent, favorable interpretation of Mun, see Poovey, 67, 79–84; and relatedly, if less recently, Joyce Oldham Appleby, *Economic Thought and Ideology in Seventeenth-Century England* (Princeton: Princeton Univ. Press, 1978), 41.

23. In order, the citations to Supple are 175–76, 58, 80, 94 (my emphases). Cf. Gould, "Trade Depression," 89.

24. Goux, *Symbolic Economies: After Marx and Freud*, trans. Jennifer Curtiss Gage (Ithaca: Cornell Univ. Press, 1990) and *The Coiners of Language*, trans. Jennifer Curtiss Gage (Norman: Univ.. of Oklahoma Press, 1994); and Shell, *The Economy of Literature* (Baltimore: Johns Hopkins Univ. Press, 1978) and *Money, Language, and Thought*.

25. In order, see Shell's *Money*, 4; cf. his *Economy*, 49–50; and then his "Issue of Representation," in Woodmansee and Osteen, eds., 53–74, here 61. Cf. Also Hawkes, 18–22, on the views of Goux and Shell; and 235–36, n. 53, on the employment of psychoanalytic concepts in semantic studies by Goux and Slavjov Žižek. While not questioning the importance of Freud and Lacan to the study of contemporary representation, Hawkes finds so little correspondence between such a theoretical frame of reference and Tudor-Stuart writers as to suggest anachronism in its application. With respect to the writing of Malynes, I agree, noting that psychoanalysis is not biology or even neo-cognitivism. The origin and bias of psychoanalytical theories are strongly and specifically (that is, historically) cultural—founded on metaphorical and metonymic transference. This is their strength and also their limitation.

26. *The Political Unconscious: Narrative as a Socially Symbolic Act* (1981; rpt. Ithaca: Cornell Univ. Press, 1988), 40, 43–44.

27. Albeit as part of a different argument, Rice Vaughan clearly registers his awareness of the consequences of lagging inflation: "*when our Meighbours* [sic] *raise their Money, then will our Money . . . go further to be coined into theirs, . . . and consequently for that profit* [our money] *will be transported until the price of their commodities do grow up unto their Money*" (219).

28. Blitz, 147. Cf. Gould, "Trade Crisis," 124–25.

29. More exactly, seigniorage, as defined by Glyn Davies, is "the difference between the total cost of producing . . . new coins and their face value" (202).

30. Citations in order: *Lex Mercatoria*, 59–60, 182; *Consuetudo, vel Lex Mercatoria, or The Ancient Law-Merchant* (London: Adam Islip, 1622), 230: that Malynes' dream has a traditional basis does not detract from its *modern* utopian resonance. Malynes' view of William Cokayne's scheme combines political and economic pragmatics with international principle: "all other nations being carefull to maintaine manufac-

tures, cannot but take an offence, if any other nation will endeauor to doe all, and to exclude others, . . . as we have found by the enterprise of the late new companie [Cokayne's], for dressing and dying [sic] of all the white clothes in England, which caused other nations to make clothes of their owne by the woolls of other nations. For (as hath been noted) it is contrarie to that common entercourse and mutall course of commodities, whereof some countries are destitute, and other countries doe abound, therby supplying the barrennesse of the one, with the superfluities of the other, maintaining a friendly correspondence and familiaritie" (1622 edition: 230).

31. E.g., *Lex Mercatoria*, 419, where Malynes might first appear to argue for a universally applied standard of fair value but turns out to want this standard to protect England's money and willingly accepts the possibility that another currency might be undervalued in England's favor: if he had his way, no man should "make any Exchanges . . . vnder the true *Par*, or value for value of our moneys, and the moneys of other countries in weight and finenesse, but at the same rate or aboue the same, . . . but neuer vnder the said rate." He might prefer true par all around, but he does not insist on it in principle. Cf. *Lex Mercatoria*, 45: "A prince ought to be a seller and not a buyer." At the same time, I would not characterize Malynes' preference as a "deliberate beggar-my-neighbor" policy, though I would Misselden's and Mun's: quotation from Blitz, 149; see also Muchmore, "Malynes," 344.

32. Supple, 179. Malynes, *Maintenance*, 104 (my emphasis): concern for "want" or "lack," I would add, is *not* the same as a desire to amass excess in this instance. There is a terminological discrepancy in my sources for economic history between those who use the term *Mercantilism* to describe the views of Malynes, Misselden, and Mun and those who use the term *Bullionism*, reserving *Mercantilism* for later developments. The terminology is controverted: e.g., see Glyn Davies, 225. The clearest and simplest solution for my purposes, which do not require the pertinent distinctions, is to use the term *Mercantilism*, period. I elect this alternative, rather than *Bullionism*, partly because the latter term has for my ear a simplistic and arguably misleading message that I do not find in allegedly *bullionist* texts.

33. Supple's argument challenges the homology Hawkes perceives between religious idolatry and mercantile "bullionism," which fetishized gold in Hawkes's view. Echoing Althusser, Hawkes defines a fetish as "an objective representation of something that is, in reality, subjective" (58, cf. 44–45). I take this reality in his view to be greed, rather than fear on the part of the bullionists. Iconoclasm, on the contrary, is based on fear. Cf. Peter Stallybrass' critique of the popular Marxian notion of fetishism: by fetishizing the commodity, he argues, capitalism precisely "*fails* to fetishize the *object*": "Worn Worlds," 290. Stallybrass' critique troubles Hawkes's homology between iconoclasm and commodity fetishism.

34. Poovey, 81. Of course the notion of "a balance of trade" that Mun embraces is itself metaphorical, as well as culturally valorized, like the balance or scale itself. Misselden's *Circle*, image in itself of completeness and perfection, is similarly so. Malynes spoils Misselden's perfect circle by arguing that it omits the actual central point, namely, gain: *Center*, 5.

35. As an additional aid to the reader in situating my discussion of *Lex Mercatoria*, I will include a parenthetical indicator of section, or "Part," and chapter, in addition to folio page, whenever this information could be useful but especially in the current portion of my discussion of *Lex Mercatoria*, where the discussion repeatedly refers to sequence in the text: e.g., here the fuller reference would be (I.v.58).

36. In "'The canker of England's Commonwealth': Gerard de Malynes and the origins of economic pathology," Jonathan Gil Harris discusses Malynes' early economic tract as a significant contribution to "the constitutive role" of the body in "shaping Western perceptions of the economic": *Textual Practice*, 13 (1999), 311–27, here 311. He also draws a parallel between Malynes' paradigm of the sick body in *Canker* and Shakespeare's in *Troilus and Cressida* (320–21).

37. Cf. Malynes, *Center*, 6, where he defends his use of figures: his treatises are "without affectation of superficiary termes of Art" and proceed "by demonstratiue reasons and infallible arguments, *illustrated by similies*" (my emphasis).

38. On this familiarity, see my chap. 6, 114–15 and n. 2; and chap. 2, n. 11: if only in emphasis, a difference is noticeable, however, between Malynes' view that a man (and especially a merchant) should have some knowledge "in most or in all things," and Mun's that "although there be no necessity that . . . a Merchant should be a great Scholar; yet is it (at least) required that in his youth he learn the Latine tongue" (*England's Treasure*, 1895, 5). If he learned Latin, he would very probably also have been exposed to some basic mythology.

39. *Lex Mercatoria*, 205, 209, 258; 1622 edition: 236.

40. In the loaded context of the spirit's infusing life, Malynes' parenthetical reference to the body of gold as "red earth" could evoke memory of a gloss on the name *Adam*, "red earth," that is often found in sermons. For example, see *The Sermons of John Donne*, ed. Evelyn M. Simpson and George R. Potter, 10 vols. (1958; rpt. Berkeley: Univ. of California Press, 1984), IX, 49, 62.

41. *Lex Mercatoria*, 275, 310; 1622 edition, 312. The phrasing of Malynes' wish "For mine owne part, although it were to be wished (which is not to be hoped) that we were of the Scithians mind . . ." is reminiscent of the end of More's *Utopia*, where money is not used and gold and silver therefore have no monetary value: "ita facile confiteor permulta esse in Vtopiensium republica, quae in nostris ciuitatibus optarim uerius, quam sperarim (But I readily admit that there are very many features in the Utopian commonwealth which it is easier for me to wish for in our countries than to have any hope of seeing realized)": St. Thomas More, *Utopia*, ed. Edward Surtz and J. H. Hexter, in *The Yale Edition of the Complete Works of St. Thomas More* (New Haven: Yale Univ. Press, 1965), IV, 245–47. *Utopia* is a text Malynes mentions in the *Mercatoria* and demonstrably knew well (see n. 111, below).

42. Malynes' explanation includes explicit reference to times when "the trialls of pixes, or of the boxes are made, and the Mint-masters make their accounts with the Prince" (282). King James in 1611 was concerned enough about the coinage to attend such a trial (an annual check on the authenticity of the intrinsic value of coins). In a provocative essay, Simon Wortham argues that James's action was based on his interest in hoarding gold, although this seems an idea hard to square with

economic conditions in the seventeenth century or with the actions of James's own Privy Council: "Sovereign Counterfeits: The Trial of the Pyx," *Renaissance Quarterly*, 49 (1996), 333–59.

43. *Lex Mercatoria*, 280–84. OED, s.v. *commonwealth*, 1–2; *common weal*, 1; *weal*, 1: "Wealth, riches, possessions. *Obs.* (as distinct from 2)"; 2: "Welfare, well-being, happiness, prosperity." Under *weal* 1, the last use listed is 1838; the previous two are 1594 and 1531. The pun in *Lex Mercatoria* activates a meaning already tending to obsolescence.

44. Other relevant instances the *OED* cites, s.v. *symbolization*, include "operation, conuersation, and simbolisation, With matter" (1607) and "That common Salt . . . doth, by symbolization, easily turn into nitre" (1658). The *OED* also notes that the cognate *symbolize* is a "technical term of early physics, said of elements or other substances having qualities in common," with instances of this use from 1591–1816. The first example given of its meaning "resembles" is 1642. The modern meaning of *symbol*, "a representation," and of its cognates dates from the seventeenth century in the main, although there are a few instances of it in the 1590s, and one, namely, *symbolist* in 1585–87, defined as a person "who holds that the elements in the Eucharist are mere symbols of the body and blood of Christ."

45. *Poetics*, 1457b7–24, here 16–18; *Rhetoric*, 1407a14–17, 1411a1–3, 1411b24–25. The availability particularly of the *Poetics* to Malynes in England is questionable, but his Continental experience, as well as his linguistic range, was considerable, and he might easily have encountered it elsewhere. Of course the *Poetics* is forward-, not backward-looking from a Renaissance point of view; that is, what "Aristotelian" means can itself be unstable, a point too often overlooked. Cf. also *De Copia* (ed. Thompson, trans. Knott), where Erasmus gives perfunctory but suggestive attention to "reciprocal metaphor": e.g., "As you can call a steersman a charioteer, so you can call a charioteer a steersman" (335). He also observes that some such "reciprocal or common" metaphors "are one-sided only," or "inconsequent."

46. Julia Kristeva's theory of the chora, for one example, encourages renewed attention to the tonal significance of rhythm: "Revolution in Poetic Language," in *The Kristeva Reader*, ed. Toril Moi (New York: Columbia Univ. Press, 1986), 89–136, here 93–98.

47. Malynes' list does not result from reading the most obvious candidate, Erasmus' *Adagia*. Yet this collection can illustrate the popularity of such compendia. Erasmus' *Adagia*, a collection of proverbs with commentaries, saw ten editions and many enlargements between 1508 and his death in 1536, and by 1700 it had gone through fifty-two complete editions and ninety-six editions in epitomized or selected form. Its popularity was almost equaled by Erasmus' other sententious collections, the early *Adagiorum Collectanea*, the *Apophthegmata*, and the *Parabolae*: Daniel Kinney, "Erasmus' *Adagia*: Midwife to the Rebirth of Learning," *Journal of Medieval and Renaissance Studies*, 11 (1981), 169–92, here 169; and *The Collected Works of Erasmus* (Toronto: Univ. of Toronto Press, 1978, 1982), XXIII, ed. Craig R. Thompson, lxiv–lxv; XXI, trans. Margaret Mann Phillips, with notes by R.A.B.

Mynors, xiii. Erasmus' collections were widely emulated, and they greatly encouraged the recording of sayings in the commonplace books of individual readers.

48. Lakoff and Johnson, *Metaphors We Live By*, 7–9; cf. their *Philosophy in the Flesh*, 163–64.

49. Lakoff and Johnson, *Metaphors We Live By*, 25–32; cf. their *Philosophy in the Flesh*, 380.

50. On "grounded" as a metaphor, cf. Spenser, *The Faerie Queene*, II.xii.1, where "this goodly frame" of Temperance "ginnes" to rise "Formerly grounded, and fast settled / On firme foundation of true bountyhed."

51. Misselden, *Circle*, 20–21, refers to an earlier use of the same image, but his point and the context of his discussion on these pages apply to the passage at hand. The word "dissimilitude," with which I take parenthetical liberties, is his.

52. *Lex Mercatoria*, 377. Misselden responds scornfully to Malynes' tripartite division: "to speake of the soule, without the spirit, or faculties of the soule, is absurd: for the soule and the faculties of the soule, are inseparable" (*Circle*, 20). In *Lex Mercatoria*, 262, Malynes observes that not only do (natural) philosophers distinguish between soul and spirit but also St. Paul does in 2 Thessalonians.

53. Helkiah Crook[e], Μιϰροϰοσμογϱαφια [*Mikrokosmographia*]: *A Description of the Body of Man, together with the Controversies and Figures thereto belonging, Collected and Translated out of the Best Authors of Anatomy, especially out of Gasper Bauhinus and Andreas Laurentius* ([London]: W. Iaggard, 1616), 173. Cf. the familiar lines in John Donne's "The Exstasie":

> . . . our blood labours to beget
>   Spirits, as like soules as it can,
> Because such fingers need to knit
>   That subtile knot, which makes us man.
>
> (61–64)

54. Crooke, 174. The coincidence of this description of the spirit's movement with that of a more familiar, non-corporeal spirit in John 3:8 of the King James version of the Bible is remarkable: "The wind bloweth where it listeth, and thou hearest the sound thereof, but canst not tell whence it cometh, and wither it goeth: so is every one that is born of the Spirit." Noting that references to the spiritual dimension of anatomy are frequent in Crooke's compendium, Jonathan Sawday relates Crooke's work to the tradition of moral anatomy found in Leiden, where Crooke had studied: *The Body Emblazoned: Dissection and the Human Body in Renaissance Culture* (London: Routledge, 1995), 167.

55. Crooke, 174. I have used the phrase "balance of payments" rather than "balance of trade" because, as Gould observes, Malynes saw trade in terms of prices and money rather than volume ("Trade Crisis," 127). Malynes was aware of the balance of trade as an issue and of the fact that it was less favorable to England than formerly, but his emphasis is always on the *prices* of imports versus exports. Harris ("Canker," 314, 316) touches on Malynes' comparing blood to money in order to distinguish his doing so from an earlier and more common relation of blood, or rather of its

loss, to a wasting consumption. (tuberculosis). In *Foreign Bodies and the Body Politic: Discourses of Social Pathology in Early Modern England* (Cambridge: Cambridge Univ. Press, 1998), Harris also remarks, though without specific reference to Malynes, a general trend in post-Reformation thought toward "more rigorous and elaborate application[s]" of the metaphor of the body politic and extension of it into areas such as law, trade, and labor (33).

56. Blitz, 147–48; Klamer and McCloskey, "Economics in the Human Conversation," in *The Consequences of Economic Rhetoric*, ed. Arjo Klamer, Donald N. McCloskey, and Robert M. Solow (Cambridge: Cambridge Univ. Press, 1988), 3–20, here 9: Klamer and McCloskey note, for example, "The mere idea that people are paid 'what they are worth'" can be expressed "in the language of historical relations and moral indignation" or "of evolution and competition," in effect producing the different economics of "classical Marxism" or "social Darwinism, [understood as] a comfort to the country club." Considering political uses, they observe that the phrase "'Marginal productivity' can justify a stony laissez-faire: 'to each according to his need' can justify a revolutionary slaughter."

57. Crooke, 174; cf. 373, 410. Crooke does not follow Galen (or at least a modern text of Galen) when he holds, as here, that spirit travels with the arterial blood: e.g. *Galen on Respiration and the Arteries*, ed. and trans. David J. Furley and J. S. Wilkie (Princeton: Princeton Univ. Press, 1984), 155–61, 177; cf. 121–33. Also *Greek Medicine: Being Extracts Illustrative of Medical Writings from Hippocrates to Galen*, trans. Arthur J. Brock (London: J. M. Dent and Sons, 1929), 19–20, 29–30, 158–59; and Galen, *On the Natural Faculties*, trans. Arthur John Brock (London: William Heinemann, 1916), xxxiv–xxxvi, 151–53. Brock explains that Galen understood *pneuma*, "breath," i.e., *spiritus*, "spirit," as (1) inspired air and (2) a vital principle, or *spiritus vitalis*, of which there are three kinds: *naturalis, vitalis,* and *animalis*. Galen's inspired air is roughly analogous to oxygen and his vital principle to blood in the body, although Galen did not realize how oxygenated blood circulates.

58. *Lex Mercatoria*, 1622 edition: III.xviii.486. Finkelstein, 36, cites Galen in connection with this passage and with Malynes' use of spirit more generally; she attributes conflation of the views of Erasistratus and Galen to Malynes, who instead appears to follow Renaissance medical tradition, which is itself more than purely Galenic. Again, Malynes tends to be a comprehensive mirror of his time, rather than an original thinker (or conflater), and even his inspiration for his central metaphor is to be found in Thomas Milles, as earlier indicated.

59. *The Cambridge History of Renaissance Philosophy*, ed. Charles B. Schmitt, et al. (Cambridge: Cambridge Univ. Press, 1988), 464–84, here 469. I have benefited from hearing and then reading talks on this subject and Spenser's *Faerie Queene* by Julia Major and Jon Quitslund: I am especially grateful to the latter for calling Park's article to my attention and to the former for directing me to Melanchthon's *Liber de Anima*, a sizeable portion of which is translated by Ralph Keen in *A Melanchthon Reader* (New York: Peter Lang, 1988), 239–89. On spirit as the instrument of the soul, see also Crooke, 410: "So wonderfull and almost so heauenly are the powers of the heate and [vital] spirit [in and from the heart], that the diuine *Senior Hippocra-*

tes applying himself to the rude capacity of the people (as *Galen* witnesseth, hee sticketh not often to doe) calleth it the Soule, that is, the chiefe instrument of the Soule." For Melanchthon's original Latin and the rest of his *De Anima*, I have consulted his *Opera*, XIII, 1–178.

60. *Melanchthon Reader*, 245, 256; also 240, 242–44, 247. Analyzing 176 inventories of books of those attached to Cambridge University who died in the sixteenth century, Åke Bergvall has found that, excepting the Bible, the three most frequently owned writers were Erasmus, Cicero, and Aristotle; the fourth was Melanchthon, with "Half the academic population of Cambridge . . . own[ing] . . . at least one book" by him. Although the *Liber de Anima* does not occur in the inventories as often as some of Melanchthon's other works, Bergvall calls its appearance "common": "Melanchthon and Tudor England," in *Cultural Exchange between European Nations during the Renaissance*, ed. Gunnar Sorelius and Michael Srigley (Uppsala, Sweden: Acta Universitatis Upsaliensis, 1994), 85–95, here 89–90. For related evidence, see Carl S. Meyer, "Melanchthon's Influence on English Thought in the Sixteenth Century," in *Miscellanea Historiae Ecclesiasticae, II* (Louvain: Publications Universitaires de Louvain, 1967), 163–85. As curious and widely read a Latinist as Malynes, who also had Continental connections, surely could have encountered Melanchthon's book *On the Soul*.

61. Park, 483–84. Park characterizes Bernardino Telesio's *De rerum natura* (1586) as most important for the notion of a single "spirit-soul." In Telesio's theory, *spiritus* is the "very substance" of the organic soul, rather than its instrument.

62. Quotation from the entry under William Harvey, by Jerome J. Bylebyl, in *Dictionary of Scientific Biography*, ed. Charles Coulston Gillispie, 16 vols. (New York: Charles Scribner's Sons, 1970–80), VI, ed. Jean Hachette and Joseph Hyrtl (1972), 150–162, here 152, cf. 151, 155–56. Finkelstein observes, "The old model of the body economic (derived from the body politic) underwent a significant shift" in the hands of Sir William Petty, Sir Joshua Child, and John Locke later in the [seventeenth] century, which "can be traced back to William Harvey's work on the circulation of the blood (though Harvey was not a mechanist) as well as to the mechanical universe of matter in motion as it was applied by Thomas Hobbes to the human mind" (5, cf. 88). She characterizes the earlier view of Malynes (and Misselden and Mun) as organicism (25).

63. Malynes summarizes his central metaphor in his address "To the Courteous Reader" before the body of his book is entered, but chap. 5 is where he first expounds it more fully.

64. *Lex Mercatoria*, 60. Misselden, *Circle*, 22–23, distorts this image in a way readers have missed. He does so by ignoring Malynes' interest in the direction and government of the ship and substituting for it the movement of the ship at all. With this substitution, the "effectual" (or efficient) cause becomes, of course, the wind in conjunction with the sails.

65. Hawkes, 79, citing Puttenham's rhetoric, asserts that "In Elizabethan English, the term 'abuse' referred to various forms of the subversion of natural teleology," whose basis was Aristotle's final cause. This is a fruitful statement, but at the very

least it is susceptible of qualification and exception. Abuse by custom and art, for example, are highly questionable cases in point. The subject of "abuse," which my previous two chapters consider at length, will recur below.

66. Notably, Malynes also refers to "the *Primum Mobile* of Exchanges" in another metaphor aimed at efficient causality: *Lex Mercatoria*, 411.

67. "Reasonable and Unreasonable Worlds: Some Expectations of Coherence in Culture Implied by the Prohibition of Mixed Metaphor," in *Beyond Metaphor: The Theory of Tropes in Anthropology*, ed. James W. Fernandez (Stanford: Stanford Univ. Press, 1991), 213–43, here 213, 218, 228, 238. Stephen C. Pepper would probably have regarded Malynes as a "formist," everywhere intuiting similarity and correspondence: *World Hypotheses* (Berkeley: Univ. of California Press, 1961), 141, 144, 180. I have argued that Malynes' view is more complicated and mixed. Malynes' procedures, mercantile as they may be, also resonate with a number of Nelson Goodman's now familiar views in *Ways of Worldmaking* (Indianapolis: Hackett, 1978): e.g., "We start . . . with some old version or world that we have on hand and that we are stuck with until we have the determination and skill to remake it into a new one" (97). Malynes' mixed views cast as much light on Goodman's observation as the reverse, making phrases like "stuck with" and "determination and skill" look simple, flat, historically insensitive.

68. *Lex Mercatoria*, I.xlii.216, cf. III.iv.272. Much of the furor over patents for monopolies related to the issue of free trade: e.g., see Robert B. Ekelund, Jr., and Robert D. Tollison, "Economic Regulation in Mercantile England: Heckscher Revisited," in Blaug, ed., 212–43, here, 233, 238–39; and Robert Ashton, "The Parliamentary Agitation for Free Trade in the Opening Years of the Reign of James I," *Past and Present*, no. 38 (1967), 40–55; and Ashton, "Jacobean Free Trade Again," *Past and Present*, no. 43 (1969), 151–57.

69. *Lex Mercatoria*, I.xlii.214, Malynes' definition is virtually the same as Misselden's in *Free Trade*, 57–58. Misselden attributes the definition to Johannes Althusius' *Politica methodice digesta* (1603) and cites his Latin. Either Misselden (*mirabile dictu*) or Althusius is conceivable as Malynes' source: cf. Finkelstein, 67, 288 n. 82. Glyn Davies, 227, thinks Malynes favors a monopolistic control of trade. This view (unsupported by citation) is puzzling with reference to the *Mercatoria*. That Davies should consider *The Canker of Englands Common Wealth* Malynes' "main publication" is equally so.

70. *Lex Mercatoria*, 194, 409. Arguably critical as well are the stories Malynes tells about noblemen and high officers under Elizabeth and James. For example, there were the "Letters Pattents [sic] graunted to the old Lord Treasurer *Burghley*, who did not execute the same in three and twentie yeares after for want of true direction, to the great losse of the Realme"; and then there was the shipment of goods that the Earl of Leicester pretended were his, while knowing perfectly well they belonged to another, who had to pay dearly to obtain them (200, 381). There was also the "alphabetical register" Malynes made of the names of men who would freely finance a Mons Pietatis, or Charitable Bank, to lend to the commoners without charging interest, which he "delivered into the hands of a great personage, who

(as it seemeth) was not worthie of the honour thereof"; or Malynes' effort to acti-vate England's mines, which was "applauded by a great personage then in authori-tie, and now deceased, who promised all the favour that he could do: but he had some other privat designs herein" (262, 335–36).

71. Although puritanism is not synonymous with iconoclasm, the two have much in common, and it is worth noting that Malynes has as visceral a dislike of puritans as does Ben Jonson: e.g., *Lex Mercatoria*, 205. For impressive recent studies of iconoclasm, see Hawkes, esp. chaps. 1–2, and Michael O'Connell, *The Idolatrous Eye: Iconoclasm & Theater in Early-Modern England* (Oxford: Oxford Univ. Press, 2000), chap. 2.

72. *Lex Mercatoria*, 364 (my emphasis). For a comprehensive review of the role of the double-entry method of bookkeeping in altering cognitive categories and legitimating capitalism, see B. Carruthers and Espeland, 31–69. James A. Aho dem-onstrates the rhetorical and specifically Ciceronian origin of the double-entry method: "Rhetoric and the Invention of Double Entry Bookkeeping," *Rhetorica*, 3 (1985), 21–43. Poovey, 33–65, develops these arguments provocatively, but her suggestion that Malynes targets double-entry bookkeeping, rather than the exchanges, is misleading (76–77).

73. *Lex Mercatoria*, 254. Cf. Thomas Culpepper, *A Tract against Usurie* (1621): "'for the rate of Usury is the measure by which all men trade, purchase, build, plant or any other waies bargaine'": cited by Robert Ashton, "Usury and High Finance in the Age of Shakespeare and Jonson," *Renaissance and Modern Studies*, 4 (1960), 14–43, here 32: Malynes appears to have been reading and appropriating again. Ash-ton pertinently observes that Culpepper's *Tract* is actually against only a high rate of usury.

74. *Cambridge Dictionary of Philosophy*, ed. Robert Audi, 2nd ed. (Cambridge: Cambridge Univ. Press, 1999), 752.

75. *Lex Mercatoria*, 307. Cf. "Certain General Rules *collected concerning* Money *and* Bullion *out of the late Consultation at Court*, 138–41,which comes at the end of '*A Speech* touching the Alteration of Coin'" (1626) that is attributed to Sir Robert Cot-ton in *A Select Collection of Scarce and Valuable Tracts on Money*, ed. J. R. McCulloch (1856; rpt. New York: Augustus M. Kelley, 1966), 121–41: "our English Mer-chants" adjust to the present value of their own money in the exchanges "the just intrinsick value of their Foreign Coin, in all barter of Commodities or Exchange except at Usance [interest]; which we [Englishmen], that are ruled and tyed by the extrinsick measure of Monies, in all our constant Reckonings and annual Bargains at home, cannot do" (140).

76. Vaughan, 8–9, 11. Cf. Cotton, "*A Speech*": "extrinsick Quality . . . is at the King's pleasure . . . to name; the other [is] the intrinsick Quality of Pure Mettal" (128). Also, *Lex Mercatoria*: "This gaine [excessive interest, usury] ariseth by the vn-derualuation of our moneys, in regard of the inhancing and ouerualuation of forreine coynes, so that the cause is extrinsique, and comprised under the said Exchange of money, and not intrinsique in the weight and finenes of moneys" (418, cf. 385).

77. *Lex Mercatoria*, 2. For the Saussurean metaphor, see Saussure, 79 (in connection with the notion of *value*, defined as "*a system for equating things of different orders*"—on the one hand labor and wages and, on the other, a signified and a signifier), and 115 (where Saussure uses a five-franc piece to illustrate the difference between linguistic value and signification).

78. *Lex Mercatoria*, Part 2, chap. 10. Ashton, "Usury," compares the medieval distinction between *res consumptibiles and res fungibiles* roughly to the modern one between current and durable goods (16–17). See also Thomas Wilson, *A Discourse Upon Usury (1572)*, ed. R. H. Tawney (New York: Harcourt Brace, 1925), 286: "what is more against nature, then that money should beget or bring forth money, which was ordained to be a pledge or right betwixt man and man, in contracts and bargayning, as a iuste measure and proporcion in bargayning, and not to increase it selfe, as a woman dothe, that bringeth foorthe a childe." Wilson's view is thoroughly Aristotelian, and medieval, as well.

79. On puritans, *Lex Mercatoria*, 205. The word *inconvenience* carries such meanings as "discordant, inconsistent with reason or rule," "inappropriate, out of place," "morally or ethically unsuitable" or "unseemly, improper": *OED*, s.v. *inconvenience*, A, 2, 3. For detailed discussion, see my essay "*Better a mischief than an inconvenience*: 'The saiyng self' in Spenser's *View*, or, How Many Meanings Can Stand on the Head of a Proverb?" in *Worldmaking Spenser: Explorations in the Early Modern Age*, ed. Patrick Cheney and Lauren Silberman (Lexington: Univ. of Kentucky Press, 2000), 219–33. On "preciseness," see *OED*, s.v. *precise*, 2.b.: "Strict or scrupulous in religious observance; in 16th and 17th c., puritanical."

80. *Lex Mercatoria*, 331. Thomas Wilson, a source whom Malynes actually acknowledges, compares the elimination of wolves in England to the (projected) elimination of usurers there, looking to a time when "there mighte bee never an usurers heade in England" (Preface, 182). But he also recognizes that Princes must do things "for very necessity, to avoyde a greater inconvenience" (186, cf. 237).

81. Tawney, ed., in Wilson, *Usury*, 119–20; see also 351–52, where Wilson's Doctor of Civil Law declares, "The best of this age, as *Bucer, Brentius, Calvyne* and *Beza*, with others, are not againste moderate usurye, but doe rather thinke it needeful to be permitted, and saye also that temperate takynge, according as it is rated by the Civill Lawe, ys not agaynste god, nor his Lawes, because it is not agaynste charitye." Malynes'ethical distinction among monetary transactions affecting the beggar, the householder, and the merchant recalls Wilson's (236), as Finkelstein points out (50). Cf. Also de Roover, "Malynes," 356; Ashton, "Usury," 24–25; and William D. Grampp, "The Controversy over Usury in the Seventeenth Century," in Blaug, ed., 245–69.

82. Cf. discussion of *Hamlet*, I.iii.130, "Breathing like sanctified and pious bonds" or else "bawds," in my chap. 2, 31, above.

83. I particularly have in mind Charles Dickens' *Hard Times*—the initial description of Coketown in chap. 5, for example: I refer to the 2nd edition of George Ford and Sylvère Monod (New York: W. W. Norton, 1990), 22.

84. See *Lex Mercatoria*, where Malynes envisions a royal banquet for the "six maner of persons," under the King, required to ensure the prosperity of the commonwealth: "Clergie-men, Noble-men, Magistrates, Merchants, Artificers, & Husband-men." Each group is asked to specify in one word "the propertie of his profession or calling," respectively, to instruct, to fight, to defend, to enrich, to furnish, and to feed (62; cf. 327–28). The increase of the traditional medieval three estates to the Aristotelian six classes of men is notable: *Politics*, 1328b6–14.

85. *Lex Mercatoria*, II.xx (treatment of bookkeeping). Ledgers prior to adoption of the double-entry method were much more narrative in form: for a telling example, see B. Carruthers and Espeland, 40. See also my chap. 2, n. 60, on Lyotard's connection of narrative form with customary knowledge.

86. *Politics*, 1257a28–1257b, 20; the rest of 1257b and 1258a1–19, is generally relevant. Also Hawkes, 27–32, on "natural teleology."

87. *Lex Mercatoria*, 381. In addition to Malynes' high regard for the institution of exchange, his attitude toward the conventions governing bills of exchange is little short of religious: for example, "The Nature of a Bill of Exchange is so noble and excelling all other dealings betweene Merchants, that the proceedings therein are extraordinarie and singular, and not subiect to any prescription by Law or otherwise; but meerely subsisting of a reuerend Custome vsed and solemnized concerning the same" (393). Bills of exchange customarily began "Laus Deo," as every double-entry page in a ledger began with "Laude Deo!" or "Christ be with you all," or with a holy cross (+Jesus and the place/date): see *Lex Mercatoria*, 393, and Aho, 28. Of course, alphabets in hornbooks and basic primers did likewise at the "cross-row." Indeed, "cross-row" is a synonym for "alphabet": *OED*, s.v. *cross-row.*

88. Raymond de Roover, "What Is Dry Exchange? A Contribution to the Study of English Mercantilism," *Journal of Political Economy*, 52 (1944), 250–66, here 260, 264. De Roover's explanation of dry exchange is authoritative, and I follow it. Additional illumination is available in de Roover's "Cambium ad Venetias: Contribution to the History of Foreign Exchange," in Kirshner, ed., 239–59.

89. *Lex Mercatoria*, 380. On those "having store of commodities at all times," see Malynes' list of the evils of bankers, among which is "To take vp money to engrosse any commoditie, either new come or whereof they haue some store, to bring the whole trade of that commoditie into their owne hands to sell both at their pleasure" (410). Although de Roover does not directly engage Malynes' explanation and examples, which are frankly difficult, he characterizes Malynes' "rather detailed description of dry exchange" in the *Mercatoria* as "fairly accurate" but "intelligible only to readers who are already familiar with the business practices of the time" ("Dry Exchange," 261–62). He therefore turns to an extensive examination of the business records of the Medici banks, leaving the problem of Malynes' actual language for others. In "Malynes," 355, de Roover indicates the synonymy on the Continent of the terms "exchange dealer," or "cambist," and "banker," a usage Malynes reflects. In the same essay, he also acknowledges that Malynes (and Thomas Wilson) "were not entirely wrong in branding bankers as parasites or as exploiters" (357, cf. 365). With obvious relevance to Malynes, if he was indeed a Fleming, Jerry

Z. Muller observes that the Dutch Reformed Church, like the Calvinists in Geneva, allowed the charging of interest up to a point but discriminated against bankers, excluding them from communion until well after Malynes' lifetime: *The Mind and the Market: Capitalism in Modern European Thought* (New York: Alfred A. Knopf, 2002), 12.

90. *Lex Mercatoria*, 382. Finkelstein, 44, apparently thinks Malynes is endorsing differential interest on the basis of distance, time, and place in this statement; while I think this is what he should be saying, I do not see that he is in this sentence. With respect to money as a merchandise, cf. Wilson, Preface, 177: men have made "the lone of moneye a kinde of merchandise, a thinge directlye against all lawe, against nature, and against god." Also Milles, *Alphabet*, sig. G2v: "Vsury in *Marchandizing Exchange*, eates out Industry and Trades; and *Marchandizing Marchants* by MONOPOLIES, conspyre to strangle trafficke"; and Cotton, "*A Speech*," 127: "*Coin* was devised, as a Rate and Measure of Merchandize and Manufactures; which if mutable, no Man can tell either what he hath, or what he oweth; no Contract can be certain; and so all Commerce, both publick and private, [is] destroyed." In sharp contrast, see "Certain General Rules," in Cotton, "*A Speech*": "Gold and Silver have a two-fold Estimation: In the extrinsick, as they are Monies, they are the Princes Measures given to his People, and this is a Prerogative of Kings: in the intrinsick, they are Commodities, valuing each other according to the plenty or scarcity; and so all other Commodities by them; and that is the sole power of Trade" (138). Mun's influence is palpable in this last citation. Puzzlingly, Hawkes, 41–42, neglects the fact that the merchandizing or commodification of money is anathema (not "epiphantic") to Malynes and asserts that the intrinsic qualities of money are irrelevant to Malynes' view.

91. Cf. Aristotle, *Nicomachean Ethics*, 1133a18–1133b28: "all things that are exchanged must be somehow commensurable. It is for this end that money has been introduced, and it becomes in a sense an intermediate; for it measures all things" (1133a18–20). Aristotle goes on to say that the unit of measure is really demand, which money represents. Subtract Aristotle's ethical emphasis on moderation of, or temperance in, demand, and presto! the "modern" economic "law" of supply and demand emerges. Aristotle's many shady examples of "useful" economic practice accord oddly with his *Ethics*, however: these are examples "which men of former days have employed or cunningly devised in order to provide themselves with money" and which might prove "useful; for a man will be able to apply some of these instances to such business as he himself takes in hand" (*Economics*, 1346a27–1353b26). For a reader of both texts, the message is mixed.

92. It is not irrelevant that one of the three concluding chapters of *Lex Mercatoria* treats "*Three Paradoxes alluding to the three Essentiall parts of Trafficke*" (477). Another chapter could be written on Malynes' final three chapters—after analysis of the preceding 84, however. I find it telling that analysis focusing on his final chapters has not yet been attempted. The ignoring of generic and rhetorical markers in Malynes' texts *has* led to some misconceiving of them.

93. If Malynes thought the same when he reported that the King might "value a peece of sterling silver weighing about foure pennie weight at twelve pence," he neglected to say so (218). His memory or awareness of contradiction, not only his motive, is questionable. His views, I have argued, are often in process—now emergent, now regressive.

94. See chap. 2, 22–23.

95. Milles, *Alphabet*, sig. K2v: after the word "beleeue," I have silently emended a period (or broken comma) to a comma. Elsewhere, I have not attempted to approximate the graphic features of other Renaissance texts in any detail, but those of Milles's text are significant enough to require approximation. They positively shout. By contrast with Milles, Malynes' relative moderation and relative clarity are notable.

96. For prejudices, see *Lex Mercatoria*, 126–27, 328. The first is a partly tongue-in-cheek story about the commandeering by the English of a Spanish ship carrying, along with other commodities, a great number of papal bulls and pardons. The second compares Christian usurers to Jews, not to the advantage of the Christians, for "The pretence of the Iewes is because we are strangers, as if wee were all Canaanites . . . but these ["Christian"] men cannot alleage any thing in their defence, but greedie lucre."

97. Milles, *Alphabet*, sig. F2r. Cf. "Vsury" in *Marchandizing Exchange*, eates out Industry and Trades (*Alphabet*, sig. G2v).

98. Misselden shares Malynes' suspicion of bankers: *Free Trade*, 9–10, as does (or once did) Mun, according to Finkelstein, 85. Finkelstein, 60–61, is exceptional in recognizing that Malynes' view is not uniquely paranoid, although de Roover, an authority on banking, earlier observes that there was *reason* for Malynes' suspicion (end of my n. 89, immediately above).

99. Vaughan, about whom little is known, is described on the title page of his book as having been a member of Gray's Inn, hence a lawyer, although the *DNB* date of his admission to Gray's came after its composition. For Mun's assessment of Malynes' proposal, see especially chaps. 12 and 14 in *England's Treasure*, 1895. In a very small book, Mun devotes these chapters (one lengthy) and more to Malynes, a testimony to Malynes' contemporary visibility. As earlier noted, Misselden and Malynes are at one another's throats all the time. On Misselden's and Mun's co-operation, see my n. 21, immediately above.

100. Cf. Spenser, *The Faerie Queene*, ed. A. C. Hamilton, 2nd ed., V.Pro.1: "Me seemes the world is runne quite out of square." Hamilton, 2nd ed., here glosses "square" as a reference "to the set square as the emblem of justice." Contemporarily, John Donne plays on Aristotle's "square" (honest, steadfast) man in the relevantly entitled poem "The Computation," which is a "square" poem (ten lines of ten syllables each) and much concerned with numbers. *OED* interpretations are not sufficient in themselves here. See *OED*, s.v. *square*, *v*.: II.4: "To regulate, frame, arrange, or direct *by, according to*, or *on* some standard or principle of action." The relevant historical examples (from 1531 on) illustrating this meaning, however, are largely moral or more general than Vaughan's use. The meaning "To bring to an

equality on both sides; . . . to balance" (5) is more apt, although not recognized by the *OED* until 1815.

101. For Spenser and Jonson, see my *Words That Matter*, chap. 4. Shakespeare's imaging of fortune by the sea is a commonplace.

102. *Lex Mercatoria*, I.xlii.214, 216; i.4, cf. xxxvii.198.

103. *Lex Mercatoria*, 327–28. *Saint George for England, Allegorically described* [sic] (London: William Tymme, 1601), 228–29. Parenthetical citation of Malynes from this point forward is to this text of *Saint George*, unless otherwise indicated.

104. Bloomfield observes the significant replacement of pride by avarice as root of the Deadly Sins in the later Middle Ages, 74–75, 223. The basis for this replacement is Timothy 6:10. Of course Malynes could have found this basis in Chaucer's Pardoner's Tale, as well: *radix malorum est cupiditas*.

105. There are several signs in *Saint George* that Malynes might have read the first book of *The Faerie Queene*. In the flashback to St. George, the King's daughter, paragon of innocence and purity, is accompanied by a lamb (51). Hangers-on of the dragon are compared to toads (as in Revelation, as well as in the instance of the vomit of Spenser's Error): these are also toads whose bowels burst from their drinking, as do those of the greedy offspring of Spenser's Error (56). With this last coincidence, the possibility that Malynes has read Spenser's Book I is stronger.

106. A. C. Hamilton, ed., 2nd ed., 716–17.

107. Cf. Gordon Teskey, *Allegory and Violence* (Ithaca: Cornell Univ. Press, 1996), chap. 1.

108. I have extended Clark's notion of external scaffolding, discussed in chap. 1, my introductory road map, and in chap. 4, above, to include the basic physical disposition, orientation, and awareness that is internal and pre-linguistic and informs language itself, an extension argued by other neo-cognitivists. Clark's curious distinguishing of language from culture (32–33) may imply such an extension, but he does not address the roots of language itself.

109. Quotations in this paragraph from *Philosophy of the Flesh*: in order, 57, 123, 350.

110. Lakoff and Johnson reject the notion that concepts are literally and truly referential and that metaphorical similarity therefore refers to objectively existing similarities, but what they thus expel from a theory of metaphor in the name of "embodied truth" and "embodied realism" returns as a conceptual similarity, and language becomes merely externalized clothing. This explains why readings of imaginative writing based on their theory tend to become taxonomic hunts for conceptual metaphors—for textual, and finally historical, levelers: e.g., George Lakoff and Mark Turner, *More than Cool Reason: A Field Guide to Poetic Metaphor* (Chicago: Univ. of Chicago Press, 1989), e.g., 1–26, and passim. See also my chap. 1, n. 4, and chap. 2, n. 47. An exception to this tendency is Crane's *Shakespeare's Brain*, but while I admire Crane's analyses of Shakespeare, I do not think they depend on such sweeping claims as Lakoff and Johnson's.

111. Besides borrowing from *The Canterbury Tales*, Malynes borrows extensively from More's *Utopia* for his description of Niobla's chief city: see Helen E. Sandison,

"An Elizabethan Economist's Method of Literary Composition," *Huntington Library Quarterly*, 6 (1943), 205–11. Sandison notes Malynes' Chaucerian borrowings and additional borrowings from *Utopia*.

112. *Saint George*, sig. B1v: Malynes refers here to a fish trap consisting of two vertical nets with wide mesh, with a fine net hanging between them; the fish enters through the wide net and then gets trapped in the fine net when it pushes the latter partly through the opposite wide net. His comparison is not so bizarre in light of the chains of fish (sequentially mouth to tail) illustrating mnemonic techniques in Mary Carruthers, *The Book of Memory: A Study of Memory in Medieval Culture* (Cambridge: Cambridge Univ. Press, 1990), 246–47 and fig. 28.

113. For another alternative that I'm relegating to an endnote, Malynes just might have seen in his travels or else heard from other merchants of one or more of those wonderful gardens on the Continent, with all sorts of exotic topiary, waterworks and mechanical forms, and giant statues: e.g., John Dixon Hunt, *Garden and Grove: The Italian Renaissance Garden in the English Imagination, 1600–1750* (Princeton: Princeton Univ. Press, 1986), esp. chap. 4.

114. In a modern classification, Malynes' comparison of nose and hills is technically a simile. As my last chapter and this one have suggested, however, the distinction between simile and metaphor is not, and should not be, hard and fast. Simile can do the work of metaphor in any given instance, although it does not do this in every instance: that is, its doing so is subject to context and demonstration. In the present instance, Malynes' simile fails as a figure for much the same reasons that would pertain to a metaphor: it is a grotesque appliqué.

115. *Saint George*, 35, 41. Treating three notices of Gargantua's mare together, Anne Lake Prescott observes that Malynes' regenders her: *Imagining Rabelais in Renaissance England* (New Haven: Yale Univ. Press, 1998), 16.

116. Put otherwise, while the allegory of a clam is an impossibility, that of a clam opening is not; the one is static, frozen into essence; the other is potentially narrative—moving, active, and temporal: cf. Stephen A. Barney, *Allegories of History, Allegories of Love* (Hamden, CT: Archon, 1979), chap. 1. I part company here with Teskey, who effectually equates allegory with abstraction and conceives of it as a static form, rather than as an embodied and narrative one. A productive view of allegory is found in Carolynn Van Dyke's argument that literary allegory is "based on the synthesis of deictic and nondeictic generic codes": *The Fiction of Truth: Structures of Meaning in Narrative and Dramatic Allegory* (Ithaca: Cornell Univ. Press, 1985), 40. In the terms *deictic* and *nondeictic*, Van Dyke includes such binaries as particular and universal, concrete and abstract, natural and emblematic, real and Real. *Deictic* itself signifies "directly pointing out" or "demonstrative." In a linguistic context, it indicates a word that particularizes and points, such as the demonstrative pronoun *this*. It derives from Greek δειϰτιϰός, "able to show, showing directly." By "genre," Van Dyke means "a set of conventions based on an inferable semiotic code" *and* "the texts that realize the code—or realize it to a significant degree" (20–21).

117. Of course a deliberate depiction of disease and disorder or a deliberate effort to unsettle, startle, or shock might use such effects. Their power to do so, however, still depends on established conventions or expectations of order. Where everything is anarchic, nothing is.

118. Vaughan, 52–53, cf. 50–51; and for other examples, 173, 176, 232–33.

119. Cf. Shell, *Money*, 7: "Credit, or belief, involves the very ground of aesthetic experience, and the same medium that seems to confer belief in fiduciary money (bank notes) and in scriptural money (created by the process of bookkeeping) also seems to confer it in literature." Shell's principle precedes his nineteenth-century historical referent, insofar as it exists in Malynes' writing and experiences with the copper farthings, for example.

Works Cited

Abrams, M. H. *A Glossary of Literary Terms*. 5th ed. New York: Holt, Rinehart, and Winston, 1988.

Abrams, Richard. "Rumor's Reign." *English Literary Renaissance* 16 (1986): 467–95.

Aers, David, and Lynn Staley. *The Powers of the Holy: Religion, Politics, and Gender in Late Medieval English Culture*. University Park: Pennsylvania State University Press, 1996.

Agnew, Jean-Christophe. *Worlds Apart: The Market and the Theater in Anglo-American Thought, 1550–1750*. Cambridge: Cambridge University Press, 1986.

Aho, James A. "Rhetoric and the Invention of Double Entry Bookkeeping." *Rhetorica* 3, no.1 (1985): 21–43.

Aitchison, Jean. *Words in the Mind: An Introduction to the Mental Lexicon*. 2nd ed. Oxford: Blackwell, 1994.

Alpers, Paul J. *The Poetry of "The Fairy Queene."* Princeton: Princeton University Press, 1967.

The American Heritage College Dictionary. 3rd ed. 1993. Rpt., Boston: Houghton Mifflin, 1997.

Anderson, Judith H. Review of *Allegory and Violence*, by Gordon Teskey. *Arthuriana* 7:4 (1997): 125–8.

———. *"Better a mischief than an inconvenience*: 'The saiyng self' in Spenser's *View*; or, How Many Meanings Can Stand on the Head of a Proverb?" In *Worldmaking Spenser: Explorations in the Early Modern Age*, ed. Patrick Cheney and Lauren Silberman. 219–33. Lexington: University of Kentucky Press, 2000.

———. *Biographical Truth: The Representation of Historical Persons in Tudor-Stuart Writing*. New Haven: Yale University Press, 1984.

———. Review of *The Ends of Allegory*, by Sayre N. Greenfield. *Spenser Newsletter* 30:2 (1999): 1–4.

———. *The Growth of a Personal Voice: "Piers Plowman" and "The Faerie Queene."* New Haven: Yale University Press, 1976.

———. "The July Eclogue and the House of Holiness." *Studies in English Literature* 10 (1970): 17–32.

———. "The Knight and the Palmer in *The Faerie Queene*, Book II." *Modern Language Quarterly* 31 (1970): 160–78.

———. " 'In liuing colours and right hew': The Queen of Spenser's Central Books." In *Critical Essays on Edmund Spenser*, ed. Mihoko Suzuki. 168–82. New York: Simon and Schuster Macmillan, 1996.

————. Review of *Reading Shakespeare's Will: The Theology of Figure from Augustine to the Sonnets*, by Lisa Freinkel. *Yearbook of Comparative and General Literature* (2002–03): 189–94.

————. "Whatever Happened to Amoret? The Poet's Role in Book IV of *The Faerie Queene*." *Criticism* 13 (1971): 180–200.

————. *Words That Matter: Linguistic Perception in Renaissance English*. Stanford: Stanford University Press, 1996.

Anderson, Marvin. "Rhetoric and Reality: Peter Martyr and the English Reformation." *Sixteenth Century Journal* 19 (1988): 451–69.

Andrewes, Lancelot. *Responsio ad apologiam Cardinalis Bellarmini*. In *The Works of Lancelot Andrews*. 11 vols. 1854. Rpt., New York: AMS, 1967.

Appleby, Joyce Oldham. *Economic Thought and Ideology in Seventeenth-Century England*. Princeton: Princeton University Press, 1978.

Aptekar, Jane. *Icons of Justice: Iconography and Thematic Imagery in Book V of "The Faerie Queene."* New York: Columbia University Press, 1969.

Aquinas, St. Thomas. *Summa Theologiae*. Blackfriars Edition. 60 vols. London: Eyre and Spottiswoode, 1964–76.

Aristotle. *The Complete Works of Aristotle*. Ed. Jonathan Barnes. 2 vols. Princeton: Princeton University Press, 1984.

Ashton, Robert. "Jacobean Free Trade Again." *Past and Present* no. 43 (1969): 151–57.

————. "The Parliamentary Agitation for Free Trade in the Opening Years of the Reign of James I." *Past and Present* no. 38 (1967): 40–55.

————. "Usury and High Finance in the Age of Shakespeare and Jonson." *Renaissance and Modern Studies* 4 (1960): 14–43.

Attridge, Derek. "Language as History/History as Language: Saussure and the Romance of Etymology." In *Post-Structuralism and the Question of History*, ed. Derek Attridge, Geoff Bennington, and Robert Young. 183–211. Cambridge: Cambridge University Press, 1987.

————. *Peculiar Language: Literature as Difference from the Renaissance to James Joyce*. Ithaca: Cornell University Press, 1988.

Augustine, Saint. *On Christian Doctrine*. Trans. D. W. Robertson, Jr. Indianapolis: Bobbs-Merrill, 1958.

————. "De catechizandis rudibus." In *Patrologia Latina*, ed. J. P. Migne. Vol. XL. Paris: Garnier, 1887.

————. *De Doctrina Christiana*. In *Sancti Aurelii Augustini Opera*. Pt. IV, *Corpus Christianorum*. ed. Joseph Martin. Series Latina XXXII. Turnhout, Belg.: Brepols, 1962.

————. *The Trinity*. Trans. Stephen McKenna. In *The Fathers of the Church*. Vol. XLV. Washington, DC: Catholic University of America Press, 1963.

Austin, J. L. *Philosophical Papers*. Oxford: Clarendon, 1961.

Ayers, P. K. "Reading, Writing, and *Hamlet*." *Shakespeare Quarterly* 44 (1993): 423–39.

Bacon, Francis. *The Works of Francis Bacon.* Ed. James Spedding, Robert Leslie Ellis, and Douglas Denon Heath. 15 vols. Boston: Brown and Taggard [imprint varies; vols. 6–10: Taggard and Thompson], 1860–64.

Baldwin, Frances Elizabeth. *Sumptuary Legislation and Personal Regulation in England.* Baltimore: Johns Hopkins Press, 1926.

Bannet, Eve Tavor. "The Scene of Translation: After Jakobson, Benjamin, de Man, and Derrida." *New Literary History* 24 (1993): 577–95.

Barkan, Leonard. *The Gods Made Flesh: Metamorphosis and the Pursuit of Paganism.* New Haven: Yale University Press, 1986.

Barney, Stephen A. *Allegories of History, Allegories of Love.* Hamden, CT: Archon, 1979.

Barthes, Roland. *Mythologies.* Trans. Annette Lavers. New York: Hill and Wang, 1972.

Bate, Jonathan. *Shakespeare and Ovid.* Oxford: Oxford University Press, 1993.

Bateson, F. W. *English Poetry and the English Language.* 1934. Rpt., New York: Russell and Russell, 1961.

Bender, John, and David E. Wellbery, eds. *The Ends of Rhetoric: History, Theory, Practice.* Stanford: Stanford University Press, 1990.

Benveniste, Emile. *Problems in General Linguistics.* Trans. Mary Elizabeth Meek. Miami Linguistics Series, no. 8. Coral Gables: University of Miami Press, 1971.

Berger, Harry, Jr. *Fictions of the Pose: Rembrandt Against the Italian Renaissance.* Stanford: Stanford University Press, 2000.

———. "Hydra and Rhizome." In *Shakespeare Reread: The Text in New Contexts,* ed. Russ McDonald. 79–104. Ithaca: Cornell University Press, 1994.

———. "Metaphor and Metonymy, and the End of the Middle Ages." Unpublished essay.

———. *Revisionary Play: Studies in the Spenserian Dynamics.* Berkeley: University of California Press, 1988.

———. "Sneak's Noise or Rumor and Detextualization in *2 Henry IV.*" The *Kenyon Review* n.s., 6 (1984): 58–78.

Bergvall, Åke. "Melanchthon and Tudor England." In *Cultural Exchange between European Nations during the Renaissance,* ed Gunnar Sorelius and Michael Srigley. 85–95. Uppsala, Sweden: Acta Universitatis Upsaliensis, 1994.

Black, Max. *Models and Metaphors: Studies in Language and Philosophy.* Ithaca: Cornell University Press, 1962.

———. "More About Metaphor." In *Metaphor and Thought,* ed. Andrew Ortony. 20–41. 2nd ed. Cambridge: Cambridge University Press, 1993.

Blitz, Rudolph. "Mercantilist Policies and the Pattern of World Trade, 1500–1750." In *The Early Mercantilists: Thomas Mun (1571–1641), Edward Misselden (1608–1634), Gerard de Malynes (1586–1623),* ed. Mark Blaug. 147–63. Pioneers in Economics, vol. 4. Aldershot, Hants, Eng.: Edward Elgar, 1991.

Bloomfield, Morton W. *The Seven Deadly Sins: An Introduction to the History of a Religious Concept, with Special Reference to Medieval English Literature.* East Lansing: Michigan State College Press, 1952.

Booth, Stephen. "Close Reading without Readings." In *Shakespeare Reread: The Text in New Contexts*, ed. Russ McDonald. 42–55. Ithaca: Cornell University Press, 1994.

Bourdieu, Pierre. *Ce que parler veut dire: l'économie des échanges linguistiques*. Paris: Fayard, 1982.

———. *Language and Symbolic Power*. Ed. John B. Thompson. Trans. Gino Raymond and Matthew Adamson. Cambridge, MA: Harvard University Press, 1991.

Boyle, Majorie O'Rourke. *Erasmus on Language and Method in Theology*. Toronto: Toronto University Press, 1977.

Bradshaw, Paul F. *The Anglican Ordinal: Its History and Development from the Reformation to the Present Day*. London: Society for Promoting Christian Knowledge, 1971.

Braun, Joseph. "Vestments." In *The Catholic Encyclopedia*. 7 July 2002 <http://www.newadvent.org/cathen/15388a.htm.>.

Breen, Quirinus. "The Subordination of Philosophy to Rhetoric in Melanchthon." *Archiv für Reformationsgeschichte* 43, no.1 (1952): 13–27.

Brock, Arthur John, ed. and trans. *Greek Medicine: Being Extracts Illustrative of Medical Writings from Hippocrates to Galen*. London: J. M. Dent and Sons, 1929.

Brook, Stella. *The Language of the Book of Common Prayer*. New York: Oxford University Press, 1965.

Brooks, Harold F. "*Richard III*: Antecedents of Clarence's Dream." *Shakespeare Survey* 32 (1979): 145–50.

Brooks, Peter Newman. *Thomas Cranmer's Doctrine of the Eucharist: An Essay in Historical Development*. 2nd ed. London: Macmillan, 1992.

Brown, Sarah Annes. *The Metamorphosis of Ovid: From Chaucer to Ted Hughes*. New York: St. Martin's Press, 1999.

Bruns, Gerald. *Inventions: Writing, Textuality, and Understanding*. New Haven: Yale University Press, 1982.

Bucer, Martin. *Censura*. In *Martin Bucer and The Book of Common Prayer*, ed. and trans. E. C. Whitaker. Great Wakering, Essex, Eng.: Mayhew-McCrimmon, 1974.

Burke, Kenneth. *A Grammar of Motives*. 1945. Rpt., Berkeley: University of California Press, 1969.

Bylebyl, Jerome J. "William Harvey." *Dictionary of Scientific Biography*. Ed. Charles Coulston Gillispie. 16 vols. New York: Charles Scribner's Sons. 1970–80. Vol. VI. Ed. Jean Hachette and Joseph Hrytl (1972). 150–62.

Bynum, Caroline Walker. *Fragmentation and Redemption: Essays on Gender and the Human Body in Medieval Religion*. New York: Zone Books, 1991.

———. *Holy Feast and Holy Fast: The Religious Significance of Food to Medieval Women*. Berkeley: University of California Press, 1987.

———. *The Resurrection of the Body in Western Christianity, 200–1336*. New York: Columbia University Press, 1995.

Byron, Brian. "From Essence to Presence: A Shift in Eucharistic Expression Illustrated from the Apologetic of St. Thomas More." In *Miscellanea Moreana: Essays for Germain Marc'hadour*, ed. Clare M. Murphy, Henri Gibaud, and Mario A. Di Cesare. 429–41. Binghamton, NY: Medieval and Renaissance Texts and Studies, 1989.

Calboli, Gualtiero. "From Aristotelian λέξις to *elocutio*." *Rhetorica* 16 (1998): 47–80.

Calvin, John. *Institutes of the Christian Religion.* Trans. Ford Lewis Battles. Ed. John T. McNeill. 2 vols. London: S. C. M., 1961.

———. *Institutio Christianae Religionis 1559.* In *Corpus Reformatorum.* Vol. XXX. Ed. Guilielmus Baum, Eduardus Cunitz, and Eduardus Reuss. Braunschweig, Ger.: Schwetschke et Filium, 1864.

———. *A Treatise on the Sacrament of the Body and Blood of Christ.* In *Writings and Translations of Myles Coverdale*, ed. George Pearson. 425–66. Cambridge: Cambridge University Press, 1844.

Cambridge Dictionary of Philosophy. Ed. Robert Audi. 2nd ed. Cambridge: Cambridge University Press, 1999.

The Cambridge History of the English Language. Ed. Roger Lass. Vol. 3. Cambridge: Cambridge University Press, 1992.

Carruthers, Bruce G., and Wendy Nelson Espeland. "Accounting for Rationality: Double-Entry Bookkeeping and the Rhetoric of Economic Rationality." *American Journal of Sociology* 97 (1991): 31–69.

Carruthers, Mary. *The Book of Memory: A Study of Memory in Medieval Culture.* Cambridge: Cambridge University Press, 1990.

Cary, Louise D. "*Hamlet* Recycled, or the Tragical History of the Prince's Prints." *ELH* 61 (1994): 783–805.

Cassell's Latin Dictionary: Latin-English and English-Latin. By J. R. V. Marchant and Joseph F. Charles, rev. ed. New York: Funk and Wagnalls, 1956.

Cassirer, Ernst. *The Philosophy of Symbolic Forms.* Vol. 1. Trans. Ralph Mannheim. 303–19. New Haven: Yale University Press, 1953.

Cave, Terence. *The Cornucopian Text: Problems of Writing in the French Renaissance.* Oxford: Clarendon, 1979.

Certeau, Michel de. *The Practice of Everyday Life.* Trans. Steven Randall. Berkeley: University of California Press, 1984.

Cicero, Marcus Tullius. *Ad C. Herennium.* Ed. and trans. Harry Caplan. 1954. Rpt., London: William Heinemann, 1981.

———. *Cicero: On the Ideal Orator.* Trans. James M. May and Jakob Wisse. New York: Oxford University Press, 2001.

———. *De legibus.* In *Cicero.* Vol. XVI. Trans. Clinton Walker Keyes. London: Heinemann, 1977.

———. *De Oratore.* Ed. G.P. Goold. Trans. E. W. Sutton. Completed H. Rackham. 2 vols. 1942. Rpt., London: Heinemann, 1988.

Clark, Andy. *Being There: Putting Brain, Body, and World Together Again.* Cambridge, MA: MIT Press, 2001.

Clayton, Thomas. "Quibbling Polonii and the Pious Bonds: The Rhetoric of *Hamlet I.iii*." *Shakespeare Studies* 2 (1966): 59–94.

Coghan, Thomas. *The Haven of Health*. London: Henrie Midleton for William Norton, 1584.

Cohen, Jeffrey Jerome. "On Saracen Enjoyment: Some Fantasies of Race in Late Medieval France and England." *Journal of Medieval and Early Modern Studies*, 31 (2001): 113–46.

Collinson, Patrick. *Elizabethan Essays*. London: Hambledon, 1994.

———. *The Elizabethan Puritan Movement*. 1967. Rpt., Oxford: Clarendon, 2000.

Cooper, Andrew M. "The Collapse of the Religious Hieroglyph: Typology and Natural Language in Herbert and Bacon." *Renaissance Quarterly* 45 (1992): 96–118.

Cooper, David E. *Metaphor*. Oxford: Basil Blackwell, 1986.

Cooper, Thomas. *Thesaurus linguae Romanae et Britannicae*. 1565. Rpt., Menston, Eng.: Scolar, 1969.

Cope, Gilbert. "Vestments." In *A Dictionary of Liturgy and Worship*, ed. J. G. Davies. New York: Macmillan, 1972.

Cotton, Sir Robert. *A Speech touching the Alteration of Coin*. In *A Select Collection of Scarce and Valuable Tracts on Money*, ed. J. R. McCulloch. 121–41. 1856. Rpt., New York: Augustus M. Kelley, 1966.

Courtenay, William J. "Cranmer as Nominalist." *Harvard Theological Review* 57 (1964): 367–80.

Courvoisier, Jacques. *Zwingli: A Reformed Theologian*. Richmond, VA: John Knox Press, 1963.

Crane, Mary Thomas. *Shakespeare's Brain: Reading with Cognitive Theory*. Princeton: Princeton University Press, 2001.

———, and Alan Richardson. "Literary Studies and Cognitive Science: Toward a New Interdisciplinarity." *Mosaic* 32 (1999): 123–40.

Cranmer, Thomas. *An Answer unto a Crafty and Sophistical Cavillation Devised by Stephen Gardiner*. In *Writings and Disputations*, ed. John Edmund Cox. 1–367. Cambridge: Cambridge University Press, 1844.

———. *A Defence of the True and Catholic Doctrine of the Sacrament of the Body and Blood of our Saviour Christ*. Ed. G. E. Duffield. Philadelphia: Fortress Press, 1965.

Crook[e], Helkiah. Μικροκοσμογραφια *[Mikrokosmographia]: A Description of the Body of Man, together with the Controversies and Figures thereto belonging, Collected and Translated out of the Best Authors of Anatomy, especially out of Gasper Bauhinus and Andreas Laurentius*. [London]: W. Iaggard, 1616.

Damasio, Antonio R. *Descartes' Error: Emotion, Reason, and the Human Brain*. New York: Avon, 1994.

Davies, Glyn. *A History of Money: From Ancient Times to the Present Day*. 3rd rev. ed. Cardiff: University of Wales Press, 2002.

Day, Angel. *The English Secretary or Methods of Writing "Epistles" and "Letters"*. 1599. Rpt., Gainesville: Scholars' Facsimiles and Reprints, 1967.

————. *The English secretary, or Methode of writing epistles and letters.* London: C. Burbie, 1599.

de Grazia, Margreta. *Shakespeare Verbatim: The Reproduction of Authenticity and the 1790 Apparatus.* Oxford: Clarendon, 1991.

Deleuze, Gilles, and Felix Guattari. *On the Line.* Trans. John Johnston. New York: Semiotext[e], 1983.

de Roover, Raymond. "Cambium ad Venetias: Contribution to the History of Foreign Exchange." In *Business, Banking, and Economic Thought in Late Medieval and Early Modern Europe: Selected Studies of Raymond de Roover,* ed. Julius Kirshner. 239–59. Chicago: University of Chicago Press, 1974.

————. "Gerard de Malynes as an Economic Writer: From Scholasticism to Mercantilism." In *Business, Banking, and Economic Thought in Late Medieval and Early Modern Europe: Selected Studies of Raymond de Roover,* ed. Julius Kirshner. 346–66. Chicago: University of Chicago Press, 1974.

————. "What Is Dry Exchange? A Contribution to the Study of English Mercantilism." *Journal of Political Economy* 52 (1944): 250–66.

Derrida, Jacques. "La mythologie blanche (la métaphore dans le texte philosophique)." *Poétique* 5 (1971): 1–52.

————. "The Retrait of Metaphor." Trans. eds. *Enclitic* 2, no. 2 (1978): 4–33.

————. "Des Tours de Babel." Trans. Joseph F. Graham. In *Difference in Translation,* ed. Joseph F. Graham. English translation, 165–207. Orig. French, 209–48. Ithaca: Cornell University Press, 1985.

————. "White Mythology: Metaphor in the Text of Philosophy." Trans. F.C.T. Moore. *New Literary History* 6 (1975): 5–74.

Dickens, Charles. *Hard Times.* 2nd ed. Ed. George Ford and Sylvère Monod. New York: W. W. Norton, 1990.

The Dictionary of National Biography. Ed. Sir Leslie Stephen and Sir Sidney Lee. 66 vols. 1885–1901. Rpt., London: Oxford University Press, 1917.

A Dictionary of Superstitions. Ed. Iona Opie and Moira Tatem. Oxford: Oxford University Press, 1989.

Donne, John. *The Complete Poetry of John Donne.* Ed. John T. Shawcross. Garden City, NY: Doubleday, 1967.

————. *Devotions upon Emergent Occasions.* Ed. Anthony Raspa. 1975. Rpt., New York: Oxford University Press, 1987.

————. *The Elegies and the Songs and Sonnets of John Donne.* Ed. Helen Gardner. 1965. Rpt., Oxford: Clarendon, 1970.

————. *The Sermons of John Donne.* Ed. George R. Potter and Evelyn M. Simpson. 10 vols. 1953. Rpt., Berkeley: University of California Press, 1984.

Duffy, Eamon. *The Stripping of the Altars: Traditional Religion in England, 1400–1580.* New Haven: Yale University Press, 1992.

Echlin, Edward P. *The Story of Anglican Ministry.* Slough, Eng.: St. Paul Publications, 1974.

Eco, Umberto. *A Theory of Semiotics.* Bloomington: Indiana University Press, 1979.

Eggert, Katherine. "Spenser's Ravishment: Rape and Rapture in *The Faerie Queene.*" *Representations* 70 (2000): 1–26.

Ekelund, Robert B., Jr., and Robert D. Tollison. "Economic Regulation in Mercantile England: Heckscher Revisited." In *The Early Mercantilists: Thomas Mun (1571–1641), Edward Misselden (1608–1634), Gerard de Malynes (1586–1623),* ed. Mark Blaug. Pioneers in Economics, vol. 4. Aldershot, Hants, Eng.: Edward Elgar, 1991.

Elsky, Martin. *Authorizing Words: Speech, Writing, and Print in the English Renaissance.* Ithaca: Cornell University Press, 1989.

Encyclopedia of Philosophy. Ed. Paul Edwards. 8 vols. London: Collier-Macmillan, 1967.

Enterline, Lynn. *The Rhetoric of the Body from Ovid to Shakespeare.* Cambridge: Cambridge University Press, 2000.

Erasmus, Desiderius of Rotterdam. *Adagia.* Trans. Margaret Mann Phillips. In *The Collected Works of Erasmus,* ed. Craig R. Thompson. Vol. XXIII. Toronto: University of Toronto Press, 1978.

———. *Annotationes.* In *Desiderii Erasmi Roterodami Opera Omnia,* ed. Jean Le Clerc. Vol. VI. Leiden: Petrus Van der Aa, 1703–06.

———. *The Collected Works of Erasmus.* Ed. Craig R. Thompson. 84 vols. Toronto: University of Toronto Press, 1974–.

———. *"Copia": Foundations of the Abundant Style.* Trans. Betty I. Knott. In *The Collected Works of Erasmus,* ed. Craig R. Thompson. Vol. XXIV. 279–659. Toronto: University of Toronto Press, 1978.

———. *De Copia Verborum ac Rerum.* Ed. Betty I. Knott. In *Opera Omnia Desiderii Erasmi Roterodami.* Vol. I, part 6. Amsterdam: North-Holland, 1988.

———. *Erasmus' Annotations on the New Testament: The Gospels.* Ed. Anne Reeve. 1535. Rpt., London: Duckworth, 1986.

———. *On the Method of Study.* Trans. Brian McGregor. In *The Collected Works of Erasmus,* ed. Craig R. Thompson. Vol. XXIV. 660–91. Toronto: University of Toronto Press, 1978.

———. *The Praise of Folly.* Trans. Betty Radice. In *Collected Works of Erasmus: Literary and Educational Writings.* Vol. XXVII. Ed. A.H.T. Levi. 77–153. Toronto: University of Toronto Press, 1986.

———. *De Ratione Studii.* In *Desiderii Erasmi Roterodami Opera Omnia,* ed. Jean Le Clerc. Vol. I. 517–30. Leiden: Petrus Van der Aa, 1703–06.

Erling, Bernhard. "*Communicatio Idiomatum* Re-examined." *Dialog* 2 (1963): 139–45.

Estienne, Robert. *Dictionarium, seu Latinae linguae thesaurus.* Paris: Robert Estienne, 1543.

Fenner, Dudley. *The Artes of Logike and Rhetorike.* Middleburg: R. Schilders, 1584.

Ferguson, Margaret. "Saint Augustine's Region of Unlikeness: The Crossing of Exile and Language." *Georgia Review* 29 (1975): 842–64.

Fincham, Kenneth. "Clerical Conformity from Whitgift to Laud." In *Conformity and Orthodoxy in the English Church, c. 1560–1660,* ed. Peter Lake and Michael Questier, 125–58. Woodbridge, Suffolk, Eng.: Boydell, 2000.

Finkelstein, Andrea. *Harmony and the Balance: An Intellectual History of Seventeenth-Century English Economic Thought.* Ann Arbor: University of Michigan Press, 2000.

The First and Second Prayer Books of Edward VI. 1549, 1552. Rpt., London: Prayer Book Society, 1999.

Fisch, Harold. "The Puritans and the Reform of Prose-Style." *ELH* 19 (1952): 229–48.

Fischer, Sandra K. *Econolingua: A Glossary of Coins and Economic Language in Renaissance Drama.* Newark: University of Delaware Press, 1985.

Fleischer, Manfred P. "Melanchthon as Praeceptor of Late-Humanist Poetry." *Sixteenth-Century Journal* 20, no. 4 (1989): 559–80.

Florio, John. *A Worlde of Wordes, or Most Copious Dictionarie in Italian and English.* London: A. Hatfield for E. Blount, 1598.

Foucault, Michel. *The Order of Things.* 1971. Rpt. New York: Random House, 1973.

Foxe, John. *Actes and Monuments.* London: Iohn Day, 1583.

———. *The Actes and Monuments of John Foxe.* Ed. Stephen Reed Cattley. 8 vols. London: R. B. Seeley and W. Burnside, 1838.

———. *Actes and Monuments.* London: John Day, 1563.

Freeman, Thomas S. "Fate, Faction, and Fiction in Foxe's *Book of Martyrs.*" *The Historical Journal* 43 (2000): 601–23.

Freinkel, Lisa. *Reading Shakespeare's Will: The Theology of Figure from Augustine to the Sonnets.* New York: Columbia University Press, 2002.

Frye, Susan. *Elizabeth I: The Competition for Representation.* Oxford: Oxford University Press, 1993.

Galen. *Galen on Respiration and the Arteries.* Ed. and trans. David J. Furley and J. S. Wilkie. Princeton: Princeton University Press, 1984.

———. *On the Natural Faculties.* Trans. Arthur John Brock. London: William Heinemann, 1916.

Garber, Marjorie. *Vested Interests: Cross-Dressing and Cultural Anxiety.* New York: Routledge, 1992.

Gardiner, Stephen. *A Detection of the Devils Sophistrie.* London: John Herforde, 1546.

———. *An Explication and assertion of the true Catholique fayth, touchyng the most blessed Sacrament of the aulter.* Rouen: Robert Caly, 1551.

Genette, Gérard. *Figures of Literary Discourse.* Trans. Alan Sheridan. New York: Columbia University Press, 1982.

Gerrish, B. A. *Continuing the Reformation: Essays on Modern Religious Thought.* Chicago: University of Chicago Press, 1993.

———. *Grace and Gratitude: The Eucharistic Theology of John Calvin.* Minneapolis: Fortress Press, 1993.

———. *The Old Protestantism and the New: Essays on the Reformation Heritage.* Chicago: University of Chicago Press, 1982.

Gilby, Anthony. *A Pleasaunt Dialogue betweene a Souldior of Barwicke and an English Chaplaine.* N.p., 1581.

Goldberg, Jonathan. "Hamlet's Hand." *Shakespeare Quarterly* 39 (1988): 307–27.

Goodman, Nelson. *Ways of Worldmaking*. Indianapolis: Hackett, 1978.

Gould, J. D. "The Trade Crisis of the Early 1620s and English Economic Thought." *The Journal of Economic History* 15 (1955): 121–33.

———. "The Trade Depression of the Early 1620s." *Economic History Review*, 2nd ser., 7 (1954): 81–90.

Goux, Jean-Joseph. *The Coiners of Language*. Trans. Jennifer Curtiss Gage. Norman: University of Oklahoma Press, 1994.

———. *Symbolic Economies: After Marx and Freud*. Trans. Jennifer Curtiss Gage. Ithaca: Cornell University Press, 1990.

Grampp, William D. "The Controversy over Usury in the Seventeenth Century." In *The Early Mercantilists: Thomas Mun (1571–1641), Edward Misselden (1608–1634). Gerard de Malynes (1586–1623)*, ed. Mark Blaug. 245–69. Aldershot, Hants,: Eng. Edward Elgar, 1991.

Greenblatt, Stephen. "Remnants of the Sacred in Early Modern England." In *Subject and Object in Renaissance Culture*, ed. Margreta de Grazia, Maureen Quilligan, and Peter Stallybrass. 337–45. Cambridge: Cambridge University Press, 1996.

Gross, Daniel M. "Melanchthon's Rhetoric and the Practical Origins of Reformation Human Science." *History of the Human Sciences* 13, no. 3 (2000): 5–22.

Guibbory, Achsah. "Donne, the Idea of Woman, and the Experience of Love." *John Donne Journal* 9 (1990): 105–12.

Hacking, Ian. *Why Does Language Matter to Philosophy?* Cambridge: Cambridge University Press, 1975.

Hall, Basil. "Cranmer, the Eucharist and the Foreign Divines in the Reign of Edward VI." In *Thomas Cranmer: Churchman and Scholar*, ed. Paul Ayris and David Selwyn. 217–58. Woodbridge, Suffolk, Eng: Boydell, 1993.

Harris, Jonathan Gil. "'The Canker of England's Commonwealth': Gerard de Malynes and the Origins of Economic Pathology." *Textual Practice* 13 (1999): 311–27.

———. *Foreign Bodies and the Body Politic: Discourses of Social Pathology in Early Modern England*. Cambridge: Cambridge University Press, 1998.

Hart, F. Elizabeth. "Cognitive Linguistics: The Experiential Dynamics of Metaphor." *Mosaic* 28 (1995): 1–23.

———. "Matter, System, and Early Modern Studies: Outlines for a Materialist Linguistics." *Configurations* 6 (1998): 311–43.

Hawkes, David. *Idols of the Market Place: Idolatry and Commodity Fetishism in English Literature, 1580–1680*. New York: Palgrave, 2001.

Heckscher, E[li] F[ilip]. *Mercantilism*. Rev. 2nd. ed. 2 vols. Ed. E. F. Söderlund. Trans. Mendel Shapiro. London: Allen and Unwin, 1955.

Helgerson, Richard. *Forms of Nationhood: The Elizabethan Writing of England*. Chicago: University of Chicago Press, 1992.

Henle, Paul. "Metaphor." In *Philosophical Perspectives on Metaphor*, ed. Mark Johnson. 83–104. Minneapolis: University of Minnesota Press, 1981.

Herbert, George. *The Works of George Herbert*. Ed. F. E. Hutchinson. 1941. Rpt., Oxford: Clarendon, 1959.

Heron, Alasdair. "*Communicatio Idiomatum* and *Deificatio* of Human Nature: A Reformed Perspective." *The Greek Orthodox Theological Review* 43 (1998): 367–76.

Historical Manuscripts Commission. *Calendar of the Manuscripts of the Most Hon. The Marquis of Salisbury*. Pt. 6. London: Eyre and Spottiswoode, 1892–95.

Hollander, Anne. *Seeing through Clothes*. 1975. Rpt., New York: Viking, 1978.

Hooper, John. "A godly Confession and protestacion of the christian faith made and sent furth by Jhon [*sic*] Hooper, wherein is declared what a christian manne is bound to beleve of God, hys King, his neibour, and hymselfe." In *Later Writings of Bishop Hooper, Together with His Letters and Other Pieces*. Ed. Charles Nevinson. 20–63, 65–92. Cambridge: Cambridge University Press, 1852.

———. "Annotations on Romans XIII." In *Later Writings of Bishop Hooper, Together with His Letters and Other Pieces*. Ed. Charles Nevinson. 93–116. Cambridge: Cambridge University Press, 1852.

———. "An Apology against the untrue and slanderous reports made against me John Hooper, late bishop of Worceter and Gloceter, that I should be a maintainer and encourager of such as cursed the Queen's Majesty's highness." In *Later Writings of Bishop Hooper, Together with His Letters and Other Pieces*. Ed. Charles Nevinson. 554–67. Cambridge: Cambridge University Press, 1852.

———. "Answer to the Bishop of Winchester's Book." In *Early Writing of John Hooper, D. D., Lord Bishop of Gloucester and Worcester, Martyr, 1555*, ed. Samuel Carr. 97–247. Cambridge: Cambridge University Press, 1843.

———. "An Oversight and Deliberation upon the Holy Prophet Jonas." In *Early Writings of John Hooper, D. D., Lord Bishop of Gloucester and Worcester, Martyr, 1555*, ed. Samuel Carr. 431–558. Cambridge: Cambridge University Press, 1843.

Hooper, Wilfred. "The Tudor Sumptuary Laws." *English Historical Review* 30 (1915): 433–49.

Hopf, C. "Bishop Hooper's 'Notes' to the King's Council, 3 October 1550." *The Journal of Theological Studies* 44 (1943): 194–99.

Horace. *Horace: Epistles, Book II and Epistle to the Pisones*. Ed. Niall Rudd. Cambridge: Cambridge University Press, 1989.

Hoskins, John. *Directions for Speech and Style*. Ed. Hoyt H. Hudson. Princeton: Princeton University Press, 1935.

Houston, Julia. "Transubstantiation and the Sign: Cranmer's Drama of the Last Supper." *Journal of Medieval and Renaissance Studies* 24 (1994): 115–30.

Howard, Jean. "Crossdressing, the Theater, and Gender Struggle in Early Modern England." *Shakespeare Quarterly* 3 (1988): 418–40.

Hudson, Anne. *The Premature Reformation: Wycliffite Texts and Lollard History*. Oxford: Clarendon, 1988.

Hunt, E. W. *The Life and Times of John Hooper (c.1500–1555) Bishop of Gloucester*. Lewiston, NY: Edwin Mellen Press, 1992.

Hunt, John Dixon. *Garden and Grove: The Italian Renaissance Garden in the English Imagination, 1600–1750*. Princeton: Princeton University Press, 1986.

Iser, Wolfgang. *The Fictive and the Imaginary: Charting Literary Anthropology*. Baltimore: Johns Hopkins University Press, 1993.

Jakobson, Roman. *Studies on Child Language and Aphasia*. The Hague: Mouton, 1971.

———, and Morris Halle. *Fundamentals of Language*. Rev. 2nd ed. 1971. Rpt., The Hague: Mouton, 1980.

James, Heather. "Ovid and the Question of Politics in Early Modern England." *ELH*, 70 (2003): 343–73.

Jameson, Fredric. *The Political Unconscious: Narrative as a Socially Symbolic Act*. 1981. Rpt., Ithaca: Cornell University Press, 1988.

Johnson, E. A. J. "Gerard de Malynes and the Theory of the Foreign Exchanges." *The American Economic Review* 22 (1933): 441–55.

Johnson, Jeffrey. *The Theology of John Donne*. Woodbridge, Suffolk, Eng.: Boydell and Brewer, 1999.

Johnson, Mark. *The Body in the Mind*. Chicago: University of Chicago Press, 1987.

———, ed. *Philosophical Perspectives on Metaphor*. Minneapolis: University of Minnesota Press, 1981.

Jones, Ann Rosalind, and Peter Stallybrass. "Dismantling Irena: The Sexualizing of Ireland in Early Modern England." In *Nationalism and Sexualities*, ed. Andrew Parker, Mary Russo, Doris Sommer, and Patricia Yaeger. 157–71. New York: Routledge, 1992.

———. *Renaissance Clothing and the Materials of Memory*. Cambridge: Cambridge University Press, 2000.

Kahn, Charles H. *The Verb 'Be' in Ancient Greek*. Pt. 6, *The Verb "Be" and its Synonyms: Philosophical and Grammatical Studies*. Foundations of Language Supplementary Series, ed. John W. M. Verhaar. Vol. 16. Dordrecht: D. Reidel, 1973.

Kavanagh, Aidan. "Liturgical Vesture in the Roman Catholic Tradition." In *Raiment for the Lord's Service: A Thousand Years of Western Vestments*, by Christa C. Mayer-Thurman. Chicago: Art Institute of Chicago, 1975.

Keats, John. *The Letters of John Keats*. Ed. Hyder Edward Rollins. Vol. 2. Cambridge, MA: Harvard University Press, 1958.

Kelly, Douglas. "*Translatio Studii*: Translation, Adaptation, and Allegory in Medieval French Literature." *Philological Quarterly* 57 (1978): 287–310.

King, John. "Fiction and Fact in Foxe's *Book of Martyrs*." In *John Foxe and the English Reformation*, ed. David Loades. 12–35. Aldershot, Hants, Eng.: Scholar Press, 1997.

Kinney, Daniel. "Erasmus' *Adagia*: Midwife to the Rebirth of Learning." *Journal of Medieval and Renaissance Studies* 11 (1981): 169–92.

Klamer, Arjo, and Donald N. McCloskey. "Economics in the Human Conversation." In *The Consequences of Economic Rhetoric*, ed. Arjo Klamer, Donald N. McCloskey, and Robert M. Solow. 3–20. Cambridge: Cambridge University Press, 1988.

Knappen, M. M. *Tudor Puritanism: A Chapter in the History of Idealism*. Chicago: University of Chicago Press, 1939.

Knott, John R. *Discourses of Martyrdom in English Literature, 1563–1694*. Cambridge: Cambridge University Press, 1993.

Kristeva, Julia. "Revolution in Poetic Language." In *The Kristeva Reader*, ed. Toril Moi. 89–136. New York: Columbia University Press, 1986.

Labriola, Albert C. " 'This Dialogue of One': Rational Argument and Affective Discourse in Donne's 'Aire and Angels.' " *John Donne Journal* 9 (1990): 77–83.

LaCapra, Dominick. "Who Rules Metaphor?" *Diacritics* 10 (winter 1980): 15–28.

Lake, Peter. "Moving the Goal Posts? Modified Subscription and the Construction of Conformity in the Early Stuart Church." In *Conformity and Orthodoxy in the English Church, c. 1560–1660*, ed. Peter Lake and Michael Questier, 179–205. Woodbridge, Suffolk, Eng.: Boydell, 2000.

Lakoff, George. *Women, Fire, and Dangerous Things: What Categories Reveal about the Mind*. Chicago: University of Chicago Press, 1987.

Lakoff, George, and Mark Johnson. *Metaphors We Live By*. Chicago: University of Chicago Press, 1980.

———. *Philosophy in the Flesh: The Embodied Mind and Its Challenge to Western Thought*. New York: Basic Books, 1999.

Lakoff, George, and Mark Turner. *More than Cool Reason: A Field Guide to Poetic Metaphor*. Chicago: University of Chicago Press, 1989.

Lanham, Richard A. *A Handlist of Rhetorical Terms: A Guide for Students of English Literature*. Berkeley: University of California Press, 1968.

Larkin, M. T. *Language in the Philosophy of Aristotle*. The Hague: Mouton, 1971.

Lewis, C. S. *English Literature in the Sixteenth Century, Excluding Drama*. Oxford: Clarendon, 1954.

Lewis, Charlton T., and Charles Short. *A Latin Dictionary*. 1879. Rpt., Oxford: Clarendon, 1966.

Liddell, Henry George, and Robert Scott. *A Greek-English Lexicon*. Rev. Henry Stuart Jones et al. Oxford: Clarendon, N.d.

Luther, Martin. "Confession Concerning Christ's Supper 1528." In *Word and Sacrament* III, ed. and trans. Robert H. Fischer. 151–372. Vol. XXXVII, *Luther's Works*, ed. Jaroslav Pelikan and Helmut T. Lehmann. Philadelphia: Concordia Publishing and Muhlenberg Press, 1961.

———. "Marburg Colloquy, 1529." In *Great Debates of the Reformation*, ed. Donald J. Ziegler. 71–107. New York: Random House, 1969.

Lyotard, Jean-François. *The Postmodern Condition: A Report on Knowledge*. Trans. Geoff Bennington and Brian Massumi. Minneapolis: University of Minnesota Press, 1984.

MacCulloch, Diarmaid. *Thomas Cranmer: A Life*. New Haven: Yale University Press, 1996.

Mahood, M. M. *Shakespeare's Wordplay*. London: Methuen, 1957.

Malynes, Gerard [Gerrard de]. *The Center of the Circle of Commerce*. London: William Jones, 1623.

———. *Consuetudo, vel Lex Mercatoria.* 1622. Rpt., Amsterdam: Theatrum Orbis Terrarum, 1979.

———. *Consuetudo, vel Lex Mercatoria, or The Ancient Law-Merchant.* London: Adam Islip, 1629.

———. *The Maintenance of Free Trade.* 1622. Rpt., New York: Augustus M. Kelley, 1971.

———. *The Merchant's Almanac of 1622, or Lex Mercatoria, the Ancient Law-Merchant.* Ed. Katie F. Hamilton. Phoenix, AZ: Metheglin Press, 1996.

———. *Saint George for England, Allegorically described.* London: William Tymme, 1601.

———. *A Treatise of the Canker of Englands Common Wealth.* London: W. Johnes, 1601.

Marcus, Leah. "Renaissance/Early Modern Studies." In *Redrawing the Boundaries,* ed. Stephen Greenblatt and Giles Gunn. 41–63. New York: Modern Language Association, 1992.

Markus, R. A. "St. Augustine on Signs." *Phronesis* 2 (1957): 60–83.

Marriott, Wharton B. *Vestiarivm Christianvm: The Origin and Gradual Development of the Dress of Holy Ministry in the Church.* London: Rivingtons, 1868.

Maskell, William. *Monumenta Ritualia Ecclesiae Anglicanae.* Vol. 2. Oxford: Clarendon, 1882.

Mayer-Thurman, Christa C. *Raiment for the Lord's Service: A Thousand Years of Western Vestments.* Chicago: Art Institute of Chicago, 1975.

McGee, Eugene K. "Cranmer and Nominalism." *Harvard Theological Review* 57 (1964): 189–216.

———. "Cranmer's Nominalism Reaffirmed." *Harvard Theological Review* 59 (1968): 192–96.

McInerny, Ralph. *Aquinas and Analogy.* Washington, DC: Catholic University of America Press, 1996.

Melanchthon, Philipp. *Liber de Anima.* In *A Melanchthon Reader,* trans. Ralph Keen. 239–89. New York: Peter Lang, 1988.

———. *Elementorum Rhetorices.* In *Philippi Melanthonis Opera quae supersunt omnia* Vol. XIII. 413–506. *Corpus Reformatorum.* Ed. Carolus Gottlieb Bretschneider. Braunschweig, Ger.: C. A. Swetschke et Filium, 1834–59.

Metz, Christian. *The Imaginary Signifier: Psychoanalysis and the Cinema.* Trans. Celia Britton, Annwyl Williams, Ben Brewster, and Alfred Guezzetti. Bloomington: Indiana University Press, 1982.

Meyer, Carl S. "Melanchthon's Influence on English Thought in the Sixteenth Century." In *Miscellanea Historiae Ecclesiasticae II: Congrès de Vienne, août-septembre 1965.* 163–85. Louvain: Publications Universitaires de Louvain, 1967.

Middle English Dictionary. Ed. Hans Kurath and Sherman M. Kuhn. Ann Arbor: University of Michigan Press, 1952–2001.

Milles, Thomas. *The Custumers Alphabet and Primer.* London: William Jaggard[?], 1608.

———. *The Customers Replie, or, Second apologie.* London: James Roberts, 1604.

Milton, John. *Areopagitica*. In *Complete Prose Works of John Milton*. Vol. II. Ed. Ernest Sirluck. New Haven: Yale University Press, 1959.

Misselden, Edward. *The Circle of Commerce or The Ballance of Trade*. 1623. Rpt., New York: Augustus M. Kelley, 1971.

———. *Free Trade or The Meanes to Make Trade Florish*. 1622. Rpt., New York: Augustus M. Kelley, 1971.

More, St. Thomas. *Utopia*. In *The Yale Edition of the Complete Works of St. Thomas More*. Vol. IV. Ed. Edward Surtz and J. H. Hexter. New Haven: Yale University Press, 1965.

Mozley, J. F. *John Foxe and His Books*. London: Society for Promoting Christian Knowledge, 1940.

Muchmore, Lynn. "Gerrard de Malynes and Mercantile Economics." *History of Political Economy* 1 (1969): 336–58.

———. "A Note on Thomas Mun's *England's Treasure by Forraign Trade*." In *The Early Mercantilists: Thomas Mun (1571–1641), Edward Misselden (1608–1634), Gerard de Malynes (1586–1623)*, ed. Mark Blaug. 187–92. Pioneers in Economics, Vol. 4. Aldershot, Hants, Eng.: Edward Elgar, 1991.

Muller, Jerry Z. *The Mind and the Market: Capitalism in Modern European Thought*. New York: Alfred A. Knopf, 2002.

Mun, Thomas. *England's Treasure by Forraign Trade*. 1664. Rpt., New York: Macmillan, 1895.

———. *England's Treasure by Forraign Trade*. 1664. Rpt., New York: Macmillan, 1928.

Norton, Glyn P. *The Ideology and Language of Translation in Renaissance France and Their Humanist Antecedents*. Genève: Librairie Droz, 1984.

Obermann, Heiko Augustinus. *The Harvest of Medieval Theology: Gabriel Biel and Late Medieval Nominalism*. Cambridge, MA: Harvard University Press, 1963.

O'Connell, Michael. *The Idolatrous Eye: Iconoclasm and Theater in Early-Modern England*. Oxford: Oxford University Press, 2000.

Oecolampadius, Johannes. *Briefe und Akten zum Leben Oekolampads*. Ed. Ernst Staehelin. Leipzig: M. Heinsius Nachfolger, Eger and Sievers, 1927.

Officer, Lawrence H. "The Purchasing-Power-Parity Theory of Gerrard de Malynes." *History of Political Economy* 14, no. 2 (1982): 256–59.

Oram, William. "Spenserian Paralysis." *Studies in English Literature* 41 (2001): 49–70.

Osteen, Mark, and Martha Woodmansee. "Introduction." In *The New Economic Criticism: Studies at the Intersection of Literature and Economics*, ed. Martha Woodmansee and Mark Osteen. 3–50. London: Routledge, 1999.

Ovid. *Metamorphoses*. 2nd ed. Trans. Frank Justus Miller. 2 vols. 1921. Rpt., London: Heinemann, 1966.

The Oxford Dictionary of English Etymology. Ed. C. T. Onions. Vol. 1. Oxford: Clarendon, 1966.

Oxford Latin Dictionary. Ed. P. G. W. Glare. 8 vols. Oxford: Clarendon, 1968–82.

Padley, G. A. *Grammatical Theory in Western Europe, 1500–1700: The Latin Tradition*. Cambridge: Cambridge University Press, 1976.

————. *Grammatical Theory in Western Europe, 1500–1700: Trends in Vernacular Grammar.* 2 vols. Cambridge: Cambridge University Press, 1985.

Papazian, Mary Arshagouni. "Donne, Election, and the *Devotions upon Emergent Occasions.*" *Huntington Library Quarterly* 55 (1992): 603–19.

Park, Katherine. "The Organic Soul." In *The Cambridge History of Renaissance Philosophy.* 464–84. Ed. Charles B. Schmitt et al. Cambridge: Cambridge University Press, 1988.

Parker, Patricia. *Literary Fat Ladies: Rhetoric, Gender, Property.* London: Methuen, 1987.

————. "Metaphor and Catachresis." In *The Ends of Rhetoric: History, Theory, Practice,* ed. John Bender and David E. Wellbery. 60–73. Stanford: Stanford University Press, 1990.

————. *Shakespeare from the Margins: Language, Culture, Context.* Chicago: University of Chicago Press, 1996.

Peacham, Henry. *The Garden of Eloquence.* London: H. Jackson, 1577.

————. *The Garden of Eloquence.* 1577; 1593. Rpt., New York: Scholars' Facsimiles and Reprints, 1954.

Peele, James. *The Pathe waye to perfectnes, in th'accomptes of Debitour, and Creditour: in manner of a Dialogue.* London: Thomas Purfoote, [1569].

Pepper, Stephen C. *World Hypotheses: A Study in Evidence.* Berkeley: University of California Press, 1961.

Pepys, Samuel. *The Diary of Samuel Pepys.* Ed. Robert Latham and William Matthews. 11 vols. Berkeley: University of California Press, 1971.

Perkins, William. *The Workes of that Famous and Worthy Minister of Christ, in the Uniuersitie of Cambridge.* Vol. 2. London: John Legatt, 1612–13.

Pesmen, Dale. "Reasonable and Unreasonable Worlds: Some Expectations of Coherence in Culture Implied by the Prohibition of Mixed Metaphor." In *Beyond Metaphor: The Theory of Tropes in Anthropology,* ed. James W. Fernandez. 213–43. Stanford: Stanford University Press, 1991.

Pierce, Charles Sanders. *Pierce On Signs.* Ed. James Hoopes. Chapel Hill: University of North Carolina Press, 1991.

Poovey, Mary. *A History of the Modern Fact: Problems of Knowledge in the Sciences of Wealth and Society.* Chicago: University of Chicago Press, 1998.

Pope, Alexander. *The Dunciad.* In *The Poems of Alexander Pope,* ed. John Butt. New Haven: Yale University Press, 1963.

Porter, H. B., Jr. *The Ordination Prayers of the Ancient Western Churches.* London: Society for Promoting Christian Knowledge, 1967.

Prescott, Anne Lake. *Imagining Rabelais in Renaissance England.* New Haven: Yale University Press, 1998.

Primus, J. H. *The Vestments Controversy.* Amsterdam: Kampen: J. H. Kok, 1960.

The Princeton Encyclopedia of Poetry and Poetics. Ed. Alex. Preminger. Enl. ed. Princeton: Princeton University Press, 1974.

Principe, Walter Henry, ed. *William of Auxerre's Theology of the Hypostatic Union.* Vol. 1, *The Theology of the Hypostatic Union in the Early Thirteenth Century.* Toronto: Pontifical Institute of Medieval Studies, 1963.

Puttenham, George. *The Arte of English Poesie 1589*. Rpt., Kent, OH: Kent State University Press, 1988.

Quintilian. *The Institutio Oratoria of Quintilian*. Ed. and trans. H. E. Butler. 4 vols. 1920. Rpt., London: William Heinemann, 1980.

———. *The Orator's Education*. Ed. and trans. Donald A. Russell. 5 vols. Cambridge, MA: Harvard University Press, 2001.

Rappaport, Steve. *Worlds within Worlds: Structures of Life in Sixteenth-Century London*. Cambridge,MA: Cambridge University Press, 1989.

Redworth, Glyn. *In Defence of the Church Catholic: The Life of Stephen Gardiner*. Oxford: Basil Blackwell, 1990.

Revel, Jacques. "Uses of Civility." In *Passions of the Renaissance*, ed. Roger Chartier. 167–205. *A History of Private Life*, Vol. 3. Ed. Philippe Ariès and Georges Duby. Cambridge, MA: Harvard University Press, 1989.

Richards, I.A. *The Philosophy of Rhetoric*. New York: Oxford University Press, 1936.

Richardson, Cyril C. "Cranmer and the Analysis of Eucharistic Doctrine." *Journal of Theological Studies* 16 (1965): 421–37.

Ricoeur, Paul. *La métaphore vive*. Paris: Seuil, 1975.

———. "The Metaphorical Process as Cognition, Imagination, and Feeling." In *On Metaphor*, ed. Sheldon Sacks. 141–57. 1978. Rpt., Chicago: University of Chicago Press, 1979.

———. *The Rule of Metaphor: Multi-Disciplinary Studies of the Creation of Meaning in Language*. Trans. Robert Czerny. 1977. Rpt., Toronto: University of Toronto Press, 1979.

Rider, John. *Bibliotheca Scholastica*. 1589. Rpt., Menston, Eng.: Scolar, 1970.

Ridley, Nicholas. "A Brief Declaration of the Lord's Supper," otherwise entitled, "A Treatise against the Error of Transubstantiation." In *The Works of Nicholas Ridley*, ed. Henry Christmas. 5–45. Cambridge: Cambridge University Press, 1843.

———. "Reply of Bishop Ridley to Bishop Hooper on the Vestment Controversy, 1550." In *The Writings of John Bradford, M. A., Fellow of Pembroke Hall, Cambridge, and Prebendary of St. Paul's, Martyr, 1555*, ed. Aubrey Townsend. 375–95. Cambridge: Cambridge University Press, 1853.

Roberts, John R. " 'Just such disparitie': The Critical Debate about 'Aire and Angels.' " *John Donne Journal* 9 (1990): 43–64.

Robinson, Forrest G. *The Shape of Things Known: Sidney's Apology in Its Philosophical Tradition*. Cambridge, MA: Harvard University Press, 1972.

Robinson, Hastings, ed. *Original Letters Relative to the English Reformation*. 2 vols. Cambridge: Cambridge University Press, 1846–47.

Roche, Thomas. *The Kindly Flame: A Study of the Third and Fourth Books of Spenser's "Faerie Queene."* Princeton: Princeton University Press, 1964.

Rosendale, Timothy. " 'Fiery Toungues': Language, Liturgy, and the Paradox of the English Reformation." *Renaissance Quarterly* 54 (2001): 1142–64.

Ross, J. F. *Portraying Analogy*. Cambridge: Cambridge University Press, 1981.

Rubin, Miri. *Corpus Christi: The Eucharist in Late Medieval Culture.* Cambridge: Cambridge University Press, 1991.

Rummel, Erika. *Erasmus' "Annotations" on the New Testament: From Philologist to Theologian.* Toronto: University of Toronto Press, 1986.

Rupp, Gordon. *Patterns of Reformation.* Philadelphia: Fortress Press, 1969.

Sandison, Helen E. "An Elizabethan Economist's Method of Literary Composition." *Huntington Library Quarterly* 6 (1943): 205–11.

Saussure, Ferdinand de. *Course in General Linguistics.* Ed. Charles Bally and Albert Sechehaye, in collaboration with Albert Reidlinger. Trans. Wade Baskin. 1959. Rpt., New York: McGraw-Hill, 1966.

Sawday, Jonathan. *The Body Emblazoned: Dissection and the Human Body in Renaissance Culture.* London: Routledge, 1995.

Schmitt, Charles B., et al. *The Cambridge History of Renaissance Philosophy.* Cambridge: Cambridge University Press, 1988.

Schoenfeldt, Michael C. "Patriarchal Assumptions and Egalitarian Designs." *John Donne Journal* 9 (1990): 23–26.

Schumpeter, Joseph Alois. *History of Economic Analysis.* New York: Oxford University Press, 1954.

Scott, William Robert. *The Constitution and Finance of English, Scottish and Irish Joint-Stock Companies to 1720.* 3 vols. 1912. Rpt., New York: Peter Smith, 1951.

Scotus, John Duns. *Opus Oxoniense.* In *Opera Omnia.* 26 vols. Paris: L. Vivès, 1891–95.

Seelig, Sharon Cadman. *Generating Texts: The Progeny of Seventeenth-Century Prose.* Charlottesville: University of Virginia Press, 1996.

Shakespeare, William. *Hamlet.* Ed. Harold Jenkins. London: Methuen, 1982.

———. *Hamlet, Prince of Denmark.* Ed. Philip Edwards. Cambridge: Cambridge University Press, 1985.

———. *The Riverside Shakespeare.* Ed. G. Blakemore Evans et al. 2nd ed. Boston: Houghton Mifflin, 1997.

Shannon, Laurie. "'His Apparel Was Done Upon Him': Rites of Personage in Foxe's *Book of Martyrs.*" *Shakespeare Studies* 28 (2000): 193–98.

Shell, Marc. *The Economy of Literature.* Baltimore: Johns Hopkins University Press, 1978.

———. "The Issue of Representation." In *The New Economic Criticism: Studies at the Intersection of Literature and Economics,* ed. Martha Woodmansee and Mark Osteen. 53–74. London: Routledge, 1999.

———. *Money, Language, and Thought: Literary and Philosophic Economies from the Medieval to the Modern Era.* 1982. Rpt., Baltimore: Johns Hopkins University Press, 1993.

Sherry, Richard. *A Treatise of the Figures of Grammar and Rhetorike.* London: Richard Tottell, 1555.

Shuger, Debora Kuller. *The Renaissance Bible: Scholarship, Sacrifice, and Subjectivity.* Berkeley: University of California Press, 1994.

Sidney, Sir Philip. *An Apology for Poetry or The Defence of Poesy.* Ed. Geoffrey Shepherd. Manchester, Eng.: Manchester University Press, 1973.

Silberman, Lauren. *Transforming Desire: Erotic Knowledge in Books III and IV of "The Faerie Queene."* Berkeley: University of California Press, 1995.

Silver, Victoria. *Imperfect Sense: The Predicament of Milton's Irony.* Princeton: Princeton University Press, 2001.

Simpson, Evelyn M. *A Study of the Prose Works of John Donne.* 2nd ed. Oxford: Clarendon, 1948.

Siraisi, Nancy G. *Medieval and Early Renaissance Medicine: An Introduction to Knowledge and Practice.* Chicago: University of Chicago Press, 1990.

Smith, Bruce R. *The Acoustic World of Early Modern England: Attending to the O-Factor.* Chicago: University of Chicago Press, 1999.

Sonnino, Lee A. *A Handbook to Sixteenth-Century Rhetoric.* New York: Barnes and Noble, 1968.

Spenser, Edmund. *The Faerie Qveene.* Ed. A. C. Hamilton. London: Longman, 1977
———. *The Faerie Queene.* Ed. A. C. Hamilton. 2nd ed. Harlow, Eng.: Longman, 2001.

———. *The Works of Edmund Spenser: A Variorum Edition.* Ed. Edwin Greenlaw, Charles Grosvenor Osgood, and Frederick Morgan Padelford. 11 vols. Baltimore: Johns Hopkins Press, 1932–57.

Sponsler, Claire. "Narrating the Social Order: Medieval Clothing Laws." *Clio* 21 (1992): 265–83.

Stallybrass, Peter. "Worn Worlds: Clothes and Identity on the Renaissance Stage." In *Subject and Object in Renaissance Culture*, ed. Margreta de Grazia, Maureen Quilligan, and Peter Stallybrass. 289–320. Cambridge: Cambridge University Press, 1996.

Starnes, DeWitt T. *Robert Estienne's Influence on Lexicography.* Austin: University of Texas Press, 1963.

Stein, Gabriele. *The English Dictionary before Cawdrey.* Tübingen: Max Niemeyer, 1985.

Steinberg, Jonathan. "The Historian and the *Questione della Lingua.*" In *The Social History of Language*, ed. Peter Burke and Roy Porter. 198–209. Cambridge: Cambridge University Press, 1987.

Strong, Roy. *The Cult of Elizabeth: Elizabethan Portraiture and Pageantry.* London: Thames and Hudson, 1977.

Sullivan, David. "The Structure of Self-Revelation in Donne's *Devotions.*" *Prose Studies* 11, no. 2 (1988): 49–59.

Supple, B. E. *Commercial Crisis and Change in England 1600–1642: A Study in the Instability of a Mercantile Economy.* Cambridge: Cambridge University Press, 1959.

Susenbrotus, Johann. Σὺν δε θεοι μάχαρες [Syn de theoi makares] Epitome troporum ac schematum et grammaticorum et rhetorum. London: Gerard Dewes, 1562.

Sweetser, Eve E. *From Etymology to Pragmatics: Metaphorical and Cultural Aspects of Semantic Structure.* 1990. Rpt., Cambridge: Cambridge University Press, 1997.

Talon, Omer. *Audomari Talaei rhetorica, e [P.] Rami, regii professoris praelectionibus obser-vata.* London: Society of Stationers, 1620.

Targoff, Ramie. "The Performance of Prayer: Sincerity and Theatricality in Early Modern England." *Representations* 60 (1997): 49–69.

Taylor, Jeremy. *The Whole Works of Jeremy Taylor.* Ed. Alexander Taylor. London. Vol. 9. Longman, Green, Longman, and Roberts, 1862.

Taylor, John R. *Linguistic Categorization: Prototypes in Linguistic Theory.* 2nd ed. Oxford: Clarendon, 1995.

Tertullian. *Tertullian adversus Marcionem.* Ed. and trans. Ernest Evans. Vol. II. Oxford: Clarendon, 1972.

Teskey, Gordon. *Allegory and Violence.* Ithaca: Cornell University Press, 1996.

Thompson, Ann, and John O. Thompson. *Shakespeare: Meaning and Metaphor.* Iowa City: University of Iowa Press, 1987.

Tobin, J. J. M. " 'Bawds' not 'Bonds.' " *Hamlet Studies* 4, nos. 1–2 (1982): 94–95.

Twycross, Meg, and Sarah Carpenter. *Masks and Masking in Medieval and Early Tudor England.* Aldershot, Hants, Eng.: Ashgate, 2002.

Tylenda, Joseph N. "Calvin's Understanding of the Communication of Properties." *The Westminster Theological Journal* 38 (1975): 54–65.

Udall, John. "A Demonstration of that trueth of the Discipline which Christ hath prescribed in his worde for the gouernment of his Church, in all times and places, vntill the end of the world." In *A parte of a register: contayninge sundrie memorable matters, written by diuers goddly and learned in our time.* Middleburg: Richard Schilders, [1593?].

———. *The Seconde parte of a register.* Ed. Albert Peel. 2 vols. Cambridge: Cambridge University Press, 1915.

Van Dyke, Carolynn. *The Fiction of Truth: Structures of Meaning in Narrative and Dramatic Allegory.* Ithaca: Cornell University Press, 1985.

Vaughan, Rice. *A Discourse of Coin and Coinage.* London: Th. Basset, 1675.

Vendler, Helen. "Reading, Stage by Stage: Shakespeare's Sonnets." In *Shakespeare Reread: The Text in New Contexts,* ed. Russ McDonald. 23–41. Ithaca: Cornell University Press, 1994.

Vermigli, Peter Martyr. *A Discourse or traictise of Petur Martyr Vermilla Florentine, the publyque reader of diuinitee in the Vniuersitee of Oxford wherin he openly declared his whole and determinate iudgemente concernynge the Sacrament of the Lordes supper.* Trans. Nicholas Udall. London: Nycolas Udall, [1550?].

Waswo, Richard. *Language and Meaning in the Renaissance.* Princeton: Princeton University Press, 1987.

Webber, Joan. *The Eloquent "I": Style and Self in Seventeenth-Century Prose.* Madison: University of Wisconsin Press, 1968.

Webster's New World College Dictionary. 3rd ed. New York: Macmillan, 1988.

Whalen, Robert. "George Herbert's Sacramental Puritanism." *Renaissance Quarterly* 54 (2001): 1273–1307.

———. *The Poetry of Immanence: Sacrament in Donne and Herbert.* Toronto: University of Toronto Press, 2002.

Wheeler, John. *A Treatise of Commerce*. Ed. George Burton Hotchkiss. 1601. Rpt., New York: New York University Press, 1931.

Wilkins, David, compiler. "Bulla Pauli papae mandans depositionem et degradationem Thomae Cranmer, archiep. Cantuar." In Vol. 4, *Concilia Magnae Britanniae et Hiberniae*. 132–6. 1737. Rpt., Brussels: Culture et Civilization, 1964.

Wilson, Thomas. *A Discourse Upon Usury (1572)*. Ed. R. H. Tawney. New York: Harcourt Brace, 1925.

———. *Wilson's Arte of Rhetorique 1560*. Ed. G. H. Mair. Oxford: Clarendon, 1909.

Wind, Edgar. *Pagan Mysteries in the Renaissance*. Rev. ed. Harmondsworth, Middlesex, Eng.: Penguin, 1967.

Winters, Yvor. *In Defense of Reason*. New York: Swallow Press and William Morrow, 1947.

Wofford, Susanne. "Gendering Allegory: Spenser's Bold Reader and the Emergence of Character in *The Faerie Queene* III." *Criticism* 30 (1988): 1–21.

Wooden, Warren W. *John Foxe*. Boston: Twayne, 1983.

Wortham, Simon. "Sovereign Counterfeits: The Trial of the Pyx." *Renaissance Quarterly* 49 (1996): 333–59.

Wright, George T. "Troubles of a Professional Meter Reader." In *Shakespeare Reread: The Text in New Contexts*, ed. Russ McDonald. 56–76. Ithaca: Cornell University Press, 1994.

Yates, Frances. *Astraea: The Imperial Theme in the Sixteenth Century*. London: Routledge and Kegan Paul, 1975.

Yeats, W. B. *The Collected Poems of W. B Yeats*. 1956. Rpt., New York: Macmillan, 1959.

Young, R. V. "Angels in 'Aire and Angels.'" *John Donne Journal* 9 (1990): 1–14.

Žižek, Slavoj. "Revisioning 'Lacanian' Social Criticism: The Law and Its Obscene Double." *The Journal for the Psychoanalysis of Culture and Society*, 1 (1996): 15–25.

———. *The Sublime Object of Ideology*. London: Verso, 1989.

Zwingli, Huldrich [Huldrych]. *Friendly Exegesis, that is, Exposition of the Matter of the Eucharist to Martin Luther*. Trans. Henry Preble. In *Writings of Huldrich Zwingli*, ed. H. Wayne Pipkin. Vol. 2. 239–385. Allison Park, PA: Pickwick Publications, 1984.

———. *On the Lord's Supper*. In *Zwingli and Bullinger*, trans. G. W. Bromiley. 185–347. Philadelphia: Westminster, 1953.

———. "Ad Theobaldi Billicani et Urbani Rhegii epistolas reponsio." In *Huldreich Zwinglis Sämtliche Werke*. Vol. IV. Ed. Emil Egli, Georg Finsler, Walter Köhler, and Oskar Farner. 893–941. Vol. XCI, *Corpus Reformatorum*. Leipzig: M. Heinsius Nachfolger, 1927.

Index

Notes are indexed if the entry is substantive or of particular interest. Consult my Works Cited for a full list of sources. There is no entry for undelimited *metaphor*, since the only reference possible would have been passim. Entries for *arch-trope* (*translatio*) and for *creative*, *dead*, and *mixed metaphor* are included, however.